ADVANCES IN KNOWLEDGE REPRESENTATION

Edited by **Carlos Ramírez Gutiérrez**

Advances in Knowledge Representation
Edited by Carlos Ramírez Gutiérrez

Published by InTech
Janeza Trdine 9, 51000 Rijeka, Croatia

Publishing Process Manager Romana Vukelic

Technical Editor Teodora Smiljanic

Cover Designer InTech Design Team

Additional hard copies can be obtained from orders@intechopen.com

Advances in Knowledge Representation, Edited by Carlos Ramírez Gutiérrez
p. cm.
ISBN 978-953-51-0597-8

For EU product safety concerns:
IN TECH d.o.o., Prolaz Marije Krucifikse Kozulić 3, 51000 Rijeka, Croatia,
info@intechopen.com or visit our website at intechopen.com.

Meet the editor

Dr Carlos Ramirez received his Ph.D. in Computer Science from The University of Kent at Canterbury, England, in December 1998. Currently, he is professor of artificial intelligence and theory of computation and research member of the Distributed and Adaptive Systems Lab for Learning Technologies Development, and of the Virtual and Robotic Agents Centre, with the faculty of the Tecnológico de Monterrey, Mexico. Dr. Ramirez research interests include cognitive informatics and computing, knowledge representation models, concept algebra, cognitive processes and inferences, dynamic concept networks, pattern and object recognition, and intelligent optimisation. He is member of several scientific organisations, has supervised numerous research and engineering projects and has publications in artificial intelligence, cognitive computing, dynamics and control and information retrieval.

Contents

Preface

What is knowledge? How can the knowledge be explicitly represented? Many scientists from different fields of study have tried to answer those questions through history, though seldom agreed about the answers. Many representations have been presented by researchers working on a variety of fields, such as computer science, mathematics, cognitive computing, cognitive science, psychology, linguistic, and philosophy of mind. Some of those representations are computationally tractable, some are not; this book is concerned only with the first kind.

Although nowadays there is some degree of success on the called "knowledge-based systems" and in certain technologies using knowledge representations, no single knowledge representations has been found complete enough to represent satisfactorily all the requirements posed by common cognitive processes, able to be manipulated by general purpose algorithms, nor to satisfy all sorts of applications in different domains and conditions—and may not be the case that such 'universal' computational representation exists--, it is natural to look for different theories, models and ideas to explain it and how to instrument a certain model or representation. The compilation of works presented here advances topics such as concept theory, positive relational algebra and k-relations, structured, visual and ontological models of knowledge representation, as well as applications to various domains, such as semantic representation and extraction, intelligent information retrieval, program proof checking, complex planning, and data preparation for knowledge modelling.

The state of the art research presented in the book on diverse facets of knowledge representation and applications is expected to contribute and encourage further advancement of the field. The book is addressed to advanced undergraduate and postgraduate students, to researchers concerned with the knowledge representation field, and also to computer oriented practitioners of diverse fields where complex computer applications based on knowledge are required.

The book is organised in three sections, starting with two chapters related to foundations of knowledge and concepts, section II includes three chapters on different views or models of how knowledge can be computationally represented, and section III presents six detailed applications of knowledge on different domains, with useful ideas on how to implement a representation in an efficient and practical way. Thus, the chapters in this book cover a spectrum of insights into the foundations of concepts and relationships, models for the representation of knowledge, development and application of all of them. By organising the book in those three sections, I have simply tried to bring together similar things, in a natural way, that may be more useful to the reader.

Dr. Carlos Ramírez
Tec de Monterrey
Querétaro,
México

Section 1

On Foundations

1

That IS-IN Isn't IS-A: A Further Analysis of Taxonomic Links in Conceptual Modelling

Jari Palomäki and Hannu Kangassalo
University of Tampere
Finland

1. Introduction

Ronald J. Brachman, in his basic article: "What IS-A Is and Isn't: An Analysis of Taxonomic Links in Semantic Networks", (1983), has analysed and catalogued different interpretations of inheritance link, which is called "IS-A", and which is used in different kind of knowledge-representation systems. This IS-A link is seen by Brachman as a relation "between the representational objects," which forms a "taxonomic hierarchy, a tree or a lattice-like structures for categorizing classes of things in the world being represented", (ibid., 30). This very opening phrase in Brachman's article reveals, and which the further analysis of his article confirms as it is done in this Chapter, that he is considering the IS-A relation and the different interpretations given to it as an *extensional* relation. Accordingly, in this Chapter we are considering an *intensional* IS-IN relation which also forms a taxonomic hierarchy and a lattice-like structure. In addition, we can consider the hierarchy provided by an IS-IN relation as a semantic network as well. On the other hand, this IS-IN relation, unlike IS-A relation, is a conceptual relation between concepts, and it is basically intensional in its character.

The purpose of this Chapter is to maintain that the IS-IN relation is not equal to the IS-A relation; more specifically, that Brachman's analysis of an extensional IS-A relation did not include an intensional IS-IN relation. However, we are not maintaining that Brachman's analysis of IS-A relation is wrong, or that there are some flaws in it, but that the IS-IN relation requires a different analysis than the IS-A relation as is done, for example, by Brachman.

This Chapter is composed as follows. Firstly, we are considering the different meanings for the IS-A relation, and, especially, how they are analysed by Brachman in (1983), and to which, in turn, we shall further analyse. Secondly, we are turning our attention to that of the IS-IN relation. We start our analysis by considering what the different senses of "in" are, and to do this we are turning first to Aristotle's and then to Leibniz's account of it. After that, thirdly, we are proceeding towards the basic relations between terms, concepts, classes (or sets), and things in order to propose a more proper use of the IS-IN relation and its relation to the IS-A relation. Lastly, as kind of a conclusion, we are considering some advances and some difficulties related to the intensional versus extensional approaches to a conceptual modelling.

2. The different meanings for the IS-A relation

The idea of IS-A relation seems to follow from the English sentences such as "Socrates is a man" and "a cat is a mammal", which provides two basic forms of using the IS-A relation. That is, a *predication*, where an individual (Socrates) is said to have a predicate (a man), and that one predicate (a cat) is said to be a *subtype* of the other predicate (a mammal). This second form is commonly expressed by the universally quantified conditional as follows: "for all entities x, if x is a cat, then x is a mammal". However, this formalization of the second use of the IS-A relation reveals, that it combines two commonly used expressions using the IS-A relation. Firstly, in the expressions of the form "x is a cat" and "x is a mammal" the IS-A relation is used as a predication, and secondly, by means of the universal quantifier and implication, the IS-A relation is used not as a predication, but as a connection between two predicates.

Accordingly, we can divide the use of the IS-A relation in to two major subtypes: one relating an individual to a species, and the other relating two species. When analysing the different meanings for the IS-A relation Brachman uses this division by calling them *generic/individual* and *generic/generic* relations, (Brachman 1983, 32).

2.1 Generic/individual relations

Brachman gives four different meanings for the IS-A relation connecting an individual and a generic, which we shall list and analyse as follows, (ibid.):

1. *A set membership relation*, for example, "Socrates is a man", where "Socrates" is an individual and "a man" is a set, and Socrates is a member of a set of man. Accordingly, the IS-A is an $\in$ -relation.
2. *A predication*, for example, a predicate "man" is predicated to an individual "Socrates", and we may say that a predicate and an individual is combined by a copula expressing a kind of function-argument relation. Brachman does not mention a copula in his article, but according to this view the IS-A is a copula.
3. *A conceptual containment relation*, for which Brachman gives the following example, "a king" and "the king of France", where the generic "king" is used to construct the individual description. In this view Brachman's explanation and example is confusing. Firstly, "France" is an individual, and we could say that the predicate "a king" is predicated to "France", when the IS-A relation is a copula. Secondly, we could say that the concept of "king" applies to "France" when the IS-A relation is an application relation. Thirdly, the phrase "the king of France" is a definite description, when we could say that the king of France is a definite member of the set of kings, *i.e.*, the IS-A relation is a converse of $\in$ -relation.
4. *An abstraction*, for example, when from the particular man "Socrates" we abstract the general predicate "a man". Hence we could say that "Socrates" falls under the concept of "man", *i.e.*, the IS-A is a falls under –relation, or we could say that "Socrates" is a member of the set of "man", *i.e.*, the IS-A is an $\in$ -relation.

We may notice in the above analysis of different meanings of the IS-A relations between individuals and generic given by Brachman, that three out of four of them we were able to interpret the IS-A relation by means of $\in$ -relation. And, of course, the copula expressing a function-argument relation is possible to express by $\in$ -relation. Moreover, in our analysis of

3. and 4. we used a term "concept" which Brachman didn't use. Instead, he seems to use a term "concept" synonymously with an expression "a structured description", which, according to us, they are not. In any case, what Brachman calls here a conceptual containment relation is not the conceptual containment relation as we shall use it, see Section 4 below.

2.2 Generic/generic relations

Brachman gives six different meanings for the IS-A relation connecting two generics, which we shall list and analyse as follows, (ibid.):

1. *A subset/superset*, for example, "a cat is a mammal", where "a cat" is a set of cats, "a mammal" is a set of mammals, and a set of cats is a subset of a set of mammals, and a set of mammals is a superset of a set of cats. Accordingly, the IS-A relation is a $\subseteq$ -relation.
2. *A generalisation/specialization*, for example, "a cat is a mammal" means that "for all entities x, if x is a cat, then x is a mammal". Now we have two possibilities: The first is that we interpret "x is a cat" and "x is a mammal" as a predication by means of copula, and the relation between them is a formal implication, where the predicate "cat" is a specialization of the predicate "mammal", and the predicate "mammal" is a generalization of the predicate "cat". Thus we can say that the IS-A relation is a formal implication $(\forall x)\ (P(x) \rightarrow Q(x))$. The second is that since we can interpret "x is a cat" and "x is a mammal" by mean of $\in$ -relation, and then by means of a formal implication we can define a $\subseteq$ -relation, from which we get that the IS-A relation is a $\subseteq$ -relation.
3. *An AKO*, meaning "a kind of", for example, "a cat is a mammal", where "a cat" is a kind of "mammal". As Brachman points out, (ibid.), AKO has much common with generalization, but it implies "kind" status for the terms of it connects, whereas generalization relates arbitrary predicates. That is, to be a kind is to have an essential property (or set of properties) that makes it the kind that it is. Hence, being "a cat" it is necessary to be "a mammal" as well. This leads us to the natural kind inferences: if anything of a kind A has an essential property ϕ, then every A has ϕ. Thus we are turned to the Aristotelian essentialism and to a quantified modal logic, in which the IS-A relation is interpreted as a necessary formal implication $\Box\ (\forall x)\ (P(x) \rightarrow Q(x))$. However, it is to be noted, that there are two relations connected with the AKO relation. The first one is the relation between an essential property and the kind, and the second one is the relation between kinds. Brachman does not make this difference in his article, and he does not consider the second one. Provided there are such things as kinds, in our view they would be connected with the IS-IN relation, which we shall consider in the Section 4 below.
4. *A conceptual containment*, for example, and following Brachman, (ibid.), instead of reading "a cat is a mammal" as a simple generalization, it is to be read as "to be a cat is to be a mammal". This, according to him, is the IS-A of lambda-abstraction, wherein one predicate is used in defining another, (ibid.). Unfortunately, it is not clear what Brachman means by "the IS-A of lambda-abstraction, wherein one predicate is used in defining another". If it means that the predicates occurring in the *definiens* are among the predicates occurring in the *definiendum*, there are three possibilities to interpret it: The first one is by means of the IS-A relation as a $\subseteq$ -relation between predicates, *i.e.*, the

predicate of "mammal" is among the predicate of "cat". The second one is that the IS-A is a $=_{df}$ -sign between *definiens* and *definiendum*, or, perhaps, that the IS-A is a lambda-abstraction of it, *i.e.*, $\lambda xy(x =_{df} y)$, although, of course, "a cat $=_{df}$ a mammal" is not a complete definition of a cat. The third possibility is that the IS-IN is a relation between *concepts, i.e.*, the concept of "mammal" is contained in the concept of "cat", see Section 4 below. - And it is argued in this Chapter that the IS-IN relation is not the IS-A relation.

5. *A role value restriction*, for example, "the car is a bus", where "the car" is a role and "a bus" is a value being itself a certain type. Thus, the IS-A is a copula.
6. *A set and its characteristic type*, for example, the set of all cats and the concept of "a cat". Then we could say that the IS-A is an extension relation between the concept and its extension, where an extension of a concept is a set of all those things falling under the concept in question. On the other hand, Brachman says also that it associates the characteristic function of a set with that set, (ibid.). That would mean that we have a characteristic function ϕ_{Cat} defined for elements $x \in X$ by $\phi_{\mathrm{Cat}}(x) = 1$, if $x \in$ Cat, and $\phi_{\mathrm{Cat}}(x) = 0$, if $x \notin$ Cat, where Cat is a set of cats, *i.e.*, Cat = $\{x \mid Cat(x)\}$, where $Cat(x)$ is a predicate of being a cat. Accordingly, Cat $\subseteq X$, ϕ_{Cat}: $X \rightarrow \{0, 1\}$, and, in particular, the IS-A is a relation between the characteristic function ϕ_{Cat} and the set Cat.

In the above analysis of the different meanings of the IS-A relations between two generics given by Brachman, concerning the relations of the AKO, the conceptual containment, and the relation between "set and its characteristic type", we were not able to interpret them by using only the set theoretical terms. Since set theory is extensional *par excellence*, the reason for that failure lies simply in the fact that in their adequate analysis some intensional elements are present. However, the AKO relation is based on a philosophical, *i.e.*, ontological, view that there are such things as kinds, and thus we shall not take it as a proper candidate for *the* IS-A relation. On the other hand, in both the conceptual containment relation and the relation between "set and its characteristic type" there occur as their terms "concepts", which are basically intensional entities. Accordingly we shall propose that their adequate analysis requires an intensional IS-IN relation, which differs from the most commonly used kinds of IS-A relations, whose analysis can be made set theoretically. Thus, we shall turn to the IS-IN relation.

3. The IS-IN relation

The idea of the IS-IN relation is close the IS-A relation, but distinction we want to draw between them is, as we shall propose, that the IS-A relation is analysable by means of set theory whereas the IS-IN relation is an intensional relation between concepts.

To analyse the IS-IN relation we are to concentrate on the word "in", which has a complex variety of meanings. First we may note that "in" is some kind of relational expression. Thus, we can put the matter of relation in formal terms as follows,

A is *in B*.

Now we can consider what the different senses of "in" are, and what kinds of substitutions can we make for *A* and *B* that goes along with those different senses of "in". To do this we are to turn first to Aristotle, who discuss of the term "in" in his *Physics*, (210a, 15ff, 1930). He lists the following senses of "in" in which one thing is said to be "in" another:

1. The sense in which a physical part is *in* a physical whole to which it belongs. For example, as the finger is *in* the hand.
2. The sense in which a whole is *in* the parts that makes it up.
3. The sense in which a species is *in* its genus, as "man" is *in* "animal".
4. The sense in which a genus is *in* any of its species, or more generally, any feature of a species is *in* the definition of the species.
5. The sense in which form is *in* matter. For example, "health is *in* the hot and cold".
6. The sense in which events center *in* their primary motive agent. For example, "the affairs of Creece center *in* the king".
7. The sense in which the existence of a thing centers *in* its final cause, its end.
8. The sense in which a thing is *in* a place.

From this list of eight different senses of "in" it is possible to discern four groups:

i. That which has to do with the *part-whole* relation, (1) and (2). Either the relation between a part to the whole or its converse, the relation of a whole to its part.
ii. That which has to do with the *genus-species* relation, (3) and (4). Either *A* is the genus and *B* the species, or *A* is the species and *B* is the genus.
iii. That which has to do with a *causal* relation, (5), (6), and (7). There are, according to Aristotle, four kinds of causes: material, formal, efficient, and final. Thus, *A* may be the formal cause (form), and *B* the matter; or *A* may be the efficient cause ("motive agent"), and *B* the effect; or, given *A*, some particular thing or event *B* is its final cause (*telos*).
iv. That which has to do with a *spatial* relation, (8). This Aristotle recognizes as the "strictest sense of all". *A* is said to be *in B*, where *A* is one thing and *B* is another thing or a place. "Place", for Aristotle, is thought of as what is occupied by some body. A thing located in some body is also located in some place. Thus we may designate *A* as the contained and *B* as the container.

What concerns us here is the second group II, *i.e.*, that which has to do with the *genus-species* relation, and especially the sense of "in" in which a genus *is in* any of its species. What is most important, according to us, it is this place in Aristotle's text to which Leibniz refers, when he says that "Aristotle himself seems to have followed the way of ideas [*viam idealem*], for he says that animal is in man, namely a concept in a concept; for otherwise men would be among animals [*insint animalibus*], (Leibniz *after* 1690a, 120). In this sentence Leibniz points out the distinction between conceptual level and the level of individuals, which amounts also the set of individuals. This distinction is crucial, and our proposal for distinguishing the IS-IN relation from the IS-A relation is based on it. What follows, we shall call the IS-IN relation an intensional containment relation between concepts.

4. Conceptual structures

Although the IS-A relation seems to follow from the English sentences such as "Socrates is a man" and "a cat is a mammal", the word "is" is logically speaking intolerably ambiguous, and a great care is needed not to confound its various meanings. For example, we have (1) the sense, in which it asserts Being, as in "*A* is"; (2) the sense of identity, as in "Cicero is Tullius"; (3) the sense of equality, as in "the sum of 6 and 8 is 14"; (4) the sense of predication, as in "the sky is blue"; (5) the sense of definition, as in "the *power set* of *A* is the set of all subsets of *A*"; etc. There are also less common uses, as "to be good is to be happy", where a relation of assertions is meant, and which gives rise to a formal implication. All this shows that the natural language is not precise enough to make clear the different meanings of the word "is", and hence of the words "is a", and "is in". Accordingly, to make differences between the IS-A relation and the IS-IN relation clear, we are to turn our attention to a logic.

4.1 Items connected to a concept

There are some basic items connected to a concept, and one possible way to locate them is as follows, see Fig. 1, (Palomäki 1994):

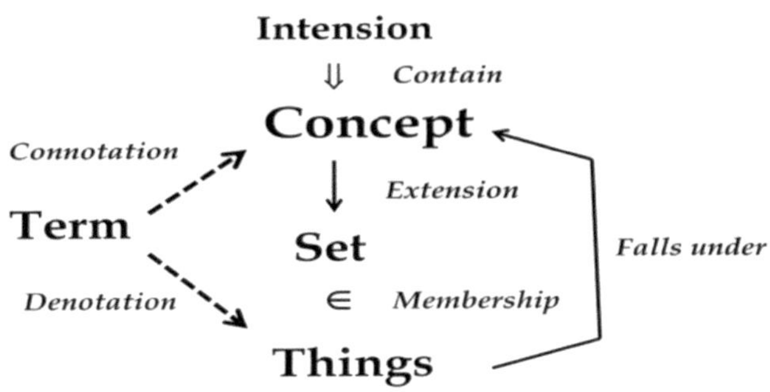

Fig. 1. Items connected to a concept

A *term* is a linguistic entity. It *denotes* things and *connotes* a concept. A concept, in turn, has an *extension* and an *intension*. The extension of a concept is a *set*, (or a *class*, being more exact), of all those things that *falls under* the concept. Now, there may be many different terms which denote the same things but connote different concepts. That is, these different concepts have the same extension but they differ in their intension. By an intension of a concept we mean something which we have to "understand" or "grasp" in order to use the concept in question correctly. Hence, we may say that the intension of concept is that knowledge content of it which is required in order to recognize a thing belonging to the extension of the concept in question, (Kangassalo, 1992/93, 2007).

Let $U = < V, C, F >$ be a universe of discourse, where i) V is a universe of (possible) individuals, ii) C is a universe of concepts, iii) $V \cap C \neq \{\}$, and iv) $F \subseteq V \times C$ is the falls under -relation. Now, if a is a concept, then for every (possible) individual i in V, either i falls under the concept a or it doesn't, *i.e*,

$$\text{if } a \in C, \text{ then } \forall i \in V : iFa \vee \sim iFa. \tag{1}$$

The extension-relation E between the set A and the concept a in V is defined as follows:

$$E_U(A,a) =_{\text{df}} (\forall i)\ (i \in A \leftrightarrow i \in V \wedge iFa). \tag{2}$$

The extension of concept a may also be described as follows:

$$i \in E_U'(a) \leftrightarrow iFa, \tag{3}$$

where $E_U'(a)$ is the extension of concept a in V, *i.e.*, $E_U'(a) = \{ i \in V \mid iFa\}$.

4.2 An intensional containment relation

Now, the relations between concepts enable us to make conceptual structures. The basic relation between concepts is an intensional containment relation, (see Kauppi 1967, Kangassalo 1992/93, Palomäki 1994), and it is this intensional containment relation between concepts, which we are calling the IS-IN relation.

More formally, let there be given two concepts *a* and *b*. When a concept *a* contains intensionally a concept *b*, we may say that the intension of a concept *a* contains the intension of a concept *b*, or that the concept *a* intensionally entails the concept *b*, or that the intension of the concept *a* entails the intension of the concept *b*. This intensional containment relation is denoted as follows,

$$a \geq b. \quad (4)$$

Then, it was observed by Kauppi in (1967) that

$$a \geq b \rightarrow (\forall i)\ (iFa \rightarrow iFb), \quad (5)$$

that is, that the transition from intensions to extensions reverses the containment relation, *i.e.*, the intensional containment relation between concepts *a* and *b* is converse to the extensional set-theoretical subset-relation between their extensions. Thus, by (3),

$$a \geq b \rightarrow E_U'(a) \subseteq E_U'(b), \quad (6)$$

where "$\subseteq$" is the set-theoretical subset-relation, or the extensional inclusion relation between sets. Or, if we put $A = E_U'(a)$ and $B = E_U'(b)$, we will get,

$$a \geq b \rightarrow A \subseteq B \quad (7)$$

[1]

For example, if the concept of a dog contains intensionally the concept of a quadruped, then the extension of the concept of the quadruped, *i.e.*, the set of four-footed animals, contains extensionally as a subset the extension of the concept of the dog, *i.e.*, the set of dogs. Observe, though, that we can deduce from concepts to their extensions, *i.e.*, sets, but not conversely, because for every set there may be many different concepts, whose extension that set is.

The above formula (6) is what was searched, without success, by Woods in (1991), where the intensional containment relation is called by him a structural, or an intensional subsumption relation.

4.3 An intensional concept theory

Based on the intensional containment relation between concepts the late Professor Raili Kauppi has presented her axiomatic intensional concept theory in Kauppi (1967), which is further studied in (Palomäki 1994). This axiomatic concept theory was inspired by Leibniz's

---

[1] In the set theory a subset-relation between sets *A* and *B* is defined by $\in$-relation between the elements of them as follows , $A \subseteq B =_{df} \forall x\ (x \in A \rightarrow x \in B)$. Unfortunately both $\subseteq$-relation and $\in$-relation are called IS-A relations, although they are different relations. On the other hand, we can take the intensional containment relation between concepts *a* and *b*, *i.e.*, $a \geq b$, to be the IS-IN relation.

logic, where the intensional containment relation between concepts formalises an "*inesse*"-relation[2] in Leibniz's logic.[3]

An intensional concept theory, denoted by *KC*, is presented in a first-order language *L* that contains individual variables *a*, *b*, *c*,..., which range over the *concepts*, and one non-logical 2-place *intensional containment relation*, denoted by "$\geq$". We shall first present four basic relations between concepts defined by "$\geq$", and then, briefly, the basic axioms of the theory. A more complete presentation of the theory, see Kauppi (1967), and Palomäki (1994).

Two concepts *a* and *b* are said to be *comparable*, denoted by $a \mathrm{H} b$, if there exists a concept *x* which is intensionally contained in both.

$$\mathrm{Df_H} \qquad a\mathrm{H}b =_{\mathrm{df}} (\exists x)\ (a \geq x \wedge b \geq x).$$

If two concepts *a* and *b* are not comparable, they are *incomparable*, which is denoted by $a \mathrm{I} b$.

$$\mathrm{Df_I} \qquad a\mathrm{I}b =_{\mathrm{df}} \sim a\mathrm{H}b.$$

Dually, two concepts *a* and *b* are said to be *compatible*, denoted by $a \perp b$, if there exists a concept *x* which contains intensionally both.

$$\mathrm{Df_\perp} \qquad a \perp b =_{\mathrm{df}} (\exists x)\ (x \geq a \wedge x \geq b)$$

If two concepts *a* and *b* are not compatible, they are *incompatible*, which is denoted by $a \mathrm{Y} b$.

$$\mathrm{Df_Y} \qquad a\mathrm{Y}b =_{\mathrm{df}} \sim a \perp b.$$

The two first axioms of *KC* state that the intensional containment relation is a *reflexive* and *transitive* relation.

$$\mathrm{Ax_{Refl}} \qquad a \geq a.$$
$$\mathrm{Ax_{Trans}} \qquad a \geq b \wedge b \geq c \rightarrow a \geq c.$$

Two concepts *a* and *b* are said to be *intensionally identical*, denoted by $a \approx b$, if the concept *a* intensionally contains the concept *b*, and the concept *b* intensionally contains the concept *a*.

$$\mathrm{Df_\approx} \qquad a \approx b =_{\mathrm{df}} a \geq b \wedge b \geq a.$$

---

[2]Literally, "*inesse*" is "being-in", and this term was used by Scholastic translator of Aristotle to render the Greek "huparchei", *i.e.*, "belongs to", (Leibniz 1997, 18, 243).

[3]Cf. "*Definition 3*. That A 'is in' L, or, that L 'contains' A, is the same that L is assumed to be coincident with several terms taken together, among which is A", (Leibniz after 1690, 132). Also, e.g. in a letter to Arnauld 14 July 1786 Leibniz wrote, (Leibniz 1997, 62): "[I]n every affirmative true proposition, necessary or contingent, universal or singular, the notion of the predicate is contained in some way in that of the subject, *praedicatum inest subjecto* [the predicate is included in the subject]. Or else I do not know what truth is." This view may be called the conceptual containment theory of truth, (Adams 1994, 57), which is closely associated with Leibniz's preference for an "intensional" as opposed to an "extensional" interpretation of categorical propositions. Leibniz worked out a variety of both intensional and extensional treatments of the logic of predicates, *i.e.*, concepts, but preferring the intensional approach, (Kauppi 1960, 220, 251, 252).

The intensional identity is clearly a reflexive, symmetric and transitive relation, hence an equivalence relation.

A concept c is called an *intensional product* of two concepts a and b, if any concept x is intensionally contained in c if and only if it is intensionally contained in both a and b. If two concepts a and b have an intensional product, it is unique up to the intensional identity and we denote it then by $a \otimes b$.

$$\text{Df}_{\otimes} \qquad c \approx a \otimes b =_{\text{df}} (\forall x)\ (c \geq x \leftrightarrow a \geq x \wedge b \geq x).$$

The following axiom $\text{Ax}_{\otimes}$ of *KC* states that if two concepts a and b are comparable, there exists a concept x which is their intensional product.

$$\text{Ax}_{\otimes} \qquad a\text{H}b \rightarrow (\exists x)\ (x \approx a \otimes b).$$

It is easy to show that the intensional product is idempotent, commutative, and associative.

A concept c is called an *intensional sum* of two concepts a and b, if the concept c is intensionally contained in any concept x if and only if it contains intensionally both a and b. If two concepts a and b have an intensional sum, it is unique up to the intensional identity and we denote it then by $a \oplus b$.

$$\text{Df}_{\oplus} \quad c \approx a \oplus b =_{\text{df}} (\forall x)\ (x \geq c \leftrightarrow x \geq a \wedge x \geq b)\ [4].$$

The following axiom $\text{Ax}_{\oplus}$ of *KC* states that if two concepts a and b are compatible, there exists a concept x which is their intensional sum.

$$\text{Ax}_{\oplus} \qquad a \perp b \rightarrow (\exists x)\ (x \approx a \oplus b)$$

The intensional sum is idempotent, commutative, and associative.

The intensional product of two concepts a and b is intensionally contained in their intensional sum whenever both sides are defined.

$$\text{Th 1} \qquad a \oplus b \geq a \otimes b.$$

Proof: If $a \otimes b$ exists, then by $\text{Df}_{\otimes}$, $a \geq a \otimes b$ and $b \geq a \otimes b$. Similarly, if $a \oplus b$ exists, then by $\text{Df}_{\oplus}$, $a \oplus b \geq a$ and $a \oplus b \geq b$. Hence, by Ax_{Trans}, the theorem follows.

A concept b is an *intensional negation* of a concept a, denoted by $\neg a$, if and only if it is intensionally contained in all those concepts x, which are intensionally incompatible with the concept a. When $\neg a$ exists, it is unique up to the intensional identity.

$$\text{Df}_{\neg} \quad b \approx \neg a =_{\text{df}} (\forall x)\ (x \geq b \leftrightarrow x\text{Y}a)\,.$$

The following axiom $\text{Ax}_{\neg}$ of *KC* states that if there is a concept x which is incompatible with the concept a, there exists a concept y, which is the intensional negation of the concept a.

[4]Thus, $a \otimes b \leftrightarrow [a] \otimes [b]$ is a greatest lower bound in $C/\approx$, whereas $a \oplus b \leftrightarrow [a] \oplus [b]$ is a least upper bound in $C/\approx$.

$$\text{Ax}_{\neg} \quad (\exists x)\ (xYa) \rightarrow (\exists y)\ (y \approx \neg a).$$

It can be proved that a concept a contains intensionally its intensional double negation provided that it exists.

$$\text{Th 2} \qquad a \geq \neg\neg a.$$[5]

Proof: By Df$_\neg$ the equivalence (1): $b \geq \neg a \leftrightarrow b\ Y\ a$ holds. By substituting $\neg a$ for b to (1), we get $\neg a \geq \neg a \leftrightarrow \neg a\ Y\ a$, and so, by Ax$_{\text{Refl}}$, we get (2): $\neg a\ Y\ a$. Then, by substituting a for b and $\neg a$ for a to (1), we get $a \geq \neg\neg a \leftrightarrow a\ Y\ \neg a$ and hence, by (2), the theorem follows.

Also, the following forms of the *De Morgan's formulas* can be proved whenever both sides are defined:

$$\text{Th 3} \quad \text{i)} \neg a \otimes \neg b \geq \neg(a \oplus b),$$
$$\text{ii)}\ \neg(a \otimes b) \approx \neg a \oplus \neg b.$$

Proof: First we are to proof the following important lemma:

Lemma 1 $\qquad a \geq b \rightarrow \neg b \geq \neg a.$

Proof: From $a \geq b$ follows $(\forall x)\ (x\ Y\ b \rightarrow x\ Y\ a)$, and thus by Df$_\neg$ the Lemma 1 follows.

i. If $a \oplus b$ exists, then by Df$_\oplus$, $a \oplus b \geq a$ and $a \oplus b \geq b$. By Lemma 1 we get $\neg a \geq \neg(a \oplus b)$ and $\neg b \geq \neg(a \oplus b)$. Then, by Df$_\otimes$, Th 3 i) follows.
ii. This is proved in the four steps as follows:
1. $\neg(a \otimes b) \geq \neg a \oplus \neg b$. Since $a \geq a \otimes b$, it follows by Lemma 1 that $\neg(a \otimes b) \geq \neg a$. Thus, by Df$_\oplus$, 1 holds.
2. $\neg(\neg\neg a \otimes \neg\neg b) \geq \neg(a \otimes b)$. Since $a \geq \neg\neg a$, by Th 2, it follows by Df$_\otimes$ that $a \otimes b \geq \neg\neg a \otimes \neg\neg b$. Thus, by Lemma 1, 2 holds.
3. $(\neg\neg a \otimes \neg\neg b) \geq \neg(\neg a \oplus \neg b)$. Since $(a \oplus b) \geq a$, it follows by Lemma 1 that $\neg a \geq \neg(a \oplus b)$, and so, by Df$_\otimes$, it follows $(\neg a \otimes \neg b) \geq \neg(a \oplus b)$. Thus, by substituting $\neg a$ for a and $\neg b$ for b to it, 3 holds.
4. $\neg a \oplus \neg b \geq \neg(a \otimes b)$. Since $\neg a \oplus \neg b \geq \neg\neg(\neg a \oplus \neg b)$, by Th 2, and from 3 it follows by Lemma 1 that $\neg\neg(\neg a \oplus \neg b) \geq \neg(\neg\neg a \otimes \neg\neg b)$, and by Ax$_{\text{Trans}}$ we get, $\neg a \oplus \neg b \geq \neg(\neg\neg a \otimes \neg\neg b)$. Thus, by 2 and by Ax$_{\text{Trans}}$, 4 holds.

From 1 and 4, by Df$_\approx$, the Th 3 ii) follows.

If a concept a is intensionally contained in every concept x, the concept a is called a *general concept,* and it is denoted by G. The general concept is unique up to the intensional identity, and it is defined as follows:

$$\text{Df}_G \qquad a \approx G =_{\text{df}} (\forall x)\ (x \geq a).$$

The next axiom of *KC* states that there is a concept, which is intensionally contained in every concept.

---

[5]This relation does not hold conversely without stating a further axiom for intensional double negation, i.e., Ax$_{\neg\neg}$: $b\ Y\ \neg a \rightarrow b \geq a$. Thus, $\neg\neg a \geq a$, and hence by Th 2, $a \approx \neg\neg a$, holds only, if the concept a is intensionally contained in the every concept b, which is incompatible with the intensional negation of the concept a.

$$\text{Ax}_G \qquad (\exists x)(\forall y)\,(y \geq x)\,.$$

Adopting the axiom of the general concept it follows that all concepts are to be comparable. Since the general concept is compatible with every concept, it has no intensional negation.

A *special concept* is a concept *a*, which is not intensionally contained in any other concept except for concepts intensionally identical to itself. Thus, there can be many special concepts.

$$\text{Df}_S \qquad S(a) =_{\text{df}} (\forall x)\,(x \geq a \rightarrow a \geq x)\,.$$

The last axiom of *KC* states that there is for any concept *y* a special concept *x* in which it is intensionally contained.

$$\text{Ax}_S \qquad (\forall y)(\exists x)\,(S(x) \wedge x \geq y)\,.$$

Since the special concept *s* is either compatible or incompatible with every concept, the *law of excluded middle* holds for *s* so that for any concept *x*, which has an intensional negation, either the concept *x* or its intensional negation $\neg x$ is intensionally contained in it. Hence, we have

$$\text{Th 4} \qquad (\forall x)S(s) \rightarrow (s \geq x \vee s \geq -x)..$$

A special concept, which corresponds Leibniz's complete concept of an individual, would contain one member of every pair of mutually incompatible concepts.

By *Completeness Theorem*, every consistent first-order theory has a model. Accordingly, in Palomäki (1994, 94-97) a model of *KC* + $\text{Ax}_{\neg\neg}$ is found to be a *complete semilattice*, where every concept $a \in C$ defines a *Boolean algebra* $B_a = \langle \downarrow a, \otimes, \oplus, \neg, G, a \rangle$, where $\downarrow a$ is an ideal, known as the *principal ideal generated by a, i.e.* $\downarrow a =_{\text{df}} \{x \in C \mid a \geq x\}$, and the intensional negation of a concept $b \in \downarrow a$ is interpreted as a *relative complement of a.*

It should be emphasized that in *KC* concepts in generally don't form a lattice structure as, for example, they do in Formal Concept Analysis, (Ganter & Wille, 1998). Only in a very special case in *KC* concepts will form a lattice structure; that is, when all the concepts are both comparable and compatible, in which case there will be no incompatible concepts and, hence, no intensional negation of a concept either.[6]

5. That IS-IN Isn't IS-A

In current literature, the relations between concepts are mostly based on the set theoretical relations between the extensions of concepts. For example, in Nebel & Smolka (1990), the conceptual intersection of the concepts of "man" and "woman" is the empty-concept, and their conceptual union is the concept of "adult". However, intensionally the common concept which contains both the concepts of "man" and of "woman", and so is their intensional conceptual intersection, is the concept of 'adult', not the empty-concept, and the concept in which they both are contained, and so is their intensional conceptual union, is the concept of "androgyne", not the concept of "adult". Moreover, if the extension of the empty-

[6]How this intensional concept theory *KC* is used in the context of conceptual modelling, *i.e.*, when developing a conceptual schemata, see especially (Kangassalo 1992/93, 2007).

concept is an empty set, then it would follow that the concepts of "androgyne", "centaur", and "round-square" are all equivalent with the empty-concept, which is absurd. Thus, although Nebel and Smolka are talking about concepts, they are dealing with them only in terms of extensional set theory, not intensional concept theory.

There are several reasons to separate intensional concept theory from extensional set theory, (Palomäki 1994). For instance: i) intensions determine extensions, but not conversely, ii) whether a thing belongs to a set is decided primarily by intension, iii) a concept can be used meaningfully even when there is not yet, nor ever will be, any individuals belonging to the extension of the concept in question, iv) there can be many non-identical but co-extensional concepts, v) extension of a concept may vary according to context, and vi) from Gödel's two Incompleteness Theorems it follows that intensions cannot be wholly eliminated from set theory.

One difference between extensionality and intensionality is that in extensionality a collection is determined by its elements, whereas in intensionality a collection is determined by a concept, a property, an attribute, etc. That means, for example, when we are creating a semantical network or a conceptual model by using an extensional IS-A relation as its taxonomical link, the existence of objects to be modeled are presupposed, whereas by using an intensional IS-IN relation between the concepts the existence of objects falling under those concepts are not presupposed. This difference is crucial when we are designing an object, which does not yet exist, but we have plenty of conceptual information about it, and we are building a conceptual model of it. In the set theoretical IS-A approach to a taxonomy the Universe of Discourse consists of individuals, whereas in the intensional concept theoretical IS-IN approach to a taxonomy the Universe of Discourse consists of concepts. Thus, in extensional approach we are moving from objects towards concepts, whereas in intensional approach we moving from concepts towards objects.

However, it seems that from strictly extensional approach we are not able to reach concepts without intensionality. The principle of extensionality in the set theory is given by a first-order formula as follows,

$$\forall A \forall B (\forall x (x \in A \leftrightarrow x \in B) \rightarrow A = B).$$

That is, if two *sets* have exactly the same members, then they are equal. Now, what is a set? - There are two ways to form a set: i) extensionally by listing all the elements of a set, for example, $A = \{a, b, c\}$, or ii) intensionally by giving the defining property $P(x)$, in which the elements of a set is to satisfy in order to belong to the set, for example, $B = \{x | \mathit{blue}(x)\}$, where the set B is the set of all blue things.[7] Moreover, if we then write "$x \in B$", we use the symbol

[7]In pure mathematics there are only sets, and a "definite" property, which appears for example in the axiom schemata of separation and replacement in the Zermelo-Fraenkel set theory, is one that could be formulated as a first order theory whose atomic formulas were limited to set membership and identity. However, the set theory is of no practical use in itself, but is used to other things as well. We assume a theory T, and we shall call the objects in the domain of interpretation of T *individuals*, (or *atoms*, or *Urelements*). To include the individuals, we introduce a predicate $U(x)$ to mean that x is an individual, and then we relativize all the axioms of T to U. That is, we replace every universal quantifier "$\forall x$" in an axiom of T with "$\forall x\ (U(x) \rightarrow ...)$ and every existential quantifier "$\exists x$" with "$\exists x\ (U(x) \wedge ...)$, and for every constant "a" in the language of T we add $U(a)$ as new axiom.

$\in$ to denote the membership. It abbreviates the Greek word *ἐστί*, which means "is", and it asserts that x *is* blue. Now, the intensionality is implicitly present when we are selecting the members of a set by some definite property $P(x)$, *i.e.*, we have to understand the property of being *blue*, for instance, in order to select the possible members of the set of all blue things (from the given Universe of Discourse).

An extensional view of concepts indeed is untenable. The fundamental property that makes extensions extensional is that concepts have the same extensions in case they have the same instances. Accordingly, if we use $\{x|\ a(x)\}$ and $\{x|\ b(x)\}$ to denote the extensions of the concepts a and b, respectively, we can express extensionality by means of the second-order principle,

$$\forall a \forall b (\forall x (a \cong b) \leftrightarrow (x \mid a(x)\} = \{x \mid b(x)\}). \qquad (*)$$

However, by accepting that principle some very implausible consequences will follow. For example, according to physiologists any creature with a heart also has a kidney, and *vice versa*. So the concepts of "heart" and "kidney" are co-extensional concepts, and then, by the principle (∗), the concepts of "heart" and "kidney" are 'identical' or interchangeable concepts. On the other hand, to distinguish between the concepts of "heart" and "kidney" is very relevant for instance in the case when someone has a heart-attack, and the surgeon, who is a passionate extensionalist, prefers to operate his kidney instead of the heart.

5.1 Intensionality in possible worlds semantic approach

Intensional notions (e.g. concepts) are not strictly formal notions, and it would be misleading to take these as subjects of study for logic only, since logic is concerned with the forms of propositions as distinct from their contents. Perhaps only part of the theory of intensionality which can be called formal is pure modal logic and its possible worlds semantic. However, in concept theories based on possible worlds semantic, (see e.g. Hintikka 1969, Montague 1974, Palomäki 1997, Duzi et al. 2010), intensional notions are defined as (possibly partial, but indeed set-theoretical) functions from the possible worlds to extensions in those worlds.

Also Nicola Guarino, in his key article on "ontology" in (1998), where he emphasized the intensional aspect of modelling, started to formalize his account of "ontology"[8] by the possible world semantics in spite of being aware that the possible world approach has some disadvantages, for instance, the two concepts "trilateral" and "triangle" turn out to be the same, as they have the same extension in all possible worlds.

---

[8]From Guarino's (1998) formalization of his view of "ontology", we will learn that the "ontology" for him is a set of axioms (language) such that its intended models approximate as well as possible the conceptualization of the world. He also emphasize that "it is important to stress that an ontology is *language-dependent*, while a conceptualization is *language-independent*." Here the word "conceptualization" means "a set of conceptual relations defined on a domain space", whereas by "the ontological commitments" he means the relation between the language and the conceptualization. This kind of language dependent view of "ontology" as well as other non-traditional use of the word "ontology" is analyzed and critized in Palomäki (2009).

In all these possible worlds approaches intensional notions are once more either reduced to extensional set-theoretic constructs in diversity of worlds or as being non-logical notions left unexplained. So, when developing an adequate presentation of a concept theory it has to take into account both formal (logic) and contentual (epistemic) aspects of concepts and their relationships.

5.2 Nominalism, conceptualism, and conceptual realism (Platonism)

In philosophy ontology is a part of metaphysics,[9] which aims to answer at least the following three questions:

1. What is there?
2. What is it, that there is?
3. How is that, that there is?

The first is (1) is perhaps the most difficult one, as it asks what elements the world is made up of, or rather, what are the building blocks from which the world is composed. A Traditional answer to this question is that the world consists of things and properties (and relations). An alternative answer can be found in Wittgenstein's Tractatus 1.1: "The world is the totality of facts, not of things", that is to say, the world consists of facts.

The second question (2) concerns the basic stuff from which the world is made. The world could be made out of one kind of stuff only, for example, water, as Thales suggests, or the world may be made out of two or more different kinds of stuff, for example, mind and matter.

The third question (3) concerns the mode of existence. Answers to this question could be the following ones, according to which something exists in the sense that:

a. it has some kind of concrete space-time existence,
b. it has some kind of abstract (mental) existence,
c. it has some kind of transcendental existence, in the sense that it extends beyond the space-time existence.

The most crucial ontological question concerning concepts and intensionality is: "What modes of existence may concepts have?" The traditional answers to it are that

i. concepts are merely predicate expressions of some language, i.e. they exist concretely, (nominalism);
ii. concepts exist in the sense that we have the socio-biological cognitive capacity to identify, classify, and characterize or perceive relationships between things in various ways, i.e. they exist abstractly, (conceptualism);
iii. concepts exist independently of both language and human cognition, i.e. transcendentally, (conceptual realism, Platonism).

If the concepts exist only concretely as linguistic terms, then there are only extensional relationships between them. If the concepts exist abstractly as a cognitive capacity, then

[9]Nowadays there are two sense of the word "ontology": the traditional one, which we may call a philosophical view, and the more modern one used in the area of information systems, which we may call a knowledge representational view, (see Palomäki 2009).

conceptualization is a private activity done by human mind. If the concepts exist transcendentally independently of both language and human cognition, then we have a problem of knowledge acquisition of them. Thus, the ontological question of the mode of existence of concepts is a deep philosophical issue. However, if we take an ontological commitment to a certain view of the mode of the existence of concepts, consequently we are making other ontological commitments as well. For example, realism on concepts is usually connected with realism of the world as well. In conceptualism we are more or less creating our world by conceptualization, and in nominalism there are neither intensionality nor abstract (or transcendental) entities like numbers.

6. Conclusion

In the above analysis of the different senses of IS-A relation in the Section 2 we took our starting point Brachman's analysis of it in (Brachman 1983), and to which we gave a further analysis in order to show that most of those analysis IS-A relation is interpreted as an extensional relation, which we are able to give set theoretical interpretation. However, for some of Brachman's instances we were not able to give an appropriate set theoretical interpretation, and those were the instances concerning concepts. Accordingly, in the Section 3 we turned our analysis of IS-IN relation following Aristotelian-Leibnizian approach to it, and to which we were giving an intensional interpretation; that is, IS-IN relation is an intensional relation between concepts. A formal presentation of the basic relations between terms, concepts, classes (or sets), and things was given in the Section 4 as well as the basic axioms of the intensional concept theory *KC*. In the last Section 5 some of the basic differences between the IS-IN relation and the IS-A relation was drawn.

So, in this Chapter we maintain that an IS-IN relation is not equal to an IS-A relation; more specifically, that Brachman's analysis of an *extensional* IS-A relation in his basic article: "What IS-A Is and Isn't: An Analysis of Taxonomic Links in Semantic Networks", (1983), did not include an *intensional* IS-IN relation. However, we are not maintain that Brachman's analysis of IS-A relation is wrong, or that there are some flaw in it, but that the IS-IN relation is different than the IS-A relation. Accordingly, we are proposing that the IS-IN relation is a conceptual relation between concepts and it is basically intensional relation, whereas the IS-A relation is to be reserved for extensional use only.

Provided that there are differences between intensional and extensional view when constructing hierarchical semantic networks, we are not allowed to identify concepts with their extensions. Moreover, in that case we are to distinguish the intensional IS-IN relation between concepts from the extensional IS-A relation between the extensions of concepts. However, only a thoroughgoing nominalist would identify concepts with their extensions, whereas for all the others this distinction is necessarily present.

7. References

Adams, R. M. (1994). *Leibniz: Determinist, Theist,* Idealist. New York, Oxford: Oxford University Press.

Aristotle, (1930). *Physics*. Trans. R. P. Hardie and R. K. Gaye, in *The Works of Aristotle*, Vol. 2, ed. W. D. Ross. Oxford: Clarendon Press.

Brachman, R. J. (1983). What IS-A Is and Isn't: An Analysis of Taxonomic Links in Semantic Networks", *IEEE Computer* 16(10), pp. 30-36.

Duzi, M., Jespersen, B. & Materna, P. (2010). *Procedural Semantics for Hyperintenisonal Logic.* Berlin etc.: Springer-Verlag.

Ganter, B. & Wille, R. (1998). *Formal Concept Analysis: Mathematical Foundations*, Berlin etc.: Springer-Verlag.

Guarino, N. (1998). Formal Ontology in Information Systems. *Formal Ontology in Information Systems. Proceedings of FOIS'98.* Ed. N. Guarino. Trento, Italy, 6-8 June 1998. Amsterdam, Washington, Tokyo: IOS Press, pp. 3-15.

Hintikka, J. (1969). *Models for Modalities.* Dordrecht: D. Reidel.

Kangassalo, H. (1992/93). COMIC: A system and methodology for conceptual modelling and information construction, *Data and Knowledge Engineering* 9, pp. 287-319.

Kangassalo, H. (2007). Approaches to the Active Conceptual Modelling of Learning. *ACM-L 2006.* LNCS 4512. Eds. P.P. Chen and L.Y. Wong. Berlin etc.: Springer-Verlag, pp. 168–193.

Kauppi, R. (1960). *Über die Leibnizsche Logic mit besonderer Berücksichtigung des Problems der Intension und der Extension.* Acta Philosophica Fennica, Fasc. XII. Helsinki: Societas Philosophica Fennica.

Kauppi, R. (1967). *Einführung in die Theorie der Begriffssysteme.* Acta Universitatis Tamperensis, Ser. A. Vol. 15. Tampere: University of Tampere.

Leibniz, G. W. (*after* 1690a). A Study Paper on 'some logical difficulties. In *Logical Papers: A Selection.* Trans. G. H. R. Parkinson. Oxford: Clarendon Press, 1966, pp. 115-121.

Leibniz, G. W. (*after* 1690b). A Study in the Calculus of Real Addition. In *Logical Papers: A Selection.* Trans. G. H. R. Parkinson. Oxford: Clarendon Press, 1966, pp. 131-144.

Leibniz, G. W. (1997). *Philosophical Writings.* Ed. G. H. R. Parkinson. Trans. M. Morris and G. H. R. Parkinson. London: The Everyman Library.

Montague, R. (1974). *Formal Philosophy.* Ed. R. Thomason. New Haven and London: Yale University Press.

Nebel, B. & Smolka, G. (1990). Representation and Reasoning with Attributive Descriptions. In *Sorts and Types in Artificial Intelligence.* Eds. Bläsius, K. H., Hedstück, U., and Rollinger, C. R. Lecture Notes in Computer Science 418. Berlin, etc.: Springer-Verlag, pp. 112-139.

Palomäki, J. (1994). *From Concepts to Concept Theory: Discoveries, Connections, and Results.* Acta Universitatis Tamperensis, Ser. A. Vol. 416. Tampere: University of Tampere.

Palomäki, J. (1997). Three Kinds of Containment Relations of Concepts. In *Information Modelling and Knowledge Bases VIII.* Eds. H. Kangassalo, J.F. Nilsson, H. Jaakkola, and S. Ohsuga. Amsterdam, Berlin, Oxford, Tokyo, Washington, DC.: IOS Press, 261-277.

Palomäki, J. (2009). Ontology Revisited: Concepts, Languages, and the World(s). *Databases and Information Systems V – Selected Papers from the Eighth International Baltic Conference, DB&IS 2008.* Eds. H.-M. Haav and A. Kalja. IOSPress: Amsterdam. Berlin, Tokyo, Washington D.C.: IOSPress, pp. 3-13.

Wittgenstein, L. (1921). *Tractatus Logico-Philosophicus.* Trans. by D. F. Pears and B. F. McGuinness. Routledge and Kegan Paul: London, 1961.

Woods, W. A. (1991). Understanding Subsumption and Taxonomy: A Framework for Progress. In *Principles of Semantic Networks – Explanations in the Representation of Knowledge.* Ed. J. Sowa. San Mateo, CA: Morgan Kaufmann Publishers, pp. 45-94.

2

K-Relations and Beyond

Melita Hajdinjak and Andrej Bauer
University of Ljubljana
Slovenia

1. Introduction

Although the theory of relational databases is highly developed and proves its usefulness in practice every day Garcia-Molina et al. (2008), there are situations where the relational model fails to offer adequate formal support. For instance, when querying *approximate data* Hjaltason & Brooks (2003); Minker (1998) or data within a given range of distance or *similarity* Hjaltason & Brooks (2003); Patella & Ciaccia (2009). Examples of such similarity-search applications are databases storing images, fingerprints, audio clips or time sequences, text databases with typographical or spelling errors, and text databases where we look for documents that are similar to a given document. A core component of such *cooperative* systems is a treatment of imprecise data Hajdinjak & Mihelič (2006); Minker (1998).

At the heart of a cooperative database system is a database where the data domains come equipped with a *similarity relation*, to denote degrees of similarity rather than simply 'equal' and 'not equal'. This notion of similarity leads to an extension of the relational model where data can be annotated with, for instance, boolean formulas (as in incomplete databases) Calì et al. (2003); Van der Meyden (1998), membership degrees (as in fuzzy databases) Bordogna & Psaila (2006); Yazici & George (1999), event tables (as in probabilistic databases) Suciu (2008), timestamps (as in temporal databases) Jae & Elmasri (2001), sets of contributing tuples (as in the context of data warehouses and the computation of lineages or why-provenance) Cui et al. (2000); Green et al. (2007), or numbers representing the multiplicity of tuples (as in the context of bag semantics) Montagna & Sebastiani (2001). Querying such *annotated* or *tagged relations* involves the generalization of the classical relational algebra to perform corresponding operations on the annotations (tags).

There have been many attempts to define extensions of the relational model to deal with similarity querying. Most utilize fuzzy logic Zadeh (1965), and the annotations are typically modelled by a membership function to the unit interval, $[0,1]$ Ma (2006); Penzo (2005); Rosado et al. (2006); Schmitt & Schulz (2004), although there are generalizations where the membership function instead maps to an algebraic structure of some kind (typically poset or lattice based) Belohlávek & V. Vychodil (2006); Peeva & Kyosev (2004); Shenoi & Melton (1989). Green et al. Green et al. (2007) proposed a general data model (referred to as the *$\mathcal{K}$-relation model*) for annotated relations. In this model tuples in a relation are annotated with a value taken from a *commutative semiring*, $\mathcal{K}$. The resulting positive relational algebra, $\mathrm{RA}^+_{\mathcal{K}}$, generalizes Codd's classic relational algebra Codd (1970), the bag algebra Montagna & Sebastiani (2001), the relational algebra on c-tables Imielinski & Lipski (1984), the probabilistic algebra on event tables Suciu (2008), and the provenance algebra Buneman et al. (2001); Cui et al. (2000). With relatively little work, the $\mathcal{K}$-relation model is also suitable as a basis for modelling data with similarities and simple, positive similarity queries Hajdinjak & Bierman (2011).

Geerts and Poggi Geerts & Poggi (2010) extended the positive relational algebra $\mathrm{RA}^+_{\mathcal{K}}$ with a difference operator, which required restricting the class of commutative semirings to commutative semirings with *monus* or *m-semirings*. Because the monus-based difference operator yielded the wrong answer for two semirings important for similarity querying, a different approach to modelling negative queries in the $\mathcal{K}$-relation model was proposed Hajdinjak & Bierman (2011). It required restricting the class of commutative semirings to commutative semirings with *negation* or *n-semirings*. In order to satisfy *all* of the classical relational identities (including the idempotence of union and self-join), Hajdinjak and Bierman Hajdinjak & Bierman (2011) made another restriction; for the annotation structure they chose *De Morgan frames*. In addition, since previous attempts to formalize similarity querying and the $\mathcal{K}$-relation model all suffered from an expressivity problem allowing only one annotation structure per relation (every tuple is annotated with a value), the *$\mathcal{D}$-relation* model was proposed in which every tuple is annotated with a tuple of values, one per attribute, rather than a single value.

Relying on the work on $\mathcal{K}$, $\mathcal{L}$-and $\mathcal{D}$-relations, we make some further steps towards a general model of annotated relations. We come to the conclusion that complete distributive lattices with finite meets distributing over arbitrary joins may be chosen as a general annotation structure. This choice covers the classical relations Codd (1970), relations on bag semantics Green et al. (2007); Montagna & Sebastiani (2001) Fuhr-Rölleke-Zimányi probabilistic relations Suciu (2008), provenance relations Cui et al. (2000); Green et al. (2007), Imielinksi-Lipski relations on *c*-tables Imielinski & Lipski (1984), and fuzzy relations Hajdinjak & Bierman (2011); Rosado et al. (2006). We also aim to define a general framework of $\mathcal{K}$, $\mathcal{L}$-and $\mathcal{D}$-relations in which all the previously considered kinds of annotated relations are modeled correctly. Our studies result in an attribute-annotated model of so called $\mathcal{C}$-relations, in which some freedom of choice when defining the relational operations is given.

This chapter is organized as follows. In §2 we recall the definitions of $\mathcal{K}$-relations and the positive relational algebra $\mathrm{RA}^+_{\mathcal{K}}$, along with $\mathrm{RA}^+_{\mathcal{K}}(\setminus)$, its extension to support negative queries. Section §3 recalls the definition of the tuple-annotated $\mathcal{L}$-relation model, the aim of which was to include similarity relations into the $\mathcal{K}$-relation framework of annotated relations. In §4 we present the attribute-annotated $\mathcal{D}$-relation model, where every attribute is associated with its own annotation domain, and we study the properties of the resulting calculus of relations. In section §5 we explore whether there is a common domain of annotations suitable for all forms of annotated relations, and we define a general $\mathcal{C}$-relation model. The final section §6 discusses the issue of ranking the annotated answers, and it gives some guidelines of future work.

2. The $\mathcal{K}$-relation model

In this section we recall the definitions of $\mathcal{K}$-relations and the positive relational algebra $\mathrm{RA}^+_{\mathcal{K}}$, along with $\mathrm{RA}^+_{\mathcal{K}}(\setminus)$, its extension to support negative queries. The aim of the $\mathcal{K}$-relation work was to provide a generalized framework capable of capturing various forms of annotated relations.

We first assume some base domains, or *types*, commonly written as τ, which are simply sets of ground values, such as integers and strings. Like the authors of previous work Geerts &

Poggi (2010); Green et al. (2007); Hajdinjak & Bierman (2011), we adopt the named-attribute approach, so a *schema*,

$$U = \{a_1\colon \tau_1, \ldots, a_n\colon \tau_n\}, \tag{1}$$

is a finite map from *attribute names* a_i to their types or domains

$$U(a_i) = \tau_i. \tag{2}$$

We represent an *U-tuple* as a map

$$t = \{a_1\colon v_1, \ldots, a_n\colon v_n\} \tag{3}$$

from attribute names a_i to values v_i of the corresponding domain, i.e.,

$$t(a_i) = v_i, \tag{4}$$

where $v_i \in \tau_i$ for $i = 1, \ldots, n$. We denote the set of all U-tuples by U-Tup.

2.1 Positive relational algebra $\mathbf{RA}^+_{\mathcal{K}}$

Consider generalized relations in which the tuples are annotated (tagged) with information of various kinds. A notationally convenient way of working with annotated relations is to model tagging by a function on all possible tuples. Green et al. Green et al. (2007) argue that the generalization of the positive relational algebra to annotated relations requires that the set of tags is a *commutative semiring*.

Recall that a *semiring*

$$\mathcal{K} = (K, \oplus, \odot, \mathbf{0}, \mathbf{1}) \tag{5}$$

is an algebraic structure with two binary operations (sum $\oplus$ and product $\odot$) and two distinguished elements ($\mathbf{0} \neq \mathbf{1}$) such that $(K, \oplus, \mathbf{0})$ is a commutative monoid[1] with identity element 0, $(K, \odot, \mathbf{1})$ is a monoid with identity element $\mathbf{1}$, products distribute over sums, and $\mathbf{0} \odot a = a \odot \mathbf{0} = \mathbf{0}$ for any $a \in K$ (i.e., $\mathbf{0}$ is an annihilating element). A semiring $\mathcal{K}$ is called commutative if monoid $(K, \odot, \mathbf{1})$ is commutative.

Definition 2.1 ($\mathcal{K}$-relation Green et al. (2007)). *Let $\mathcal{K} = (K, \oplus, \odot, \mathbf{0}, \mathbf{1})$ be a commutative semiring. A $\mathcal{K}$-relation over a schema $U = \{a_1\colon \tau_1, \ldots, a_n\colon \tau_n\}$ is a function $A\colon U\text{-Tup} \rightarrow K$ such that its support,*

$$\operatorname{supp}(A) = \{t \mid A(t) \neq \mathbf{0}\}, \tag{6}$$

is finite.

Taking this extension of relations, Green et al. proposed a natural lifting of the classical relational operators over $\mathcal{K}$-relations. The tuples considered to be 'in' the relation are tagged with $\mathbf{1}$ and the tuples considered to be 'out of' the relation are tagged with $\mathbf{0}$. The binary operation $\oplus$ is used to deal with union and projection and therefore to combine different tags of the same tuple into one tag. The binary operation $\odot$ is used to deal with natural join and therefore to combine the tags of joinable tuples.

Definition 2.2 (Positive relational algebra on $\mathcal{K}$-relations Green et al. (2007)). *Suppose $\mathcal{K} = (K, \oplus, \odot, \mathbf{0}, \mathbf{1})$ is a commutative semiring. The operations of the positive relational algebra on $\mathcal{K}$, denoted $RA^+_{\mathcal{K}}$, are defined as follows:*

[1] A monoid consists of a set equipped with a binary operation that is associative and has an identity element.

Empty relation: *For any set of attributes U, there is* $\emptyset_U : U\text{-}Tup \to K$ *such that*

$$\emptyset_U(t) \stackrel{\text{def}}{=} \mathbf{0} \tag{7}$$

for all U-tuples t.[2]

Union: *If* $A, B : U\text{-}Tup \to K$, *then* $A \cup B : U\text{-}Tup \to K$ *is defined by*

$$(A \cup B)(t) \stackrel{\text{def}}{=} A(t) \oplus B(t). \tag{8}$$

Projection: *If* $A : U\text{-}Tup \to K$ *and* $V \subset U$, *we write* $f \downarrow V$ *to be the restriction of the map f to the domain V. The projection* $\pi_V A : V\text{-}Tup \to K$ *is defined by*

$$(\pi_V A)(t) \stackrel{\text{def}}{=} \sum_{(t' \downarrow V) = t \text{ and } A(t') \neq \mathbf{0}} A(t'). \tag{9}$$

Selection: *If* $A : U\text{-}Tup \to K$ *and the selection predicate* $\mathbf{P}$ *maps each U-tuple to either* $\mathbf{0}$ *or* $\mathbf{1}$, *then* $\sigma_{\mathbf{P}} A : U\text{-}Tup \to K$ *is defined by*

$$(\sigma_{\mathbf{P}} A)(t) \stackrel{\text{def}}{=} A(t) \odot \mathbf{P}(t). \tag{10}$$

Join: *If* $A : U_1\text{-}Tup \to K$ *and* $B : U_2\text{-}Tup \to K$, *then* $A \bowtie B$ *is the* $\mathcal{K}$*-relation over* $U_1 \cup U_2$ *defined by*

$$(A \bowtie B)(t) \stackrel{\text{def}}{=} A(t \downarrow U_1) \odot B(t \downarrow U_2). \tag{11}$$

Renaming: *If* $A : U\text{-}Tup \to K$ *and* $\beta : U \to U'$ *is a bijection, then* $\rho_\beta A : U'\text{-}Tup \to K$ *is defined by*

$$(\rho_\beta A)(t) \stackrel{\text{def}}{=} A(t \circ \beta). \tag{12}$$

Note that in the case for projection, the sum is finite since A has finite support.

The power of this definition is that it generalizes a number of proposals for annotated relations and associated query algebras.

Lemma 2.1 (Example algebras on $\mathcal{K}$-relations Green et al. (2007))**.**

1. *The classical relational algebra with set semantics Codd (1970) is given by the* $\mathcal{K}$*-relational algebra on the boolean semiring* $\mathcal{K}_{\mathbb{B}} = (\mathbb{B}, \vee, \wedge, \mathsf{false}, \mathsf{true})$.
2. *The relational algebra with bag semantics Green et al. (2007); Montagna & Sebastiani (2001) is given by the* $\mathcal{K}$*-relational algebra on the semiring of counting numbers* $\mathcal{K}_{\mathbb{N}} = (\mathbb{N}, +, \cdot, 0, 1)$.
3. *The Fuhr-Rölleke-Zimányi probabilistic relational algebra on event tables Suciu (2008) is given by the* $\mathcal{K}$*-relational algebra on the semiring* $\mathcal{K}_{prob} = (\mathcal{P}(\Omega), \cup, \cap, \emptyset, \Omega)$ *where* Ω *is a finite set of events and* $\mathcal{P}(\Omega)$ *is the powerset of* Ω.
4. *The Imielinksi-Lipski algebra on c-tables Imielinski & Lipski (1984) is given by the* $\mathcal{K}$*-relational algebra on the semiring* $\mathcal{K}_{c\text{-}table} = (\mathsf{PosBool}(X), \vee, \wedge, \mathsf{false}, \mathsf{true})$ *where* $\mathsf{PosBool}(X)$ *is the set of all positive boolean expressions over a finite set of variables X in which any two equivalent expressions are identified.*

[2] As is standard, we drop the subscript on the empty relation where it can be inferred by context.

5. *The provenance algebra of polynomials with variables from X and coefficients from* $\mathbb{N}$ *Cui et al. (2000); Green et al. (2007) is given by the* $\mathcal{K}$*-relational algebra on the provenance semiring* $\mathcal{K}_{prov} = (\mathbb{N}[X], +, \cdot, 0, 1)$.

The positive relational algebra $\mathrm{RA}^+_{\mathcal{K}}$ satisfies many of the familiar relational equalities Ullman (1988; 1989).

Proposition 2.1 (Identities of $\mathcal{K}$-relations Green et al. (2007); Hajdinjak & Bierman (2011)). *The following identities hold for the positive relational algebra on* $\mathcal{K}$*-relations:*

- *union is associative, commutative, and has identity* $\emptyset$;
- *selection distributes over union and product;*
- *join is associative, commutative and distributive over union;*
- *projection distributes over union and join;*
- *selections and projections commute with each other;*
- *selection with boolean predicates gives all or nothing,* $\sigma_{\mathsf{false}}(A) = \emptyset$ *and* $\sigma_{\mathsf{true}}(A) = A$;
- *join with an empty relation gives an empty relation,* $A \bowtie \emptyset_U = \emptyset_U$ *where* A *is a* $\mathcal{K}$*-relation over a schema* U;
- *projection of an empty relation gives an empty relation,* $\pi_V(\emptyset) = \emptyset$.

It is important to note that the properties of idempotence of union, $A \cup A = A$, and self-join, $A \bowtie A = A$, are missing from this list. These properties fail for the bag semantics and provenance, so they fail to hold for the more general model.

Green et al. only considered positive queries and left open the problem of supporting negative query operators.

2.2 Relational algebra $\mathrm{RA}^+_{\mathcal{K}}(\setminus)$

Geerts and Poggi Geerts & Poggi (2010) recently proposed extending the $\mathcal{K}$-relation model by a difference operator following a standard approach for introducing a monus operator into an additive commutative monoid Amer (1984). First, they restricted the class of commutative semirings by requiring that every semiring additionally satisfy the following pair of conditions.

Definition 2.3 (GP-conditions Geerts & Poggi (2010)). *A commutative semiring* $\mathcal{K} = (K, \oplus, \odot, \mathbf{0}, \mathbf{1})$ *is said to satisfy the* GP conditions *if the following two conditions hold.*

1. *The preorder* $x \preceq y$ *on* K *defined as*

$$x \preceq y \text{ iff there exists a } z \in K \text{ such that } x \oplus z = y \tag{13}$$

   is a partial order.[3]

2. *For each pair of elements* $x, y \in K$*, the set* $\{z \in K; x \preceq y \oplus z\}$ *has a smallest element. (As* $\preceq$ *defines a partial order, this smallest element must be unique, if it exists.)*

Definition 2.4 (m-semiring Geerts & Poggi (2010)). *Let* $\mathcal{K} = (K, \oplus, \odot, \mathbf{0}, \mathbf{1})$ *be a commutative semiring that satisfies the GP conditions. For any* $x, y \in K$*, we define* $x \ominus y$ *to be the smallest element* z *such that* $x \preceq y \oplus z$*. A (commutative) semiring* $\mathcal{K}$ *that can be equipped with a* monus *operator* $\ominus$ *is called a* semiring with monus *or* m-semiring.

---

[3] While a *preorder* is a binary relation that is reflexive and transitive, a *partial order* is a binary relation that is refleksive, transitive, and antisymmetric.

Geerts and Poggi identified two equationally complete classes in the variety of m-semirings, namely

(1) m-semirings that are a boolean algebra (i.e., complemented distributive lattice with distinguished elements **0** and **1**), for which the monus behaves like set difference, and
(2) m-semirings that are the positive cone of a lattice-ordered commutative ring, for which the monus behaves like the truncated minus of the natural numbers.

Recall that a *lattice-ordered ring* (or l-ring) is an algebraic structure $\mathcal{K} = (K, \vee, \wedge, \oplus, -, \mathbf{0}, \odot)$ such that $(K, \vee, \wedge)$ is a lattice, $(K, \oplus, -, \mathbf{0}, \odot)$ is a ring, operation $\oplus$ is order-preserving, and for $x, y \geq \mathbf{0}$ we have $x \odot y \geq \mathbf{0}$. An l-ring is commutative if the multiplication operation $\odot$ is commutative. The set of elements x for which $\mathbf{0} \leq x$ is called the *positive cone* of the l-ring.

Lemma 2.2 (Example m-semirings Geerts & Poggi (2010)).

1. *The boolean semiring, $\mathcal{K}_{\mathbb{B}} = (\mathbb{B}, \vee, \wedge, \mathsf{false}, \mathsf{true})$, is a boolean algebra. We have*

$$\mathsf{false} \ominus \mathsf{false} = \mathsf{false},\ \mathsf{false} \ominus \mathsf{true} = \mathsf{false},\ \mathsf{true} \ominus \mathsf{false} = \mathsf{true},\ \mathsf{true} \ominus \mathsf{true} = \mathsf{false}. \tag{14}$$

2. *The semiring of counting numbers, $\mathcal{K}_{\mathbb{N}} = (\mathbb{N}, +, \cdot, 0, 1)$, is the positive cone of the ring of integers, $\mathbb{Z}$. The monus corresponds to the truncated minus,*

$$x \ominus y = \max\{0, x - y\}. \tag{15}$$

3. *The probabilistic semiring, $\mathcal{K}_{prob} = (\mathcal{P}(\Omega), \cup, \cap, \emptyset, \Omega)$, is a boolean algebra. The monus corresponds to set difference,*

$$X \ominus Y = X \setminus Y. \tag{16}$$

4. *In the case of the semiring of c-tables, $\mathcal{K}_{c\text{-}table} = (\mathsf{PosBool}(X), \vee, \wedge, \mathsf{false}, \mathsf{true})$, the monus cannot be defined unless negated literals are added to the base set, in which case we get a boolean algebra. For any two expressions $\phi_1, \phi_2 \in Bool(X)$ we then have*

$$\phi_1 \ominus \phi_2 = \phi_1 \wedge \neg\phi_2, \tag{17}$$

where negation $\neg$ over boolean expressions takes truth to falsity, and vice versa, and it interchanges the meet and the join operation.

5. *The provenance semiring, $\mathcal{K}_{prov} = (\mathbb{N}[X], +, \cdot, 0, 1)$, is the positive cone of the ring of polynomials from $\mathbb{Z}[X]$. The monus of two polynomials $f[X] = \sum_{\alpha \in I} f_\alpha x^\alpha$ and $g[X] = \sum_{\alpha \in I} g_\alpha x^\alpha$, where I is a finite subset of $\mathbb{N}^n$, corresponds to*

$$f[X] \ominus g[X] = \sum_{\alpha \in I} (f_\alpha \dot{-} g_\alpha) x^\alpha, \tag{18}$$

where $\dot{-}$ denotes the truncated minus on $\mathbb{N}$.

Given an m-semiring, the positive relational algebra $\mathrm{RA}^+_{\mathcal{K}}$ can be extended with the missing difference operator as follows.

Definition 2.5 (Relational algebra on $\mathcal{K}$-relations Geerts & Poggi (2010)). *Let $\mathcal{K}$ be an m-semiring. The algebra $RA^+_{\mathcal{K}}(\setminus)$ is obtained by extending $RA^+_{\mathcal{K}}$ with the operator:*

Difference *If $A, B : U\text{-}Tup \to K$, then the difference $A \setminus B : U\text{-}Tup \to K$ is defined by*

$$(A \setminus B)(t) \stackrel{\text{def}}{=} A(t) \ominus B(t). \tag{19}$$

Geerts and Poggi show that their resulting algebra coincides with the classical relational algebra, the bag algebra with the monus operator, the probabilistic relational algebra on event tables, the relational algebra on c-tables, and the provenance algebra.

3. The $\mathcal{L}$-relation model

In this section we recall the definition of the $\mathcal{L}$-relation model, the aim of which was to include similarity relations into the general $\mathcal{K}$-relation framework of annotated relations.

3.1 Domain similarities

In a similarity context it is typically assumed that all data domains come equipped with a similarity relation or similarity measure.

Definition 3.1 (Similarity measures Hajdinjak & Bierman (2011)). *Given a type τ and a commutative semiring $\mathcal{K} = (K, \oplus, \odot, \mathbf{0}, \mathbf{1})$, a* similarity measure *is a function $\rho\colon \tau \times \tau \to K$ such that ρ is reflexive, i.e. $\rho(x,x) = \mathbf{1}$.*

Following earlier work Shenoi & Melton (1989), only reflexivity of the similarity measure was required. Other properties don't hold in general Hajdinjak & Bauer (2009). For example, symmetry does not hold when similarity denotes driving distance between two points in a town because of one-way streets. Another property is transitivity, but there are a number of non-transitive similarity measures, e.g. when similarity denotes likeness between two colours.

Allowing only $\mathcal{K}$-valued similarity relations, Hajdinjak and Bierman Hajdinjak & Bierman (2011) modeled an answer to a query as a $\mathcal{K}$-relation in which each tuple is tagged by the similarity value between the tuple and the *ideal tuple*. (By an ideal tuple a tuple that perfectly fits the requirements of the similarity query is meant.) Prior to any querying, it is assumed that each U-tuple t has either desirability $A(t) = \mathbf{1}$ or $A(t) = \mathbf{0}$ whether it is in or out of A.

Example 3.1 (Common similarity measures). *Three common examples of similarity measures are as follows.*

1. *An equality measure $\rho\colon \tau \times \tau \to \mathbb{B}$ where $\rho(x,y) \stackrel{\text{def}}{=} \mathsf{true}$ if x and y are equal and false otherwise. Here, $\mathbb{B} = \{\mathsf{false}, \mathsf{true}\}$ is the underlying set of the commutative semiring*

$$\mathcal{K}_{\mathbb{B}} = (\mathbb{B}, \vee, \wedge, \mathsf{false}, \mathsf{true}), \tag{20}$$

   called the boolean semiring.

2. *A fuzzy equality measure $\rho\colon \tau \times \tau \to [0,1]$ where $\rho(x,y)$ expresses the degree of equality of x and y; the closer x and y are to each other, the closer $\rho(x,y)$ is to 1. Here, the unit interval $[0,1]$ is the underlying set of the commutative semiring*

$$\mathcal{K}_{[0,1]} = ([0,1], \max, \min, 0, 1), \tag{21}$$

   called the fuzzy semiring.

3. *A distance measure $\rho\colon \tau \times \tau \to [0, d_{max}]$ where $\rho(x,y)$ is the distance from x to y. Here, the closed interval $[0, d_{max}]$ is the underlying set of the commutative semiring*

$$\mathcal{K}_{[0,d_{max}]} = ([0, d_{max}], \min, \max, d_{max}, 0), \tag{22}$$

   called the distance semiring.

Because of their use the commutative semirings from this example were called similarity semirings.

A predefined environment of similarity measures that can be used for building queries is assumed—for every domain $\mathcal{K} = (K, \oplus, \odot, \mathbf{0}, \mathbf{1})$ and every $\mathcal{K}$-relation over a schema $U = \{a_1 \colon \tau_1, ..., a_n \colon \tau_n\}$ there are similarity measures

$$\rho_{a_i} : \tau_i \times \tau_i \to K, 1 \leq i \leq n. \tag{23}$$

3.2 The selection predicate

In the original Green et al. model (Definition 2.2) the selection predicate maps U-tuples to either the zero or the unit element of the semiring. Since in a similarity context we expect the selection predicate to reflect the relevance or the degree of membership of a particular tuple in the answer relation, not just the two possibilities of full membership ($\mathbf{1}$) or non-membership ($\mathbf{0}$), the following generalization to the original definition was proposed Hajdinjak & Bierman (2011).

Selection: If $A \colon U\text{-Tup} \to K$ and the selection predicate

$$\mathbf{P} \colon U\text{-Tup} \to K \tag{24}$$

maps each U-tuple to an element of K (instead of mapping to either $\mathbf{0}$ or $\mathbf{1}$), then $\sigma_{\mathbf{P}} A \colon U\text{-Tup} \to K$ is (still) defined by

$$(\sigma_{\mathbf{P}} A)(t) = A(t) \odot \mathbf{P}(t). \tag{25}$$

Selection queries can now be classified on whether they are based on the attribute values (as is normal in non-similarity queries) or whether they use the similarity measures. Selection queries can also use constant values.

Definition 3.2 (Primitive predicate Hajdinjak & Bierman (2011))**.** *Suppose in a schema $U = \{a_1 \colon \tau_1, \ldots, a_n \colon \tau_n\}$ the types of attributes a_i and a_j coincide. Then given a commutative semiring $\mathcal{K} = (K, \oplus, \odot, \mathbf{0}, \mathbf{1})$, for a given binary predicate θ, the* primitive predicate *$[a_i \, \theta \, a_j] \colon U\text{-Tup} \to K$ is defined as follows.*

$$[a_i \, \theta \, a_j](t) \stackrel{\text{def}}{=} \chi_{a_i \theta a_j}(t) = \begin{cases} \mathbf{1} & \text{if } t(a_i) \, \theta \, t(a_j), \\ \mathbf{0} & \text{otherwise.} \end{cases} \tag{26}$$

In words, $[a_i \, \theta \, a_j]$ behaves as the characteristic map of θ, where θ may be any arithmetic comparison operator among $=, \neq, <, >, \leq, \geq$.

Definition 3.3 (Similarity predicate Hajdinjak & Bierman (2011))**.** *Suppose in a schema $U = \{a_1 \colon \tau_1, \ldots, a_n \colon \tau_n\}$ the types of attributes a_i and a_j coincide. Given a commutative semiring $\mathcal{K} = (K, \oplus, \odot, \mathbf{0}, \mathbf{1})$, the* similarity predicate *$[a_i \texttt{ like } a_j] \colon U\text{-Tup} \to K$ is defined as follows.*

$$[a_i \texttt{ like } a_j](t) \stackrel{\text{def}}{=} \rho_{a_i}(t(a_i), t(a_j)). \tag{27}$$

A symmetric version is as follows.

$$[a_i \sim a_j] \stackrel{\text{def}}{=} [a_i \texttt{ like } a_j] \cup [a_j \texttt{ like } a_i], \tag{28}$$

where union ($\cup$) of selection predicates is defined below.

Definition 3.4. *Given a commutative semiring* $\mathcal{K} = (K, \oplus, \odot, \mathbf{0}, \mathbf{1})$*, union and intersection of two selection predicates* $\mathbf{P}_1, \mathbf{P}_2 \colon U\text{-}Tup \to K$ *is defined as follows.*

$$(\mathbf{P}_1 \cup \mathbf{P}_2)(t) \stackrel{\text{def}}{=} \mathbf{P}_1(t) \oplus \mathbf{P}_2(t), \tag{29}$$

$$(\mathbf{P}_1 \cap \mathbf{P}_2)(t) \stackrel{\text{def}}{=} \mathbf{P}_1(t) \odot \mathbf{P}_2(t). \tag{30}$$

3.3 Relational difference

Whilst the similarity semirings support a monus operation in the sense of Geerts and Poggi Geerts & Poggi (2010), the induced difference operator in the relational algebra does not behave as desired.

- The fuzzy semiring, $\mathcal{K}_{[0,1]} = ([0,1], \max, \min, 0, 1)$, satisfies the GP conditions, and the monus operator is as follows.

$$x \ominus y = \min\{z \in [0,1]; x \leq \max\{y,z\}\} = \begin{cases} 0 & \text{if } x \leq y, \\ x & \text{if } x > y. \end{cases} \tag{31}$$

  This induces the following difference operator in the relational algebra.

$$(A \setminus B)(t) = \begin{cases} 0 & \text{if } A(t) \leq B(t), \\ A(t) & \text{if } A(t) > B(t). \end{cases} \tag{32}$$

  Hajdinjak and Bierman Hajdinjak & Bierman (2011) regret that this is not the expected definition. First, fuzzy set difference is universally defined as $\min\{A(t), 1 - B(t)\}$ Rosado et al. (2006). Secondly, in similarity settings only totally irrelevant tuples should be annotated with 0 and excluded as a possible answer Hajdinjak & Mihelič (2006). In the case of the fuzzy set difference $A \setminus B$, these are exclusively those tuples t where $A(t) = 0$ or $B(t) = 1$, and certainly not where $A(t) \leq B(t)$.
- The distance semiring, $\mathcal{K}_{[0,d_{\max}]} = ([0, d_{\max}], \min, \max, d_{\max}, 0)$, satisfies the GP-conditions, and the monus operator is as follows.

$$x \ominus y = \max\{z \in [0, d_{\max}]; x \geq \min\{y,z\}\} = \begin{cases} d_{\max} & \text{if } x \geq y, \\ x & \text{if } x < y. \end{cases} \tag{33}$$

  This induces the following difference operator in the relational algebra.

$$(A \setminus B)(t) = \begin{cases} d_{\max} & \text{if } A(t) \geq B(t), \\ A(t) & \text{if } A(t) < B(t). \end{cases} \tag{34}$$

  Again, in the distance setting, we would expect the difference operator to be defined as $\max\{A(t), d_{\max} - B(t)\}$. Moreover, this is a continuous function in contrast to the step function behaviour of the operator above resulting from the monus definition.

Rather than using a monus-like operator, Hajdinjak and Bierman Hajdinjak & Bierman (2011) proposed a different approach using *negation*.

Definition 3.5 (Negation). *Given a set L equipped with a preorder, a* negation *is an operation* $\neg \colon L \to L$ *that reverts order,* $x \leq y \implies \neg y \leq \neg x$*, and is involutive,* $\neg\neg x = x$.

Definition 3.6 (n-semiring Hajdinjak & Bierman (2011)). *A (commutative) n-semiring* $\mathcal{K} = (K, \oplus, \odot, \mathbf{0}, \mathbf{1}, \neg)$ *is a (commutative) semiring* $(K, \oplus, \odot, \mathbf{0}, \mathbf{1})$ *equipped with negation,* $\neg\colon K \to K$ *(with respect to the preorder on K).*

Provided that $\mathcal{K} = (K, \oplus, \odot, \mathbf{0}, \mathbf{1}, \neg)$ is a commutative n-semiring, the difference of $\mathcal{K}$-relations $A, B : U\text{-Tup} \to K$ may be defined by

$$(A \setminus B)(t) \stackrel{\text{def}}{=} A(t) \odot \neg B(t). \tag{35}$$

Each of the similarity semirings has a negation operation that, in contrast to the monus, gives the expected notion of relational difference.

Example 3.2 (Relational difference over common similarity measures).

- *In the boolean semiring,* $\mathcal{K}_{\mathbb{B}} = (\mathbb{B}, \vee, \wedge, \mathsf{false}, \mathsf{true})$, *negation can be defined as complementation.*

$$\neg x \stackrel{\text{def}}{=} \begin{cases} \mathsf{true} & \textit{if } x = \mathsf{false}, \\ \mathsf{false} & \textit{if } x = \mathsf{true}. \end{cases} \tag{36}$$

  From the above we get exactly the monus-based difference of $\mathcal{K}_{\mathbb{B}}$*-relations.*

$$A(t) \odot \neg B(t) = A(t) \ominus B(t) = \begin{cases} \mathsf{false} & \textit{if } B(t) = \mathsf{true}, \\ A(t) & \textit{if } B(t) = \mathsf{false}. \end{cases} \tag{37}$$

- *In the fuzzy semiring,* $\mathcal{K}_{[0,1]} = ([0,1], \max, \min, 0, 1)$, *ordered by relation* $\leq$, *we can define a negation operator as*

$$\neg x \stackrel{\text{def}}{=} 1 - x. \tag{38}$$

  In the generalized fuzzy semiring $\mathcal{K}_{[a,b]} = ([a,b], \max, \min, a, b)$, *we can define* $\neg x \stackrel{\text{def}}{=} a + b - x$. *In the fuzzy semiring we thus get*

$$A(t) \odot \neg B(t) = \min\{A(t), 1 - B(t)\}, \tag{39}$$

  and in the generalized fuzzy semiring we get $A(t) \odot \neg B(t) = \min\{A(t), a + b - B(t)\}$. *These coincide with the fuzzy notions of difference on* $[0,1]$ *and* $[a,b]$, *respectively Rosado et al. (2006).*
- *In the distance semiring,* $\mathcal{K}_{[0,d_{max}]} = ([0, d_{max}], \min, \max, d_{max}, 0)$, *ordered by relation* $\geq$, *we can define a negation operator as*

$$\neg x \stackrel{\text{def}}{=} d_{max} - x. \tag{40}$$

  We again get the expected notion of difference.

$$A(t) \odot \neg B(t) = \max\{A(t), d_{max} - B(t)\}. \tag{41}$$

  This is a continuous function of $A(t)$ *and* $B(t)$, *and it calculates the greatest distance* d_{max} *only if* $A(t) = d_{max}$ *or* $B(t) = 0$.

Moreover, the negation operation gives the same result as the monus when $\mathcal{K}$ is the boolean semiring, $\mathcal{K}_{\mathbb{B}}$, the probabilistic semiring, $\mathcal{K}_{\text{prob}}$, or the semiring on c-tables, $\mathcal{K}_{c\text{-table}}$. Unfortunately, while the provenance semiring, $\mathcal{K}_{\text{prov}}$, and the semiring of counting numbers, $\mathcal{K}_{\mathbb{N}}$, both contain a monus, neither contains a negation operation. In general, not all m-semirings are n-semirings. The opposite also holds Hajdinjak & Bierman (2011).

3.4 Relational algebra on $\mathcal{L}$-relations

We have seen that the $\mathcal{K}$-relational algebra does not satisfy the properties of idempotence of union and self-join because, in general, the sum and product operators of a semiring are not idempotent. In order to satisfy *all* the classical relational identities (including idempotence of union and self-join) and to allow a comparison and ordering of tags, Hajdinjak and Bierman Hajdinjak & Bierman (2011) have restricted commutative n-semirings to De Morgan frames (with the lattice join defined as sum and the lattice meet as product). Recall that the lattice supremum $\vee$ and infimum $\wedge$ operators are always idempotent.

Definition 3.7 (De Morgan frame Salii (1983)). *A De Morgan frame, $\mathcal{L} = (L, \bigvee, \wedge, \mathbf{0}, \mathbf{1}, \neg)$, is a complete lattice $(L, \bigvee, \wedge, \mathbf{0}, \mathbf{1})$ where finite meets distribute over arbitrary joins, i.e.,*

$$x \wedge \bigvee_i y_i = \bigvee_i (x \wedge y_i), \tag{42}$$

and $\neg\colon L \to L$ is a negation operation.

Proposition 3.1 (De Morgan laws Salii (1983)). *Given a De Morgan frame $\mathcal{L} = (L, \bigvee, \wedge, \mathbf{0}, \mathbf{1}, \neg)$, the following laws hold.*

$$\neg\mathbf{0} = \mathbf{1} \tag{43}$$

$$\neg\mathbf{1} = \mathbf{0} \tag{44}$$

$$\neg(x \vee y) = \neg x \wedge \neg y \tag{45}$$

$$\neg(x \wedge y) = \neg x \vee \neg y \tag{46}$$

The similarity semirings from Example 3.1 are De Morgan frames, the same holds for the probabilistic semiring and the semiring on c-tables.

Definition 3.8 ($\mathcal{L}$-relation Hajdinjak & Bierman (2011)). *Let $\mathcal{L} = (L, \bigvee, \wedge, \mathbf{0}, \mathbf{1}, \neg)$ be a De Morgan frame. An $\mathcal{L}$-relation over a schema $U = \{a_1 \colon \tau_1, \ldots, a_n \colon \tau_n\}$ is a function $A\colon U\text{-}Tup \to L$.*

Definition 3.9 (Relational algebra on $\mathcal{L}$-relations Hajdinjak & Bierman (2011)). *Suppose $\mathcal{L} = (L, \bigvee, \wedge, \mathbf{0}, \mathbf{1}, \neg)$ is a De Morgan frame. The operations of the relational algebra on $\mathcal{L}$, denoted $RA_{\mathcal{L}}$, are defined as follows:*

Empty relation: *For any set of attributes U there is $\emptyset_U\colon U\text{-}Tup \to L$ such that*

$$\emptyset(t) \stackrel{\text{def}}{=} \mathbf{0} \tag{47}$$

for all U-tuples t.

Union: *If $A, B\colon U\text{-}Tup \to L$ then $A \cup B : U\text{-}Tup \to L$ is defined by*

$$(A \cup B)(t) \stackrel{\text{def}}{=} A(t) \vee B(t). \tag{48}$$

Projection: *If $A\colon U\text{-}Tup \to L$ and $V \subset U$, the projection of A on attributes V is defined by*

$$(\pi_V A)(t) \stackrel{\text{def}}{=} \bigvee_{(t' \downarrow V) = t \text{ and } A(t') \neq \mathbf{0}} A(t'). \tag{49}$$

Selection: *If $A\colon U\text{-}Tup \to L$ and the selection predicate $\mathbf{P}\colon U\text{-}Tup \to L$ maps each U-tuple to an element of $\mathcal{L}$, then $\sigma_{\mathbf{P}} A\colon U\text{-}Tup \to L$ is defined by*

$$(\sigma_{\mathbf{P}} A)(t) \stackrel{\text{def}}{=} A(t) \wedge \mathbf{P}(t). \tag{50}$$

Join: *If* $A\colon U_1$*-Tup* $\rightarrow L$ *and* $B\colon U_2$*-Tup* $\rightarrow L$*, then* $A \bowtie B$ *is the* $\mathcal{L}$*-relation over* $U_1 \cup U_2$ *defined by*

$$(A \bowtie B)(t) \stackrel{\text{def}}{=} A(t) \wedge B(t). \tag{51}$$

Difference: *If* $A, B\colon U$*-Tup* $\rightarrow L$*, then* $A \setminus B\colon U$*-Tup* $\rightarrow L$ *is defined by*

$$(A \setminus B)(t) \stackrel{\text{def}}{=} A(t) \wedge \neg B(t). \tag{52}$$

Renaming: *If* $A\colon U$*-Tup* $\rightarrow L$ *and* $\beta\colon U \rightarrow U'$ *is a bijection, then* $\rho_\beta A : U'$*-Tup* $\rightarrow L$ *is defined by*

$$(\rho_\beta A)(t) \stackrel{\text{def}}{=} A(t \circ \beta). \tag{53}$$

Unlike for $\mathcal{K}$-relations, we need not require that $\mathcal{L}$-relations have finite support, since De Morgan frames are complete lattices, which quarantees the existence of the join in the definition of projection.

It is important to note that since $\mathrm{RA}_\mathcal{L}$ satisfies *all* the main positive relational algebra identities, in terms of query optimization, all algebraic rewrites familiar from the classical (positive) relational algebra apply to $\mathrm{RA}_\mathcal{L}$ without restriction. Matters are a little different for the negative identities Hajdinjak & Bierman (2011). In fuzzy relations Rosado et al. (2006) many of the familiar laws concerning difference do not hold. For example, it is not the case that $A \setminus A = \emptyset$, and so it is not the case in general for the $\mathcal{L}$-relational algebra. Consequently, some (negative) identities from the classical relational algebra do not hold any more.

4. The $\mathcal{D}$-relation model

Notice that all tuples across all the $\mathcal{K}$-relations or the $\mathcal{L}$-relations in the database and intermediate relations in queries must be annotated with a value from the same commutative semiring $\mathcal{K}$ or De Morgan frame $\mathcal{L}$. To support simultaneously several different similarity measures (e.g., similarity of strings, driving distance between cities, likelihood of objects to be equal), and use these different measures in our queries (even within the same query), Hajdinjak and Bierman Hajdinjak & Bierman (2011) proposed to move from a tuple-annotated model to an attribute-annotated model. They associated every attribute with its own De Morgan frame. They generalized an $\mathcal{L}$-relation, which is a map from a tuple to an annotation value from a De Morgan frame, to a $\mathcal{D}$*-relation*, which is a map from a tuple to a corresponding tuple containing an annotation value for every element in the source tuple, referred to as a *De Morgan frame tuple*.

Definition 4.1 (De Morgan frame schema, De Morgan frame tuple, $\mathcal{D}$-relation Hajdinjak & Bierman (2011)).

- *A* De Morgan frame schema, $\mathcal{D} = \{a_1\colon \mathcal{L}_1, ..., a_n\colon \mathcal{L}_n\}$, *maps an attribute name,* a_i*, to a De Morgan frame,* $\mathcal{L}_i = (L_{a_i}, \bigvee_{a_i}, \wedge_{a_i}, \mathbf{0}_{a_i}, \mathbf{1}_{a_i}, \neg_{a_i})$.
- *A* De Morgan frame tuple, $s = \{a_1\colon l_1, ..., a_n\colon l_n\}$, *maps an attribute name,* a_i*, to a De Morgan frame element,* l_i.
- *Given a De Morgan frame schema,* $\mathcal{D}$*, a schema* U*, then a tuple* s *is said to be a* De Morgan frame tuple matching $\mathcal{D}$ over U *if* $dom(s) = dom(U) = dom(\mathcal{D})$*. The set of all De Morgan frame tuples matching* $\mathcal{D}$ *over* U *is denoted* $\mathcal{D}(U)$*-Tup.*
- *An* $\mathcal{D}$-relation over U *is a finite map from* U*-Tup to* $\mathcal{D}(U)$*-Tup.* Its support needs *not* be finite.

Definition 4.2 (Relational algebra with similarities Hajdinjak & Bierman (2011)). *The operations of the* relational algebra with similarities, *$RA_{\mathcal{D}}$, are defined as follows:*

Empty relation: *For any set of attributes U and corresponding De Morgan frame schema, $\mathcal{D}$, the empty $\mathcal{D}$-relation over U, $\emptyset_U$, is defined such that*

$$\emptyset_U(t)(a) \stackrel{\text{def}}{=} \mathbf{0}_a \tag{54}$$

where t is a U-tuple and $\mathcal{D}(a) = (L_a, \bigvee_a, \wedge_a, \mathbf{0}_a, \mathbf{1}_a, \neg_a)$.

Union: *If $A, B\colon U\text{-}Tup \to \mathcal{D}(U)\text{-}Tup$, then $A \cup B\colon U\text{-}Tup \to \mathcal{D}(U)\text{-}Tup$ is defined by*

$$(A \cup B)(t)(a) \stackrel{\text{def}}{=} A(t)(a) \vee_a B(t)(a) \tag{55}$$

where $\mathcal{D}(a) = (L_a, \bigvee_a, \wedge_a, \mathbf{0}_a, \mathbf{1}_a, \neg_a)$.

Projection: *If $A\colon U\text{-}Tup \to \mathcal{D}(U)\text{-}Tup$ and $V \subset U$, the projection of A on attributes V is defined by*

$$(\pi_V A)(t)(a) \stackrel{\text{def}}{=} \bigvee\nolimits_{(t' \downarrow V)=t \text{ and } A(t')(a) \neq \mathbf{0}_a} A(t')(a) \tag{56}$$

where $\mathcal{D}(a) = (L_a, \bigvee_a, \wedge_a, \mathbf{0}_a, \mathbf{1}_a, \neg_a)$.

Selection: *If $A\colon U\text{-}Tup \to \mathcal{D}(U)\text{-}Tup$ and the selection predicate $\mathbf{P}\colon U\text{-}Tup \to \mathcal{D}(U)\text{-}Tup$ maps each U-tuple to an element of $\mathcal{D}(U)$-Tup, then $\sigma_{\mathbf{P}} A\colon U\text{-}Tup \to \mathcal{D}(U)\text{-}Tup$ is defined by*

$$(\sigma_{\mathbf{P}} A)(t)(a) \stackrel{\text{def}}{=} A(t)(a) \wedge_a \mathbf{P}(t)(a) \tag{57}$$

where $\mathcal{D}(a) = (L_a, \bigvee_a, \wedge_a, \mathbf{0}_a, \mathbf{1}_a, \neg_a)$.

Join: *Let $\mathcal{D}_1 = \{a_1\colon \mathcal{L}_1, ..., a_n\colon \mathcal{L}_n\}$ and $\mathcal{D}_2 = \{b_1\colon \mathcal{L}'_1, ..., b_m\colon \mathcal{L}'_m\}$ be De Morgan frame schemata. Let their union, $\mathcal{D}_1 \cup \mathcal{D}_2$, contain an attribute, $c_i\colon \mathcal{L}_i$, as soon as $c_i\colon \mathcal{L}_i$ is in $\mathcal{D}_1$ or $\mathcal{D}_2$ or both. (If there is an attribute with different corresponding De Morgan frames in $\mathcal{D}_1$ and $\mathcal{D}_2$, a renaming of attributes is needed.) If $A\colon U_1\text{-}Tup \to \mathcal{D}_1(U_1)\text{-}Tup$ and $B\colon U_2\text{-}Tup \to \mathcal{D}_2(U_2)\text{-}Tup$, then $A \bowtie B$ is the $(\mathcal{D}_1 \cup \mathcal{D}_2)$-relation over $U_1 \cup U_2$ defined as follows.*

$$(A \bowtie B)(t)(a) \stackrel{\text{def}}{=} \begin{cases} A(t \downarrow U_1)(a) & \text{if } a \in U_1 - U_2 \\ B(t \downarrow U_2)(a) & \text{if } a \in U_2 - U_1\,. \\ A(t \downarrow U_1)(a) \wedge_a B(t \downarrow U_2)(a) \end{cases} \tag{58}$$

Difference: *If $A, B\colon U\text{-}Tup \to \mathcal{D}(U)\text{-}Tup$, then $A \setminus B\colon U\text{-}Tup \to \mathcal{D}(U)\text{-}Tup$ is defined by*

$$(A \setminus B)(t)(a) \stackrel{\text{def}}{=} A(t)(a) \wedge_a (\neg_a B(t)(a)) \tag{59}$$

where $\mathcal{D}(a) = (L_a, \bigvee_a, \wedge_a, \mathbf{0}_a, \mathbf{1}_a, \neg_a)$.

Renaming: *If $A\colon U\text{-}Tup \to \mathcal{D}(U)\text{-}Tup$ and $\beta\colon U \to U'$ is a bijection, then $\rho_\beta A\colon U'\text{-}Tup \to \mathcal{D}(U')\text{-}Tup$ is defined by*

$$(\rho_\beta A)(t)(a) \stackrel{\text{def}}{=} A(t)(\beta(a)). \tag{60}$$

As in the case of $\mathcal{L}$-relations it is required that every tuple outside of a similarity database is ranked with the minimal De Morgan frame tuple, $\{a_1\colon \mathbf{0}_1, \ldots, a_n\colon \mathbf{0}_n\}$, and every other tuple is ranked either with the maximal De Morgan frame tuple, $\{a_1\colon \mathbf{1}_1, \ldots, a_n\colon \mathbf{1}_n\}$, or a smaller De Morgan frame tuple expressing a lower degree of containment of the tuple in the database.

Proposition 4.1 (Identities of $\mathcal{D}$-relations Hajdinjak & Bierman (2011)). *The following identities hold for the relational algebra on $\mathcal{D}$-relations:*

- *union is associative, commutative, idempotent, and has identity $\emptyset$;*
- *selection distributes over union and difference;*
- *join is associative and commutative, and distributes over union;*
- *projection distributes over union and join;*
- *selections and projections commute with each other;*
- *difference has identity $\emptyset$ and distributes over union and intersection;*
- *selection with boolean predicates gives all or nothing, $\sigma_{\mathsf{false}}(A) = \emptyset$ and $\sigma_{\mathsf{true}}(A) = A$, where $\mathsf{false}(\mathsf{t})(\mathsf{a}) = \mathbf{0}_\mathsf{a}$ and $\mathsf{true}(\mathsf{t})(\mathsf{a}) = \mathbf{1}_\mathsf{a}$ for $\mathcal{D}(a) = (L_a, \bigvee_a, \bigwedge_a, \mathbf{0}_a, \mathbf{1}_a, \neg_a)$;*
- *join with an empty relation gives an empty relation, $A \bowtie \emptyset_U = \emptyset_U$ where A is a $\mathcal{D}$-relation over a schema U;*
- *projection of an empty relation gives an empty relation, $\pi_V(\emptyset) = \emptyset$.*

Each of the similarity measures associated with the attributes maps to its own De Morgan frame. Again, a predefined environment of similarity measures that can be used for building queries is assumed—for every $\mathcal{D}$-relation over U, where $\mathcal{D} = \{a_1 \colon \mathcal{L}_1, ..., a_n \colon \mathcal{L}_n\}$ and $\mathcal{L}_i = (L_i, \bigvee_i, \bigwedge_i, \mathbf{0}_i, \mathbf{1}_i, \neg_i)$ and $U = \{a_1 \colon \tau_1, ..., a_n \colon \tau_n\}$ there is a similarity measure

$$\rho_{a_i} \colon \tau_i \times \tau_i \to L_i, 1 \le i \le n. \tag{61}$$

In the $\mathcal{D}$-relation model, primitive and similarity predicates need to be redefined.

Definition 4.3 (Primitive predicates Hajdinjak & Bierman (2011)). *Suppose in a schema $U = \{a_1 \colon \tau_1, \ldots, a_n \colon \tau_n\}$ the types of attributes a_i and a_j coincide. Then for a given binary predicate θ, the* primitive predicate

$$[a_i\, \theta\, a_j] \colon U\text{-}Tup \to \mathcal{D}(U)\text{-}Tup \tag{62}$$

is defined as follows.

$$[a_i\, \theta\, a_j](t)(a_k) \stackrel{\text{def}}{=} \begin{cases} \chi_{a_i \theta a_j}(t) & \text{if } k = i \text{ or } k = j, \\ \mathbf{1}_k & \text{otherwise.} \end{cases} \tag{63}$$

In words, $[a_i\, \theta\, a_j]$ has value **1** in every attribute except a_i and a_j, where it behaves as the characteristic map of θ defined as follows.

$$\chi_{a_i \theta a_j}(t) \stackrel{\text{def}}{=} \begin{cases} \mathbf{1}_k & \text{if } t(a_i)\, \theta\, t(a_j), \\ \mathbf{0}_k & \text{otherwise.} \end{cases} \tag{64}$$

Similarity predicates annotate tuples based on the similarity measures.

Definition 4.4 (Similarity predicates Hajdinjak & Bierman (2011)). *Suppose in a schema $U = \{a_1 \colon \tau_1, \ldots, a_n \colon \tau_n\}$ the types of attributes a_i and a_j coincide. The similarity predicate $[a_i \texttt{ like } a_j] \colon U\text{-}Tup \to \mathcal{D}(U)\text{-}Tup$ is defined as follows.*

$$[a_i \texttt{ like } a_j](t)(a_k) \stackrel{\text{def}}{=} \begin{cases} \rho_{a_i}(t(a_i), t(a_j)) & \text{if } a_k = a_i, \\ \rho_{a_j}(t(a_i), t(a_j)) & \text{if } a_k = a_j, \\ \mathbf{1}_k & \text{otherwise.} \end{cases} \tag{65}$$

In words, $[a_i \texttt{ like } a_j]$ *measures similarity of attributes* a_i *and* a_j*, each with its own similarity measure. The symmetric version is defined as follows.*

$$[a_i \sim a_j] \stackrel{\text{def}}{=} [a_i \texttt{ like } a_j] \cup [a_j \texttt{ like } a_i]. \tag{66}$$

Now union and intersection of selection predicates are computed component-wise.

Given the similarity measures associated with attributes, it is possible to define similarity-based variants of other familiar relational operators, such as similarity-based joins Hajdinjak & Bierman (2011). Such an operator joins two rows not only when their join-attributes have equal associated values, but when the values are similar.

5. A common framework

In this section we explore whether there is a common domain of annotations suitable for all kinds of annotated relations, and we define a general model of $\mathcal{K}$, $\mathcal{L}$-and $\mathcal{D}$-relations.

5.1 A common annotation domain

We have recalled two notions of difference on annotated relations: the monus-based difference proposed by Geerts and Poggi Geerts & Poggi (2010) and the negation-based difference proposed by Hajdinjak and Bierman Hajdinjak & Bierman (2011). We have seen in §3.3 that the monus-based difference does not have the qualities expected in a fuzzy context. The negation-based difference, on the other hand, does agree with the standard fuzzy difference, but it is not defined for bag semantics (and provenance). More precisely, the semiring of counting numbers, $\mathcal{K}_{\mathbb{N}} = (\mathbb{N}, +, \cdot, 0, 1)$, cannot be extended with a negation operation. (The same holds for the provenance semiring.)

We could try to modify the semiring of counting numbers in such a way that negation can be defined. For instance, if we replace $\mathbb{N}$ by $\mathbb{Z}$, we get the ring of integers, $(\mathbb{Z}, +, \cdot, 0, 1)$, where negation can be defined as $\neg x \stackrel{\text{def}}{=} -x$. This implies $(A \setminus B)(t) = -A(t) \cdot B(t)$, which is not equal to the standard difference of relations annotated with the tuples' multiplicities Montagna & Sebastiani (2001). Some other modifications would give the so called *tropical semirings* Aceto et al. (2001) whose underlying carrier set is some subset of the set of real numbers $\mathbb{R}$ equipped with binary operations of minimum or maximum as sum, and addition as product.

Let us now study the properties of the annotation structures of both approaches.

Proposition 5.1 (Identities in an m-semiring Bosbach (1965)). *The notion of an m-semiring is characterized by the properties of commutative semirings and the following identities involving* $\ominus$.

$$x \ominus x = \mathbf{0}, \tag{67}$$

$$\mathbf{0} \ominus x = \mathbf{0}, \tag{68}$$

$$x \oplus (y \ominus x) = y \oplus (x \ominus y), \tag{69}$$

$$x \ominus (y \oplus z) = (x \ominus y) \ominus z, \tag{70}$$

$$x \odot (y \ominus z) = (x \odot y) \ominus (x \odot z). \tag{71}$$

Notice that even in a De Morgan frame a difference-like operation may be defined,

$$x \div y \stackrel{\text{def}}{=} x \wedge \neg y. \tag{72}$$

Clearly, negation is then expressed as $\neg x = 1 \div x$.

Proposition 5.2 (Identities in a De Morgan frame). *In a De Morgan frame the following identities involving $\div$ hold.*

$$\mathbf{1} \div \mathbf{0} = \mathbf{1}, \tag{73}$$
$$\mathbf{1} \div \mathbf{1} = \mathbf{0}, \tag{74}$$
$$\mathbf{1} \div (x \vee y) = (\mathbf{1} \div x) \wedge (\mathbf{1} \div y), \tag{75}$$
$$\mathbf{1} \div (x \wedge y) = (\mathbf{1} \div x) \vee (\mathbf{1} \div y), \tag{76}$$
$$\mathbf{0} \div x = \mathbf{0}, \tag{77}$$
$$\mathbf{1} \div (\mathbf{1} \div x) = x, \tag{78}$$
$$x \div (\mathbf{1} \div y) = x \wedge y, \tag{79}$$
$$\mathbf{1} \div (\mathbf{1} \div (x \vee y)) = x \vee y, \tag{80}$$
$$\mathbf{1} \div (x \div y) = (\mathbf{1} \div x) \vee y, \tag{81}$$
$$(x \div y) \wedge y = x \wedge (y \div y), \tag{82}$$
$$(x \div y) \vee y = (x \vee y) \wedge (\mathbf{1} \div (y \div y)). \tag{83}$$

Proof. The first four identities are exactly the De Morgan laws from Proposition 3.1. The rest holds by simple expansion of definitions and/or is implied by the De Morgan laws. □

Notice the differences between the properties of the monus-based difference $\ominus$ in an m-semiring and the properties of the negation-based difference $\div$ in a De Morgan frame. For instance, in a De Morgan frame we do *not* have $x \div x = \mathbf{0}$ in general.

However, since neither of the proposed notions of difference give the expected result for all kinds of annotated relations, an annotation structure different from m-semirings and De Morgan frames is needed. Observe that by its definition, a complete (even bounded) distributive lattice, $\mathcal{L} = (L, \vee, \wedge, \mathbf{0}, \mathbf{1})$, is a commutative semiring with the natural order $\preceq$ being the lattice order, $a \oplus b = a \vee b$ and $a \odot b = a \wedge b$ for every a, b in L. Because lattice completeness assures the existence of a smallest element in every set and hence the existence of the monus (see Definition 2.3 on GP-conditions), a complete distributive lattice is an m-semiring. On the other hand, if a commutative semiring, $\mathcal{K} = (K, \oplus, \odot, \mathbf{0}, \mathbf{1})$, is partially ordered by $\preceq$ and any two elements from K have an infimum and a supremum, it is a lattice, not necessarily bounded Davey & Priestley (1990). The lattice meet and join are then determined by the partial order $\preceq$, and they are, in general, different from $\oplus$ and $\odot$. Since $\mathbf{0} \oplus a = a$, we have $\mathbf{0} \preceq a$ for any $a \in K$, and $\mathbf{0}$ is the least element of the lattice. In general, a similar observation does not hold for $\mathbf{1}$, which is hence not the greatest element of the lattice.

The underlying carrier sets of all the semirings considered are partially ordered sets, even distributive lattices. The unbounded lattices among them (i.e., $\mathcal{K}_{\mathbb{N}}$ and $\mathcal{K}_{\text{prov}}$) can be converted into bounded (even complete) lattices by adding a greatest element. To achieve this we just need to replace $\mathbb{N} \cup \{\infty\}$ for $\mathbb{N}$ and define appropriate calculation rules for ∞.

Lemma 5.1 (Making unbounded partially ordered semirings bounded).

1. *The semiring of counting numbers,* $\mathcal{K}_{\mathbb{N}} = (\mathbb{N}, +, \cdot, 0, 1)$*, partially ordered by*

$$n \preceq m \iff n \leq m, \tag{84}$$

may be extended to the partially ordered commutative semiring $(\mathbb{N} \cup \{\infty\}, +, \cdot, 0, 1)$ *by defining* $\infty + n = \infty$ *and* $\infty \cdot n = \infty$ *except* $\infty \cdot 0 = 0$*. The partial order* $\preceq$ *now determines a complete lattice structure,* $(\mathbb{N} \cup \{\infty\}, \max, \min, 0, \infty)$.

2. *The provenance semiring,* $\mathcal{K}_{prov} = (\mathbb{N}[X], +, \cdot, 0, 1)$*, partially ordered by*

$$f[X] \preceq g[X] \iff f_\alpha \leq g_\alpha \textit{ for all } \alpha \in I, \tag{85}$$

where $f[X] = \sum_{\alpha \in I} f_\alpha x^\alpha$ *and* $g[X] = \sum_{\alpha \in I} g_\alpha x^\alpha$*, may be extended to the commutative semiring* $((\mathbb{N} \cup \{\infty\})[X], +, \cdot, 0, 1)$ *by defining* $x^\infty \cdot x^n = x^\infty$ *as well as* $\infty + n = \infty$ *and* $\infty \cdot n = \infty$ *except* $\infty \cdot 0 = 0$ *as before. The partial order* $\preceq$ *now determines a complete lattice structure on* $(\mathbb{N} \cup \{\infty\})[X]$ *with*

$$f[X] \wedge g[X] = \sum_{\alpha \in I} \min\{f_\alpha, g_\alpha\} x^\alpha, \tag{86}$$

$$f[X] \vee g[X] = \sum_{\alpha \in I} \max\{f_\alpha, g_\alpha\} x^\alpha. \tag{87}$$

The least element of the lattice is the zero polynomial, 0, and the greatest element is the polynomial with all coefficients equal to ∞.

To summarize, a complete distributive lattice is an m-semiring. If the lattice even contains negation, we have two difference-like operations; monus $\ominus$ and $\div$, which is induced by negation. There is a class of annotated relations when only one of them ($\ominus$ for bag semantics and provenance, $\div$ for fuzzy semantics) gives the standard notion of relational difference, and there is a class of annotated relations when they both coincide (e.g., classical set semantics, probabilistic relations, and relations on c-tables).

Proposition 5.3 (General annotation structure)**.** *Complete distributive lattices with finite meets distributing over arbitrary joins are suitable codomains for all considered annotated relations.*

Proof. The boolean semiring, the probabilistic semiring, the semiring on c-tables, the similarity semirings as well as the semiring of counting numbers and the provenance semiring (see Lemma 5.1) can all be extended to a complete distributive lattice in which finite meets distribute over arbitrary joins. The later property allows to model infinite relations satisfying all the desired relational identities from Proposition 4.1, including commuting selections and projections. Relational difference may be modeled with the existing monus, $\ominus$, or $\div$ if the lattice is a De Morgan frame where a negation exists. The other (positive) relational operations are modeled using lattice meet, $\wedge$, and join, $\vee$, or semiring sum, $\oplus$, and product, $\odot$. □

5.2 A common model

Recall that Green et al. Green et al. (2007) defined a $\mathcal{K}$-relation over $U = \{a_1 \colon \tau_1, \ldots, a_n \colon \tau_n\}$ as a function $A \colon U\text{-Tup} \to K$ with finite support. The finite-support requirement was made to ensure the existence of the sum in the definition of relational projection. When the commutative semiring $\mathcal{K} = (K, \oplus, \odot, \mathbf{0}, \mathbf{1})$ was replaced by a De Morgan frame, $\mathcal{L} = (L, \bigvee, \wedge, \mathbf{0}, \mathbf{1}, \neg)$, the finite-support requirement became unnecessary; the existence of the join in the definition of projection was guaranteed by the completeness of the codomain.

To model similarity relations more efficiently, Hajdinjak and Bierman Hajdinjak & Bierman (2011) introduced a $\mathcal{D}$-relation over U as a function from U-Tup to $\mathcal{D}(U)$-Tup assigning every element of U-Tup (row of a table) a tuple of different annotation values. We adopt Definition 4.1 to the proposed general annotation structure, and show that a tuple-annotated model may be injectively mapped to an attribute-annotated model.

Definition 5.1 (Annotation schema,annotation tuple,$\mathcal{C}$-relation).

- *An* annotation schema, $\mathcal{C} = \{a_1 \colon \mathcal{L}_1, ..., a_n \colon \mathcal{L}_n\}$, *over* $U = \{a_1 \colon \tau_1, ..., a_n \colon \tau_n\}$ *maps an attribute name,* a_i, *to a complete distributive lattice in which finite meets distribute over arbitrary joins,* $\mathcal{L}_i = (L_{a_i}, \bigvee_{a_i}, \wedge_{a_i}, \mathbf{0}_{a_i}, \mathbf{1}_{a_i})$.
- *An* annotation tuple, $s = \{a_1 \colon l_1, ..., a_n \colon l_n\}$, *maps an attribute name,* a_i, *to an element of a complete distributive lattice in which finite meets distribute over arbitrary joins,* l_i. *The set of all* annotation tuples *matching* $\mathcal{C}$ *over* U *is denoted* $\mathcal{C}(U)$*-Tup.*
- *An* $\mathcal{C}$-relation over U *is a finite map from* U*-Tup to* $\mathcal{C}(U)$*-Tup.*

Proposition 5.4 (Injection of a tuple-annotated model to an attribute-annotated model). *Let* $\mathcal{A}$ *be the class of all functions* $A \colon U$*-Tup* $\to L$ *where* U *is any relational schema and* $\mathcal{L} = (L, \bigvee, \wedge, \mathbf{0}, \mathbf{1})$ *is any complete distributive lattice with finite meets distributing over arbitrary joins. Let* $\mathcal{B}$ *be the class of all* $\mathcal{C}$*-relations over* U, $B \colon U$*-Tup* $\to \mathcal{C}(U)$*-Tup, where* $\mathcal{C}$ *is an annotation schema. There is an injective function* $F \colon \mathcal{A} \to \mathcal{B}$ *defined by*

$$F(A)(t)(a_i) \stackrel{\text{def}}{=} A(t) \tag{88}$$

for all attributes a_i *in* U *and tuples* $t \in U$*-Tup.*

Proof. For $A_1, A_2 \in \mathcal{A}$ with $A_1(t) \neq A_2(t)$ we clearly have $F(A_1)(t)(a_i) \neq F(A_2)(t)(a_i)$. □

Proposition 5.4 says that moving from tuple-annotated relations to attribute-annotated relations does not prevent us from correctly modeling the examples covered by the $\mathcal{K}$-relation model in which each tuple is annotated with a single value from $\mathcal{K}$. The annotation value just appears several times. We thus propose a model of $\mathcal{C}$-relations, a common model of $\mathcal{K}$, $\mathcal{L}$-and $\mathcal{D}$-relations, that is attribute annotated. The definitions of union, projection, selection, and join of $\mathcal{C}$-relations may be based on the lattice join and meet operations (like in Definitions 3.9 and 4.2) or, if there exist semiring sum and product operations different from lattice join and meet, the positive relational operations may be defined using these additional semiring operations (like in Definition 2.2). The definition of relational difference may be based on the monus or, when dealing with De morgan frames where a negation exists, the derived $\div$ operation

Definition 5.2 (Relational algebra on $\mathcal{C}$-relations). *Consider* $\mathcal{C}$*-relations where all the lattices* $\mathcal{L}_i = (L_{a_i}, \bigvee_{a_i}, \wedge_{a_i}, \mathbf{0}_{a_i}, \mathbf{1}_{a_i})$ *from annotation schema* $\mathcal{C} = \{a_1 \colon \mathcal{L}_1, ..., a_n \colon \mathcal{L}_n\}$ *are complete distributive lattices in which finite meets distribute over arbitrary joins. Let* $\bigtriangledown_{a_i}$ *and* $\vartriangle_{a_i}$ *stand for either the lattice* $\vee_{a_i}$ *and* $\wedge_{a_i}$ *or some other semiring* $\oplus_{a_i}$ *and* $\odot_{a_i}$ *operations defined on the carrier set* L_{a_i} *of a* $\mathcal{L}_i$*, respectively. Let* $-_{a_i}$ *stand for either the monus* $\ominus_{a_i}$ *or a* $\div_{a_i}$ *operation defined on* L_{a_i}*. The operations of the relational algebra on* $\mathcal{C}$*, denoted* $RA_{\mathcal{C}}$*, are defined as follows.*

Empty relation: *For any set of attributes* U *and corresponding annotation schema,* $\mathcal{C}$*, the empty* $\mathcal{C}$*-relation over* U, $\emptyset_U$*, is defined by*

$$\emptyset_U(t)(a) \stackrel{\text{def}}{=} \mathbf{0}_a. \tag{89}$$

Union: *If $A, B\colon U$-Tup $\to \mathcal{C}(U)$-Tup, then $A \cup B\colon U$-Tup $\to \mathcal{C}(U)$-Tup is defined by*

$$(A \cup B)(t)(a) \stackrel{\text{def}}{=} A(t)(a) \nabla_a B(t)(a). \tag{90}$$

Projection: *If $A\colon U$-Tup $\to \mathcal{C}(U)$-Tup and $V \subset U$, the projection of A on attributes V is defined by*

$$(\pi_V A)(t)(a) \stackrel{\text{def}}{=} \nabla_{(t' \downarrow V)=t \text{ and } A(t')(a) \neq \mathbf{0}_a} A(t')(a). \tag{91}$$

Selection: *If $A\colon U$-Tup $\to \mathcal{C}(U)$-Tup and the selection predicate $\mathbf{P}\colon U$-Tup $\to \mathcal{C}(U)$-Tup maps each U-tuple to an element of $\mathcal{C}(U)$-Tup, then $\sigma_{\mathbf{P}} A\colon U$-Tup $\to \mathcal{C}(U)$-Tup is defined by*

$$(\sigma_{\mathbf{P}} A)(t)(a) \stackrel{\text{def}}{=} A(t)(a) \ \Delta_a \ \mathbf{P}(t)(a). \tag{92}$$

Join: *Let $\mathcal{C}_1 = \{a_1\colon \mathcal{L}_1, ..., a_n\colon \mathcal{L}_n\}$ and $\mathcal{C}_2 = \{b_1\colon \mathcal{L}'_1, ..., b_m\colon \mathcal{L}'_m\}$ be annotation schemata. If $A\colon U_1$-Tup $\to \mathcal{C}_1(U_1)$-Tup and $B\colon U_2$-Tup $\to \mathcal{C}_2(U_2)$-Tup, then $A \bowtie B$ is the $(\mathcal{C}_1 \cup \mathcal{C}_2)$-relation over $U_1 \cup U_2$ defined as follows.*

$$(A \bowtie B)(t)(a) \stackrel{\text{def}}{=} \begin{cases} A(t \downarrow U_1)(a) & \text{if } a \in U_1 - U_2 \\ B(t \downarrow U_2)(a) & \text{if } a \in U_2 - U_1 \ . \\ A(t \downarrow U_1)(a) \ \Delta_a \ B(t \downarrow U_2)(a) & \end{cases} \tag{93}$$

Difference: *If $A, B\colon U$-Tup $\to \mathcal{C}(U)$-Tup, then $A \setminus B\colon U$-Tup $\to \mathcal{C}(U)$-Tup is defined by*

$$(A \setminus B)(t)(a) \stackrel{\text{def}}{=} A(t)(a) -_a B(t)(a). \tag{94}$$

Renaming: *If $A\colon U$-Tup $\to \mathcal{C}(U)$-Tup and $\beta\colon U \to U'$ is a bijection, then $\rho_\beta A\colon U'$-Tup $\to \mathcal{C}(U')$-Tup is defined by*

$$(\rho_\beta A)(t)(a) \stackrel{\text{def}}{=} A(t)(\beta(a)). \tag{95}$$

Relational algebra $\text{RA}_{\mathcal{C}}$ still satisfies *all* the main positive relational algebra identities.

Proposition 5.5 (Identities of $\mathcal{C}$-relations). *The following identities hold for the relational algebra on $\mathcal{C}$-relations:*

- *union is associative, commutative, idempotent, and has identity $\emptyset$;*
- *selection distributes over union and difference;*
- *join is associative and commutative, and distributes over union;*
- *projection distributes over union and join;*
- *selections and projections commute with each other;*
- *difference has identity $\emptyset$ and distributes over union and intersection;*
- *selection with boolean predicates gives all or nothing, $\sigma_{\mathsf{false}}(A) = \emptyset$ and $\sigma_{\mathsf{true}}(A) = A$, where $\mathsf{false(t)(a)} = \mathbf{0}_{\mathsf{a}}$ and $\mathsf{true(t)(a)} = \mathbf{1}_{\mathsf{a}}$ for $\mathcal{C}(a) = (L_a, \bigvee_a, \wedge_a, \mathbf{0}_a, \mathbf{1}_a)$;*
- *join with an empty relation gives an empty relation, $A \bowtie \emptyset_U = \emptyset_U$ where A is a $\mathcal{C}$-relation over a schema U;*
- *projection of an empty relation gives an empty relation, $\pi_V(\emptyset) = \emptyset$.*

Proof. If the lattice join and meet are chosen to model the positive relational operations, the above identities are implied by Proposition 4.1. On the other hand, if some other semiring sum and product operations are chosen, the identities are implied by Proposition 2.1. □

The properties of relational difference are implied by the identities involving $\ominus$ (see Proposition 5.1) and/or the identities involving $\div$ (see Proposition 5.2), depending on the selection we make.

6. Conclusion

Although the attribute-annotated approach has many advantages, it also has some disadvantages. First, it is clear that asking all attributes to be annotated requires more storage than simple tuple-level annotation. Another problem is that since the proposed general annotation structure, complete distributive lattices with finite meets distributing over arbitrary joins, may not be linearly ordered, an ordering of tuples with falling annotation values is not always possible. Even if each lattice used in an annotation schema is linearly ordered, it is not necessarily the case that there is a linear order on the annotation tuples. Hence, it may not be possible to list query answers (tuples) in a (decreasing) order of relevance. In fact, a suitable ordering of tuples may be established as soon as the lattice of annotation values, $\mathcal{L} = (L, \bigvee, \wedge, \mathbf{0}, \mathbf{1})$, is *graded* Stanley (1997). Recall that a graded or ranked poset is a partially ordered set equipped with a rank function $\rho : L \to \mathbb{Z}$ compatible with the ordering, $\rho(x) < \rho(y)$ whenever $x < y$, and such that whenever y covers x, then $\rho(y) = \rho(x) + 1$. Graded posets can be visualized by means of a Hasse diagram. Examples of graded posets are the natural numbers with the usual order, the Cartesian product of two or more sets of natural numbers with the product order being the sum of the coefficients, and the boolean lattice of finite subsets of a set with the number of elements in the subset. Notice, however, that the ranking problem simply reflects a fact about ordered structures and not a flaw in the model.

The work on attribute-annotated models is very new and has, as far as we know, not been implemented yet Hajdinjak & Bierman (2011). A prototype implementation by means of existing relational database management systems is thus expected to be performed in short term. Another guideline for future research is the study of standard issues from relational databases in the general setting, including data dependencies, redundancy, normalization, and design of databases, optimization issues.

7. References

Aceto, L.; Ésik, Z. & Ingólfsdóttir, A. (2001). *Equational Theories of Tropical Semirings*, BRICS Report Series RS-01-21, University of Aarhus, Denmark.

Amer, K. (1984). Equationally Complete Classes of Commutative Monoids with Monus. *Algebra Universalis*, Vol. 18, No. 1, Jan 1984, -129 – -131, ISSN 0002-5240.

Belohlávek, R. & Vychodil, V. (2006). Relational Model of Data Over Domains with Similarities: An Extension for Similarity Queries and Knowledge Extraction, *Proceedings of the 2006 IEEE International Conference on Information Reuse and Integration*, pp. 207-213, ISBN 0-7803-9788-6, Waikoloa, USA, Sept 2006, IEEE Press, Piscataway, USA.

Bordogna, G. & Psaila, G. (2006). *Flexible Databases Supporting Imprecision and Uncertainty*, Springer-Verlag, Berlin Heidelberg, Germany.

Bosbach, B. (1965). Komplementäre Halbgruppen: Ein Beitrag zur instruktiven Idealtheorie kommutativer Halbgruppen. *Mathematische Annalen*, Vol. 161, No. 4, Dec 1965, -279 – -295, ISSN 0025-5831.

Buneman, P.; Khanna, S. & Tan, W. C. (2001). Why and Where: A Characterization of Data Provenance, *Proceedings of the 8th International Conference on Database Theory*, pp. 316-330, ISBN 3-540-41456-8, London, UK, Jan 2001, Springer-Verlag, London, UK.

Calì, A.; Lembo, D. & Rosati, R. (2003). On the Decidability and Complexity of Query Answering over Inconsistent and Incomplete Databases, *Proceedings of the 22nd Symposium on Principles of Database Systems*, pp. 260–271, ISBN 1-58113-670-6, San Diego, USA, June 2003, ACM Press, New York, USA.

Codd, E. F. (1970). A Relational Model of Data for Large Shared Data Banks. *Communications of the ACM*, Vol. 13, No. 6, June 1970, -377 – -387, ISSN 0001-0782.

Cui, Y.; Widom, J. & Wiener, J. L. (2000). Tracing the Lineage of View Data in a Warehousing Environment. *ACM Transactions on Database Systems*, Vol. 25, No. 2, June 2000, -179 – -227, ISSN 0362-5915.

Davey, B. A. & Priestley, H. A. (1990). *Introduction to Lattices and Order*, Cambridge University Press, Cambridge, UK.

Garcia-Molina, H.; Ullman, J. & Widom, J. (2008). *Database Systems: The Complete Book*, 2nd edition, Prentice Hall, New York, USA.

Geerts, F. & Poggi, A. (2010). On Database Query Languages for *K*-Relations. *Journal of Applied Logic*, Vol. 8, No. 2, June 2010, -173 – -185, ISSN 1570-8683.

Green, T. J.; Karvounarakis, G. & Tannen, V. (2007). Provenance Semirings, *Proceedings of the 26th Symposium on Principles of Database Systems*, pp. 31-40, ISBN 978-1-59593-685-1, Beijing, China, June 2007, ACM Press, New York, USA.

Hajdinjak, M. & Mihelič, F. (2006). The PARADISE Evaluation Framework: Issues and Findings. *Computational Linguistics*, Vol. 32, No. 2, June 2006, -263 – -272, ISSN 0891-2017.

Hajdinjak, M. & Bauer, A. (2009). Similarity Measures for Relational Databases. *Informatica*, Vol. 33, No. 2, May 2009, -135 – -141, ISSN 0350-5596.

Hajdinjak, M. & Bierman, G. M. (2011). Extending Relational Algebra with Similarities. To appear in *Mathematical Structures in Computer Science*, ISSN 0960-1295.

Hjaltason, G. R. & Samet, H. (2003). Index-Driven Similarity Search in Metric Spaces. *ACM Transactions on Database Systems*, Vol. 28, No. 4, Dec 2003, -517 – -580, ISSN 0362-5915.

Hutton, B. (1975). Normality in Fuzzy Topological Spaces. *Journal of Mathematical Analysis and Applications*, Vol. 50, No. 1, April 1975, -74 – -79, ISSN 0022-247X.

Imielinski, T. & Lipski, W. (1984). Incomplete Information in Relational Databases. *Journal of the ACM*, Vol. 31, No. 4, Oct 1984, -761 – -791, ISSN 0004-5411.

Jae, Y. L. & Elmasri, R. A. (2001). A temporal Algebra for an ER-Based Temporal Data Model, *Proceedings of the the 17th International Conference on Data Engineering*, pp. 33-40, ISBN 0-7695-1001-9, Heidelberg, Germany, April 2001, IEEE Computer Society, Washington, USA.

Ma, Z. (2006). *Studies in Fuzziness and Soft Computing: Fuzzy Database Modeling of Imprecise and Uncertain Engineering Information*, Vol. 195, Springer-Verlag, Berlin Heidelberg, Germany.

Ma, Z. & Yan, L. (2008). A Literature Overview of Fuzzy Database Models. *Journal of Information Science and Engineering*, Vol. 24, No. 1, Jan 2008, -189 – -202, ISSN 1016-2364.

Minker, J. (1998). An Overview of Cooperative Answering in Databases, *Proceedings of the 3rd International Conference on Flexible Query Answering Systems*, pp. 282-285, ISBN 3-540-65082-2, Roskilde, Denmark, May 1998, Springer-Verlag, Berlin Heidelberg.

Montagna, F. & Sebastiani, V. (2001). Equational Fragments of Systems for Arithmetic. *Algebra Universalis*, Vol. 46, No. 3, Sept 2001, -417 – -441, ISSN 0002-5240.

Patella, M. & and Ciaccia, P. (2009). Approximate Similarity Search: A Multi-faceted Problem. *Journal of Discrete Algorithms*, Vol. 7, No. 1, March -2009, -36 – -48, ISSN 1468-0904.

Peeva, K. & Kyosev, Y. (2004). *Fuzzy Relational Calculus: Theory, Applications And Software (Advances in Fuzzy Systems)*, World Scientific Publishing Company, ISBN 9-812-56076-9.

Penzo, W. (2005). Rewriting Rules to Permeate Complex Similarity and Fuzzy Queries within a Relational Database System. *IEEE Transactions on Knowledge and Data Engineering*, Vol. 17, No. 2, Feb 2005, -255 – -270, ISSN 1041-4347.

Rosado, A.; Ribeiro, R. A.; Zadrozny, S. & Kacprzyk, J. (2006). Flexible Query Languages for Relational Databases: An Overview, In: *Flexible Databases Supporting Imprecision and Uncertainty*, Bordogna, G. & Psaila, G. (Eds.), pp. 3-53, Springer-Verlag, ISBN 978-3-540-33288-6, Berlin Heidelberg, Germany.

Salii, V. N. (1983). Quasi-Boolean Lattices and Associations. In: *Lectures in Universal Algebra: Proceedings of Colloquia Mathematica Societatis János Bolyai*, Vol. 43, Szabo, L. & Szendrei, A. (Eds.), pp. 429-454, North-Holland, ISBN xxx, Amsterdam, The Nerherlands.

Schmitt, I. & Schulz, N. (2004). Similarity Relational Calculus and its Reduction to a Similarity Algebra, In: *Lecture Notes in Computer Science: Foundations of Information and Knowledge Systems - FoIKS 2004*, Vol. 2942, Seipel, D. & Turull Torres, J. M. (Eds.), pp. 252-272, Springer-Verlag, ISBN 3-540-20965-4, Berlin Heidelberg, Germany.

Shenoi, S. & Melton, A. (1989). Proximity Relations in the Fuzzy and Relational Database Model. *Fuzzy Sets and Systems*, Vol. 31, No. 3, July 1989, -285 – -296, ISSN 0165-0114.

Stanley, R. (1997). *Cambridge Studies in Advanced Mathematics 49: Enumerative Combinatorics*, Vol. 1., Cambridge University Press, Cambridge, England.

Suciu, D. (2008). Probabilistic Databases. *SIGACT News*, Vol. 39, No. 2, June 2008, -111 – -124, ISSN 0163-5700.

Ullman, J. D. (1988). *Principles of Database and Knowledge-Base Systems*, Vol. I, Computer Science Press, Inc., Rockville, USA.

Ullman, J. D. (1989). *Principles of Database and Knowledge-Base Systems: The New Technologies*, Vol. II, Computer Science Press, Inc., Rockville, USA.

Van der Meyden, R. (1998). Logical Approaches to Incomplete Information: A Survey, In: *Logics for Databases and Information Systems*, Chomicki, J. & Saake, G. (Eds.), page numbers (307-356), Kluwer Academic Publishers, ISBN 0-7923-8129-7, Norwell, USA.

Yazici, A. & George, R. (1999). *Fuzzy Database Modeling*, Physica-Verlag, Heidelberg, Germany.

Zadeh, L. A. (1965). Fuzzy Sets. *Information and Control*, Vol. 8, No. 3, June 1965, -338 – -353, ISSN 0019-9958.

Section 2

Representations

3

A General Knowledge Representation Model of Concepts

Carlos Ramirez and Benjamin Valdes
Tec of Monterrey Campus Queretaro, DASL4LTD Research Group
Mexico

1. Introduction

Knowledge is not a simple concept to define, and although many definitions have been given of it, only a few describe the concept with enough detail to grasp it in practical terms; knowledge is sometimes seen as a *thing* out in the real word waiting to be uncovered and taken in by the receptive mind; however, knowledge is not a *thing* to be encountered and taken in, no knowledge can be found in any mind without first have been processed by cognition. Knowledge is not something just to be uncovered or transmitted and stored, it has to be constructed. The construction of knowledge involves the use of previous knowledge and different cognitive processes, which play an intertwined function to facilitate the development of association between the new concepts to be acquired and previously acquired concepts. Knowledge is about information that can be used or applied, that is, it is information that has been contextualised in a certain domain, and therefore, any piece of knowledge is related with more knowledge in a particular and different way in each individual.

In this chapter, a model for the representation of conceptual knowledge is presented. Knowledge can have many facets, but it is basically constituted by static components, called concepts or facts, and dynamic components, called skills, abilities, procedures, actions, etc., which together allow general cognition, including all different processes typically associated to it, such as perceiving, distinguishing, abstracting, modelling, storing, recalling, remembering, etc., which are part of three primary cognitive processes: learning, understanding and reasoning (Ramirez and Cooley, 1997). No one of those processes can live isolated or can be carried out alone, actually it can be said that those processes are part of the dynamic knowledge, and dynamic knowledge typically requires of conceptual or factual knowledge to be used.

In the first section of this chapter, a review of the basic concepts behind knowledge representation and the main types of knowledge representation models is presented; in the second section, a deep explanation of the components of knowledge and the way in which they are acquired is provided; in the third section, a computer model for knowledge representation called Memory Map (MM) that integrates concepts and skills is explained, and in section four, a practical application for the MM in a learning environment is presented.

2. What is knowledge?

There is not a unified definition for the concept of knowledge, diverse definitions from different backgrounds and perspectives have been proposed since the old times; some definitions complement each other and some prove more useful in practical terms. In philosophy we find the very first definitions of knowledge, one of the most accepted ones was provided by Sir Thomas Hobbes in 1651: knowledge is the evidence of truth, which must have four properties: first knowledge must be integrated by concepts; second, each concept can be identified by a name; third, names can be used to create propositions, and fourth, such propositions must be concluding (Hobbes, 1969). Hobbes is also credited with writing the most intuitively and broadly used definition of concept in his book "Leviathan", Hobbes's definition has its origins in the traditional Aristotelian view of ideas; this is known as the Representational Theory of the Mind (RTM), till this day RTM continues to be used by most works in Cognitive Science. It must be taken into account that Hobbes's works were of a political, philosophical and religious nature, for this reason there is not one simple hard interpretation of RTM, in this work we will refer to the most common one which is the following: RTM states that knowledge is defined as the evidence of truth composed by conceptualisations product of the imaginative power of the mind, i.e., cognitive capabilities; ideas here are pictured as objects with mental properties, which is the way most people picture concepts and ideas as abstract objects. RTM is complemented at a higher cognitive level by the Language of Thought Hypothesis (LOTH) from Jerry Fodors proposed in the 70's (Fodors, 1975). LOTH states that thoughts are represented in a language supported by the principles of symbolic logic and computability, this language is different form the one we to use to speak, it is a separate in which we can *write* our thoughts and we can validate them using symbolic logic. This definition is much more useful for computer science including Artificial Intelligence and Cognitive Informatics, since it implies that reasoning can be formalised into symbols; hence thought can be described and mechanised, and therefore, theoretically a machine should be able to, at least, emulate thought. The idea that thought in itself has a particular language is not unique, in fact there are previous works such as Vygotsky's Language and Thought (1986) that propose a similar approach. The difference between Vygotsky's and Fodor's approach is that LOTH's is based on a logic system and logic systems can, to an extent, be used for computation, whereas Vygotsky's work is based more on his observations of experiments with children and how this affects their learning processes and general development. The first approach can be directly linked to knowledge in the hard branch of A.I., for example project CYC which will be discussed in future sections of this chapter, while the second one can be put to better use in the development of practical tools in soft A.I., such as in Intelligent Tutoring Systems and more application oriented agents.

Not as old as Philosophy but still directly relevant to knowledge is Psychology, particularly the branches of Psychology that study the learning process. In Psychology through more empirical methods, a vast number of theories to understand and interpret human behaviour in relation to knowledge have been developed, among the most relevant theories for knowledge representation systems are associative theories also referred to as connectionist theories, cognitive theories and constructivist theories. There is also a group of theories that study behaviour by itself know as behaviourist theories, these theories did have a strong impact on Psychology in general and how humans were perceived to learn. In their classic posture behaviourists do not contemplate an internal cognitive process, only external behaviour, i.e., behavioural responses to different stimulus, for this reason behaviourist theories cannot explain thought (Chomsky, 1967) or knowledge in the desired depth, and will not be studied here. Connectionist theories state that knowledge can be described as a number of interconnected concepts, each concept is connected through associations, these are the roots of semantics as means for knowledge representation (Vygotsky, 1986), i.e., what we know today as semantic knowledge representation. Semantic knowledge representation has been proven to be the main driver along with similarity behind reasoning for unstructured knowledge (Crisp-Bright, 2010), traditional connectionist approaches do not account for causality; they just focus on the presence or absence of associations and their quantity. This proves that connectionist theories are not wrong, but they still can't explain higher cognitive processes and therefore higher types of knowledge. Constructivist theories on the other hand do contemplate more complex reasoning drivers such as causality, probability and context. Most constructivist theories therefore complement connectionist approaches by stating that each group of associations integrate different layers of thought where the difference between in each level is the strength of the associations. As a result, the highest layer is the concept, i.e., an organised and stable structure of knowledge and the lowest layer are loosely coupled heaps of ideas (Vygotsky, 1986). This layered structure for knowledge and the way it is built is the reason why constructivism is so relevant to semantic knowledge, because it presents mechanisms complex enough to represent how semantic knowledge is built to our current understanding.

Cognitive Science has focused on modelling and validating previous theories from almost every other science ranging from Biology and Neuroscience to Psychology and Artificial Intelligence (Eysenck, 2010); because of this, Cognitive Science is positioned as the ideal common ground where knowledge definitions from all of the above disciplines can meet computer oriented sciences, this has in fact been argued by Laird in his proposition of mental models (Laird, 1980) though this theory in reasoning rather than in knowledge. Cognitive Science is therefore a fertile field for new theories or for the formalisation of previous ones through computer models (Marr, 1982). It is common for knowledge in this field to be described through equations, mathematical relations and computer models, for this reason approaches like connectionism in Psychology have been retaken through the modelling of neural networks and similar works (Shastri, 1988). In this more oriented computer approach knowledge is treated as the structure in terms of association's strength, we will discuss the approach with more detail in the following section. Other famous approaches in this field include Knowledge Space Theory (Doignon & Falmagne, 1999) which defines knowledge as a group of questions which are combined with possible answers to form knowledge states. The possible permutations of operations through set theory of these states are used to create a congruent framework for knowledge, based on the assumption that knowledge can be described as questions and correct answers in its most basic form. Ackoff's (1989) distinction between data information and knowledge is helpful in providing a practical definition for knowledge in real life. Data are symbols without significance, such as numbers, information is data that also includes basic relations between such symbols in a way that provide meaning, and knowledge is context enriched information that can be used or applied, and serves a purpose or goal. Brown (1989) in her studies of knowledge transfer, states that knowledge in its learning continuum, is composed of theories, causal explanation, meaningful solutions and arbitrary solutions, where theories are networks of concepts, causal explanations are facts, meaningful solutions are isolated pieces of knowledge and arbitrary solutions are random decisions.

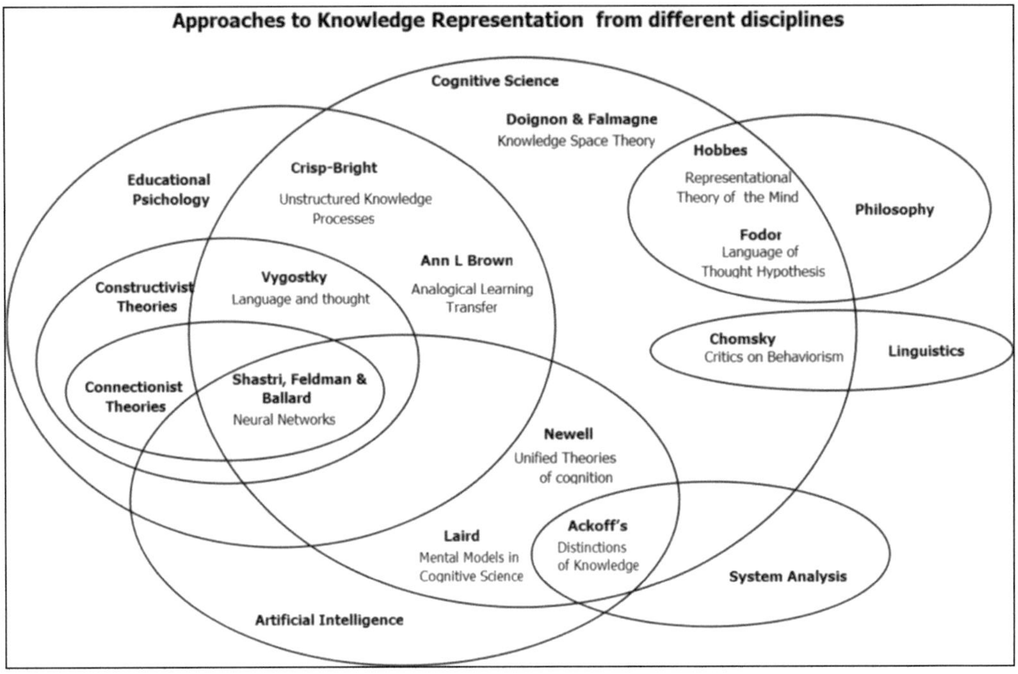

Fig. 1. Approaches to Knowledge Representation from different disciplines

As it shown in figure 1 there are several approaches to describe and define knowledge, though most of them come different fields we can compare them through Cognitive Science which has served as a common ground for similar issues in the past. What is of interest here is not to get the most complete specific definition, but a generic definition that can be worked with and used in a computer model. For this reason this work focuses on the common elements in every presented theory, these elements represent a common ground for knowledge representation and any system or model for knowledge representation should consider them:

i. Knowledge is composed of basic units, which we shall refer to as *concepts*. Some authors use attributes as basic units and others use network structures, however all of them agree on the existence of concepts. The approaches for representing those basic structures will be discussed in section 2.3.
ii. Concepts have *associations* or relations to other concepts. On this point there is general consensus, the debate on associations is about the representational aspects regarding to the following issues: a) What information should an association contain and b) What elements should be used to describe such information i.e., type, directionality, name, intension, extension, among others. These characteristics will be addressed in section 2.3 and 4.
iii. Associations and concepts build dynamic structures which tend to become stable through time. These structures are the factual or conceptual knowledge. The representation of such structures of knowledge is what varies most, in section 2.1 we will explore several different approaches used to model these structures.

From the consensus it can be assumed that these three key points are the core components of knowledge, other characteristics can be included to create more complete definitions, but these will be context dependent. With a basic notion of what knowledge *is*, more interesting questions can be posed in the following sections.

2.1 What types of knowledge do exist?

There are several ways to classify knowledge; the most common distinction is closely related to human memory: the memories related to facts and the memories related to processes, i.e., factual and procedural. Factual or declarative knowledge explains what things are e.g., *the dogs eats meat* or *a dog has a tail.* Procedural knowledge explains how things work for example what the dog needs to do in order to eat, e.g. *if dog hungry -> find food, then chew food, then swallow, then find more food if still hungry.*

We use both types of knowledge in our everyday life; in fact it is hard to completely separate them; however, many computer models can only represent abstract ideal situations with simplified contexts in which each type of knowledge can be clearly identified, but trading off completeness for simplification. The three characteristics of knowledge, discussed in section 2, hold true for both types of knowledge, although they are easier to observe in declarative knowledge because on procedural knowledge concepts are integrated into processes, usually referred to as skills and competences, and the relations between them are imbued in rule sets. An example of declarative knowledge representation and procedural knowledge representation can be seen in figure 2.

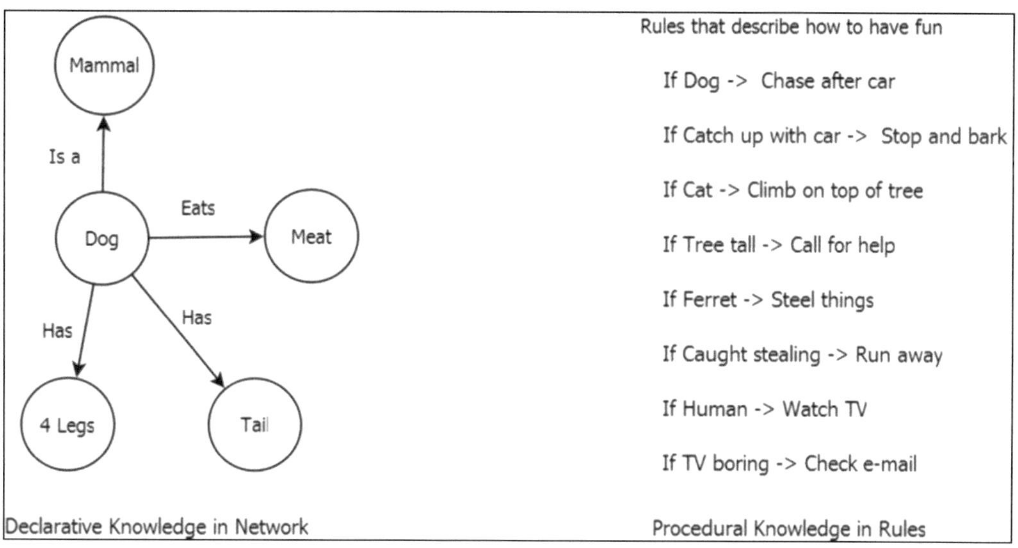

Fig. 2. Example of declarative and procedural knowledge.

Another important distinction is between structured and unstructured knowledge, since this has a strong implication on our reasoning processes. Structured knowledge relies strongly on organisation and analysis of information using higher cognitive processes, unstructured knowledge relies in lower cognitive processes such as associative knowledge and similarity (Crisp-Bright, 2010; Redher, 2009; Sloman, 1996). In order for unstructured knowledge to become structured there needs to be a higher cognitive process involved in its acquisition and ordering knowledge such as taxonomy knowledge, domain knowledge, direction of causality, and description of the type of association, among others. Though some computer systems already do this in their knowledge representation such as semantic networks and Bayesian causality networks, they do so mainly on intuitive bases (Crisp-Bright A. K., 2010), where the particular reasoning process used is imbued in the heuristic or algorithm employed for information extraction and processing.

Both of these distinctions are important because they can strongly influence the way in which knowledge is represented, other common types of knowledge include domain specific knowledge which can be regarded as a categorisation of knowledge by subject, such as taxonomic knowledge domain, ecological knowledge domain and causality knowledge domain, among others (Crisp-Bright A.K., 2010).

2.2 What are knowledge representation models?

The purpose of understanding what knowledge is, and what types of knowledge exist, is to allow us to use it in artificial systems. This long standing ambition has been fuelled by the desire to develop intelligent technologies that allow computers to perform complex tasks, be it to assist humans or because humans cannot perform them. In this section it will be explained how knowledge can be used in computer systems by representing it through different knowledge representation models.

Knowledge representation is deeply linked to learning and reasoning processes, as Crisp-Bright states when defining knowledge as "the psychological result of perception, learning and reasoning" (2010). In other words, in order to have any higher level cognitive process, knowledge must be generated, represented, and stored. The works of Newell (1972, 1982, 1986, 1994) and Anderson (1990, 2004) provide comprehensive explanations for the relations between these processes, as well as computer frameworks to emulate them. Both Newell's Unified theories of Cognition (1994) and Anderson's Adaptive Character of Thought (1990) theory have strongly influenced today's knowledge representation models in cognitive and computer sciences, examples include the components of the Cognitive Informatics Theoretical Framework (Wang, 2009). Models are representations of theories that allows us to run simulations and carry out tests that would render outputs predicted by the theory, therefore when we speak of knowledge representation models, we are referring to a particular way of representing knowledge that will allow the prediction of what a system knows and what is capable of with knowledge and reasoning mechanisms. Since most knowledge representation models have been designed to emulate the human brain and its cognitive processes, it is common to find knowledge representation models that focus on long term memory (LTM), short term memory (STM) or combine both types of memory (Newell, 1982).

Having computers that can achieve complex tasks such as driving a car require intelligence. Intelligence involves cognitive processes like learning, understanding and reasoning, and as has been said before, all of these processes require knowledge to support or guide them. As Cognitive Informatics states if computers with cognitive capabilities are desired (Wang, 2003), then computerised knowledge representations are required.

To understand how generic knowledge can be represented in abstract systems we must also understand the types of possible representations, it is important to consider that these representations are descriptions of the types of knowledge; therefore they are usually akin to particular types of knowledge. A helpful metaphor is to picture types of knowledge as ideas and types of representations as languages, not all languages can express the same ideas with the same quality, there are words which can only be roughly translated.

2.3 Types of knowledge representation models

A distinction should be made between types of knowledge and types of knowledge representation models. Types of knowledge were described in the section 2.1 as *declarative* vs. *procedural* and *structured* vs. *unstructured*. Types of models are the different ways each type of knowledge can be represented.

The types of representation models used for knowledge systems include distributed, symbolic, non-symbolic, declarative, probabilistic, ruled based, among others, each of them suited for a particular type of reasoning: inductive, deductive, analogy, abduction, etc (Russell & Norvig, 1995). The basic ideas behind each type of knowledge representation model will be described to better understand the complex approaches in current knowledge representation models. Since this is a vast field of research, the focus will be directed to monotonic non probabilistic knowledge representations models.

Symbolic systems are called that way because they use human understandable representations based on symbols as the basic representation unit, each symbols means something i.e., a word, a concept, a skill, a procedure, an idea. Symbolic systems were in fact the original and predominant approach in AI until the late 80's (Haugeland, 1989). Non-symbolic systems use machine understandable representations based on the configuration of items, such as numbers, or nodes to represent an idea, a concept, a skill, a word, non-symbolic systems are also known as distributed system. Symbolic systems include structures such as semantic networks, rule based systems and frames, whereas distributed systems include different types neural or probabilistic networks, for instance. An example of a symbolic system in the way of semantic network and non-symbolic model in the way of a neural network can be seen in Figure 3.

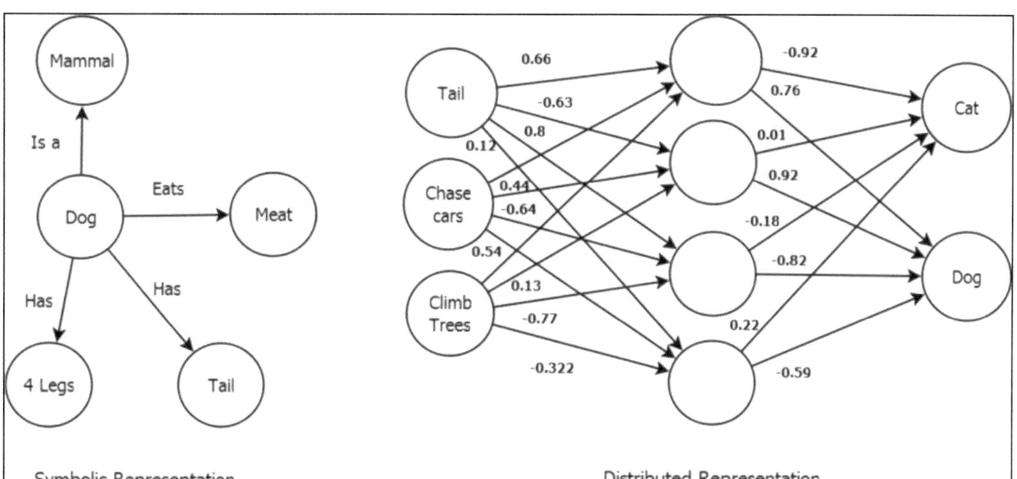

Fig. 3. Example of a semantic network for symbolic representation and a neural network for distributed representation.

As their names states, semantic networks are concept networks where concepts are represented as nodes and associations are represented as arcs (Quillian, 1968), they can be defined as a graphical equivalent for propositional logic (Gentzen, 1935). This type of knowledge representation models rely strongly on similarity, contrast and closeness for conceptual representation or interpretation. In semantic networks, associations have a grade which represents knowledge or strength of the association; learning is represented by increasing the grade of the association or creating new associations between concepts. Semantic networks are commonly used to model declarative knowledge both in structured and an unstructured way, but they are flexible enough to be used with procedural knowledge. When modelling structured knowledge the associations must be directed and have information of causality or hierarchy. Figure 3 on the left shows an example of a semantic network. Semantic networks are based in traditional RTM and associative theories.

Ruled based systems are symbolic representation models focused in procedural knowledge, they are usually organised as a library of rules in the form of condition - action, e.g., *if answer is found then stop else keep looking*. Rule systems proved to be a powerful way of representing skills, learning and solving problems (Newell's & Simon's, 1972, Anderson, 1990), rule based systems are frequently used when procedural knowledge is present. Rule systems might also be used for declarative knowledge generally with classification purposes, e.g., *if it barks then is dog else not dog*. The *else* component is not actually necessary, when there is no *else* component systems do nothing or go to the next rule, an example of a rules can be seen on the right side of figure 2.

A frame is a data-structure for representing a stereotyped situation (Minsky, 1975). Frames can be considered as a type of semantic network which mixes declarative knowledge and structured procedural knowledge. Frames are different from other networks because they are capable of including procedures (fragments of code) within each symbol. This means that each symbol in the network is a frame which contains a procedure, which is called a 'demon' (Minsky, 1975), and a group of attributes for the description of the situation. The idea behind the frame is to directly emulate human memory which stores situations that mix procedural and declarative knowledge. When we find ourselves in a situation similar to one we have lived before, we allude to the stereotype stored in our memory so we can know how to react to this new situation. This theory is an attempt at joining unifying several other approaches proposed by psychology, linguistics and Artificial Intelligence.

Very similar and contemporary theory to Minsky's theory of frames is Shank's theory of scripts. Scripts are language oriented as their name suggests they resemble a long sentence that describes an action. Scripts are part of the description of a larger plan or goal, which can also be used to model networks similar to those of semantic networks (Shank, 1975). Script theory was originally oriented toward the understanding of human language and focusing on episodic memory, he later used it in his Dynamic Memory Model (1982) to explain higher aspects of cognition. Since scripts and frames have theories resemble so much they are both treated as part of a same sub-group of semantic networks.

Neural networks are the most popular type of distributed knowledge representation models, instead of using a symbol to represent a concept they use an activation pattern over and entire network. A simple way to understand how neural networks work, is by looking at the place from where the idea came, i.e., the human brain. Humans have a number of neurons connected in a highly complex structure, each time a person thinks thousands or millions of neurons in a localised part of the brain activate. This pattern of activation can be used then to identify a concept or an idea; hence if a tiny specific part of the concept is lost, is does not affect the general idea because what matters is the overall pattern. The pattern is strengthened each time we think about it, we refer to this as training of a network. Neural Networks emulate this cognitive process of mental reconstruction.

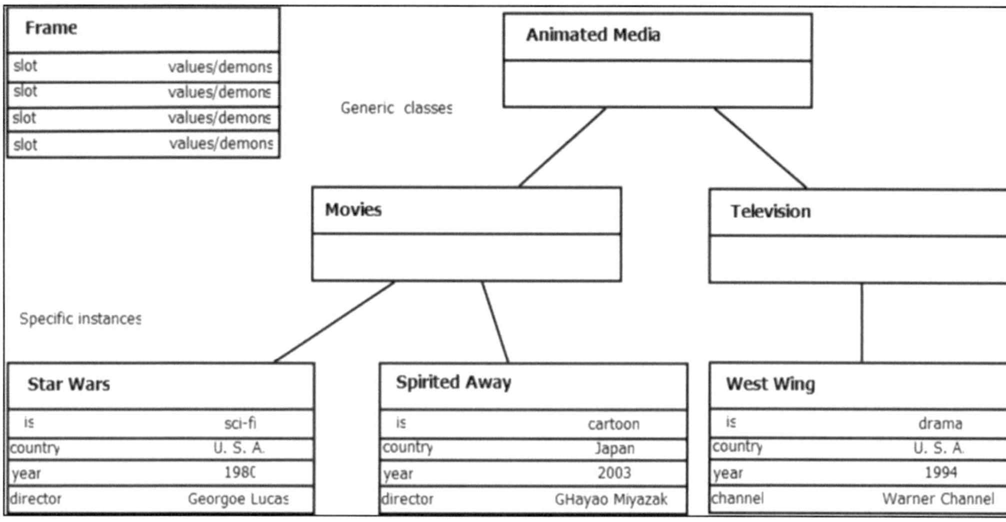

Fig. 4. Frames as a type of symbolic representation.

As shown in the right side of figure 3, in a Neural Network attributes are used as basic inputs. The combination of these inputs will activate an input layer and will generate a pattern of propagation until it reaches the last layer where it will return the result of a function which could be a concept. Even though neural networks are very flexible and robust for knowledge representation of certain structures, they cannot be used for vast amount of knowledge, since they become too complex for implementation over a small amount of time. The second reason why neural networks are not used as large scale knowledge representation models is that they must be trained so they can learn the patterns which will identify specific concepts; this means that knowledge must be previously modelled as training sets before it can fed unto the net , thus it becomes unpractical for average knowledge retrieval. Also it is worth mentioning that the black box nature of the neural networks does not show to get to the knowledge, it only shows that some inputs will render this and that output ,i.e., its representation is non-symbolic. The real advantage of neural networks are their capacity to emulate any function, this implies that the entire network will specialize in that particular function therefore it cannot specialize on everything. Among the common types of Neural Network the following can be found: perceptrons which don not have hidden layers; Feed forward networks, back propagation and resilient propagation which are networks with the same structure but differ in the approach used to adjust the weights of the networks; Radio based function networks; Hopfield networks, which are bidirectional associative networks; and self-organizing feature maps, which are a kind of network that does not require much training per se; among others (Rojas 1996, Kriesel, 2011). Neural networks indeed are of very different natures but in the end they are all based on connectionist theory and are inspired on biological neural networks, in particular the human, brain science.

Ontologies remain a debate issue in two aspects, first as to what is to be considered an ontology, and second how it should be used in computer science (Weller, 2007). Some authors argue that simple hierarchical relations in a structure is not enough as to call it an ontology (Gauch & et. al 2007), while others use these simple structures and argument they are (Weller, 2007). The most relevant insights in artificial intelligence as to how to define ontologies in computer systems are provided by Grubber: "An ontology is an explicit specification of a conceptualisation ... A conceptualisation is an abstract, simplified view of the world that we want to represent... For AI systems, what 'exists' is that which can be represented." (Gruber, 1993). Gruber also notes that "Ontologies are not about truth or beauty, they are agreements, made in a social context, to accomplish some objectives, it's important to understand those objectives, and be guided by them." (Gruber, 2003) However this definition has created a new debate since it also applies to folksonomies (Gruber, 2007), especially since ontologies and folksonomies (Medelyan & Legg 2008) became popular in the context of semantic web through RDF and OWL (McGuiness & Harmelen, 2004) specifications. Weller (2007) and Gruber (2007) present a deeper explanation of this debate as well as the differences and advantages of each of both folksonomies and ontologies. In practical sense ontology are flexible hierarchical structures that define in terms that a computer can understand, the relations between its elements, a language often used for this purpose is first order logic. In reality, ontologies have been used mostly as enhanced controlled vocabularies with associated functionalities and categorisation. Computational implementations of ontologies tend to resemble taxonomies or concept networks (Helbig, 2003, Chen 2009), i.e., semantic networks with formal conceptual descriptions for their associations, and therefore can be considered symbolic systems. Some examples of Ontology include those defined as part of an interaction communication protocol in multi agent systems (FIPA, 2000), those built though ontology edition tools for ontology web language (OWL) like *protégé* which are used to build *the semantic net*, and project CYC which will be addressed in section 4.

All representation models presented satisfy the three basic characteristics placed above. Both symbolic and distributed systems recognise a concept as a unit of knowledge, the main difference between them is that one approach models it as a symbol and the other as a pattern. Both approaches agree on the need for associations between concepts and both recognise that the configuration of the associations also represents knowledge. It should be noted that some symbolic models like ontologies include instances as another layer for representation of the embodiment of a concept, however not every models includes them and therefor even though they will be mentioned in future sections they will not be included within the basic characteristics that all knowledge representation models have in common. With this we conclude a basic introduction of what knowledge is and how it is represented in computers, now we will analyse each of the basic units that compose knowledge: concepts, skills and associations.

3. Concepts, skills and their acquisition

We have already explained that knowledge is divided in two types: factual and procedural; Roughly speaking factual knowledge in a higher cognitive dimension can represent concepts, and procedural knowledge in higher cognitive scale can be used to represent skills. As was mentioned in section 1, this does not mean that any fact can be considered a concept or any procedure a skill, the inter-association between each of these components as well as the structures they build must also be considered. To get a deeper understanding of knowledge we now review each of these components in more depth.

3.1 Definition of concept

The definition of a concept is closely related to the discussion of knowledge, in fact most of the theories attempting to explain one also explain the other. The most traditional definitions of concepts are based on Aristotelian philosophy and can be considered as revisions and complements previous works in the same line, Representational Theory of the Mind (Hobbes, 1651) was the first formalisation of this philosophy and Language of Though hypothesis (Fodor, 2004) is the latest extension added to it.

The Representational Theory of the Mind (RTM) states concepts and ideas as mental states with attributes sometimes defined as images, the Language of Thought (LOT) hypothesis states that thoughts are represented in a language which is supported by the principles of symbolic logic and computability. Reasoning can be formalised into symbols and characters; hence it can be described and mechanised. In other words RTM states that concepts exist as mental objects with attributes, while LOT states that concepts are not images but words in a specific language of the mind subject to a unique syntax. A complete and practical definition of concept should be influenced by those two aspects, and therefore be as follows: A concept is considered as the representation of a mental object and a set of attributes, expressed through a specific language of the mind which lets it be represented through symbols or patterns which are computable. Such approach defines concepts as objects formed by a set of attributes, in the same atomic way as the Classic Theory of Concept Representation does (Osherson & Smith, 1981), but also considers descriptive capabilities of the role of a concept in the same as the approach of Concepts as Theory Dependent (Carey, 1985; Murphy and Medin, 1985; Keil,1987). This definition is useful for declarative knowledge since it can be easily included to most existing models and remains specific enough to be computationally implemented as will be shown in section 4.

3.2 Definition of skill

Philosophic views such as (Dummet 1993, Kenny 2010) propose that abilities and concepts are the same thing, however, these approaches have not been very popular in computer and cognitive sciences, because of studies made in learning theories from Cognitive Science provide a more practical and empirical approach which instead support the Aristotelian view of concepts. Skills are practical manifestations of procedural knowledge, the most popular definitions of skills used today are based on constructivist theories and variations of Bloom's Taxonomy of Skills, this comes as a historic consequence of research in education, were skills is a core interest in educational psychology. Therefore, it is then not strange that the most referenced theories for skill development are found in this social science. Vygotsky's constructivist theory (Vygotsky, 1986) explains how skills are developed through a complex association process and upon construction of dynamic structures which can be traced through internal language or speech. Bloom's taxonomy for skills provides perhaps the most practical classification and enumeration of cognitive, social and physical skills. The combination of those works establishes enough theoretical insight to build more complex models for skill representation, such as those used in Cognitive Informatics for the Real Time Process Algebra (Wang, 2002), Newell's Soar cognitive architecture (Newell, 1990) and Anderson's ACT-R cognitive architecture (Anderson, 1994).

In Thought and Language, Vygostky (1986) explains several processes used to learn and create ideas. Ideas stated as concepts and skills dynamic in nature behave as processes in continual development which go through three evolution stages starting at the basic stage of syncretism heaps, which are loosely coupled ideas through mental images, and concluding in formal abstract stable ideas, which are fully developed concepts and skills that manifest in language.

Benjamin Bloom (1956) developed a taxonomy for skills with a very practical approach, in which three domains are specified: cognitive, affective, and psychomotor. Each domain contains different layers depending on the complexity of the particular skill. Bloom's taxonomy is widely used, however, as with any other taxonomy, criticisms have been raised; Spencer Kagan (2008) made the following observations:

1. A given skill can have different degrees of complexity; hence a layer model might not provide an adequate representation.
2. Skill integration in complexity order does not always keep true.

These observations imply that if there is a hierarchy in skills it must be dynamic in nature and this characteristic must be taken into account when defining what a skill is. The idea of flexible structure can also be found in Vygotsky's theories. In the framework for Cognitive Informatics, Wang (2002) proposes an entire system for describing processes, according to what we now know of procedural knowledge we can use such system to define skills in computational terms, thus under this train of thought skills are pieces of computer code located in an action buffer, such processes are composed by sub-processes and are described using Real Time Process Algebra (RTPA). RTPA is oriented to a structured approach where a skill is not as flexible as Kagan's observations suggest, the types of data, processes, meta-processes and operations between skills, should be included in a comprehensive definition of skills.

Using constructivist theories as a basis, Bloom's taxonomies for organisation and the cognitive architectures for mappings to computational terms, a generic definition for skills in computer systems can be stated as: A cognitive process that interacts with one or more concepts as well as other skills through application and has a specific purpose which produces internal or external results. Skills have different degrees of complexity and may be integrated or composed by other skills. In contrast with concepts which are factual entities by nature, skills are process oriented, they are application/action related by nature and it is common to describe them using verbs.

3.3 Associations between concepts and skills

Of the three basic common characteristics of knowledge stated in section 1, perhaps the second characteristic: *Concepts have relations or associations to other concepts,* is the most agreed upon. Every theory and model reviewed so far agrees that associations are vital to knowledge (Hobbes, 1651, Fodors, 1975, Vygotsky, 1986, Bloom, 1956, Kagan, 2003, Newell,

1990, Anderson, 1994, Quillian, 1968, Wang, 2002, Helbig, 2003, among others); the differences appear when defining their properties and implications, these are better observed in cognitive or computer models, since more general theories tend to be vague in this regard and detailed specification is a requirement for computer models (Marr, 1982). Most declarative knowledge representation models rely on propositional logic or its graphical equivalents in network representations e.g., Cyc (Read & Lenat, 2002), WordNet (Miller, 1990) , OAR (Wang, 2006), Multinet (Helbig, 2003) and Telos (Paquette, 1990) among others, the specific type of the network is determined by aspects such as directionality of associations (Helbig, 2003), the type of association (Wang, 2006), if the associations allows cycles, if they are hierarchical in nature (Paquette, 1990) or mixed and if there is a grouping or filtering scheme for them.

Traditional semantic networks only used presence or absence of associations; current semantic networks such as MultiNet or Object Attribute Relation OAR (Wang, 2007) provide deeper types of associations and integrate layers for knowledge composition. Examples of deeper type of association can be seen in MultiNet where associations are defined as a third type of node that contain procedural knowledge similar to Minsky frames, or OAR associations which are described as types of relations which can be grouped into several categories: Inheritances, Extension, Tailoring, Substitute, Composition, Decomposition, Aggregation and Specification. OAR categories are in fact operations for Concept Algebra (Wang, 2006), i.e., a mathematical way to describe how knowledge structures are integrated. Concept algebra does not include procedural knowledge, for this reason RTPA has a different set of associations which describe a hierarchy for composition of processes; both real time process and concept algebras are integrated in a higher framework called system algebra (Wang, 2009).

Associations are important because they create the context and embody semantic meaning for each context, some authors refer to this as sense (Vygostky, 1986), others discriminate between intrinsic knowledge, i.e., knowledge inherent to that concept, and context knowledge i.e., knowledge inferred from the associations and other concepts surrounding the original concept (Helbig, 2008). Understanding these approaches we can then summarise that an association is a relation between two elements, which can be skills or concepts that contain a particular function and a directionality that explains the nature of the relation. Groups of associations are what create contexts and each of these contexts may provide a uniquely different sense to a concept or skill which should reflect upon interpretation and inference process.

4. A model for the representation of concepts and skills In different contexts

An important functionality for knowledge representation models is the capacity to represent multiple contexts in a single instantiation, as well as the impact that context changes have on a concept's meaning. Approaches such as micro-theories models used in Cyc contemplate this and have successfully managed to combine multiple facts of a subjective nature into a coherent knowledge base, however, Cyc requires understanding of its own native language which is based on predicate logic semantics for information modelling and for information extraction as well, this has proven a problem for most users (Lenat, 2006). Simpler graphical representations which retain this context flexibility and can be represented in computers present an attractive alternative for average users, such as domain experts not versed in CYC language. Graphical oriented models such as Multinet or OAR have been used for natural language processing and for knowledge composition and process specification respectively, but their focus is not to represent several contexts a time.

Multinet for example has specific context differentiation based on grammar attributes such as singular or plural elements, however, it does not have differentiators for the concepts meaning when the context changes. In these models when a new context is to be created only a small fraction of the information of concepts is reused and most of it has to be re-instantiated for each domain, this is a common trait of knowledge representation models that have instances as part of their model. OAR presents a similar situation since the context is defined as the relation between objects and its attributes in a given set (Wang, 2006). OAR is more flexible and does contemplate multiple contexts for the instantiations of the concepts, but not for the concepts themselves, which means that what are dynamic are not the concepts themselves but the objects in regard to the context. The implication for this is that a concept will have several different instantiations depending on the context, however this issue does not represent the impact the context has on the formation of a concept as was described by Vygotsky (1986).

4.1 The memory map model

The Memory Map (MM) is a knowledge representation model for concepts and skills, its main goal is to represent the interaction of these elements in different contexts, including the representation of concepts which meaning changes according to the context, i.e., semantic environments. The MM can be visualised as a semantic network which is compliant with the theoretical views presented in section 1 and 2. The main difference between the MM and other models is that the MM strongly focuses in context flexibility, because of this approach, in the MM concepts and skills must have an open granularity subject to the modeller's criteria; an arbitrary level of atomicity which can be specified for each concept, and dynamic hierarchies which can change for different domains of knowledge. The implementation of the MM is a directed graph, very similar to the more flexible types of semantic networks and to ontologies.

4.2 Memory map components

There are three main components in the MM which were developed using the theoretical bases for knowledge stated in section 1:

1. **Concepts** referred to as Concept Representation Units (Concept-RU), they are represented as the round nodes in the network.
2. **Skills** referred to as Skill Representation Units (Skill-RU), they are represented as the round nodes in the network.
3. **Associations** between the members of Concept-RUs, between the members of Skill-RUs and associations among Concept-RUs and Skill-RUs, they are the arcs in the network.

4.2.1 Concept representation units

The basic definition for concept in the MM can be described by the elements of section 2. Syntactically, each concept is enclosed in its particular Concept-RU which has associations to other Skill-RUs and Concept-RUs. The attributes of concepts and skills together with their associations define their semantics, therefore any skill or concept is described and defined by the associations it has with other skills and concepts. This means that a Concept-RU has little intrinsic knowledge, and almost all the knowledge is provided from its context through its associations which are also its attributes. A concept's meaning changes depending on the group of attributes that are tagged for each different domain. Using the domain tags for attributes allows a Concept-RU to represent an indeterminate amount of meanings for that concept, since ultimately the concept is in fact a structure; an example of this is presented in figure 5, where the concept *cell* is represented for 3 different contexts: *Biology, Buildings* and *Communications*. A similar approach for attributes can be found in distributed systems with local representation (Eysenck, 2010), which could be closest thing to a hybrid representation model between the symbolic and the distributed systems.

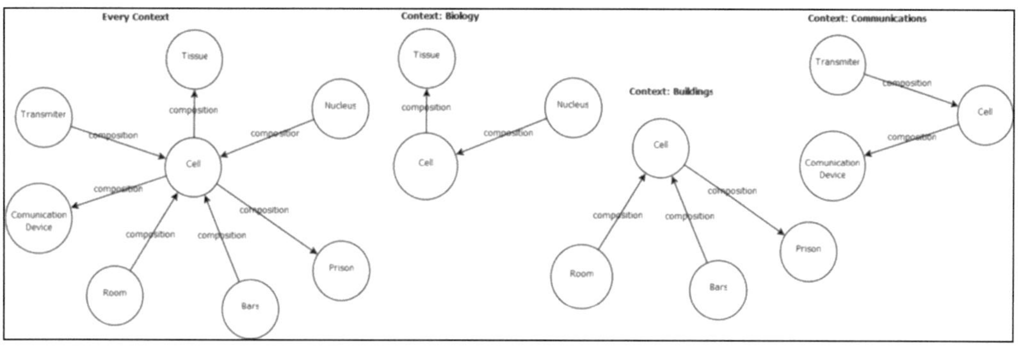

Fig. 5. Example of concept representation unit in three different contexts

Formally a Concept Representation Unit is defined as:

$$c(n,A,x) \tag{1}$$

where c is a concept with a name or identifier n, a set of attributes A, and a numerical level of knowledge x, where A is

$$A = \{a_1, a_2, a_3, \dots a_n\} \tag{2}$$

each a is an association from the concept to other concepts or skills, and n is the total number associations that the Skill-RU has. Two associated concepts or skills will share an association for each context, so the intersection of both concepts must return all the associations by which they are related. Hence if c_a and c_b are associated as follows:

$$c_a(n,\{a_1,a_2,a_{3\dots}a_n\},x) \cap c_b(n,\{b_1,b_2,b_{3\dots}b_n\},x) \neq 0 \tag{3}$$

The context representation is handled within each association and will be explained in 4.2.4 and 4.3.

4.2.2 Skill representation units

In accordance to what was established in section 2, a skill in the MM is a cognitive process that interacts with one or more concepts and other skills, usually through application, which has a specific purpose and produces a certain result, be it internal or external. Skills have different degrees of complexity and can be integrated with other skills. Skills are process oriented, they are action related by nature, for this reason they are described using verbs. Figure 5 shows the representation for two different versions of Bloom's taxonomy, versions of skills can also be modelled as different contexts, this way combinations of trees and domains of concepts can be used to model knowledge domains in a flexible way re-using most of the information already contained in the model. To represent the dynamicity described by Vygotsky, Skill-RU have knowledge levels which indicate how evolved a Skill-RU or a Concept-RU is, this number can be mapped using thresholds to indicate if a structure is weak, i.e., syncretic or strong and stable, i.e., conceptual. The way in which knowledge is extracted and calculated is explained in 4.2.4.

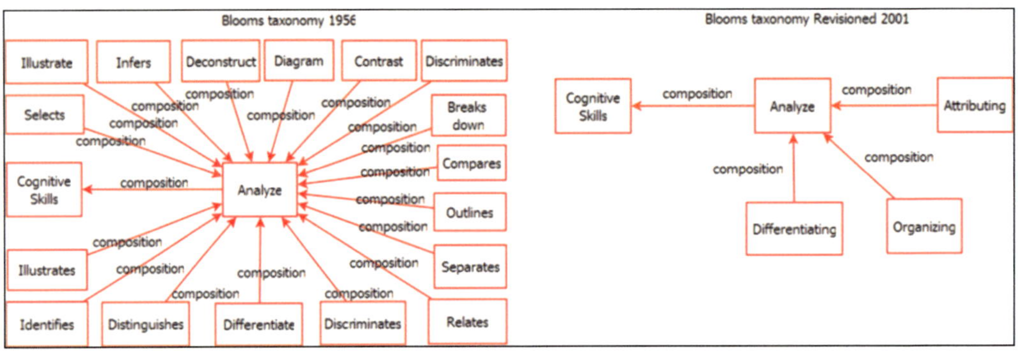

Fig. 6. The structure to the left is a skill representation in the MM of a segment of Bloom's (1956) original taxonomy based on keywords, the structure to the right is a representation of a revision made in 2001 of Bloom's work (L. Anderson et al., 2001).

In a formal definition a Skill-RU is similar to the Concept-RU, the main difference is the type of associations skills have which reflect a more application oriented nature. A skill is defined as follows:

$$s(n,A,x) \tag{4}$$

Two associated concepts or skills will share an association for each different context, so the intersection of both skills must return all the associations by which they are related. Hence if Sa and Sb are associated:

$$s_a(n,\{a_1,a_2,a_{3\ldots}a_n\},x) \cap s_b(n,\{b_1,b_2,b_{3\ldots}b_n\},x) \neq 0 \tag{5}$$

4.2.3 Associations

Skill-RUs and Concept-RUs are the constituents in the MM and are glued through associations, there is only one restriction in the associations and that is that only Skill-RUs can have application oriented roles. Skill-RUs and Concept-RUs have independent organisation structures within the MM structure, this is used to represent composition of skill and of concepts as is shown in figure 7.

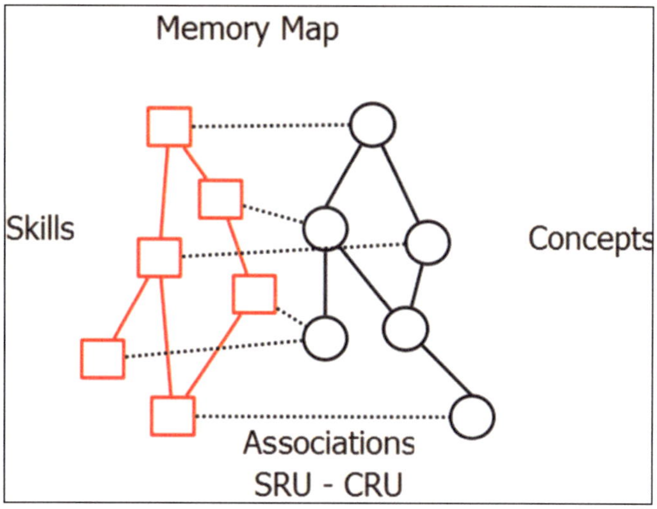

Fig. 7. Associations between skills and concepts in a Memory Map

The purpose of the associations is to represent how concepts and skills relate to each other to generate knowledge. Knowledge is not only a group of stored concepts, but the structure of associations itself. An association therefore must:

- Provide information of the nature of the relation, knowing that the nature of a relation allows us to understand how the structure is to behave and enables more complex reasoning processes.
- Provide information of the directionality of causality, the inheritance of attributes in directly dependent on this factor, when we say inheritance of attributes we also mean inheritance of associations.
- Provide information as to the domain where it is valid, so the structure can be context sensitive and discriminate which associations hold true for a domain and which do not.
- Provide quantitative information of the strength of the association, knowing the strength of an association will allow probabilistic estimation of how much is known of a concept or skill, this is letting the structure know how much does it know regarding that specific relation.

An association **a** is defined as a relationship between two representation units which may be either a Concept-RU or a Skill-RU, the first unit is predecessor *pre* and the second is successor *suc*. The association role **r** contains specific information that describes the nature of the relationship and the set of domains *D* where the association holds true and **y** indicates the strength of the association.

$$a\left(u_{pre,}u_{suc}, r, D, y\right) \tag{6}$$

where u represents a unit which might either be a concept or a skill, this holds true for groups as well:

$$U\left(u_1,u_2,u_{3,\dots}\right) = C\left(c_1,c_2,c_4, \dots\right) \cup S\left(s_1,s_2,s_3, \dots\right) \tag{7}$$

An example of associations with the information attributes presented above is presented in figure 8.

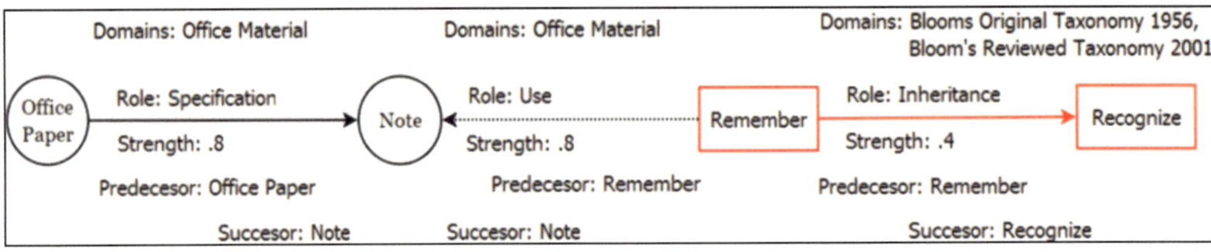

Fig. 8. Three types of associations: left Concept-RU-Concept-RU, middle Concept-RU-Skill-RU and right Skill-RU-Skill-RU.

Two representation units can share more than one association as is shown in figure 9, the only restriction is that there can only be one association per domain with the same role and between the same RUs, this avoids two things: the first is direct contradictions within the same domain in case the directionality for that role is inversed, the second is redundancy of information in the case of two associations with the same directionality and the same role which will result in unnecessary repeated information.

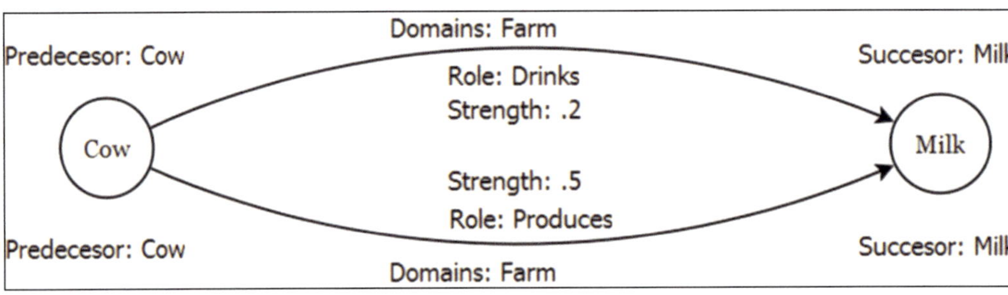

Fig. 9. Two concepts in the same domain share two associations with different roles.

Role types:	Description
inheritance	the successor unit inherits all the associations and hence the attributes of the predecessor representation unit.
extension	the precursor unit integrates single individual attribute
tailoring	the predecessor unit cannot inherit a specific association to the successor if a group of associations are inherited from it.
composition	the precursor unit is a component of the successor unit; the successor unit inherits the composition associations of the precursor unit.

Table 1. Examples of association types of OAR used as Roles in the MM. \

Since associations contain the information regarding the domain, they change when the domain changes, examples are presented in figures 5 and 6. Roles or types of associations can be freely defined and integrated into the model as long as they have a consistent functionality; MultiNet presents a similar approach for its types of relations (Helbig, 2003), the main difference being that MultiNet focuses on natural language and requires more types of relation to describe lexical and grammatical rules. A solid and economic base to describe knowledge composition can be found in OARs types of associations, with only 8 types of associations and an instantiation OAR provides congruent mathematical explanations of concept composition. The MM can use any type and number of roles to describe the basic composition for Concept-RUs and Skill-RUs; several examples based on OARs associations are shown in table 1. On the other hand, the MM does not create objects and instantiations as OAR does, in the MM both are treated as the same thing, for this reason some of the types of associations used in OAR become redundant in the MM as is shown in table 2.

Role types:	Description
decomposition	the inverse behaviour of composition, it is rarely used since it can be substituted by backtracking the directionality of composition.
aggregation	the same behaviour as the tailoring role, it can be substituted since due to the nature of the MM model it has no application.
specification	the same behaviour as the extension role, it can be substituted since due to the nature of the MM model it has no application.
substitution	attributes change for different instantiations, this is not necessary in the MM for domain filtering naturally and transparently handles this substitution.

Table 2. Association types of OAR that becomes redundant or Useless in MM.

A graphical representation of how each association role is presented in figure 10.

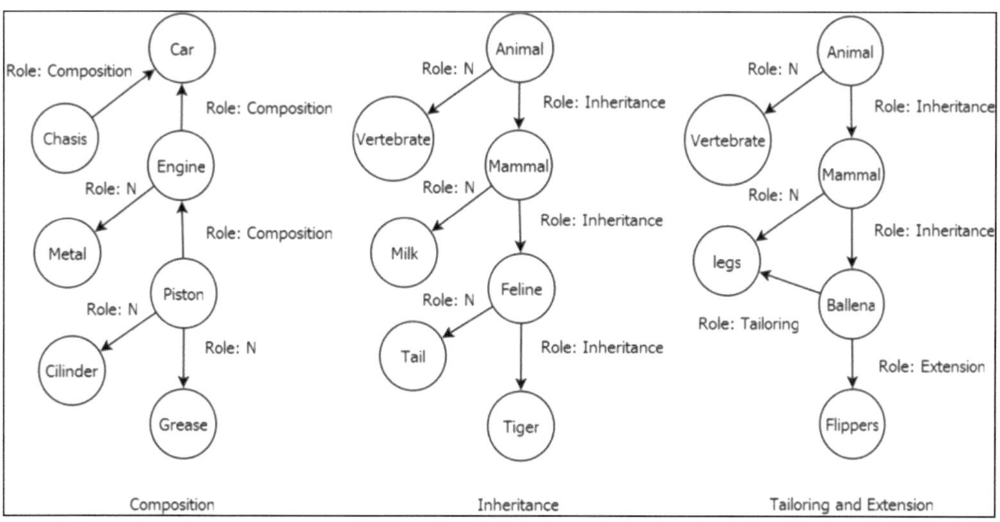

Fig. 10. Examples of OAR types of associations Composition, Inheritance, Tailoring and Extension integrated into MM model as roles.

4.3 Context and inter context associations

Context is the embodiment of semantic knowledge, that is, the way in which groups of ideas are associated. In the MM a context is the body of knowledge composed by one or more domains of knowledge, associations are subject to the domains they belong to, an association between two RUs must belong to at least one domain, using the combination of multiple domains different contexts may be built. A domain cannot present a contradiction within itself, however built contexts can present contradictions since each domain included in a context may have contradictory knowledge in the form of a same rol with inverse directionality, because of this when combining several domains into a mixed context, priority mechanisms for contradictions should be defined as well. Contradictions may generate problems such as creating cyclic structure in MM, this is a common problem for flexible low restriction model like Ontology Web Language OWL (McGuinness & Harmelen, 2004). OWL in its first two levels establishes mainly treelike structures, but at its most expressive and flexible level OWL cannot guaranty computability (McGuinness & Harmelen, 2004), this seems to be a common fault for which workarounds can be made in implementations such as memory stacks or limits in searches, but there seems to be no model solution in sight which does not compromise the models flexibility.

4.4 Knowledge extraction

If the model used for knowledge representation is flexible enough then complex information may be extracted using simple functions or algorithms, such is the case of the MM. Queries or knowledge extraction in the model are performed through simple unguided recursive searches that return relevant segments of the MM, it must be stated that the main focus of this knowledge representation model is to be able to easily access information for open questions such as: *what does this MM know about concept A or skill B? What are the attributes of concept A? How are concepts A and B related under this particular domain of knowledge? What attributes of A hold for every domain? What concepts are related by type of association a?* Each of these questions can be answered using the domain or combination of domains, the roles of associations, the depth of knowledge, the directionality knowledge and the combination of all of the above.

Basic knowledge extraction in the MM can be described by the recursive function:

$$f\left(\left((u)(n,A,x)\right)_i, r_j, d_k\right) = f\left(\left((u)_,(n,A,x)\right)_{i-1}, r_{i+1}, d_{k+1}\right)$$

$$i=0, 1, 2, ..., n \qquad j=0, 1, 2, ..., m \qquad k=0, 1, 2, ..., l \tag{8}$$

Where n is the number of existing concepts or skill levels that the search can reach, m is the number of existing roles and l is the number of existing domains. The function in turn will return a group of associations, because the associations themselves represent the structure of knowledge that is sought. We now provide different examples of how the function works for some of the questions presented above:

What does this MM know? If the MM is queried with function setting as parameter n, m, and l, then the function returns the whole MM as is shown in figures 11, 12 and 13.-*What is concept*

A composed of or what class does it belong to? If the MM is queried with the function from *i* to *n*, the search will return a structure of units for a domain k with the role j, as is shown in figure 10. This represents a hierarchy or a chain of composition, though this will be subject to what role j is.

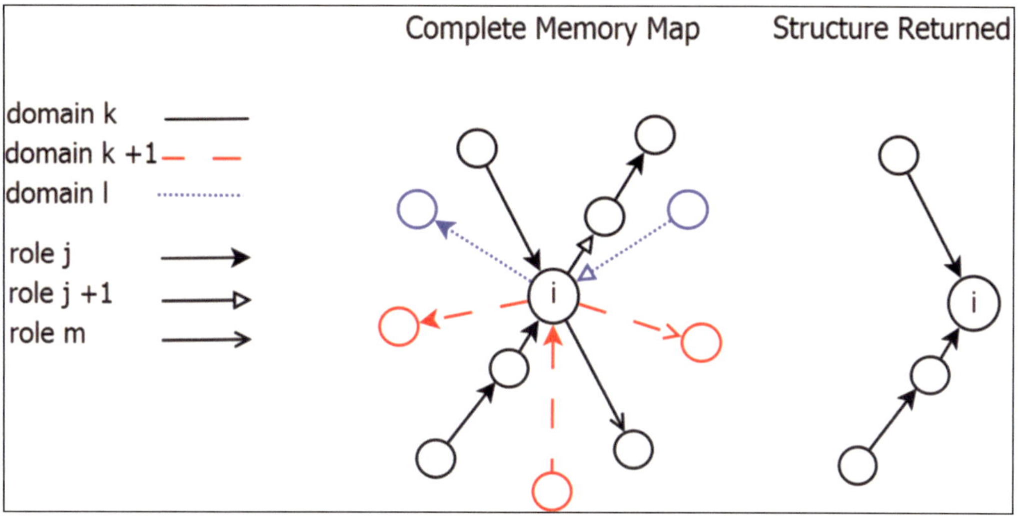

Fig. 11. The search result for an every concept or limitless search with one role and in one domain.

What are the attributes of concept A? If the MM is queried with the function from *j* to *m*, the search will return every role associated to the concept *i* in the domain *k*, as is shown in figure 12. This represents the direct attributes of the central concept.

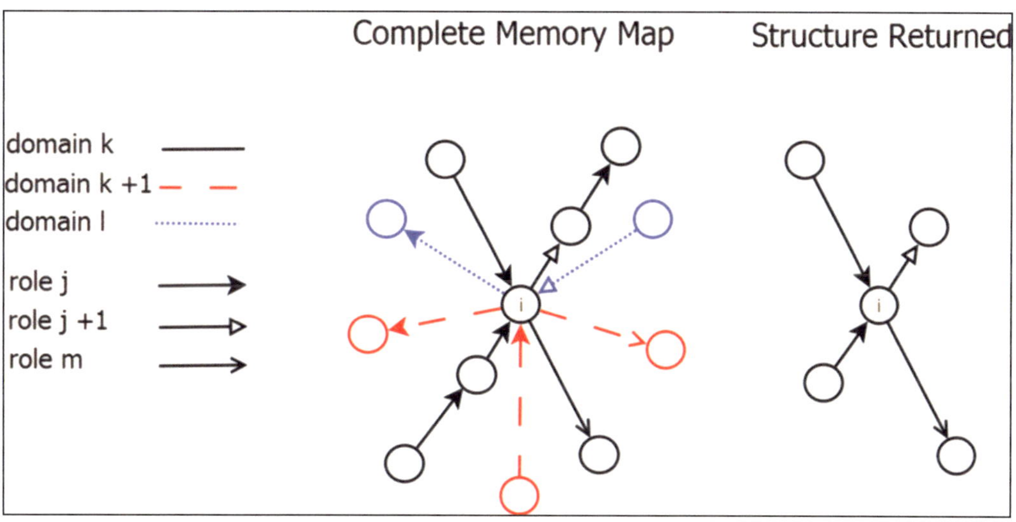

Fig. 12. The result for an every role or attributes search for one concept and in one domain.

What attributes does concept A hold for in different domains? If the MM is queried with the function from *k* to *l*, the search will return every association with role j associated to the concept *i* in every domain, as is shown in figure 13. This represents every possible meaning the concept might take in a completely open context.

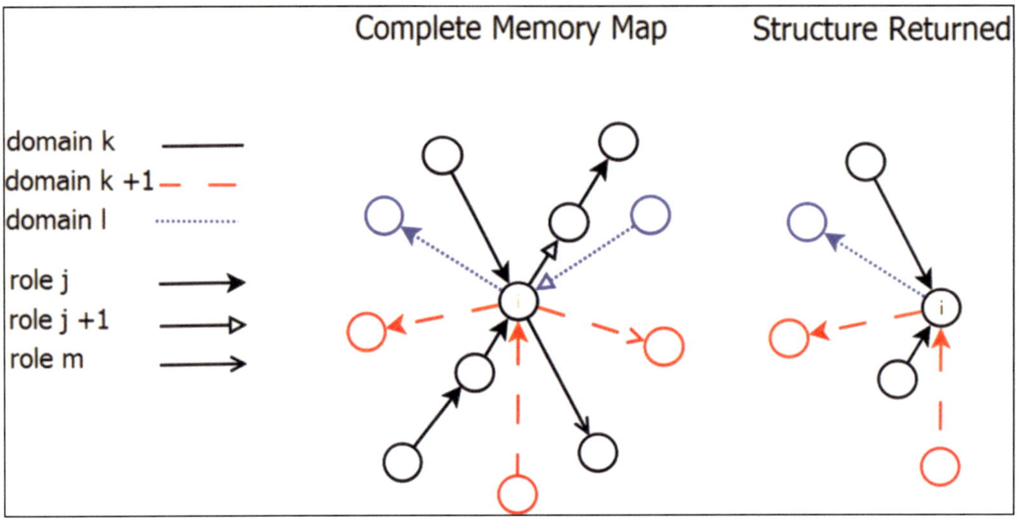

Fig. 13. The result for an every domain or open context search for one concept and with one role.

The rest of the questions can be answered with combinations of these criteria.

4.5 Knowledge acquisition

New knowledge is acquired by associating it to previous knowledge. Acquisition in the MM also follows this principle, new representation units must be integrated with the main body of representation units that are already known, this follows also the constructivist principle that knowledge is constructed upon more knowledge, hence the more we know the easier it is to learn and retain knowledge in long term memory. This approach establishes then some restrictions:

- For a concept or skill to be considered as part of knowledge it must be associated to the structure of knowledge. A domain can appear to have sparsity, i.e., secluded knowledge, however it is because there is an association that link's that concept or skill to the whole structure which cannot be seen because it is part of a different domain. Though the domain seems disconnected, other domains complement it in a natural way and therefore the MM is congruent in general. A real life example of this can be seen in academic courses where requirements come from different fields, e.g., knowledge of programming as well as propositional logic are required for the understanding of artificial intelligence, though they might not be directly related between each other, a novice's MM in the domain of artificial intelligence would appear fragmented since some of the concepts would not be yet related through this domain, however, knowledge of both programming and logic must be associated through other currently hidden domains in the novice's MM because they cannot be completely secluded. If knowledge is found to be completely secluded through every context then this represents a memorised fact instead of knowledge.

- Associations must always be linked to representation units, an association cannot be linked to an empty unit or remain unlinked.
- If a new concept or skill is to be integrated, then the representation units must be created first and the association later. If a structure is to be integrated, then this process is repeated recursively for each unit of the structure.

In general the integration of new knowledge to the structure is described in figure 14.

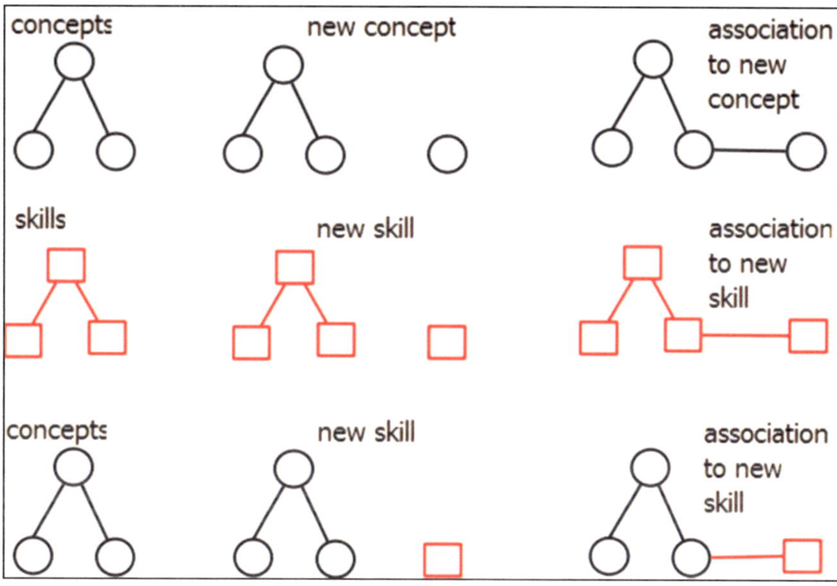

Fig. 14. Integration of new concepts and skills to the structure of knowledge.

4.6 Knowledge measuring

Knowledge measuring in the MM is subject to context, only in few occasions will it be desired to know all the information from a concept in every domain, most of the time the interest will be in knowing the level of knowledge for a concept in regard to a context. There are two scenarios for knowledge measuring: the first when knowledge is measured in an absolute way, and second when knowledge is measured through a query. The differences between them will now be explained.

To know the general knowledge grade of a concept the average of numeric value v of each association is multiplied by an associative factor determined by:

$$\text{Associative Factor} = 1 + (\#@) * 0.1 \tag{9}$$

where #@ is the number of selected associations, the factor represents the increment of impact of a more associated concept, this means that if two concepts have the same average of association strength, the associative factor will give a higher grade to the more associated concept. The general knowledge measurement for a representation unit would be calculated by:

$$\text{Representation Unit K} - \text{level} = \left(\text{Average}(\text{v})\right) * \text{AssociativeFactor} \tag{10}$$

where v is the numerical value of a group of associations that were selected.

When measuring knowledge for the general case, 10 will be used for the concept with every existing association, when measuring knowledge for a specific context only those associations included in the domains will be used, therefore a concept will have a different knowledge value for each context. When measuring the knowledge of a group of representation units, a similar approach is used:

$$\text{Segment K} - \text{level} = \left(\text{Average}(\text{RUK} - \text{level})\right) * \ 1 + (\#\text{RU}) * 0.1 \tag{11}$$

Where RU level is the representation unit knowledge level, and the average of all the selected concepts are multiplied by a factor determined by representation units, hence if two segments have an equal amount of knowledge level in their representation units, then the segment having more representation units, i.e., concepts and skills is said to have more knowledge.

4.7 Properties of the MM

The fact that every attribute is considered as a mixture between a concept and an association in the memory and that depending on the current context, this change generates properties which make the MM flexible and expressive:

- **Open/Unlimited Granularity.** Since the composition of knowledge is a network structure, there can be an indeterminate number of levels to specify composition. A field expert can determine the level of granularity specification for any unit, this means different units within the structure can have different granularities.
- **Dynamic Hierarchy.** Concept and skill representation units can be integrated into proper hierarchies through roles and directionality of associations; a unit can be placed in several taxonomies, i.e., in several hierarchies, where each hierarchy belongs to a different context, the combination of several domains with different hierarchy structures generate in turn new hierarchies, making the hierarchies dynamic and context dependent. This enables the use of semantic information contained in the taxonomy for a context that includes that taxonomy.
- **Economy of Knowledge.** The structure is developed in a way to avoid information redundancy, i.e. the same nodes are used for different knowledge structures, each one of them delimited by a different context.
- **Informativeness Capability.** There is no limit to the amount of Concept-RUs or Skill-RUs in a structure, nor is there a limit to the depth of the knowledge represented, that is, there is no limit for the hierarchy of attributes and associations.
- **Flexibility.** The structure can create associations between any Concept-RU and Skill-RU, and each association can have several roles each offering a unique behaviour.

5. Application of the MM in an advanced learning environment

The problems and challenges found in the development of smart tools for education remain attractive and closely linked to knowledge representation models in general, for this reason the MM was instrumented as part of an Advance Learning Environment where it is used for the adaptation of learning resources. The adaptation is done through user profiles that contain user knowledge, interest, learning styles and emotional profiles. Similar approaches have been presented in (Carchiolo, Longheu & Malgeri, 2002, Van Marcke, 1998) where integral user profiles are used to model generic personalisation of learning environments. Knowledge Representation models have been used for education successfully in Intelligent Computer Aided Instruction ICAI (Nwanna, 1990), Adaptive Hypermedia (Brusilovsky, 2004) and Intelligent Tutoring System ITS (Nwanna, 1990) fields, the frameworks and architectures established in theese fields can be described as generic adaptation processes, these greatly eases the transition of a purely theoretical models to practical implementations in human learning environments.

5.1 Proposed architecture

The architecture for an Advance Learning Environment is meant to provide optimal learning conditions both physical: by adjusting settings such as environment noise, temperature and illumination, as well as cognitive conditions: through the personalisation of learning resources, media, activities, sequencing, evaluation methods and content. To achieve this, the architecture requires physical sensors and algorithms to process the user physical information, such methods are described in (Ramirez, Concha, & Valdes, 2010, Arroyo & Cooper, 2009) and include body temperature, posture detection, heart rate, facial expression recognition, among others. Each of these methods pass the processed input information to a group of algorithms which will decide what adaptations need to be made to achieve optimal learning conditions.

The complete architecture is presented in figure 15, the cycle that describes the operation of the system is the following:

1. Starting on the side of the figure we can observe tools for editing the MM, integrating Learning Objects (LO) and Learning Services (LS), modifying student portfolios and creating assessments. The tools are meant to assist teachers in the development of the MMs to be used in their courses, and for students to consult and partially edit their own portfolios. The student portfolios include their cumulative MM from every course they have taken, their emotional-cognitive mappings, their learning profile and their explicit interest and learning goals. Through these editors information is manually captured into the entire system.
2. Once the system has a complete user portfolio, a MM of the course designed by expert and enough LOs and LSs, the system can start the personalisation process. If the student is new to the system and does not have a MM, the process starts with an initial evaluation. The evaluation can be either a regular test, automated observation or through expert direct assessment, with this information the student's MM is created, or updated if a MM already exists.
3. Using heuristics based on the user knowledge level and the course MM, the system determines the next concepts to present. This is done through an overlay approach, i.e., the student knowledge must be a subset of the expert knowledge, (Brusilovsky, 2007).

4. Knowing what the next concept or skill to be taught should be, the system selects from a library of LOs and LSs the most adequate object for the user's profile from a group the group of LSs and LOs that match the selected knowledge.
5. Once the object is selected it passes onto a learning management system (LMS) (Alcorn, & et al. 2000) where the learning object will be integrated into the main sequence of activities to be presented to the student, in this stage smaller modifications regarding the presentation of the object such as colour, font size, layout and duration are also made.
6. Depending on the activity, the student must go through a knowledge evaluation regarding the content just presented either through behaviour observation during activity or through a post-test.
7. With the feedback obtained from this evaluation the student's MM is updated and the cycle begins again until the desired concepts in MM of the course are learnt.

While this is all taking place, physical sensors are continually observing and gathering data to estimate the users emotional condition and with this information the user profile is updated as to determine what factors in the learning process affect the student's emotional state, with enough information on this regard patterns can be established as to predict what will cause undesirable stress in the student. This factor is considered into the algorithms in charge of conceptual selection and those in charge of content personalisation. We will now review each of these applications of the memory map in the advance learning environment with more detail.

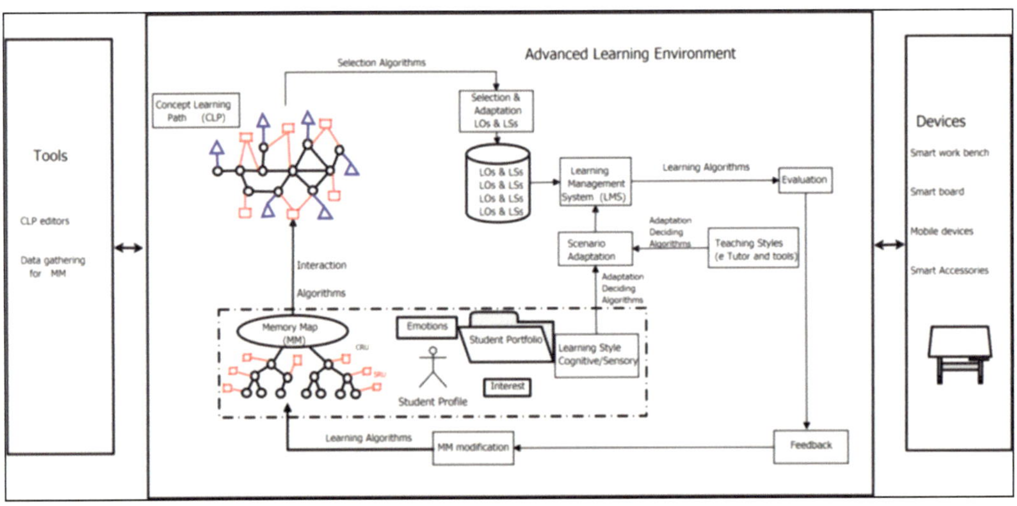

Fig. 15. The architecture of the Advanced Learning Environment

5.2 Knowledge representation for apprentice/student modelling

If personalisation is desired then a source of information is required, a knowledge representation model is the ideal source of information for advanced adaptations. This is because a knowledge representation model, usually a concept or semantic network, contains key information on how ideas are related and how to present them to a student through a complex negotiation process which can be described through algorithms supported on learning theories, in particular the constructivist theory (Vygotsky, 1986).

In education systems architectures, user modelling is divided into two categories: student model and expert model (Nwanna, 1990, Murray, 1999), whereas their name states the student model contains the information regarding student knowledge and the expert model contains all the information an expert should know for that context. In the advanced learning environment the MM is used to model both the expert model and the student model. The MM is used to model the concepts and associations that a group of students is expected to learn during an academic course or subject to be learnt, this is called the course-MM and would be equivalent to the expert model on cognitive agent architecture; each association and representation unit is taken to be an implicit learning objective which will be mapped to LOs and LSs. For the student a MM is created for her/his particular knowledge, the students MM are built and expanded using academic tests with specifically designed questions to inquire if an association between particular concepts exists, this approach, where a set of specifically designed questions reflect the knowledge of a user on a domain, is used in knowledge spaces theory as well (Doignon & Falmagne 1999).

The fact that both knowledge structures are represented using the same knowledge representation model makes the use of an overlay approach natural for detecting differences between what the student knows and what the courses conceptual contents are, i.e., what the student knows and what he/she must learn in the course. Almost any knowledge representation model can be used to represent both the student model and the expert model, however the context management attributes of the MM allow it to represent several different student domains of the same student for different courses, this is, each context dynamically established in the MM can be treated as a different knowledge domain either for student or for the expert. For example if learner A enrols in course B, only the knowledge in student A's MM that is labelled under the domain (of the course) B or the representation units that are detected to be equivalent to those found in B, will be used for the content selection in the system, as shown in figure 16. The updates to student A's MM will be labelled under the domain B, therefore incrementing A's MM, both in this particular context and in general. A more detail explanation as to the methods used for the personalisation of the learning path can be found in (Ramirez & Valdes 2011).

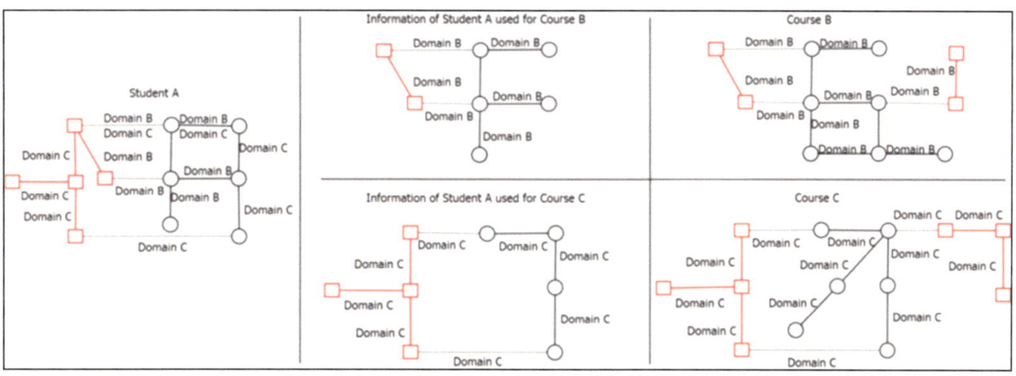

Fig. 16. Example of one student memory map. *Student A* is being used for an overlay approach in two courses: *course A* and *course B*.

Several courses and topics such as: Artificial Intelligence, Theory of Computation and Search Algorithms have been modelled using the MM and have been used in preliminary tests of the presented architecture, segments of each of the MMs are shown in figures 17, 18 and 19. Only

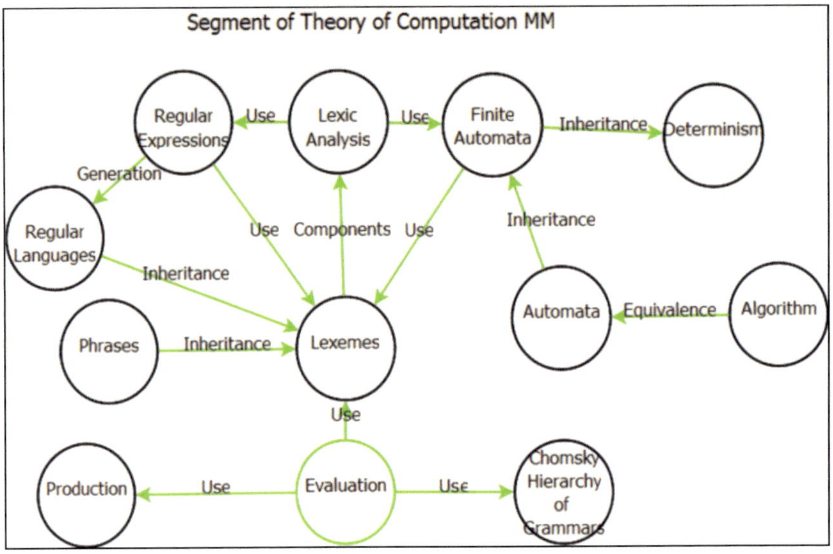

Fig. 17. Segments of MMs for Theory of Computation.

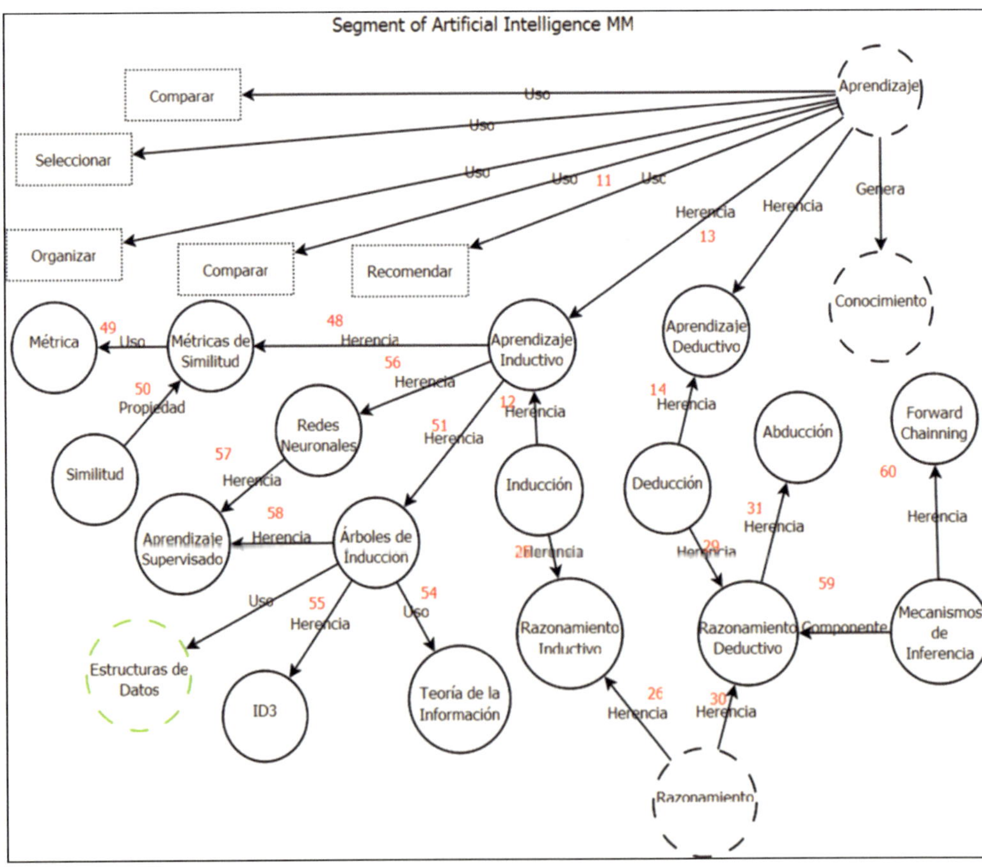

Fig. 18. Segments of MMs for Artificial Intelligence course.

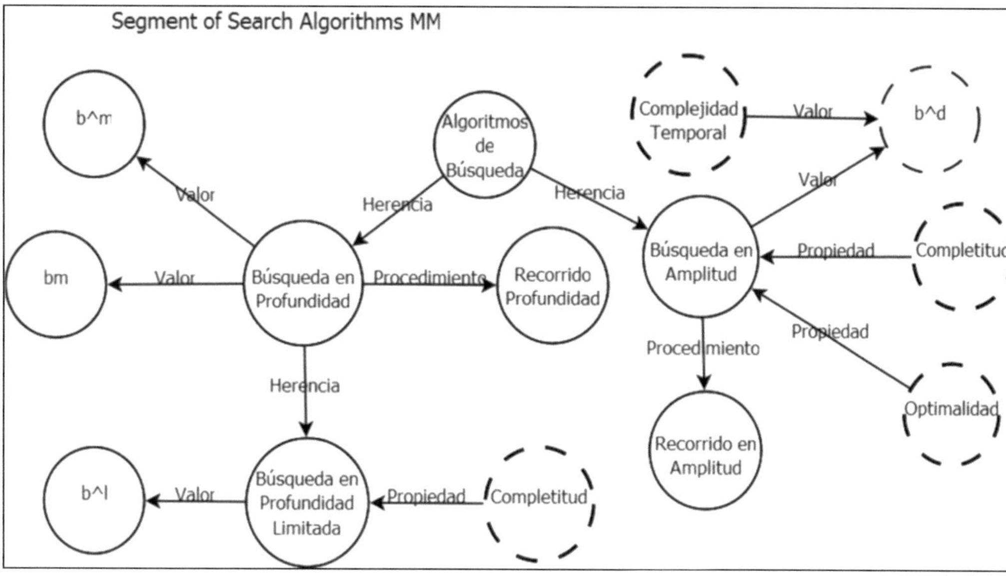

Fig. 19. Segments of MMs for Search Algorithms .

segments are shown because the real MMs are much bigger, the largest map is of an entire course on Artificial Intelligence, it has over 90 associations just between Concept-RUs and 40 mixed associations between the Concept-RUs and Skill-RUs. In this map there are no associations between Skill-RUs and Skill-RUs. The ABET skill taxonomy was used --although any taxonomy can be used--, ABET taxonomy is based on Bloom's but has no real hierarchy for skill composition.

5.3 Knowledge representation working with emotional feedback

In recent years affective learning has becomes one of the main focuses for learning research (Arroyo & Cooper, 2009, Hernández, Sucar & Conati 2009, Ramirez, Concha & Valdes, 2010a, 2010b), it has been proven that emotional conditions have a strong impact in the learning process of students and furthermore certain combination of emotions have been detected on which optimal learning takes place and reduces learning curve (Csikszentmihalyi, 1991). The advanced learning environment architecture contemplates this factor by using non-invasive sensors matching physical and physiological signals through correlations between temporal emotions and subject's learning processes. Diverse physical and physiological variables can be used to trace the emotional condition of a person, such as cardiac pulse, respiratory rate, posture, facial and voice expressions, etc. The cardiac pulse in particular is a reliable signal that carries useful information about the subject's emotional condition, it is detected using a classroom chair adapted with non-invasive EMFi sensors and an acquisition system that generates ballistocardiogram (BCG) signals, which are analysed to obtain cardiac pulse statistics. If emotions can be successfully monitored then a relation can be established between the emotional state, performance and characteristics of learning activities such as difficulty, time constrains and presentation style among others.

On another facet, Steels (2004) demonstrated that the level of difficulty in a task does have an impact in the emotional process. Difficulty can be associated with the contents presented in learning activities to students and their previous experience, i.e., the student's skills and concepts. It is common in current "industrial" education systems to find students that lack previous context specific knowledge to comprehend new ideas, this generates stress and frustration and hinders the learning process. To help the learner get into an adequate emotional state for learning, not only the physical environment should be appropriate; but also the content of the learning subject itself and the order in which it is presented. Altering the order of learning activities might prove to be cheaper and more effective, the problem is to know the most appropriate order for each individual. The main goal is to create a positive emotional impact through personalisation; in order to do this we need to detect and avoid stress barriers due to an excess of difficulty and the lack of proper basis for the learning of complex concepts.

Keeping a record of the emotional feedback and the current LO or LS being presented enables a mapping between the emotions and the content. Negative emotional conditions can be predicted and avoided through pre-emptive adaptations. For example, if a student is presented with very advanced content that she is unable to understand, it is probable that she will experience frustration and anxiety; on the other hand, if she is presented with basic content which she already knows, it is probable the she will experience apathy or boredom (Steels, 2005). On the first case a previous learning activity to develop required skills before entering the scheduled learning activity is introduced in her learning flow; on the second case the learning activity can be skipped or eliminated. A second option in either case would consist of changing the difficulty level of the activity to better suit her. Detection of emotional condition and according reaction in the sequence of learning activities adaptation can be used to check if a previous adaptation is adequate. For example, if frustration is detected in a student while performing an activity, her MM would be checked to verify that she indeed has the required skills for the activity, in case the content is too advanced, assistance would be provided in the way of an AI tutor or an assistance signal could be emitted to the professor if deemed necessary.

6. Summary

In this chapter it was presented the basic concepts behind Knowledge Representation and types of knowledge going from traditional theories such as RTM to modern ones such as LOTH and showing not only how each discipline or science, including Philosophy, Psychology, Cognitive Science, Brain Science and Computer Science, has its own approach and limitations, but also that most of them complement each other and are situated upon three similar bases. We have also analysed the theoretical foundations for the explanation of the components of knowledge: concepts, skills and associations, including the way in which these are acquired, the way they interact, and their impact in other processes of cognition which in turn allow us to understand the reasons why computer models for knowledge representation are the way they are, and also, how each of these models can and have been used in recent years, in general terms. Additionally, we presented an original computer model for general knowledge representation, called Memory Map (MM). MM integrates both, skills and concepts into dynamic hierarchies defined by domains that reflect knowledge as context dependent. The MM was compared with similar models like MultiNet and OAR, showing similarities and differences, particularly regarding the representation of context. A practical application of the MM model was presented within a learning environment architecture, showing several examples of domains of knowledge modelled with the it. Finally some applications of the MM model for the development of an information system for the personalisation of learning considering affective-cognitive aspects were discussed.

7. Acknowledgment

The authors are members of the DASL4LTD research group would like to thank the Tec of Monterrey Campus Querétaro as well as CONACYT for supporting their financial support.

8. References

Ackoff, R. L. (1989). "From Data to Wisdom", Journal of Applies Systems Analysis, Volume 16, p 3-9.

Alcorn, R. L., Cane, D. E., Chasen, M. L., Chi, T. R., Gilfus, S. R., Perian, S., et al. (2000, June). Internet-based education support system and methods.

Anderson, J. R., Bothell, D., Byrne, M. D., Douglass, S., Lebiere, C., & Qin, Y. (2004). An integrated theory of the mind. *Psychological Review, 111, (4),* 1036-1060

Anderson, J. R. (1990). *The Adaptive Character of Thought (Studies in Cognition Series)* (p. 304). Psychology Press

Anderson, L. W., Krathwohl, D. R., Airasian, P. W., Cruikshank, K. A., Mayer, R. E., Pintrich, P. R., et al. (2000). *A Taxonomy for Learning, Teaching, and Assessing: A Revision of Bloom's Taxonomy of Educational Objectives, Complete Edition* (p. 384). Allyn & Bacon.

Arroyo, I., & Cooper, D. (2009). Emotion sensors go to school. *Proceedings of 14th Annual Conference on Artificial Intelligence in Education.* Retrieved July 25, 2011, from

Bloom, B. (1956). *Taxonomy of Educational Objectives, Handbook I: The Cognitive Domain.* (D. McKay, Ed.). New York: David McKay Co Inc.

Brown, Ann L. (1989). *Similarity and Analogical Reasoning.* (S. Vosniadou & A. Ortony, Eds.). Cambridge: Cambridge University Press. doi:10.1017/CBO9780511529863

Brusilovsky, P. (2004). Adaptive Navigation Support : From Adaptive Hypermedia to the Adaptive Web and Beyond. *Knowledge Creation Diffusion Utilization,* 2(1), 7 - 23.

Brusilovsky, P. (2007). Adaptive Navigation Support. In P. Brusilovsky, W. Nejdl, & A. Kobsa (Eds.), *The adaptive web* (pp. 263 - 290). Berlin, Heidelberg: Springer Verlag.

Carchiolo, V., Longheu, A., & Malgeri, M. (2002). Adaptive Formative Paths in a Web-based Learning Environment. *Educational Technology & Society,* 5(4), 64–75.

Card, S. K., Moran, T. P., & Newell, A. (1986). *The Psychology of Human-Computer Interaction.* Hillsdale, NJ: Lawrence Erlbaum Associates. Retrieved from http://www.amazon.com/Psychology-Human-Computer-Interaction-Stuart-Card/dp/0898598591.

Chen, C. M. (2009). Ontology-based concept map for planning a personalised learning path. *British Journal of Educational Technology,* 40(6), 1028–1058. Wiley Online Library. doi: 10.1109/ICCIS.2008.4670870.

Chomsky, N. (1967). A Review of B. F. Skinner's Verbal Behavior. In L. A. J. A. M. S. Miron. (Ed.), *Readings in the psychology of language* (pp. 142 - 143). Englewood Cliffs, N.J.: Prentice-Hall psychology.

Crisp-bright, A. K. (2010a). The Effects of Domain and Type of Knowledge on Category-Based Inductive Reasoning. *Memory*, 67-72.

Crisp-bright, A. K. (2010b). *Knowledge Selection in Category-Based Inductive Reasoning. Cognitive Science*. Durham University.

Doignon, J.-P., & Falmagne, J.-C. (1999). *Knowledge Spaces. Knowledge Spaces*. New York: Springer Verlag.

Dummett, M. (1993). *Seas of Language*, Oxford: Oxford University Press.

Eysenck, M. W., & Keane, M. T. (2010). *Cognitive Psychology A Student's Handbook*, (6th ed.). East Sussex: Psychology Press. Retrieved September 3, 2010.

FIPA. (2000). *FIPA Ontology Service Specification*. Geneva, Switzerland. Retrieved from http://www.lsi.upc.edu/~bejar/aia/fipa/FIPA_Ontology_Service_SpecificationX C00086C.pdf

Fodors, J. A. (1975). *The Language of Thought* (p. 214). Cambridge: Harvard University Press.

Gauch, S., Speretta, M., Chandramouli, A., & Micarelli, A. (2007). User profiles for personalized information access. In P. Brusilovsky, A. Kobsa, & W. Nejdl (Eds.), *The Adaptive Web* (p. 54–89). Berlin, Heidelberg: Springer-Verlag.

Gentzen, Gerhard (1935) "Untersuchungen über das logische Schließen," translated as "Investigations into logical deduction" in *The Collected Papers of Gerhard Gentzen*, ed. and translated by M. E. Szabo, North-Holland Publishing Co., Amsterdam, 1969, pp. 68-131.

Gruber, T. R. (1993). Toward Principles for the Design of Ontologies Used for Knowledge Sharing. *International Journal Human-Computer Studies*, *43*, 907-928.

Gruber, T. (2003, March). It Is What It Does: The Pragmatics of Ontology. doi: http://tomgruber.org/writing/cidoc-ontology.htm.

Gruber, T. (2007). Ontology of Folksonomy: A Mash-up of Apples and Oranges. (A. Sheth, Ed.)*International Journal on Semantic Web Information Systems*, *3*(2), 1-11. CILIP. Retrieved from http://tomgruber.org/writing/ontology-of-folksonomy.htm

Helbig, Hermann. (2008). Layer Structures and Conceptual Hierarchies in Semantice Representation for NLP. In A. Gelbukh (Ed.), *Computational Linguistics and Intelligent Text Processing* (Vol. 4919). Berlin, Heidelberg: Springer Berlin Heidelberg. doi: 10.1007/978-3-540-78135-6.

Hernández, Y., Sucar, L. E., & Conati, C. (2009). Incorporating an Affective Behavior Model into an Educational Game. *FLAIRS* (p. 448–453).

Hobbes, T. (1651). *leviathan*. Oxford: Clarendon Press.

Hobbes, T. (1969). *Elements of Law, Natural and Political* (p. 186). Routledge.

Haugeland, J. (1989) *Artificial intelligence: the very idea* (p. 287). MIT Press. Retrieved from http://books.google.com/books?id=zLFSPdIuqKsC&pgis=1

Johnson-Laird, P. N. (1980). Mental models in cognitive science. *Cognitive science*, 4(1), 71–115. Wiley Online Library. Retrieved from http://onlinelibrary.wiley.com/doi/10.1207/s15516709cog0401_4/abstract

Kagan, D. S. (2008). Rethinking Thinking Does Bloom's Taxonomy Align with Brain Science? *SPENCERS THINKPAD*.

Keil, F. C. (1987). Conceptual Development and Category Structure. In U. Neisser (Ed.), *Concepts and Conceptual Development: The ecological and intellectual factors in categorization*. Cambridge: Cambridge University Press.

Kenny, A. (2010). Concepts, Brains, and Behaviour, *Grazer Philosophische Studien*, 81 (1): 105–113.

Kriesel, D. (2011). *A brief introduction to Neural Networks. Neural Networks* (p. 244). dkriesel.com. Retrieved from http://www.dkriesel.com/en/science/neural_networks

Lenat, D. (2006). Computers versus Common Sense. *Google Tach Talks*. Retrieved from http://video.google.com/videoplay?docid=-7704388615049492068

Marr, D. (1982). *Vision*. CA San Francisco: W. H. Freeman.

McGuinness, D. L., & Harmelen, F. van. (2004). OWL Web Ontology Language Overview. Retrieved from http://www.w3.org/TR/owl-features/.

Medelyan, O., & Legg, C. (2008). Integrating Cyc and Wikipedia: Folksonomy meets rigorously defined common-sense. *Proceedings of the WIKI-AI: Wikipedia and AI Workshop at the AAAI* (Vol. 8).

Miller, G. A., Beckwith, R., Fellbaum, C., Gross, D., & Miller, K. J. (1990). Introduction to WordNet: An On-line Lexical Database. *International Journal of Lexicography, 3*, 235-244.

Minsky, M. (1975). A Framework for Representing Knowledge. *The Psychology of Computer Vision*. Massachusett: McGrawHill. Carey, S. (1985). *Conceptual Change in Childhood*. Cambridge: MIT Press.

Murphy, G. L., & Medin, D. L. (1985). The role of theories in conceptual coherence. *Psychological review, 92*(3), 289-316.

Murray, T. (1999). Authoring Intelligent Tutoring Systems : An Analysis of the State of the Art. *International Journal of Artificial Intelligence in Education, 10*, 98-129.

Newell, A., & Simon, H. A. (1972). *Human Problem Solving* (p. 784). NJ: Prentice Hall. Retrieved September 3, 2010, from http://www.amazon.com/Human-Problem-Solving-Allen-Newell/dp/0134454030.

Newell, A. (1982). The knowledge level. *Artificial Intelligence, 18*, 87-127.

Newell, A. (1994). *Unified Theories of Cognition*. MA: Harvard University Press.

Nwana, H. (1990). Intelligent tutoring systems: an overview. *Artificial Intelligence Review*, 4(4), 251-277. doi: 10.1007/BF00168958.

Quillian, M. R. (1968). Semantic Information Processing. In M. Minsky (Ed.), (p. 227–270.). Cambridge, Massachusetts: MIT Press.

Ramirez, C., Concha, C., & Valdes, B. (2010). Cardiac Pulse Detection in BCG Signals Implemented on a Regular Classroom Chair Integrated to an Emotional and Learning Model for Personalization of Learning Resources. In L. G. Richards & K. Curry (Eds.), *The 40th Annual Frontiers in Education (FIE) Conference*. Arlington Virginia: IEEE.

Ramirez, C., Concha, C., & Valdes, B. (2010). Non-Invasive Technology on a Classroom Chair for Detection of Emotions used for the Personalization of Learning Resources. *International Conference on Educational Technology ICET 2010*. Paris France: IEEE.

Ramirez, C., & Valdes, B. (2011). Memory Map a Knowledge Representation Model Used for Intelligent Personalization of Learning Activities Sequences. *International Conference on Cognitive Informatics 2011* (pp. 1-9).

Reed, S. L., & Lenat, D. B. (2002). Mapping ontologies into Cyc. *AAAI 2002 Conference Workshop on Ontologies For The Semantic Web* (p. 1–6).

Rehder, B. (2009). Causal-based property generalization. *Cognitive science, 33*(3), 301-44. doi: 10.1111/j.1551-6709.2009.01015.x.

Rojas, R. (1996). *Neural networks: a systematic introduction. Neural Networks* (p. 509). Springer. Retrieved from http://books.google.com/books?hl=en&lr=&id=txsjjYzFJS4C&oi=fnd&pg=PA3&dq=Neural+Networks+A+systematic+Introduction&ots=fl22SGHDAR&sig=yNm2kotq9R9RQvOyOvCtB1X2_-k

Russell, S. J., & Norvig, P. (1995). *Artificial Intelligence: A Modern Approach* (p. 960). Prentice Hall. Retrieved from http://www.amazon.com/Artificial-Intelligence-Approach-Stuart-Russell/dp/0131038052

Schank, R. C. (1975). *Conceptual Information Processing*. New York, NY USA: Elsevier Science Inc. Retrieved from http://dl.acm.org/citation.cfm?id=540279

Schank, R. C. (1982). *Dynamic Memory: A theory of reminding and learning in computers and people*. Cambriedge: Cambriedge University Press.

Shastri, L. (1988). A connectionist approach to knowledge representation and limited inference. *Cognitive Science, 12*(3), 331–392. Elsevier. Retrieved from http://www.sciencedirect.com/science/article/pii/0364021388900274

Sloman, S. A. (1996). The empirical case for two systems of reasoning. Psychological Bulletin, 119, 3–23

Steels, L. (2004) An Architecture of Flow. M. Tokoro and L. Steels. A Learning Zone of One's Own. Amsterdam : IOS Press , pp. 137-150.

Van Marcke, K. (1998). GTE: An epistemological approach to instructional modelling. *Instructional Science, 26*(3), 147–191. Springer. Retrieved May 9, 2011, from http://www.springerlink.com/index/k12667t738160225.pdf.

Vygotsky, L. (1986). *Thought and Language*. (A. Kozulin, Ed.). New York, USA: MIT Press.

Wang, Y. (2002). The Real-Time Process Algebra (RTPA). *Annals of Software Engineering, 14*(1).

Wang, Y. (2003). On Cognitive Informatics. *Brain and Mind, 4,* 151-167. doi: 10.1002/jbm.a.33145.

Wang, Y. (2006). On Concept Algebra and Knowledge Representation. In Y. W. Y.Y. Yao Z.Z. Shi & W. Kinsner (Eds.), *5th*

Wang, Y. (2007). The OAR Model of Neural Informatics for Internal knowledge Representation in the Brain. *Int'l Journal of Cognitive Informatics and Natural Intelligence, 1*(3), 66-77.

Wang, Y. (2009). The theoretical framework of cognitive informatics. *Simulation, 8*(March), A5. *IEEE Int. Conf on Cognitive Informatics* (pp. 320-330).

Weller, K. (2007). Folksonomies and ontologies: two new players in indexing and knowledge representation Folksonomies: metadata for. *Online Information* (pp. 108-115).

4

A Pipe Route System Design Methodology for the Representation of Imaginal Thinking

Yuehong Yin, Chen Zhou and Hao Chen
Institute of Robotics, Shanghai Jiao Tong University, Shanghai, China

1. Introduction

Human beings have long been fascinated by figuring out the accurate answer to what the essential characteristic of human thinking really is. Besides, how knowledge is represented in human mind is also a mystery. However, limitations of development of traditional Artificial Intelligence framing of human thinking: logical thinking and intuitive thinking have deterred this process. Furthermore, such traditional AI framing has been challenged by Brooks' action-based AI theory with nontraditional symbolic representations and reasoning. Radically different from the above traditional views, we consider thinking in terms of images is the fundamental characteristics of human thinking and memory and knowledge are all stored as high dimensional images. Thereby we define this kind of thinking style as imaginal thinking.

Humans often think by forming images based on experience or knowledge and comparing them holistically and directly. Experimental psychologists have also shown that people actually use images, not descriptions as computers do, to understand and respond to some situations. This process is quite different from the logical, step-by-step accurate massive computation operations in a framed world that computers can perform. We argue that logical thinking and intuitive thinking are partial understanding to human thinking in AI research history which both explain part of, not all, the features of the human thinking. Though the applications of these descriptions helped the AI researchers to step forward to the essence of human thinking, the gap between the two totally different thinking styles still provokes vigorous discussions. We believe that the real human brain uses images as representation of experience and knowledge from the outer world to generate connection and overlap these two thinking styles. The images mentioned here are generalized, including not only the low level information directly apperceived by the sensing apparatus of human body, but also high level information of experiences and knowledge by imitating and learning. Imitation is the way human brain mainly learns experience and knowledge from the outer environment, which played an extraordinary role in helping human brain reach present intelligence through the millions of years of evolution. By imitating human imaginal thinking, a novel AI frame is founded trying to solve some complicated engineering problems, which is possible to take both advantages of human intelligence and machine calculation capability. Brooks' achievements in action-based AI theory also show indirect evidence of some basic ideas of human imaginal thinking, which is different in approach but equally satisfactory in result.

Just as the above mentioned, an effective AI frame has been constructed to solve some complicated engineering problems. Actually, when facing difficult engineering problems, lots of bio-inspired approaches, such as naturalistic biological synthesis approach and evolution inspired methodology have been tried and exhibited great advantage over traditional logical mathematic algorithms in improving system adaptability and robustness in uncertain or unpredictable situation. Take pipe-routing system for example, pipe-routing system design like aero-engine, not only a typical NP-hard problem in limited 3D space, must also extraordinarily depend on human experience. So as for pipe-routing, experienced human brain is often capable of providing more reasonable solutions within acceptable time than computer. So in the rest of this chapter, we'll focus on our current research: pipe route design based on imaginal thinking. A complete methodology will be given, and how computer simulates this process is to be discussed, which is mainly about the optimal path for each pipe. Furthermore, human's imaginal thinking is simulated with procedures of knowledge representation, pattern recognition, and logical deduction.The pipe assembly planning algorithm by imitating human imaginal thinking is then obtained, which effectively solved the problem of conceiving the shortest pipe route in 3D space with obstacles and constraints. Finally, the proposed pipe routing by imitating imaginal thinking is applied in an aero-engine pipe system design problem to testify the effectiveness and efficiency of the algorithm.

The main idea of this chapter is by intercrossing investigations of the up-to-date research accomplishments in biology, psychology, artificial intelligence and robotics, trying to present the truth of human thinking so as to understand the fundamental processing style of human brain and neural network and explain the problems which has been confusing the artificial intelligence research, such as what the human thinking is, how human thinks, how human learns and how knowledge is represented and stored. Our work may bring us closer to the real picture of human thinking , then a novel design methodology of pipe-routing system integrating the human imaginal thinking and logic machine computation capability is presented. The holistic layout of pipes is represented as images of feasible workspace, which reflect human experience and knowledge; the optimal path for each pipe is quickly decided by applying the translational configuration space obstacle and the improved visibility graph imitating human pipe-routing behavior. The simulation demonstrated the effectiveness and high efficiency of our pipe-routing design method.

2. Imaginal thinking: It's origin and style

In this part, we will discuss what human thinking is, from step-by-step analysis, the mystery of human thinking style will be revealed and people will find imaginal thinking exist in the whole thinking process. First, human thinking does not exist without intermedium, instead the real biological organs are the hardware which human thinking relies on. Therefore, we will introduce the biological foundation for human thinking: neurons and neural network. After that, we will generally define the human thinking process, and definition here is descriptive. As a biological process the human thinking is, we will discuss what really happens during the thinking in detail. At last, we will classify the human thinking styles with reference of past research in artificial intelligence. Among all the thinking styles, the most fundamental also the most important style is called imaginal thinking, as it covers all the other thinking styles which makes other thinking style a special appearance of imaginal thinking.

2.1 What is human thinking?

2.1.1 The biological basis of human thinking

A neuron (also called a neurone or nerve cell) which is an electrically excitable cell can process and transmit information by electrical and chemical signaling. The synapses, specialized connections with other cells make chemical signaling possible. These connections by neurons to each other can further form networks. Neurons are fundamental elements of the nervous system, which includes the brain, spinal cord, and peripheral ganglia. We can classify neurons according to their specific functions like sensory neurons, motor neurons, and interneurons. A typical neuron is made up of a cell body (often known as the soma), dendrites, and an axon. Dendrites are filaments generating from the cell body which often stretch for hundreds of microns and branches multiple times, resulted in a complicated "dendritic tree". An axon, known as a special cellular filament, arises from the cell body at a site called the axon hillock and extends for a distance, as far as 1 m in humans or even more in other species. Multiple dendrites can be frequently brought about by the cell body of a neuron, although the axon may branch hundreds of times before ending but never more than one axon can be generated. As for most synapses, signals are usually transmitted from the axon of one neuron to a dendrite of another. However, as we know, nature is fed up with specialties, the same applies to neurons which means many neurons violate these rules: neurons lacking dendrites, neurons having no axon, synapses connecting an axon to another axon or a dendrite to another dendrite, etc are all examples of this kind of exception.

All neurons are electrically excitable which denotes that they can maintain voltage gradients across their membranes. This mechanism is realized by metabolically driven ion pumps, which manipulate ion channels embedded in the membrane to generate intracellular-versus-extracellular concentration differences of ions such as sodium, potassium, chloride, and calcium. The function of voltage dependent ion channels can be altered by changes in the cross-membrane voltage. An all-or-none electrochemical pulse called an action potential is generated when the voltage changes large enough. This pulse traveling rapidly along the cell's axon activates synaptic connections with other cells when arriving.

As we can see, the neurons and the networks they form are fundamental hardware for human thinking. Although lots of mysteries haven't been solved, we believe multiple networks and various patterns of connection are relevant to people' thinking style which is denoted as imaginal thinking in this article. To some extent, we propose people's thoughts and memories are actually projections of these numerous structures of networks.

2.1.2 Definition of human thinking

First, it is important to clarify that human thinking are forms and images created in the mind, rather than the forms perceived through the five senses. Thought and thinking are the processes by which these imaginary sense perceptions arise and are manipulated. Thinking allows beings to model the world and to represent it according to their objectives, plans, ends and desires. Similar concepts and processes include cognition, sentience, consciousness, ideas, and imagination.

The general definition of human thinking: representative reactions towards stimuli from internal chemical reactions or external environmental factors. This definition precludes the notion that anything inorganic could ever be made to "think": An idea contested by such computer scientists as Alan Turing. Different research domains have different research methods and focuses on human thinking.

Philosophy of mind is a branch of modern analytic philosophy that studies the nature of the mind, mental events, mental functions, mental properties, consciousness and their relationship to the physical body, particularly the brain. The mind-body problem, i.e. the relationship of the mind to the body, is commonly seen as the central issue in philosophy of mind, although there are other issues concerning the nature of the mind that do not involve its relation to the physical body[1].

Our perceptual experiences depend on stimuli which arrive at our various sensory organs from the external world and these stimuli cause changes in our mental states, ultimately causing us to feel a sensation, which may be pleasant or unpleasant. Someone's desire for something to eat, for example, will tend to cause that person to move his or her body in a specific manner and in a specific direction to obtain what he or she wants. The question, then, is how it can be possible for conscious experiences to arise out of a lump of gray matter endowed with nothing but electrochemical properties. A related problem is to explain how someone's propositional attitudes (e.g. beliefs and desires) can cause that individual's neurons to fire and his muscles to contract in exactly the correct manner.

Psychologists have concentrated on thinking as an intellectual exertion aimed at finding an answer to a question or the solution of a practical problem. Cognitive psychology is a branch of psychology that investigates internal mental processes such as problem solving, memory, and language. The school of thought arising from this approach is known as cognitivism which is interested in how people mentally represent information processing. It had its foundations in the Gestalt psychology of Max Wertheimer, Wolfgang Köhler, and Kurt Koffka [2], and in the work of Jean Piaget, who provided a theory of stages/phases that describe children's cognitive development. Cognitive psychologists use psychophysical and experimental approaches to understand, diagnose, and solve problems, concerning themselves with the mental processes which mediate between stimulus and response. They study various aspects of thinking, including the psychology of reasoning, and how people make decisions and choices, solve problems, as well as engage in creative discoveries and imaginative thoughts. Cognitive theory contends that solutions to problems take the form of algorithms - rules that are not necessarily understood but promise a solution, or heuristics - rules that are understood but that do not always guarantee solutions. Cognitive science differs from cognitive psychology in that algorithms that are intended to simulate human behavior are implemented or implementable on a computer.

In conclusion, we know that thinking is a mental process, by which living creatures connect themselves to the outer world and form cognition styles. Thinking can also be considered as the information processing when forming concepts, making solutions, deduction and decisions. Thinking is possibly an idea, an image, a sound or even a desire aroused in mind.

2.1.3 Human thinking

In artificial intelligence history, people use their own methods to study on human mental activity and intelligence. Therefore, there are many different assumptions to artificial intelligence, such as symbolism, connectionism, and behaviorism [3]. Symbolism and connectionism have a long history with more supporters, meanwhile, arguments and divergences lie between the two main widely accepted research domains of artificial intelligence. Different from traditional artificial intelligence, behaviorism takes a new path, which is supported by convincing experimental results.

Here we introduce some of the basic assumptions and ideas of symbolism, connectionism, and behaviorism, and then we propose our assumption on human thinking.

2.1.3.1 Symbolism

Symbolism has the longest history in AI, also the widest application and influence. The name of 'artificial intelligence' was firstly proposed by symbolism believers. The symbolism still takes the leading position in AI, and the successful applications include problem solving, computer gambling, theorem proving, and expert systems which bring historical breakthrough to symbolism applications. Symbolism, also called as symbol method or logicism, is the AI theory based on symbol processing which was first proposed by Newell and Simon in their 'Physical Symbol System Hypothesis'. The hypothesis considers all the intelligent creatures as a symbolic systems, the intelligence comes from symbol processing. By using symbols to represent knowledge and deduction based on symbols, intelligence may be fulfilled.

There are some challenges to symbolism. First, human does not rely merely on logical thinking to solve problems; no-logical deduction also plays an important role in human mental activities. For example, the visionary senses are mainly based on images which can hardly be represented as symbols. Second, when the knowledge database reaches such a huge volume that how to manage and search in the database in acceptable time is a main technical problem, known as 'frame problem', which some affirm never to be solved. Finally, even the frame problem was solved, the intelligent system realized by symbolism still could not own human intelligence. After all, searching the database is not the way human deals with problems.

2.1.3.2 Connectionism

Connectionism is also called connection method or neural calculation, which imitates human neuron structure as the main method to realize intelligence. The major tool being used is called artificial neural networks, which is also formed by connections between large volumes of neurons.

Connectionism uses a concept opposite to symbolism, which focuses on the structure of the intelligent machine. Connectionism, a bottom up concept, believes only if the machine has the same structure as human brain, it will own the possibility to have intelligence. Symbolism, a top down concept, considers that the high level intelligence has nothing to do with the low level mechanism; as long as the intelligence is obtained, it does not matter to use what kind of structure.

A prototype of artificial neural network is a piece of empty paper which has no intelligence. Learning and training are essential in adjusting the network structure and weights of connections between the neurons, so as to obtain the knowledge to solve the problems. Therefore, in connectionism, the learning problem is more crucial than the structure problem. To solve the problem, study on machine learning is unavoidable.

2.1.3.3 Behaviorism

Behaviorism, also called behavioral intelligence or behavioral method or cyberneticsism, is the intersection between cybernetics and AI. Behaviorism is based on 'perception-action' model, which considers the intelligence is from perception to action, also from the adaptation to the complex outer environment, rather than representation or deduction. Thereby, the fundamental units of intelligence are simple behavior, such as obstacle avoiding and moving forward. More complicated behavior generates in interaction with the simple actions. Another point of view of connectionism is: since it is difficult to realize human level intelligence, why not lower the requirements, just make low level intelligence similar as insects. Then, with biological evolution, maybe we can realize the required artificial intelligence.

With these ideas, the most influential scientist of connectionism, Rodney A Brooks, made a six-leg insect-like robot with 150 sensors and 23 actuators. The mechanical insect robot has no deduction or planning capability as humans, but it showed much better performance in handling the complex environment than former robots. It has agile bumping prevention and cruising capability in non-structural or framed world. In 1991, Brooks published the paper 'intelligence without representation' and 'Intelligence without reason', challenging the traditional AI beliefs and opened a door to a new research direction in AI.

Brooks' revolutionary work has roused both support and challenge in behaviorism. Some consider the success in robot insect cannot guarantee high level intelligence, and the evolution from the insect to human is just an illusion. Despite all, the behaviorism is still a feasible and necessary method to realize AI.

2.1.4 Human thinking: Our attempted hypothesis

From the above discussion we can see, the traditional AI theory in understanding human thinking is limited. Such traditional AI frame [4-5] provoked vigorous discussion, and has especially been challenged by Brooks' action-based AI theory which uses a direct and tight connection from perception to action with nontraditional symbolic representation and reasoning [5-6]. Experimental psychologists have also shown that people actually use images, not descriptions as computers do, to understand and respond to some situations [7]. Hereby, we propose our hypothesis on human thinking, as shown in Figure 2.5.

First, human thinking must be a stimuli-responding process from perception to action. The stimuli can be external, such as sight, touch, taste, smell, and sound; or internal, such as hunger, pain. Both the external and internal stimuli are sensed by neural excitations (although some of the correspondences between the neural excitation and internal stimuli are still not clear, the existence of such correspondence is pretty sure); such process is defined as perception. The stimulated sensory neurons generate neural signals and propagate in neural networks through synapses of interneurons in a certain style which forms the action potential in motor neurons so as to cause muscle contraction (although how neuron excitation accurately controls muscle contraction is still not clear, we know that certain action somehow corresponds to the stimulation by external observation); such process is defined as action. Such perception to action process is similar as Brooks' ideas and definition in behaviorism. Human thinking happens during the process of perception to action.

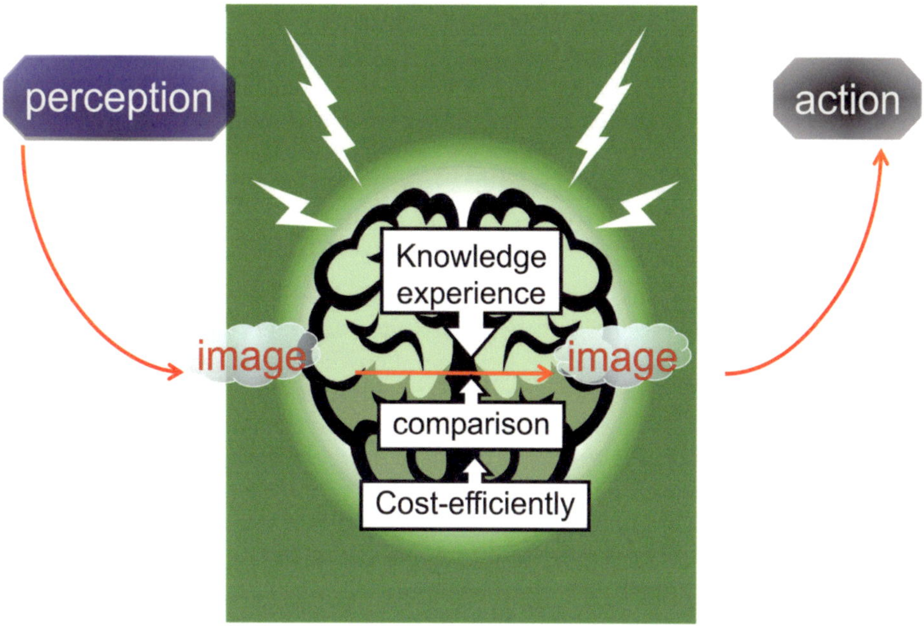

Fig. 2.5. Human thinking processes

Second, the information in thinking process is high dimensional images. Of course, the information discussed here is not referred to single neuron signaling. As known to all, a single neuron signal is caused by changing voltage difference between inner and outer sides of membrane by opening the ion channel. The information discussed here represents signals in the huge neural network formed by synapses when humans respond to a certain perception. Every single neuron signal is one dimensional. With average 10^{11} neurons and 7000 synapses of each neuron, the one dimensional signals may present high dimensional information by coordination among all kinds of neurons (some neurons transmit the signal one way, others transmit multi-ways). Such high dimensional information is defined as images. However it's important to clear that the information is not limited to real images, this definition applies to all the information that can be understood in human mind as forms of images. Any signal form like sound, perception and emotion can all be images, as long as the high dimensional information stimulates various neuron architecture models formed by certain synapses and neurons in neuron networks (or a neural excitation graphics) to express different modes of information.

Third, the high dimensional neural network, namely the activated synapses and corresponding neurons by responding to certain high dimensional signals, can be formed in two major ways. One is by in heritage of biological evolution. Some vital knowledge of surviving in the out world has been recorded in human DNA, so some of the synapses are formed in fetus phase, such as spinal reflection mechanism, crying, breathing and milking. The other way is the interaction with the out environment based on one single purpose - survival. Such animal instinct leads to a more fundamental biological behavior, which is consuming less energy to accomplish more activities. Such process trains human neural network and forms synapses. The network is formed when human finally reaches mature phase which can be proved by the changing numbers of human neural synapses indirectly.

Human neural synapses increase as growing up, which means the inherited neural network may not be sufficient in surviving the environment so new synapses continue to grow. At 3 years old, human synapses' number reaches the peak of 10^{15}. This number decrease ever since, meanwhile human interacts with the environment and forms corresponding network excitation to stimuli, such network must use lowest energy and therefore high energy consumption synapses disappear. Based on evolution and survival instinct, human gets training and learning in the environment and forms the responding neural network structure, such process is the way human forms intelligence.

At last, human thinking is the process by comparing the past knowledge and experiences, also the process from lowest energy consumptive neural network to highest ones. During the interaction between human and environment, knowledge and experience are absorbed corresponding to specific stimulations respectively, which are presented and memorized as groups of synapses and their neural networks. The knowledge and experience can be obtained as high dimensional images which map to different neural network structures and solutions to different kinds of problems and tasks with different levels of energy consumptions. Humans always try to solve any problem by using low energy consumptive solutions; only if the feedback shows an uncompleted task, the higher energy consumptive solutions will be taken into consideration. When all the stored experience and knowledge cannot fulfill the requirements of problem solving, human will feel incapable and tired of thinking since metabolism in neural system has reached an unusually high level. One thing noticeable is that the handling of using what kind of energy consumptive level of neural networks is also represented as neural networks, which use same forms and functions of structure in memory, information management, calculation, perception, signaling, generating motion potential, and motion control, which is totally different from the infrastructure of computers.

To sum up, we may conclude human thinking as a process of generating responses to the stimuli starting from perception, by trying different solutions with the sequence of from low energy to high energy through signaling in neural networks, thus finally generating motion potentials meeting specific responsive needs and controlling the motor neurons to actuate or restrain the actions through motion neurons from specific neuron networks.

2.2 Imaginal thinking style

2.2.1 Definition to imaginal thinking

Human thinking is one kind of animal instincts for survival, which is acquired through inheritage or learning, to respond to the outer or inner stimuli. The different energy consumptive neural networks corresponding to different knowledge and experience. The motion potential is formed by searching and comparing the neural networks from low energy to high energy so as to actuate or restrain the motions to fulfill biological demands.

Since the information and signals processed during thinking are represented as high dimensional neural images which are appreciable and imaginable, so we define such thinking style as imaginal thinking. The confusion needs to be clarified with traditional thinking style in form of images. The images in imaginal thinking are generalized, which not only include the low level perceptive information, but also cover the high level experiential information. The word image in imaginal thinking is a metaphor, similar as the definition of hyper-dimensional concepts. Human intelligence is formed by millions of years of evolution, which makes it impossible for anything non-biological to have such thinking style, unless it has biological neural network functions or characteristics.

2.2.2 What happens in imaginal thinking?

The ultimate purpose of imaginal thinking is forming motion potentials, so as to actuate or restrain the motor neurons. Such thinking procedures can be further divided into two categories as learning and non-learning. The non-learning procedure can also be considered as problem solving procedure.

2.2.2.1 Learning procedure

Learning procedure, as shown in Figure 2.6, happens when the former experience and knowledge are insufficient to satisfy the responding demands. Human has two major ways of learning which are imitation and observation. Both the experiments on capuchin monkeys [8-9] and the study on the social learning show solid evidences for the importance of imitation in learning[10-11]. The existence of mirror neurons shows that when human imitates or observes a certain action, mirror neurons in human brain will excite unexceptionally. By using the modern scanning and imaging technology, the distinct functional areas are found in cortex mapping the respondents to different stimuli which includes the five senses. The learning experiment on mice shows that the repeating stimuli will cause growing new dendrites, connections and synapses, so as to form new neural network to represent new knowledge and experience.

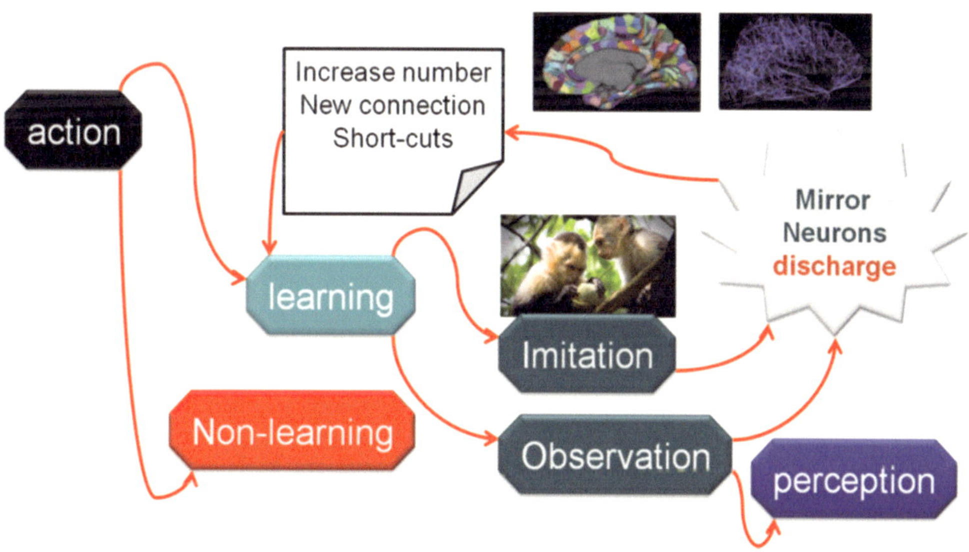

Fig. 2.6. Learning procedure of imaginal thinking

2.2.2.2 Non-learning procedure

Non-learning procedure, also called problem solving action, aims at finding the appropriate knowledge and experience to solve the demanding problem so as to meet biological desires and requirements. The detailed processes are shown in Figure 2.7.

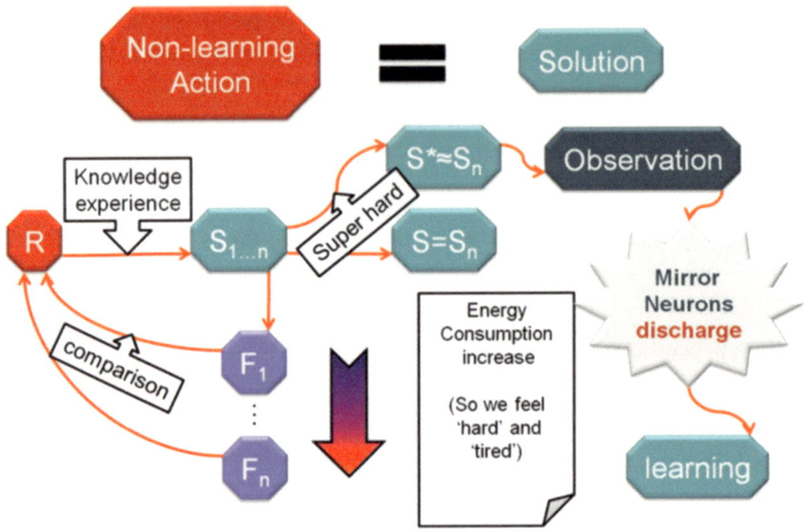

Fig. 2.7. Non-learning procedure

Survival instinct generates a requirement when humans perceive stimuli of outer or inner environment, which is denoted as R. By scanning the former knowledge and experience from low to high consumptive energy, a series of solutions are generated, denoted as S_1, …, S_n. Of course all the possible solutions can't be generated immediately, instead whenever a solution is obtained, human brain converts it to the potential function, denoted as F_1,…, F_n. Once a function is generated, human brain compares it with the previous requirement; if it fulfills the requirement, the corresponding solution will be the final solution, denoted as $S=S_n$. If all the solutions cannot satisfy the requirement, human brain will try to find the most closer solution as $S^* \approx S_n$, and apply the solution. At the same time humans observe the performance, which forms new neural synapses causing excitation of mirror neurons. Such procedure is similar as learning procedure which provides knowledge and experience for future tasks.

2.2.3 Imaginal thinking vs logical thinking

The symbolism emphasizes on logical thinking, the logic can be considered as a special type of high dimensional image in imaginal thinking frame. Such image is represented with mathematical logic procedures with each step still an imaginal thinking one, figure 2.8. So logical thinking can be considered as a certain level of imaginal thinking, namely a specific neural network level representing the mathematical logics, and the memory and knowledge lying in this network level are unexceptionally stored as high dimensional images. Therefore, logical thinking is a special type of imaginal thinking.

2.2.4 Imaginal thinking vs intuitive thinking

The connectionism emphasizes intuitive thinking which has no clear representation between the requirements and solution, only the result is respected. Actually, such procedure only happens when the searching of past knowledge and experience cannot meet the requirement, denoted as $S_{1 \cdots n} \neq S$, so the human brain goes for blind search trying to find a similar neural network pattern to solve the similar problem. Such procedure is searching for metaphors or analogies. The searching continues until a sudden stimulus generates a neural network which meets the requirement, then human takes this solution to generate motion potential, denoted as $S^* \approx S$. It does not matter why this neural network results in a satisfactory solution, however what's really significant is to meet the survival requirements. Such thinking which cannot be represented by mathematical logic or existed knowledge or experience is intuitive thinking, the essence of which is still a special type of imaginal thinking.

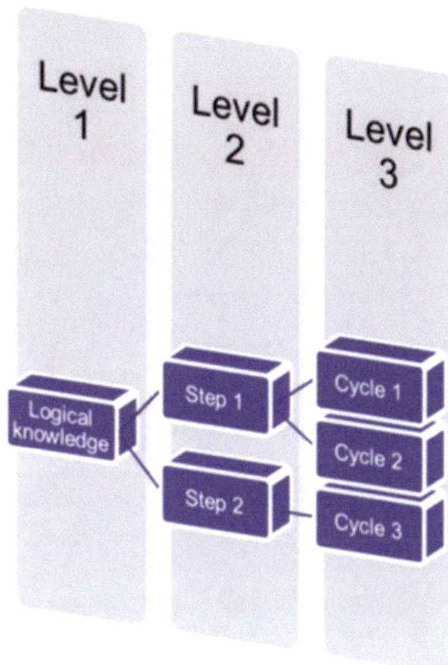

Fig. 2.8. Logical thinking structure

2.2.5 Role of imaginal thinking

As is shown in figure 2.9, behaviorism, characterized by a simple perception-action process, is a lower level of human thinking which is most common in initial development phrase of human intelligence. The two basic elements of behaviorism, perception and action can be both denoted as images thus the whole procedure can be seen as transformation of one image to another to generate a satisfied image guiding the future action. Without image, the essential interaction between perception and action certainly doesn't exist, so a proper act is almost impossible to happen.

As humans interact more and more with outer environments trying to solve problems to meet desires and requirements, knowledge and experiences stored as high dimensional images are accumulated which lays a foundation for logical thinking favored by symbolism. This logic can be considered as a special type of high dimensional image in imaginal thinking. With ascending ability to reasoning and deducting and expanding knowledge and experience base, humans tend to handle more complicated problems. Sometimes past knowledge and experience cannot meet present requirement, as intuitive thinking accentuated by connectionism describes, human brain goes for blind search trying to find a similar neural network pattern to solve the similar problem. This process is actually finding the best matching of requirements and solutions both denoted by images, the innate logic is still based on past knowledge and experience represented by numerous images in human mind only this transformation of images isn't clear.

Thereby, as figure 2.9 shows, we can conclude that imaginal thinking actually includes the characteristics of all other thinking styles, logical thinking and intuitive thinking. It also solves the conflicts between different ideas and assumptions of artificial intelligence, symbolism, connectionism and behaviorism. Besides, neural functions and human thinking are bonded tight by imaginal thinking and it addresses the origin of human thinking from an aspect that none of the former theories has proposed. It's reasonable to reach the conclusion that imaginal thinking is fundamental to human thinking and can lead us into the truth of human thinking.

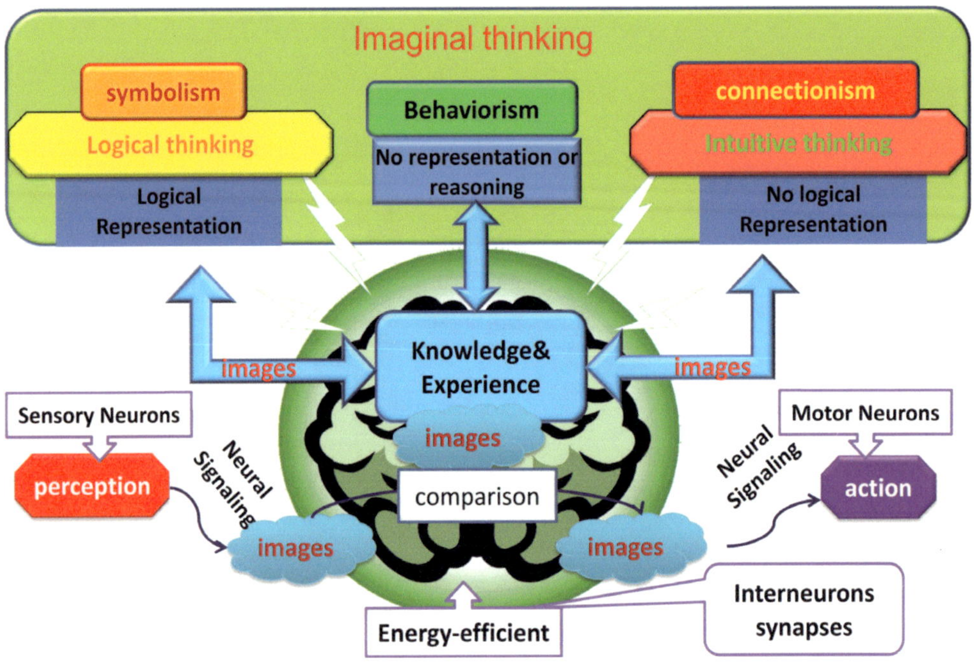

Fig. 2.9. relations between imaginal thinking and other thinking styles

3. A novel visible graph methodology integrating imaginal thinking

When faced with difficult engineering problem, lots of bio-inspired approaches, such as naturalistic biological synthesis approach and evolution inspired methodology have been tried and exhibited great advantage over traditional logical mathematic algorithms in improving system adaptability and robustness in uncertain or unpredictable situation[12,13]. As for pipe-routing, a typical NP-hard problem in limited 3D space, experienced human brain is often capable of providing more reasonable solution within acceptable time than computer. In this section, we will present a novel design methodology of visible graph integrating human imaginal thinking.

3.1 human imaginal thinking in pipe-routing

Pipe-routing is actually far more complicated that it appears to be, not only it's a typical NP-hard problem in limited 3D space, but also most of it relies on human experience. Besides, there exist strict restrictions in pipe-routing which can't be expressed by standard statistics. So experts' advice and opinions are totally indispensible in pipe-routing. The present platform in pipe-routing can't be fully self-dependent, instead people need to guide the whole design process based on their knowledge and experience.

Faced up with difficult engineering problems and math questions, experienced human mind always offers more practical solutions within limited and accepted time. It's important to notice that people recognize the whole pattern of pipe-routing through imaginal thinking. So if we want to get a smart pipe-routing system or a algorithm, we must first understand how humans recognize the whole space.

Human mind represents knowledge and experience by forming the holistic image of feasible workspace. This holistic image cognizing the layout of all pipes is achieved by decomposing, comparing and coordinating among the images which reflect human knowledge and experience. The experience includes pipe functions, piping order, manufacturability, vibration concerns and leakage protection, while knowledge consists of obstacle shape, pipe size, liquid velocity, temperature, thermal deformation, etc.

Firstly, a predetermined piping order is decided by human engineering experience: from inside to outside, from dense part to sparse part, from thick pipe to thin pipe, from short pipe to long pipe. The pipes locating on relative inner side are harder to replace and maintain due to the intervention of the covered pipes outside. Therefore, the pipes which need frequently replacement or maintenance should be arranged in outer layers which are easier to reach and manipulate. According to geometric knowledge, a geodesic line can be connected from the start point to the end point which shows the optimal path for each pipe. All the geodesic lines of pipes holistically form a path-net image which shows spatial density of the piping system. Human always deals with dense parts first while the sparse parts are left to behind, since that the pipe-routing is more complicated in dense parts due to smaller average free space, more obstacles and more complex constraints. The routes of thick pipes are always decided before the thin pipes, as the thick pipes are not as 'flexible' as thin pipes and are not allowed to be manufactured with many elbows.

Secondly, the effective obstacles and limitations along the geodesic line should be found for each pipe. The effective physical obstacles which consist of auxiliary equipments and other pipes are determined by checking whether these obstacles get in the way of geodesic line. In addition, virtual limitations of electric protection, deformation, temperature, vibration, etc are also taken into consideration. The pipes are divided into groups according to pipe functions, such as fuel, lubrication, gas, water, electrical signal. The pipes in the same group have similar virtual limitations. The effective physical obstacles and virtual limitations are dynamic, since they change with the different groups and pipes. All the requirements for routing each pipe are decomposed to a series of images of dynamic obstacles and limitations in human brain. By comparing those images to experience and knowledge, human acknowledges the perspective situation for each pipe respectively.

Finally, immediate coordination on those images of dynamic obstacles gets the holistic image of the pipe-routing problem. The images of dynamic obstacles and limitations are coordinated, which transfers all those intricate experience and knowledge into an easy distinguishable decision-making problem: feasible space or unfeasible space. Every piece of human experience or knowledge is correlated to some unfeasible space with the rules in human mind. Such correlations can be considered as mapping the experience and knowledge to images representing the information of how to route the pipe. By recognizing the unfeasible space, the feasible space is achieved for each pipe. The finding path problem is consequently as same as finding the shortest path in the holistic feasible space which contains all the human experience and knowledge.

As we have understood every step in pipe-routing using imaginal thinking, we notice that human imaginal thinking in pipe-routing is direct, effective and intentional which is different from the blind computer-based route algorithm. Especially, imaginal thinking is characterized by images representing, converting and transferring information which guarantees high efficiency. Next, to combine the advantages of both human intelligence and computer's massive accurate calculation, we need to endow computer with human intelligence in pipe-routing.

The biggest obstacle for computer to imitate imaginal thinking is that the hardware is fundamentally different from the structure that enables human to react to outside environments. Computer has independent control, transport, memory parts. Output and input appliance are only connected by memory. So computer can only work according to programs and isn't able to learn and adapt to environment. Both the experiments on capuchin monkeys and the study on the social learning show solid evidences for the importance of imitation in learning. Thus it's highly reasonable to teach computer how to imitate and the knowledge computer can grab through imitation. Of course this needs a language that can be understood by computer, although we're restricted by the Von Neumann structure, this doesn't mean that imitation of human thinking is meaningless. Since it's impossible to render computer gain human-like neural network and study ability at present, we can help computer to imitate human thinking instead. Though every step is accomplished by humans rather than computer, like study function, variable structure ability, processing and etc, the whole imitation of thinking can make us get closer to real artificial intelligence. So next we will present the elaborate steps about how computer can imitate human thinking to obtain shortest path more efficiently.

3.2 Visible graph method based on imaginal thinking

Pipe-routing can be seen as searching for the pipe path meeting requirements in 3D space given starts and ends. Configuration space and visibility graph are common methods in path plan. In this part we will present a novel visibility graph based on human imaginal thinking to lower computation complexity of traditional visibility graph and increase efficiency. Euclidean Shortest Path—ESP is a famous NP problem which can be defined as searching for a path avoiding all obstacles given two points S, T and a set of obstacles in Euclidean space. Shortest path in 3D space have been paid much attention since 1970s, in this article, we mainly concentrate on situation where obstacles are mainly convex polyhedrons. Lots of algorithms have been put up, from which we can conclude that two basic questions in obtaining shortest path in 3D space: finding possible edge sequences that optimal path can travel along and determining the shortest path on edge sequences are coupling. How to handle this problem effectively is crucial to construct an efficient shortest path algorithm. In the rest of this part, we will give detailed procedures of refined visible graph method integrating imaginal thinking.

3.2.1 Design of feasible workspace

Aero-engine pipe routing can be seen as searching for the path meeting obstacle restrictions given the starts and ends of pipes. All restrictions can be classified as physical obstacles and virtual obstacles. The physical obstacles include equipments, auxiliaries and other pipes; while the virtual limitations consist of manufacture, installation, maintenance requirements, or manual pipe function divisions and area divisions, or vibration and thermal deformation. The physical obstacles are easy to be represented as 3D images because they actually exist. With the vertices of each obstacle, convex hull can be calculated in polynomial time to represent the space that the obstacle covers. Concave obstacles can be decomposed as a union of several polyhedral. Every obstacle can be denoted as an unfeasible space by $U_p^{\,i}$ where p represents the physical obstacle and i denotes ith obstacle.

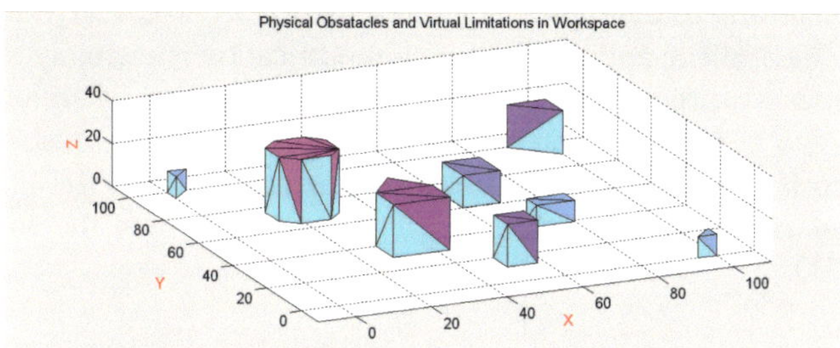

Fig. 3.1. physical obstacles and virtual limitations in workspace

The virtual limitations need to be represented as visible images based on either human experience or engineering knowledge. Although they are invisible, the invisible limitations need to be transferred to visible unfeasible workspaces. Taking electric protection as an example, the water pipes should be nowhere around the electric auxiliaries in case the malfunction caused by leakage. Then the space that encloses the electric parts is considered as one kind of unfeasible space for those water pipes, also denoted as visible unfeasible space U^j, where v represents the virtual and j denotes jth limitation. Due to the limit of the chapter length, we cannot list all the procedures of transferring the experience to unfeasible spaces, although different experience and knowledge have their distinct methods to be represented as images.

With all the physical obstacles and the virtual limitations denoted as a closed set and U^j, if we assume the whole workspace as S, and the feasible workspace F_k for the kth pipe is expressed by Eq. (1):

$$F_k = S - \sum_i U_p^{\,i} - \sum_j U_v^{\,j} \tag{1}$$

The feasible workspace F_k is also dynamic for each pipe since each pipe has different $\{U_p^{\,i}\}$ and $\{U^j\}$. Fig 3.1 shows the 3D explanation of the feasible space F_k for one pipe. The array $\{F_k\}$ forms a holistic image which not only makes human experience and knowledge visible but also represents human perspective concept in system design. By overlapping the images of the feasible workspaces of all the pipes represented as $\{F_k\}$, the holistic layout of all pipes is obtained. The pipe system design is based on such layout by routing the pipe with predetermined pipe order.

3.2.2 Decomposing global information for each pipe to generate local images

When planning a route for each pipe according to the pipe order, human also uses global concept to route. The computer route-planning algorithms in next section are conceived by imitating such human behavior. The optimal path for each pipe is decided by decomposing its feasible workspace to local images, comparing the local images, and coordinating the possible routes.

The holistic image of feasible workspace $\{F_k\}$ needs to be modified by imitating human knowledge of interference of the pipe size. Human sees all the unfeasible space with an offset boundary according to the pipe size to be routed. Such boundary ensures no physical conflicts between the obstacle and the pipe. The modification is virtually shrinking the pipe to its centre line and growing all the obstacles with the pipe size. Therefore, among several existing methods, we here apply translational configuration space obstacle (TCSO) to the feasible workspace $\{F_k\}$ to generate modified $\{F_{k'}\}$ which imitates the human thinking in forming images of obstacles with pipe size [14]. Fig. 3.2 shows the image of obstacles modified with TCSO.

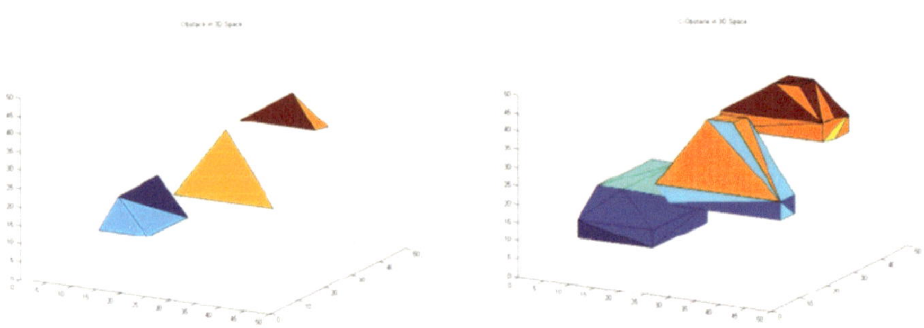

Fig. 3.2. Translational configuration space obstacles with pipe dia.5

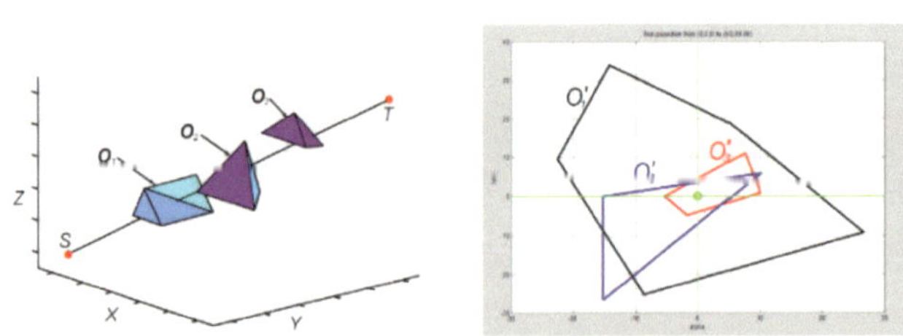

Fig. 3.3. 2D Projection of 3D Convex Obstacles

It has been proved that the shortest path connecting the start point S and the termination point T avoiding all the convex obstacles is through the obstacle edges in 3D case. When the global information is not available, human has to make decisions based on what can be seen at the present position. From one edge to the next, human only goes to those visible edges. Therefore, the visible graph is the method to generate the candidate edge sequences for the shortest path. Each modified feasible workspace $F_{K'}$ needs to be further decomposed to a series images to describe what human sees along the global routing direction.fig 3.3 describes three obstacles in 3D space and their first projection from start S to destination T.

The traditional visible graph uses computer logic that generates all the visible nodes or edges on the obstacle considered to be possible nodes or edges, while a lot of which are never seemed to be the candidate for the shortest path. By imitating human global optimal routing concept, we here improve the visible graph to find only the reasonable candidate nodes or edges through the path and delete as many the redundant nodes or edges as possible, so as to shorten the calculation time.

The 3D visible graph expresses the visibility among edges of polyhedral by connecting all the edge pair that sees each other fully or partially without blocks in between. The visibility is determined by comparing a series projected images which show 2D explanation of 3D information. The images in projection plane are polygons, therefore only the vertices need to be transformed. The projection of a polyhedron is received by projecting the vertices of the polyhedron to the image plane. This image plane is perpendicular to the direction from the initial projecting node to the termination node. The projected polyhedral images are used to produce the visible edges for a single node. After the projection, the obstacle space coordinates are transformed to image plane coordinates, a transform matrix ensures the collineation. The collineation provides a proper way to project vertices from the 3D space to the 2D image planes. The outline of the image can be obtained by connecting the appropriate vertices using the theorem.

Theorem 1: Given an object space R and an image plane R', let a convex polyhedron Oi be projected onto R' as Oi' by collineation. Then the outline of Oi' forms a closed edge loop on Oi[15].

3.2.3 Comparing among the local images to generate edge sequences

In 3D feasible workspace, as the shortest path only exists along some of the edges of the convex polyhedra obstacles, the main purpose of comparing the visible graph is to find the visible relationship between edges. The four rules to find the reasonable candidate nodes or edges through the path and delete all the redundant nodes or edges are as follows:

Rule 1: Only the polyhedra in $\{U_p^i\}$ and $\{U^j\}$ that block the direction from the start point S to the termination point T are taken into account as obstacles of visible graph. Human only considers the blocks that are in the way as the obstacles.

Rule 2: If the termination point T is visible from any edge, then the termination point will be the only visible point for this edge, any other edges are no longer considered as visible. Human goes directly to the destination from any position and never goes to intermedial points if the direct path is accessible.

Rule 3: If any edge sees an edge that has been seen by its ancestor edges before, then this edge is considered as invisible. Human avoids the points that have been reached before and only goes to those points have not been attempted.

Rule 4: For each visible edge, if on the different positions along the edge, the visible sub-edges are different; this edge has to be further divided into several segments to replace the original edge, by viewing from the termination point T to the edge according to the obstacles in between.

On the basis of visible graph, the edge sequences in 3D can be achieved as shown in Fig. 3.2, by representing as edge sequence tree. Every possible route is one branch from the root (the start point S) to the leaf (the termination point T).

3.2.4 Coordinating the edge sequence tree to obtain optimal path

The local shortest path via every branch of the edge sequence tree needs to be locally optimized first. After all the local shortest paths are specified, the global optimal route is chosen by comparing the lengths of the routes.

Theorem 2 :In 3D space distributed with convex polyhedra, the shortest path between two points has the property that if it turns on an edge, the angles formed by two adjacent path segments and the edge subtend. (Due to length of this chapter, the detailed proof of the widely accepted [Theorem 1] and [Theorem 2] is omitted here; similar proof may be found in Mitchell's survey paper [15])

Local optimization is based on Theorem 2 with following procedures:

Firstly, checking each edge sequence, if the equal diagonal angle condition cannot satisfy on any edge by adjusting three related turning points, discard the sequence.

Secondly, for those possible sequences, as shown in Fig. 3.4, calculate the turning point T_1 on E_1. Based on start point S and the middle point M_1 of E_2, the diagonal equation $a_l = b_1$ should be satisfied. Unfold the two triangle plane formed with the four points (vertices of E_1, S and midpoint on E_2) into the same plane then connect S to M_1 with a line. This line either intercrosses the edge E_1 in its visible range, or at one end of the range closer to $a_l = b_1$ (in case the range is not long enough). Find the visible range of E_2, from the new turning point on E_1 and the middle point on E_3, adjust the turning point on E_2. Carrying on the process until the turning point on En is adjusted.

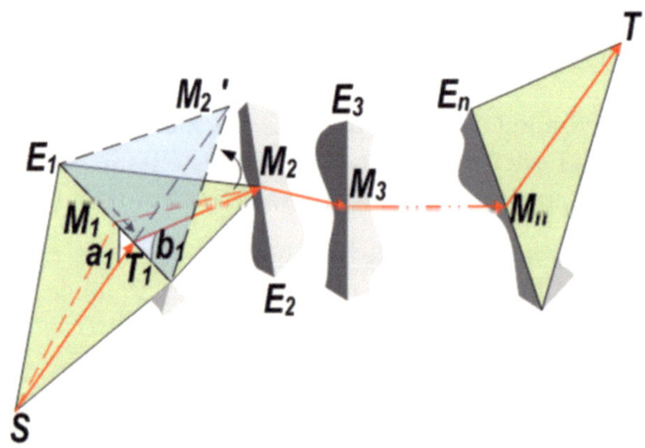

Fig. 3.4. Adjusting the edge sequence in the turning points

Thirdly, repeat the second process to adjust the turning points from E_1 to En several times. After i times, the comparative error δ will be within a certain amount ε, where $\delta = |(l -l$

$_{i+1})/l_i| \leq \varepsilon$, li is the length of the path at ith computation. Then the path image formed by the representing links is the shortest path via this edge sequence with certain precision.

With all the local shortest path images being determined considering the experience and knowledge represented in feasible workspace, the global optimization is mainly computational comparison by selecting the global shortest path from the local shortest paths via different edge sequences. This process is a typical logical thinking, since there is no better way rather than accurate calculation to select the best path from all the possible candidates, and obviously computer does this much more efficient than human.

It's obvious that after introduction of some rules imitating human thinking, visible graph method integrating imaginal thinking reduces the complexity of computation and can obtain optimal path more efficiently. So searching for optimal path in 3D space, a highly logical process can be successfully represented by processing of high-dimensional images as mentioned in former section. This proves imaginal thinking is basically a fundamental style reflected by other thinking styles. Besides although refined visible graph method is presented under the circumstances of pipe-routing, it's also applicable in path plan for robot and printing circuit board (PCB) planning.

4. Pipe-routing algorithm by imitating imaginal thinking

In this part, human's imaginal thinking is further simulated with procedures of knowledge representation, pattern recognition, and logical deduction; the algorithm transforms the physical obstacles and constraints into 3D pipe routing space and then into 2D planar projection, by using convex hull algorithm onto the projection, the shortest pipe route is found efficiently. The pipe-routing algorithm by imitating human imaginal thinking is then obtained, which effectively solved the problem of conceiving the shortest pipe route in 3D space with obstacles and constraints.

4.1 Overview of algorithms concerning pipe-routing

Pipe assembly planning is a problem, which very much relies on a pipe routing algorithm that decides the pipe paths and affects the pipe assembly feasibility. Pipe routing algorithm has been a popular research field in the past several decades in different industrial applications, such as printing circuit board (PCB) planning, chemical plant layout, ship pipe system design, and aero-engine pipe route design. The pipe routing problem can be generally defined as the problem of planning the shortest path connecting two ends of the pipe in a limited workspace by avoiding all obstacles with the given pipe size for each pipe, meanwhile considering all the constraints that affect the pipe system. Much effort has been put into creating new algorithms and improving the efficiency of the existing ones.

The maze algorithm presented by Lee (1961)[16] was the earliest research in pipe routing problems. The algorithm was developed to find the shortest path in logical electronic circuit design (Lee, 1961). The workspace was meshed into units, and the algorithm was based on wave propagation principle. Each path was found by generating a wave from the start unit and propagating through all the meshed units until the wave reaches the end unit. The maze algorithm requires massive memory space to find the shortest path of each single pipe in 2D space, since every single meshed unit has to be covered. The computational complexity of the maze algorithm in 2D space is O(n2), where n represents the problem scale such as number of meshed units. To improve the efficiency of the maze algorithm, Hightower (1969)[17] introduced an escape algorithm by using two orthogonal lines instead of wave propagation which was widely used in PCB design. Although the escape algorithm used less memory space than the maze algorithm, it does not guarantee to find the shortest path even if sometimes the path is quite obvious. Wangdahl et al. (1974)[18] improved the escape algorithm by defining intervisible points and intervisible lines to guide the escape lines so as to find the shortest connection to avoid obstacles. This kind of algorithm, known as network optimization, needs experts to define such nodes that pipes intercross, connect, and swerve, therefore, the pipe routing results depend very much on human's experiences. Zhu [19] and Latombe (1991) proposed a pipe routing algorithm by transferring the pipe routing problem into robot route planning with several constraints; whereas the algorithm has to backtrack when it fails to find a channel for the "robot." The genetic algorithm (GA) was first applied into pipe routing problem by Ito (1999, 1998)[20,21] in 2D space with satisfactory results. Ito's algorithm used single and two-point crossover which led to lots of unacceptable solutions. Adaptive genetic algorithm (AGA) was developed to comprise the contradiction between diversity and convergence of traditional GA. By use of adaptive probabilities of crossover and mutation, AGA realized the twin goals of maintaining diversity and sustaining the convergence capacity (Srinivas and Patnaik, 1994). Simulated annealing GA is another adaptive GA which was applied in ship pipe system design with suboptimum results (Fan et al., 2007a). GA is robust and random, however, different definition and rule of fitness functions yields different solutions, some of which are far not optimal. By research on ant social behavior, ant colony optimization (ACO) was introduced into industrial applications as revolutionary computation method by Dorigo et al. (1996) and Bonabeau et al. (2000). To overcome the deficiency of cooperation in GA, ACO was applied in ship pipe route planning with better results comparing to GA (Fan et al., 2007b). Fuzzy function (Wu et al., 1998) and expert system (Kang et al., 1999) are two tools used to extend the limitation of the existed automated pipe routing computer-aided design systems. Although attempts have been made to provide the pipe routing problem with reasonable solutions, more work is still needed before real breakthrough.

All the above algorithms focus on avoiding physical obstacles, and pipe routes are calculated in orthogonal directions which are not theoretically shortest. Practical constraints such as maintenance requirements and manufacturability are not well recognized, consequently human still cannot be replaced by computer and human is still needed to guide computer to complete the design.

4.2 Knowledge representation

4.2.1 Workspace definition

Human imaginal thinking is limited to R^3 space and tends to use 2D graphs to display 3D information. Most of the complicated workspace shapes can be divided into two main kinds: cubic and cylindrical. In the cubic space, such as chemical plant, PCB, and indoor pipe systems, coordinates can be defined easily by using orthogonal (x, y, z) coordinates which are parallel to the cubic edges. In the cylindrical space, such as sub-marine, aero-engine, and coordinates can be defined as (θ, r, h) cylindrical frame. With equation (1), the absolute (x, y, z) coordinates can be achieved, and the coordinate definition is shown in Figure 4.1:

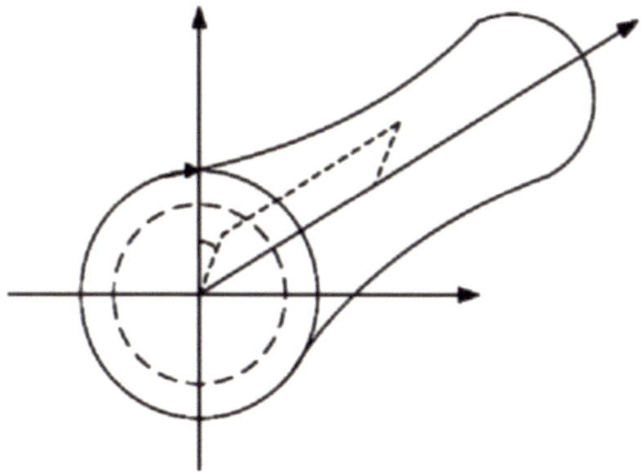

Fig. 4.1. Cylindrical coordinate definition

$$\begin{bmatrix} x \\ y \\ z \end{bmatrix} = \begin{bmatrix} r \cdot \cos\theta \\ r \cdot \sin\theta \\ h \end{bmatrix} \quad (1)$$

The cylindrical space can be unrolled to cubic space as shown in Figure 4.2 which is similar to the correspondence between the globe and the 2D world map. By unrolling the cylinder, the 3D pipe route is calculated in the cubic space which is easy for meshing and projection.

The above definition is universal to most the algorithms, therefore different algorithms can be applied to the same model.

4.2.2 3D inaccessible space definition

By defining the inaccessible space, the accessible space is achieved for each pipe. Every constraint is converted into an inaccessible space, which reflects real physical obstacles and hypothetic limitations. The real physical obstacles include equipments, auxiliaries, and other pipes; while the hypothetic limitations consist of manufacture, installation, maintenance requirements, or manual pipe level divisions and area divisions, or vibration and thermal deformation. Every inaccessible space is denoted as a closed set Ui where I denote different constraint and the accessible space F for each pipe yields by equation (2). Figure 4.2 shows the 2D explanation of the inaccessible spaces:

$$F = \overline{U_1 \cup U_2 \cup U_3 \cup \ldots U_i \ldots \cup U_n} \quad (2)$$

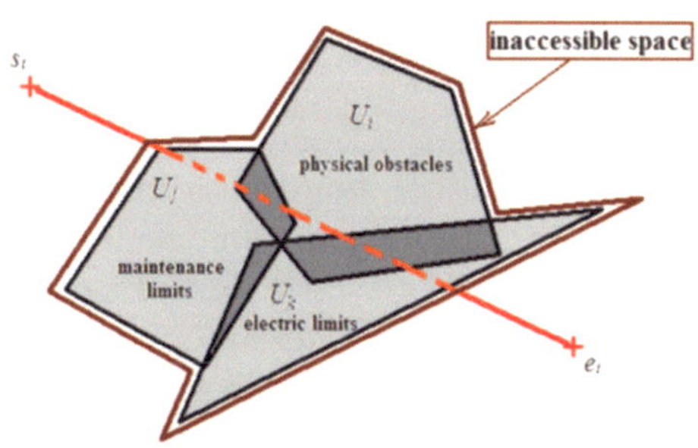

Fig. 4.2. Generalized inaccessible space

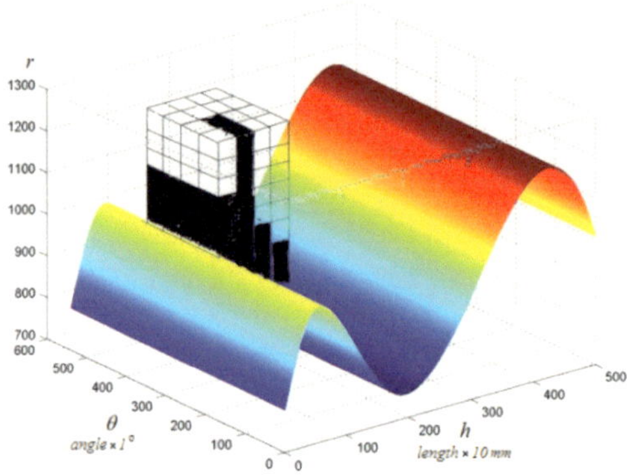

Fig. 4.3. 3D inaccessible space division

In practical use, the cubic space is meshed with cubic unit ($d\theta$, dr, dh), and every cube has two statuses: accessible and inaccessible which are denoted as "0" and "1." As shown in Figure 4.3, white cubes denote "0" indicating accessible and black cubes denote "1" indicating inaccessible.

For each ($d\theta$, dh), sum up all the continuous accessible cubes along r direction, and the max accessible width vertically is denoted with 1. If the pipe diameter is d, when $\varepsilon<d$, set the corresponding grid in 2D pipe map as inaccessible; when $\varepsilon \geq d$, set the corresponding grid in 2D pipe map as accessible. All the 3D constraint information is expressed in the 2D pipe map. In addition, pipe system always designed as several layer divisions. Each layer can be also projected to the pipe map as shown in Figure 4.4.

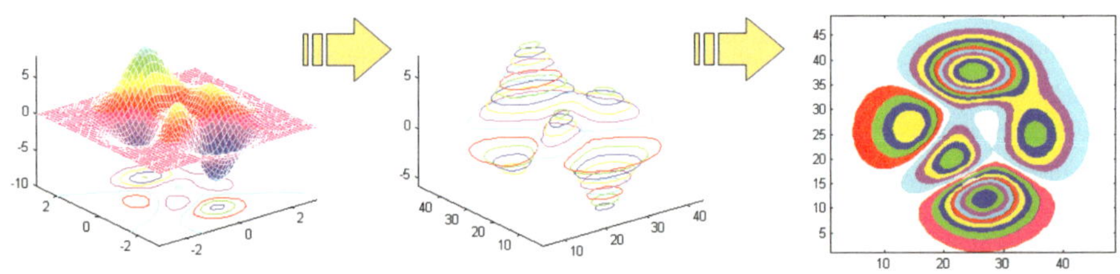

Fig. 4.4. 2D projection of pipe layer division

4.3 Pattern representation

4.3.1 Pipe routes density recognition

When human designs a pipe system, a predetermined piping order is decided by experience, which is from inside to outside, from dense part to sparse part, thick pipe to thin pipe, short pipe to long pipe. These long-time accumulated experiences, lacking an accurate reasoning and deduction process, can be best represented by intuitive thinking style emphasized by connectionism. As is mentioned in 1.2.4, we believe intuitive thinking is actually a special kind of imaginal thinking. From the following analysis, we will find these spontaneous thoughts in pipe-routing can be represented by images to solve problems. Here, follows elaborate justification and explanation of the experienced order chose rules.

4.3.1.1 Inside to outside

The pipe routing space, no matter cubic space or cylinder space, can always find a direction which points from inside layers to outside layers and the pipes are routed on respective layers. The pipe lies on relative inner layers are harder to replace and maintain due to the intervention of the covered pipes in outer layers. Therefore, the pipes which need frequently replacement or maintenance should be arranged in outer layers which are easier to reach and manipulate. Pipes on inner layers are those need little replacement.

4.3.1.2 Dense to sparse

Within one pipe layer, the positions of starts and ends of pipes determine the pipes locations. A skillful pipe route design engineer always deals with dense pipe intercrossing parts first while the sparse parts are left to the end, that is because in those dense parts, pipes have to share not only the free routing space but also the obstacles and the constraints of each pipe, which interferes with each other. This makes the pipe routing more complicated in dense parts due to smaller average free space, more obstacles and more complex constraints. The route design of the pipe in sparse part is relatively easy since each pipe has bigger free routing space to travel and less obstacles to bypass.

4.3.1.3 Thick to thin, short to long

Pipe diameter is another key parameter in pipe routing order chosen. The routes of thick pipes are always decided before the thin ones. The main reason for this is because the thick pipes are not as "flexible" as thin pipes which means thick pipes are not allowed to manufacture to the shape of many elbows. The gap between each pair of adjacent elbows has a minimum length of straight pipe. The lack of flexibility of the thick pipe makes it harder to conceive the path from the start

point to the end point than those thin ones. Another reason for designing the routes of thin pipes after the thick ones is that the thin pipe can be fixed along the thick pipes which are installed already, so the routes of thin pipes somehow decided by the thick pipes installed before them. The lengths of pipes are the last order chosen parameter of those pipes with same diameter. Similarly, short pipes are always preferential to long pipe due to smaller numbers of possible elbows along the way. The order chosen of the pipe with human experience is recognized by computer as follows.

4.3.1.4 Inside to outside

Divide the works pace to n+1 layers along the vertical direction r or z, the lower and upper boundaries are denoted as: $[r_{inner}, r_1), [r_1, r_2), [r_2, r_3), ..., [r_{n-1}, r_n), [r_n, r_{outer})$ (2)

Where:

$$r_{inner} < r_1 < r_2 < r_3 <, ..., < r_{n-1} < r_n < r_{outer}$$

Define every layer from inside to outside as $L_1, L_2, L_3, ..., L_{n-1}, L_n, L_{n+1}$; sort the pipe by its replacement time; assign the pipe with long replacement time to inner layer and the pipe with short replacement time to outer layer. Every pipe is assigned to a layer and every layer contains a group of pipe(s).When pipe routing, the inner layer is prior to outer layer.

4.3.1.5 Dense to sparse

For each layer Li, connect the start point s_i and the end point e_i of the each pipe with geodesic lines (explain below), ignoring all the obstacles. By using output sensitive balanced binary search tree algorithm (de Berg et al., 2005)[22], the intersections of lines are obtained. Use a sweep line l scans the pipe map along the increasing directions of θ (or x) or h (or y). The lines that intercross the sweep line l are stored in one of the leaves of balanced binary search tree T. By inputting starts set, all the intersections and the relevant lines are achieved.

Mesh the pipe map along (θ, h) or (x, y), set the mesh grid as maximum diameter of the pipe in such layer $d\theta=dh=3 \cdot D_{max}$, where D_{max} is the maximum diameter. Every start, end and intersection locates in a grid of (dθ, dh) or (dx, dy). Number the grid by the quantity of the starts, ends, and intersections of the lines. The grid with bigger number contains more pipes, as shown in Figure 4.5. The dense area is prior than the sparse area.

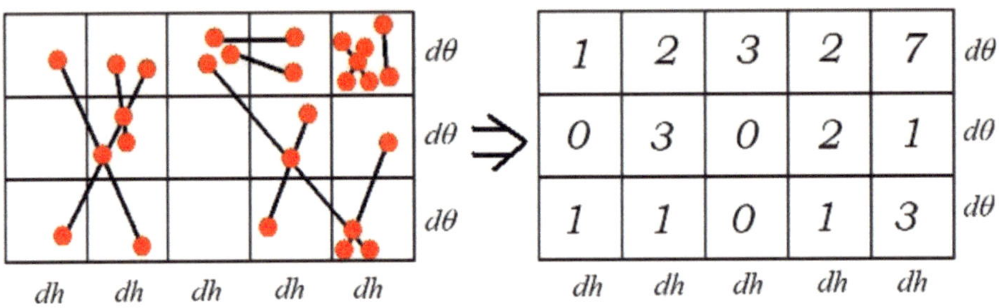

Fig. 4.5. Pipe density division in the same layer

4.3.1.6 Thick to thin, short to long

For same density area in a layer, pipe with bigger diameter is preferred and the pipe with thin diameter route along the thick pipes and clamped to the thick pipe. For same diameter pipes, the shorter pipe is prior to longer ones. The so-called shorter pipe is defined as pipe with shorter line connecting start and end points. Diameters of pipes and lengths of lines connecting start and end points are the last factordetermining pipe order. Diameters and lengths of pipes are display quantitative index, as for which human thinking and logic of computer have no difference.

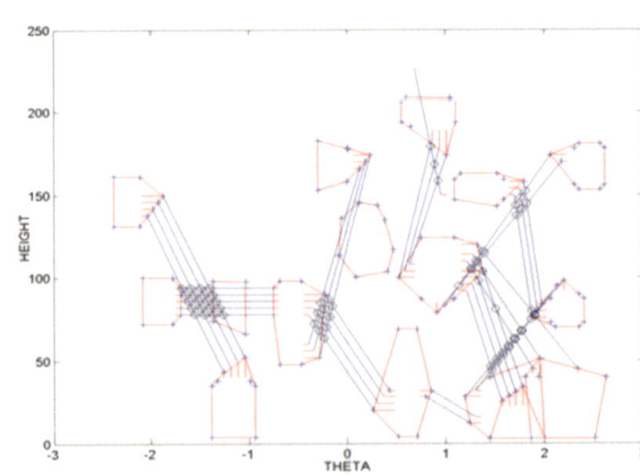

Fig. 4.6. Pipe density area

Figure 4.6 shows the actual application of these rules. Where red closed curves represent obstacles, blue cross dots symbolize vertexes of obstacles, blue crossing are geodesic lines connecting start and end points, blue circle dots are interaction points of pipe paths.

Fig. 4.7. the shortest path on the surface: geodesic line

4.3.2 Geodesic line

It is known from knowledge of differential geometry that the shortest path connecting two points on a curved plane is called the geodesic line. As shown in Figure 4.7, the flying trace of plane is the geodesic line of the earth which is the shortest path though it looks like a curve on the planar map. So, when bypassing obstacles in the workspace, the pipe should follow or as close as possible to the geodesic line so as to find the shortest route. As for the revolved surface, the geodesic line can be expressed as equation (4):

$$\int_{\theta_0}^{\theta} d\theta = \int_{h_0}^{h} \frac{c\sqrt{r'^2_i(h)+1}}{r_i(h)\sqrt{r_i^2(h)-c^2}} dh \tag{4}$$

where: $r_i(h)$ the rotational meridian. c the constant.

4.4 Logical deduction

4.4.1 Pipe routing

With the pipe map and the pipe orders in hand, the remaining pipe route concerns finding shortest path bypassing inaccessible spaces in 2D feasible workspace.

The simplest situation is shown as Figure 4.8(a) that the geodesic line penetrates one closed inaccessible space, and the pipe routing algorithm is as follows:

Algorithm Shortest Path (s_i, e_i,Obi)

Input. Start point s_i , end point e_i , collection of obstacles Obi
Output. Shortest path connecting start and end points

1. Connect start s_i and end e_i of the pipe with geodesic line, and mark entrance point and exit point of the inaccessible space U_i on the geodesic line as $k_1(\theta_{k1}, h_{k1}), k_2(\theta_{k2}, h_{k2})$
2. mark the midpoint of k_1, k_2 as $k_{1,2}$.((($\theta_{k1} + \theta_{k2}$)/2,(($h_{k1} + h_{k2}$)/2))
3. $k_{1,2}$ is obviously an inner point of inaccessible space U_i; put all the adjacent points inside U_i in closed set K.
4. Apply convex hull algorithm (explained below) on set K so that the boundary of the inaccessible space U_i is obtained and denoted as convex set B.
5. Apply convex hull algorithm to $B \cup s_i \cup e_i$ again to get the following points sequence: $P = [s_i, p_1, p_2, p_3, ..., p_n, e_i, p_{n+1}, ...]$, where the sub-sequence from s_i to e_i is the shortest path bypassing the inaccessible space U_i
6. Return P'

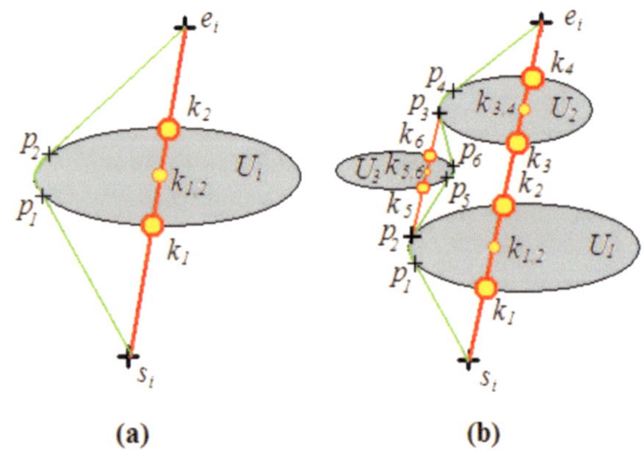

Fig. 4.8. Planar convex hull shortest path algorithm

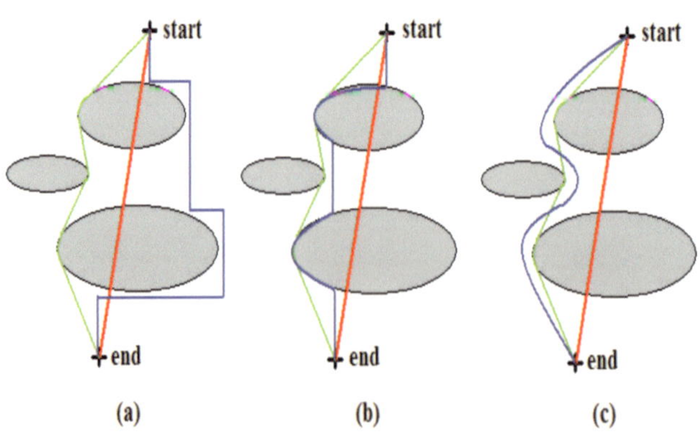

Fig. 4.9. The shortest pipe route

A more complicated situation is that the geodesic line penetrates several closed inaccessible spaces as shown in Figure 4.9(b). The pipe routing algorithm for this situation can be expressed as follows:

Algorithm Shortest Path (s_i, e_i,Obi)
Input. Start point s_i , end point e_i , collection of obstacles Obi **Output.** Shortest path connecting start and end points
Connect start s_i and end e_i of the pipe with geodesic line, and mark all the entrance points and exit points of every inaccessible space $U_1, U_2, U_3, \dots, U_n$ on the geodesic line as: $k_1(\theta_{k1},h_{k1}),k_2(\theta_{k2},h_{k2}),$ $k_3(\theta_{k3},h_{k3}),k_4(\theta_{k4},h_{k4}),$ ... $k_{2n-1}(\theta_{k2n-1},h_{k2n-1}),k_{2n}(\theta_{k2n},h_{k2n})$ totally n pairs of points where n denotes the number the inaccessible spaces. 7. Calculate all the midpoints of each pair of points and denote as: $k_{1,2}(\frac{\theta_{k1}+\theta_{k2}}{2},\frac{h_{k1}+h_{k2}}{2}),$ $k_{3,4}(\frac{\theta_{k3}+\theta_{k4}}{2},\frac{h_{k3}+h_{k4}}{2}),$ ... $k_{2n-1,2n}(\frac{\theta_{k2n-1}+\theta_{k2n}}{2},\frac{h_{k2n-1}+h_{k2n}}{2}),$ 8. All the midpoints are obviously the inner points of inaccessible space $U_1, U_2, U_3, \dots, U_n$; put all the adjacent point inside $U_1, U_2, U_3, \dots, U_n$ in closed set matrix: $[K_1,K_2,K_3,...,K_n]$ 9. Apply convex hull algorithm on set matrix $[K_1, K_2, K_3, \dots, K_n]$ so that the boundary of the inaccessible space $U_1, U_2, U_3, \dots, U_n$ is obtained and denoted as convex set matrix: $[B_1,B_2,B_3,...,B_n]$ 10. Apply convex hull algorithm to $B1 \cup B2 \cup B3 \cup \cdots \cup B_n \cup s_i \cup e_i$ again to get the following points sequence: $P=[s_i,p_1,p_2,p_3,...,p_n,e_i,p_{n+1},...]$ 11. Extract the sub-sequence from s_i to e_i out of sequence P, in which every pair of points that enters and exits each inaccessible space can be found; together with the pipe start and end points s_i to e_i, form a new sequence denote as: $P'=[s_i,p_1,p_2,p_3,p_4,...,p_{2n-1},p_{2n},e_i]$ where p_1, p_2, p_{2n} are the n pairs of entrances and exits as shown in Figure 3.9(b). 12. Extract： $p_2(\theta_{p2},h_{p2}),p_3(\theta_{p3},h_{p3}),$ $p_4(\theta_{p4},h_{p4}),p_5(\theta_{p5},h_{p5}),$ ... $p_{2n-2}(\theta_{p2n-2},h_{p2n-2}),p_{2n-1}(\theta_{p2n-1},h_{p2n-1})$ totally n-1 pairs of points, as new pipe starts and ends to repeat Steps 1-6 until no inaccessible space is penetrated.

As shown in Figure 4.9, the route from s_i to e_i which bypasses the inaccessible areas is the final path. Comparing with orthogonal route, polygonal route and curved route calculated by other algorithms as shown in Figure 4.9 (a)-(c), respectively, the geodesic route generated by this chapter is shorter; in addition, the routing algorithm proposed by this chapter starts with shortest geodesic line and bypasses every inaccessible space with length incensement as short as possible, therefore the obtained pipe route is the shortest path.

The algorithm conducted in this chapter imitates human thinking, which is with low-computational complexity of O($nlogn$) where n is the scale of the problem. The computational complexity of Step 1 that calculates the intersection points with the inaccessible spaces is no bigger than O(n); the computational complexity of Step 2 that generates the midpoints and boundaries of the inaccessible spaces is also less than O(n); the computational complexity is determined by the convex hull algorithm which is less than O($nlogn$) (de Berg *et al.*, 2005).

In this section, through imitation of human thinking, we use images to serve as medium of information to propose a 3D pipe-routing algorithm based on human imaginal thinking. From the above procedures filled with human experiences guiding pipe-routing which reflect intuitive thinking underscored by connectionism, we can see intuitive thinking styles can be presented with processing of images. Thus in turn our conclusion that essence of intuitive thinking is imaginal thinking is confirmed.

5. Simulation platform of pipe routing in aero-engine

During the design of pipes of aero-engine, various subjects like mathematical modeling, arrangement algorithm, static and dynamic strength, fluid, vibration and noise and fluid structure interaction are involved. These fields will use respective simulation software during the design and simulation process and tons of data will be generated. The data needs to be circulated frequently between design and simulation process to fulfill the goal that design offers information to analysis and in turn analysis amends design. However, the present data generated by design can only be used by manufacturing and assembly rather than simulation platforms; the results gained by simulation are mainly transformed into feedback manually which means the efficiency is very low. In a word, we lack a comprehensive design and simulation platform to do integrated management about the design tools, design process, simulation tools, data and simulation process.

In this part, we will introduce a platform suitable for design and simulation of aero-engine pipes, build advisable pipe design and assessment system, to let different design departments complete simulation and assessment of aero-engine pipes more efficiently and achieve optimization of pipe system; at the same time , we will consider comprehensively the practicability, routing ability, maintenance, reliability (including vibration check and strength check) ,durability and various design factors to construct proper pipe design and check system. So we can complete the simulation, assessment and check of aero-engine pipe system faster and more efficiently.

5.1 Problem description

Aero-engine is the "heart" of a plane determining the carrying capacity and performance of an aircraft. According to the accident reports on aircraft engines such as CF6 and CFM56 of general electric, half of the engine accidents in the air are caused by pipe system and accessory system. The pipe system design of aircraft engine is extraordinarily difficult since the design is mostly based on human experience and knowledge. The pipe system of aero-engine has following features:

Big quantity vs small space. The average number of the pipes in an aero-engine is 100 , 200 together with hundreds of pipe clamps; while the installation space for the multi-layer 3D pipe system is a 150 , 250mm thick cylindrical space between the engine jacket and the engine cabin.

Connecting multi-functional accessory system. The model aero-engine has more than 50 accessories with all kinds of functions and various outer shape and material. The pipe system has to connect all the accessories and transfer fuel, lubricant, coolant, and control signals.

Many constraints. The pipe system of aero-engine should meet the requirements of manufacturability, installation, maintenance and replacement, vibration and stiffness, thermal fatigue and distortion, and electrical limitations.

The proposed pipe routing algorithm is applied in an aero engine pipe system design problem to testify the effectiveness and efficiency of the algorithm.

5.2 Structure of design and simulation platform

The platform is mainly made up of two modules, the pipe design module and the pipe simulation module. Figure 5.1 presents an overall structure of the whole system.

The design module is responsible for reorganization of geometric information of the aero-engine 3D UG model, accessories and starting and ending points of pipes. In the UG pipe laying plug-in mode, based on diameter and timber of every pipe, liquid in pipe, velocity of flow and life of pipe, the module can automatically recognize the dense and sparse sections, planning proper sequence of pipe-laying. Besides, the path of every pipe is also generated by using the shortest path principle or quadrature rules without breaking laws of design of pipes and design process.

The pipe simulation module transfers geometric data of the 3D UG models of pipes to simulation system of aero engine pipe through interface with 3D UG model, fluid structure interaction, strength, vibration and life to generate files concerning adjustment about pipe-routing which can be turned back into pipe design module to further remedy the path of pipes in the aero engine pipe system simulation platform. Every big module consists of several small parts, figure 5.1. gives an complete structure of the platform and information flow.

5.3 Pipe design module

Both the above visible graph method and 3D pipe-routing algorithm are realized by pipe design module.

5.3.1 3D UG Model

Aero-engine 3D UG model is a present universal 3D model including geometric and processing parameters of aero-engine and corresponding accessories generalized by UNIGRAPHHICS 3D mechanical design software. This software contains all the mechanical parts design information except from pipes and is a useful guide model for design of aero-engine and later period of production, as figure 5.1 shows.

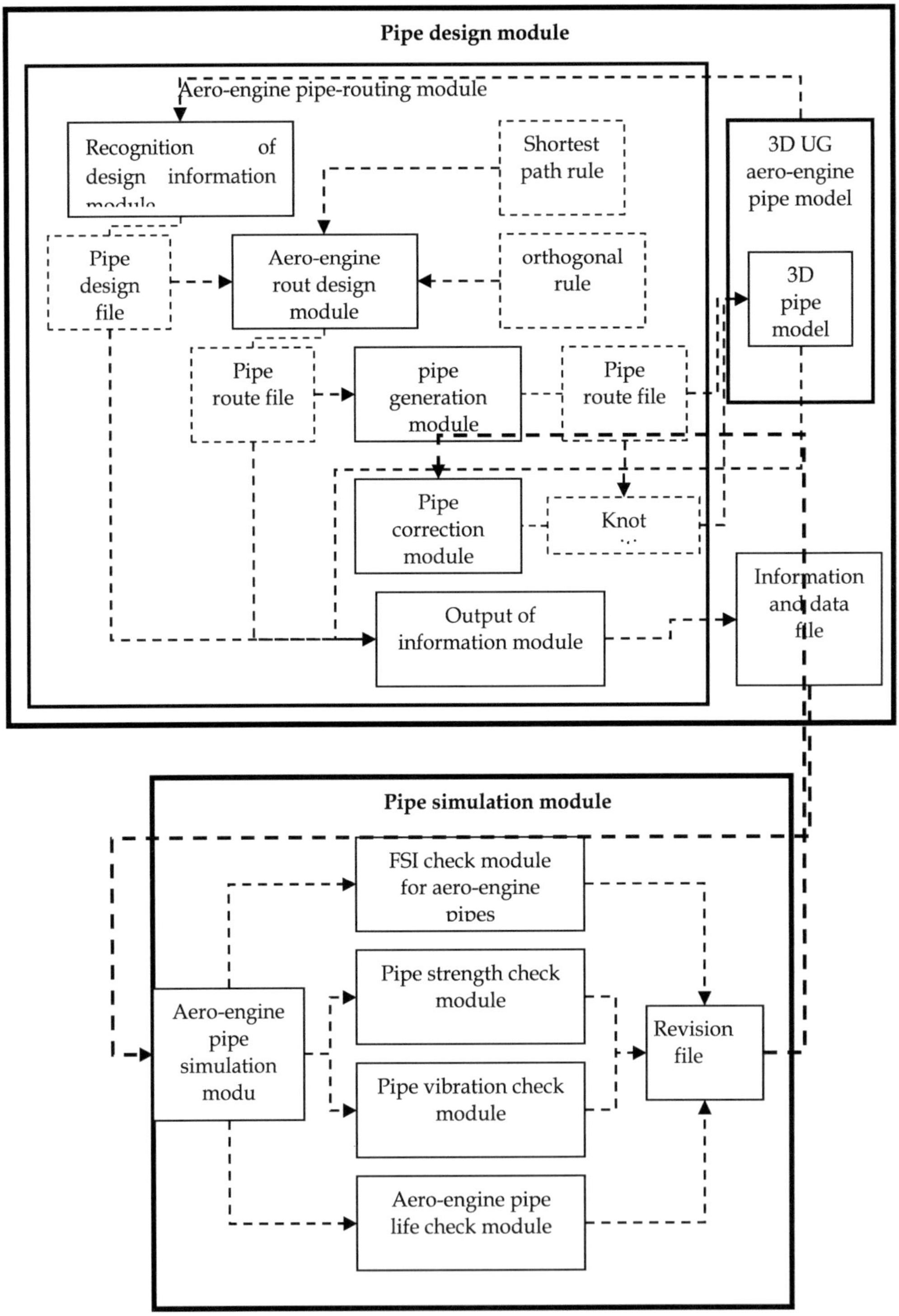

Fig. 5.1. Design & simulation platform structure for aero-engine pipe system

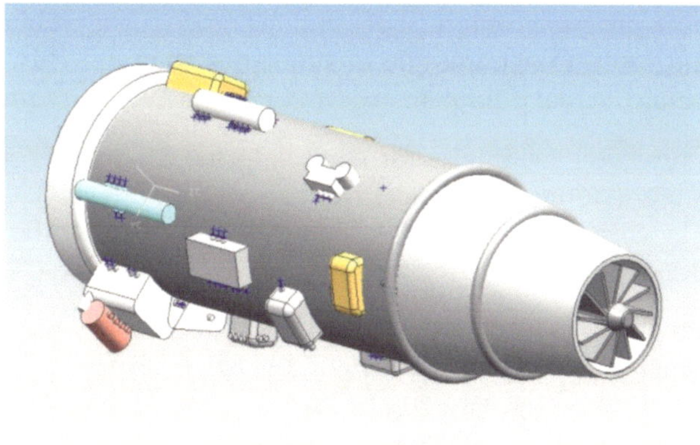

Fig. 5.2. 3D UG model of aero-engine

5.3.2 UG pipe-laying plug-in model

UG pipe-laying plug-in model is an OPEN API or OPEN GRIP interface using C language or GRIP language for programming in UG which is made up of recognition of aero-engine design information module, pipe-routing module, pipe-generating module, pipe-correcting module and output of aero-engine information and processing parameters module.

Recognition of aero-engine design information module is responsible for reading and storing of the starting and ending information of pipes of aero-engine 3D UG model. This model can recognize hundreds of pipes with various information of starting and ending points and store it in a information file using a general format. As figure 5.3 shows, this module can use UG grip file sweep.grx to scan UG aero-engine casing model to generate unified aero-engine casing geometric information text file and transfer this information to MATLAB for later application by employing inputting file load_layer.m and transforming file base_data.m in MATLAB. The similar approach applies to pipe geometric information which enters MATLAB by transforming pipe_info.grx to pipe_info.txt and further obtaining load_pipe.m using pipe-inro.m.

The aero-engine pipe-routing module can accomplish pipe-routing based on the information of starting and ending points in recognition module and geometric data of aero-engine casing and accessories by using the 3D pipe-routing algorithm in section 4.

This module can allow choosing whether the principle of pipe-routing is the shortest pipe path principle or the traditional orthogonal rule. The shortest pipe path principle focuses attaining the shortest path while the orthogonal rule emphasizes to lay pipes according the engine casing's equidistant surface thereby ensure the beautiful orthogonal pipe routes. Here we use the shortest path rule to produce pipe-routing file. The detailed information flow can be seen figure 5.4. and the algorithms in all the parts can be referred to mathematical modeling and algorithms in section 4.

Aero-engine pipe generating module is based on the above recognition of aero-engine design information module and aero-engine pipe-routing module. On the one hand, it uses the information stored in these two modules to output pipe_route_final.txt by pipe output transform file, further produces the corresponding axis of pipes in aero-engine 3D UG model by UG interface program centerline.grx and 3D model using tubing.grx; on the other hand it outputs pipe_route_final.frame file to simulation module. This module's final UG pipe models will decide the real pipe geometric and manufacturing information.

Aero-engine pipe correction module is for correcting the 3D models generated by aero-engine pipe generating module. This model can correct the nodes in centerline of pipes to change pipe routes by correcting pipe_route_final.m, it also can alter the diameters of pipes to change appearance of pipes, as figure 5.1 shows.

Output of aero-engine pipe information and process parameters module can output and store the final aero-engine design information and process parameters. This model uses TXT format to store and output all the aero-engine pipe 3D models' information of starting and ending points, diameters, paths (stored in nodes in centerlines). Any pipe's design information and process parameters can be searched by this txt, namely pipe data and process parameters file.

5.4 Pipe simulation module

The pipe simulation module is developed based on fluid structure interaction simulation analysis and strength, vibration, life detecting and simulating software. It achieves automatic transferring of various simulation data and integrates multiple databases, like database of pipe materials properties, database of fluid parameters and database of pipe parts (pipes, clamps, joints and other parts) finite element models. Thus it can fulfill the concurrence of simulation of solid structure interaction of pipe system [23-26], strength verifying, vibration check, and life adjustment.

Pipe detection module contains detection module of fluid structure interaction of pipe routes in aero-engine, module for strength verification, module for vibration check of aero-engine pipe system, module for life check of aero-engine pipe system. The following part will give a detailed account about detection module of fluid structure interaction.

5.4.1 Detection module of Fluid Structure Interaction (FSI)

5.4.1.1 Importance of FSI analysis

Static index needs to be considered in a pipe filled with fluid, besides as for pipe system requiring strict working conditions (aero-engine pipe system, nuclear reactor pipes) transient index also is needed. When velocity of fluid in pipe changes drastically, fluid structure interaction needs to be taken into account to verify pipes' safety accurately. The most common transient phenomenon in pipe is the water hammer phenomenon, a fluid impact effect caused by the sudden closure of valve. When it happens, the whole system is susceptible to movement due to its massive impact. At this time, we can't separate fluid from structure to build models, so FSI analysis is implemented instead [27].

5.4.1.2 FSI problem in pipe system of aero-engine

As for cases of unstable pipes, as figure 5.3 shows, the traditional water hammer effect analysis, a combination of elasticity and pressure wave, isn't applicable. When pressure wave in figure (a) passes the twist on the right, the difference of pressure in corners on both sides result in movement in figure (b). Due to this reason pressure in right corner decreases while pressure in left corner increases. This movement causes transmitting of pressure wave in pipes, and in turn causes movement of pipes, repetition of which forms vibration [28].

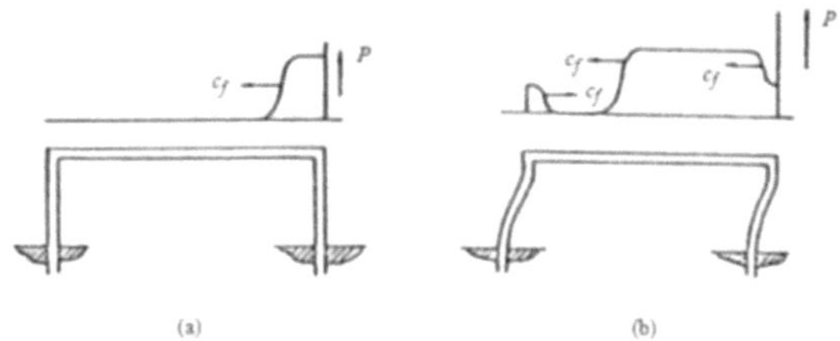

Fig. 5.3. Junction coupling of un-mounted pipes[57]

The above situation seldom happens in aero-engine pipes for pipes are usually fixed on jacket surface of aero-engine with clamps firmly. Of course FSI is possible if accidents occur to cause loose and failure of clamps, and the possibility of failure of pipes is also augmenting. Apart from this the following FSI situation is worth considering.

As figure 5.4 shows, fluid moves with velocity V in figure (a), reference pressure P at this time is 0; in figure (b), as fluid suddenly stops, the pressure is correspondingly rocketing quickly and pressure wave is transmitted with velocity c_f accompanying with expansion of pipe walls, as figure (c) shows. This kind of expansion spreads across the surface of pipe with velocity c_t and causes constriction of pipe walls in other places. This contraction generates a second increase of pressure spreading with velocity c_t (c_t is usually greater than c_f)which is often called precursor of wave, as figure (b) shows.

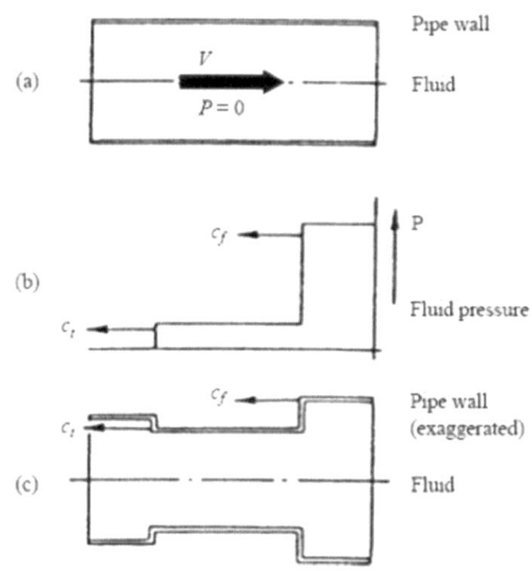

Fig. 5.4. Poisson coupling in normal case [57]

5.4.2 Feedback information of FSI analysis

Based on the FSI analysis, we can find working conditions need to be considered in design of pipes. Based on results of FSI analysis and the possible operations like operation of valves and sudden change of velocity of fluid and impact (lateral and axial impact) we can decide whether straight pipe or elbow pipe is a proper solution. When faced up with frequent axial impact, it's more feasible to replace straight pipes with elbow pipes and to use more pipe supports; while there are more lateral impacts, results of FSI analysis should be taken care of to meet working needs of pipes and increasing use of pipes according to specific conditions is reasonable.

What kind of pipe should be used at the start and end point of pipe? How many clamps and what kind of clamps is proper? To solve these questions, we can't simply rely on vibration analysis and strength analysis, FSI analysis is indispensible to decide the suitable structure of pipes. If a straight pipe must be substituted by an elbow type based on FSI analysis, we can regard results of FSI analysis as human experience and knowledge which can be transformed to a virtual obstacle between two endpoints of the pipe added to unfeasible workspace. Thus based on the pipe-routing algorithm in section 4, it's natural to obtain an alternative strategy, namely the replacement of straight pipes with elbow pipes to preclude failure of pipes in FSI analysis.

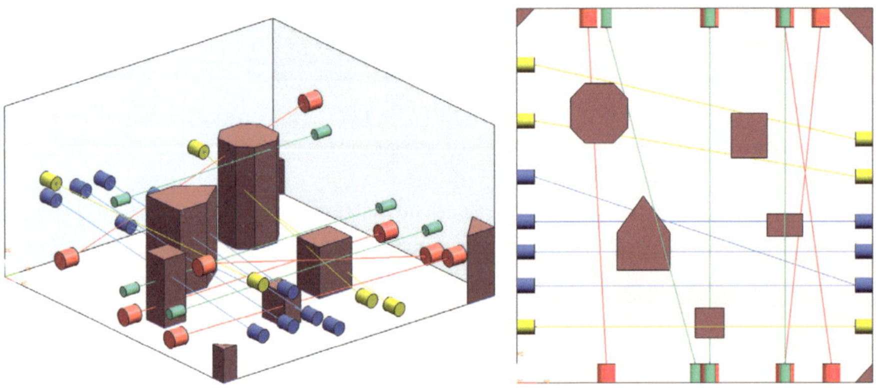

Fig. 5.5. Pipe route configuration based on FSI analysis

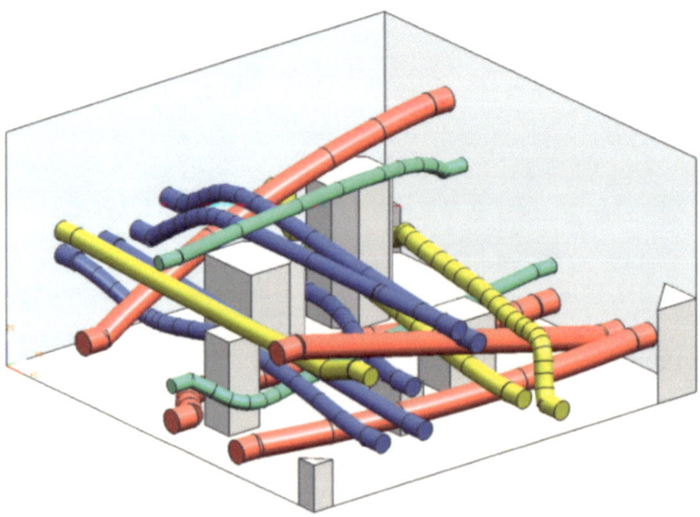

Fig. 5.6. Pipe routing results after FSI analysis

As figure 5.5 shows, the blue circles signify start and end points of pipe. This pipe is initially supposed to be straight, however based on FSI analysis, this pipe can't withstand massive axial impact, it needs to be replaced by an elbow pipe and a support needs to be added in the bending section. So an obstacle symbolized by a red circle can be added to force generation of elbow pipe to meet results of FSI analysis. The ultimate result of pipe-routing can be seen in figure 5.6 with arrow denoting the effect after modification.

From the above successful application of FSI analysis results in optimization of pipe-routing, we can find FSI results, based on knowledge and logical deduction which are accentuated by symbolism , can be finally employed in solving problems by make virtual imaginal changes integrating mathematical deduction and knowledge of the predesigned solution. So this application illustrates our former conclusion that logical thinking is a special type of imaginal thinking.

5.5 Simulation results

The aero-engine mechanical model is set up in UG NX4, by using self-developed interface, the geometry data of the aero-engine and pipe starts, ends and diameter information are transferred into MATLAB database as input of calculation. The algorithm is written with MATLAB language and the calculated pipe route result is feed back to UG module to generate 3D pipe modules[29-31].

5.5.1 pipe-routing without obstacles

As shown in Figure 5.7, the algorithm is applied to a non-obstacle aero-engine model.

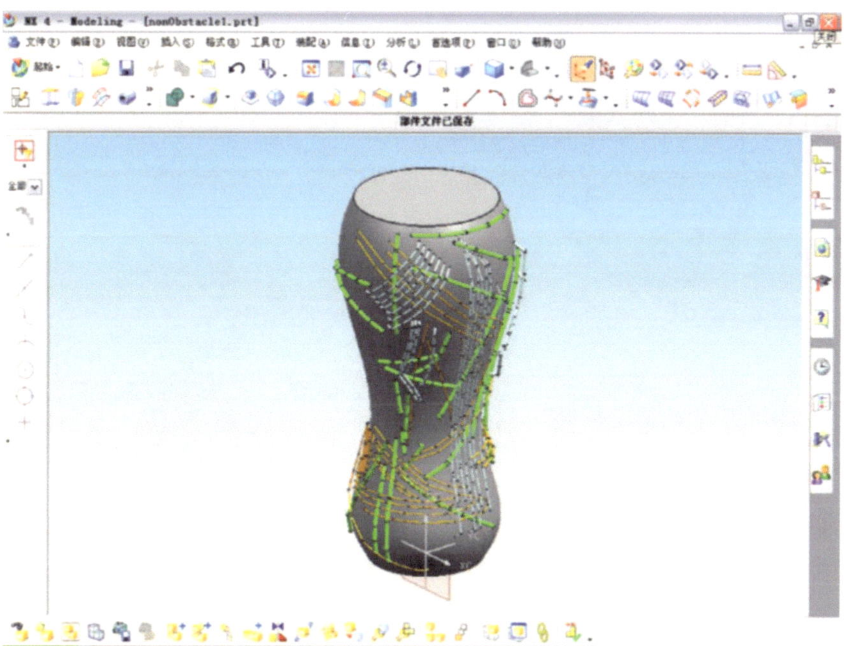

Fig. 5.7. Non-obstacle pipe routing

The aero-engine model is a revolved body with no accessories, the length (Z-direction, namely the air flow direction) is 5,000 mm, the diameter of the body is from 1,520 to 2,400mm; the free space gap of the aero-engine is no bigger than 150mm (from the outer surface according to the engine to the installation cabin inner surface). 67 pipes of functions as lubrication, cooling, information transmission, fuel, etc. are divided into three layers, from inside to outside displayed with different colors (green, orange, and white).

5.5.2 Pipe-routing with obstacles

As shown in Figure 5.8 and 5.9, the algorithm is applied to an aero-engine with all kinds of shapes of equipments.

The aero-engine model is very much similar to the real situation (real engine model is not allowed to display according to local government regulations), the length (Z-direction, namely the air flow direction) is 3,000mm, the diameter of the engine jacket is from 250 to 1,290 mm, six accessories of simplified shapes are included, the free space gap between the engine jacket and the installation cabin is no bigger than 150mm. 86 pipes of functions as lubrication, cooling, information transmission, fuel, etc. 86 pipes are assigned into five layers, from inside to outside displayed with different colors (yellow, green, blue, white, and red).

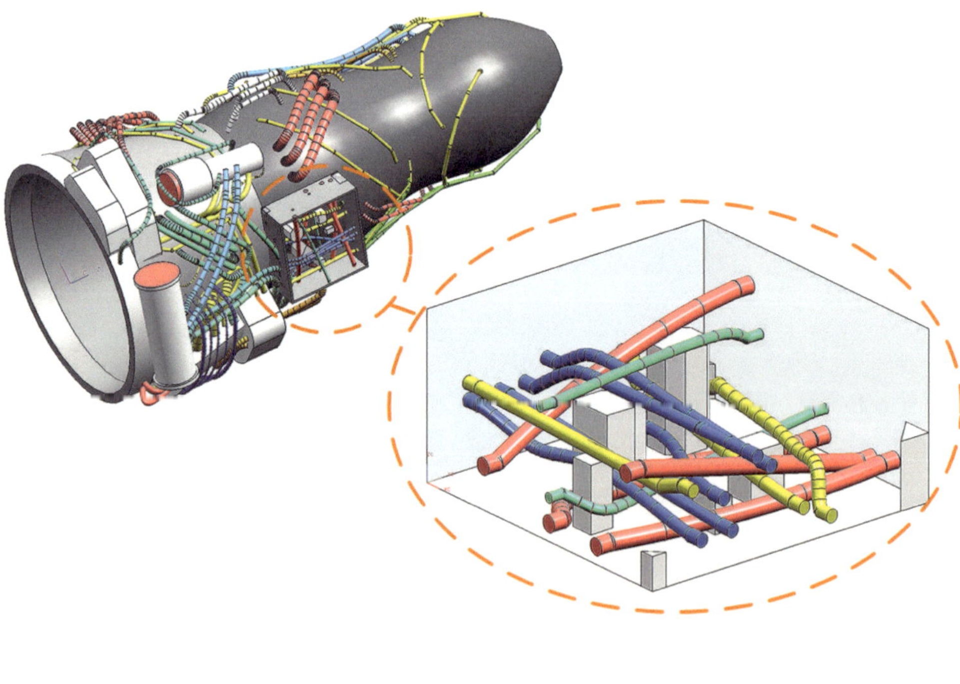

Fig. 5.8. Simulation of pipe routes planning for an aero-engine model

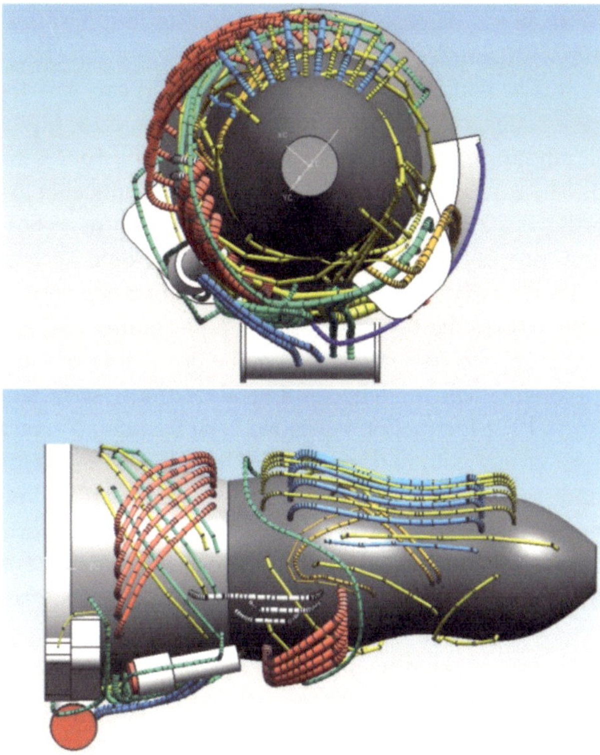

Fig. 5.9. Simulation of pipe routes planning for an aero-engine model (back & front view)

6. Epilogue

There exist serious conflicts between different schools of human thinking style. Meantime many engineering problems still heavily rely on human knowledge and experience for instruction so imitation of human thinking is a valuable and urgent job. Because information transmitted by the whole human thinking and the expression of it are both based on high dimension neural images which can be perceived and imagined, so we hope by imitating human thinking, we can find a way to solve engineering problems.

Autonomous pipe-routing system problem like aero-engine with hundreds of pipes within a limited gap, extraordinarily depends on human experience, is hard to solve by traditional AI frame. This article discussed a new kind of fundamental thinking style: imaginal thinking by forming images and comparing them holistically and directly. Moreover, we imitate human imaginal thinking to develop a novel pipe-routing design methodology, which combines the accurate massive computational capability of computer with the pipe-routing experiences or knowledge of skillful human.

By imitating human's imaginal thinking and using the graphs as information media, a novel pipe assembly planning algorithm has been introduced. Different from other computer logic algorithms, the human's imaginal thinking algorithm quantifies the skillful technicians' experience and intuitions while planning pipe routes. Comparing with other algorithms, this algorithm takes all kinds of pipe routing constraints into account and automatically conceives pipe routes with simpler computational complexity which is more effective and efficient. For a certain pipe routing problem, the algorithm can sort the pipes with order chosen rules and translate the obstacles and constraints into pipe routing map (the inaccessible area distribution), subsequently, the output pipe routes are very much alike human brain's work. The results of the article are generally applicable to all kinds of routing problems, and thus have a wide range of applications, such as robot collision-free path planning, PCB design, process plant layout planning, ship pipe system design, and aero-engine pipe routing. Particularly, it is used in this chapter to design an aero-engine pipe line system. On this basis, two results for non-obstacle pipe routing and obstacle pipe routing are presented. During the actual design of aero-engine pipes, tons of information concerning various areas like mathematical models, routing algorithms, static and mobile strength, fluid, vibration noise and FSI interaction is needed. The frequent interaction and transfer of information call for a common simulation platform to manage design tools, design process, data of simulation and simulation process. Thereby we put up a platform suitable for design of aero-engine pipes and simulation process. Correlations between former algorithms and modules of platform are explicated. Besides, another crucial question in pipe-routing, FSI problem is accentuated and pipe-route method based on FSI analysis is presented. The simulation based case studies demonstrated the effectiveness and high efficiency of our pipe-routing design method and led us to a better understanding of some of the essence of human thinking.

Our future work is to build a complete AI frame of imaginal thinking, on the basis of the effective and efficient pipe-routing system integrating vibration analysis and fluid - structure interaction (FSI) examination as the knowledge and experience for aero-engine will be extended to application in aero-engine assembly. We believe, with combination of human imaginal thinking style and machine computation capability, computers may finally have higher intelligence than humans in solving some complicated engineering problem like aero-engine assembly.

7. References

[1] Kim, J. (1995). Honderich, Ted. Ed, Problems in the Philosophy of Mind,Oxford Companion to Philosophy,Oxford: Oxford University Press.

[2] Max Wertheimer, Gestalt Theory, Published by Hayes Barton Press, 1944, ISBN 1593776950.

[3] Xiabi Liu, Introduction to Artificial Intelligence-method & system, Chinese National Defense Industry Press

[4] Newell A, Simon H A, Computer science as empirical enquiry: Symbols and search, Communications of the ACM, 1976, 19(3): 113–126

[5] Brooks R A, The Relationship Between Matter and Life, Nature, 2001, 409(6818): 409–411

[6] Brooks R A, New Approaches to Robotics, Science, 1991, 253(5025): 1227–1232

[7] Dreyfus H, Dreyfus S, Why Expert Systems Do Not Exhibit Expertise, IEEE Expert, 1986, 1(2): 86-90

[8] Paukner A, Suomi S J, Visalberghi E et al., Capuchin Monkeys Display Affiliation Toward Humans Who Imitate Them, Science, 2009,325(5942): 880-883
[9] Call J, Carpenter M, Monkeys Like Mimics, Science, 2009, 325(5942): 824-82
[10] Hurley S, Chater N, Perspectives on imitation: from cognitive neuroscience to social science, MIT press, 2005
[11] Rendell L, Boyd R, Cownden D et al., Why Copy Others? Insights from the Social Learning Strategies Tournament, SCIENCE, 2010, 328: 208-213
[12] Y. Jin, G.E. Zouein and S.C.-Y. Lu, A Synthetic DNA Based Approach to Design of Adaptive Systems, Annals of the CIRP 58 (1) (2009), pp. 153–156.
[13] R. Roy, Y.T. Azene, D. Farrugia, C. Onisa and J. Mehnen, Evolutionary Multi-objective Design Optimisation with Real Life Uncertainty and Constraints, Annals of the CIRP 58 (1) (2009), pp. 169–172.
[14] T. Lozano-Perez, Spatial Planning: A Configuration Space Approach, IEEE Transactions on Computers C-32 (2) (1983), pp. 108–120.
[15] J.S.B. Mitchell, Geometric Shortest Paths and Network Optimization, Handbook of Computational Geometry (2000), pp. 633–701.
[16] Lee C Y, An algorithm for path connections and its applications, IRE Transactions on Electronic Computers, 1961, EC-10:346-365
[17] Hightower D W, A solution to line routing problems on the continuous plane, Proceedings of Sixth Design Automation Workshop, IEEE 1969: 1-24
[18] Wangdahl G E, Pollock S M, Woodward J B. Minimum trajectory pipe routing, Journal of Ship Research, 1974, 18(1):44-49
[19] Zhu D, Latombe J, Pipe routing=path planning (with many constraints), Proceedings of the 1991 IEEE International Conference on Robotics and Automation, Sacramento, California, 1991: 1940-1947
[20] Ito T, A genetic algorithm approach to piping route path planning, Journal of Intelligent Manufacturing, 1999, 10: 103-114
[21] Ito T, Piping layout wizard: basic concepts and its potential for pipe route planning, International conference on industrial & engineering applications of artificial intelligence & expert systems, Castellon, Spain, 1998, 1:438-447
[22] Berg M, Kreveld M, Overmars M, et al., Computational Geometry Algorithms and Applications (Second Edition), Tsinghua University Express, 2005
[23] Brooks R A, Solving the Find-Path Problem by Good Representation of Free Space, IEEE Systems, Man and Cybernetics, SMC, 1983, 13: 190-197
[24] Brooks R A, Model-Based Three Dimensional Interpretations of Two Dimensional Images, IEEE Pattern Analysis and Machine Intelligence, 1983, 140-150
[25] Tusseling A S, Fluid-structure interaction in liquid-filled piping systems: a review, Journal of Fluids and Structures, 1996, 10:109 - 146
[26] Kwon Y W, Jo J C, 3D Modeling of Fluid-Structure Interaction With External Flow Using Coupled LBM and FEM, Journal of Pressure Vessel Technology, 2008, 130/021301: 1-8
[27] Gale J, Tiselj I, Godunov's Method for Simulations of Fluid-Structure Interaction in Piping Systems, Journal of Pressure Vessel Technology, 2008, Vol. 130/031304: 1-12

[28] Kwon Y W, Jo J C, 3D Modeling of Fluid-Structure Interaction With External Flow Using Coupled LBM and FEM, Journal of Pressure Vessel Technology, 2008, 130/021301: 1-8
[29] Lavooij C S W, Tijsseling A S, Fluid-structure interaction in liquid-filled piping systems, Journal of Fluids and Structures, 1991, 5:573-595

5

Transforming Natural Language into Controlled Language for Requirements Elicitation: A Knowledge Representation Approach

Carlos Mario Zapata J and Bell Manrique Losada
Universidad Nacional de Colombia
Universidad de Medellín
Colombia

1. Introduction

Requirements elicitation is one of the first processes of the requirements engineering for software development. At the beginning of this process, a team of analysts and stakeholders must capture the requirements belonging to the domain—expressed in natural language—in which the future software application must work. Then, the analyst must transform the captured information into artifacts—mostly diagrams—(Leite, 1987), which specify this domain.

The requirements engineering research community proposes some models for understanding the requirements elicitation process. We discover such models in the state-of-the-art review. The models are used for representing knowledge on this conceptual domain by using a formalization that specifies the most common concepts. Among these models we can cite ontologies, meta-ontologies, and meta-models.

With a model, we can represent, describe, or specify something. In the requirements engineering field of knowledge, we can use a domain-model to describe the concepts of a domain and its interrelations, as well as a business-model to represent the business rules of a company. Ontologies, meta-models, and meta-ontologies are examples of models. A descriptive, structural model, representing reality by a set of concepts, their interrelations, and constraints ruled by open-world assumption (Assmann, 2006) is called *ontology*. A *meta-model* is the definition of a set of valid models, facilitating their transformation and exchange. In meta-models, statements are made about what can be expressed in the valid models of a certain modeling language (Seidewitz, 2003). Basically, a meta-model is the description of a set of other models and tries to describe the language elements that can be used to create models, along with aspects related to the modeling technique, the modeling language, and the modeling procedure. Finally, a *meta-ontology* is a model that formalizes the relationships among several categories of formal and semi-formal concepts and also the connection of these theories to the informal concepts of a domain.

The representation of the conceptual domain knowledge related to the requirements elicitation has been addressed by several models. Most of them fail to describe some issues: the elements represented in the natural language discourse vs. the models and diagrams (specifications) expressed in controlled languages, the process followed by analysts for transforming the natural language discourse into controlled language specifications, and the relationship between structural and dynamic elements within the process.

In the search for a solution to these drawbacks, in this Chapter we present a meta-model to represent knowledge about these issues by using a pre-conceptual schema. The analysts can use this meta-model for improving the implementation of requirements elicitation processes in several domains.

The remainder of the Chapter is organized as follows: in Section 2 we describe the conceptual framework about requirements elicitation, knowledge representation, natural language, and controlled language. In Section 3 we review knowledge representation related to the requirements elicitation process and we discuss existing approaches to follow this process. In Section 4 we present the proposed meta-model and, then, we describe this kind of knowledge representation. Finally, in Section 5, we present the conclusions.

2. Conceptual framework

2.1 Requirements elicitation

Requirements elicitation is one of the first phases of requirements engineering for software development. The primary goal of the requirements engineering process is focused on discovering all the requirements which the future system needs to satisfy for being considered successful. In order to achieve this goal, two major activities—requirements elicitation and requirements analysis—are iteratively and incrementally carried out, involving an informal Natural Language and a formal modeling language (Li *et al.*, 2003).

The requirements elicitation phase has several activities, including: understanding the domain, capturing and classifying requirements, establishing priorities, resolving conflicts, and negotiating system requirements (Robertson & Robertson, 2006).

Requirements elicitation is primarily concerned with the communication between the analyst and the stakeholder (customer, end-user, domain expert, and so on,) as a way to gather the essential and relevant domain information. Such information is considered the basis for the requirements elicitation process.

2.2 Natural language and controlled language in requirements elicitation

The requirements elicitation process needs, as a basis for the entire process, the usage of two kinds of languages: Natural Language and Controlled Language, which are explained as follows.

2.2.1 Unrestricted grammars

Grammars are intended to describe the structure of a language. They provide a precise and understandable syntactic specification. A grammar comprises mainly a set of production rules describing syntactically valid phrases made by using the language (Jiang & Li, 1998).

Chomsky defined a hierarchy (1995) with four classes of grammar (0-3). Type 0 is the unrestricted grammar and the other types are derived by increasing restrictions on the form of the productions that may be used. Languages generated by using type 0 grammars are recognized by Turing machines. Also, they are called computably enumerable languages (CE-languages; Ruohonen, 2009).

2.2.2 Natural Language (NL)

The following issues are commonly addressed when working with NL: i) lexical ambiguity related to alternative parts of speech and word classes (article, preposition, adjective, noun, pronoun, adverb, verb, etc.) and ii) syntactic ambiguity, due to the complexity of sentence structure to avoid redundancy.

According to Berry (2003), the vast majority of requirements are written in natural language. The identification of the concepts used by the domain expert and the relationships among them are very important for the analyst. These concepts and relationships are considered the basis for the common language understanding used by the requirements engineer and the domain expert. According to Li *et al.* (2003), NL is highly informal in nature, because speakers and writers frequently create new forms and combinations of a language. This inventiveness is unfolded especially by the continuous evolution of nouns.

2.2.3 Controlled Language (CL)

Controlled Language is used—in requirements engineering and other similar knowledge areas—to improve the clarity of expression in the source text and the quality of the analysis phase (Mitamura & Nyberg, 1995).

The definition of a controlled language based on some subset of the natural language is important to establish a controlled vocabulary and a controlled grammar. The controlled languages restrict the translation so that only a pre-defined vocabulary is used. With this vocabulary, an analyst can write and standardize rule-based readable texts. If the grammatical constraints of the source language are formally specified, then a machine translation system may take advantage of less-complex and less-ambiguous texts (Mitamura & Nyberg, 1995).

2.3 Knowledge representation

The requirements elicitation and other similar processes are intended to gather information, which must be organized and modeled, in order to create a meaningful whole: the conceptual model. Either the clarification or the solution of a problem can apply the definition of a concept as a structure, derived from the information acquired. Consequently, the first task in creating a knowledge representation in a specific domain is the conceptualization, defined as the usage of concepts and relationships to deal with—and probably solve—a problem (Andrade *et al.*, 2003). Accordingly, a conceptual model is an abstraction of the universe of discourse, as well as a kind of knowledge representation, and a possible model of a possible solution for the problem.

Knowledge representation requires all the information elements to be identified from the analysis, and classified or grouped into levels, depending on what function they must fulfill in the specific domain. According to Andrade *et al.* (2003), such levels are: *static information*, which comprises the structural or declarative domain information about the problem (*i.e.*, concepts, properties, relationships, and constraints), and *dynamic information*, needed to conform the behavior that takes place in the domain (functionality, actions, etc.)

Requirements elicitation is a negotiation process in which knowledge is intensively captured, combined, and disseminated (Falbo *et al.*, 2004). In this process, analysts and stakeholders should exchange information about the context and the activities to be supported by the software application under development. This process involves knowledge representation actions—from all possible information available—including the behavioral analysis of previous systems.

Zapata *et al.* (2006) propose the pre-conceptual schemas (PS) as knowledge representation models. The PS is an intermediate schema for facilitating the mapping process between natural language specifications and Unified Modeling Language (UML) diagrams. The main PS symbols are concepts (rectangles), relationships (ovals), connections (thin arrows), and implications (thick arrows). Also, conditionals in PS are expressed by rhombs.

3. State-of-the-art review

In the requirements elicitation process, analysts and stakeholders should exchange information concerning the context and activities from the domain. This information is useful to understand how we can obtain conceptual schemas from it. Obtaining a controlled language from the natural language discourse can be considered a useful idea to facilitate and improve this elicitation process. Along this line of thought, several approaches have been proposed.

Commonly, some approaches to knowledge representation have been identified in the requirements elicitation process. Because of this diversity, the state of the art encompasses a number of models from different viewpoints. These models are categorized as meta-models, meta-ontologies, and ontologies. The following are models of some currently deployed approaches, reflecting this trend.

The KAOS meta-model (Dardenne *et al.*, 1991) is made up of meta-concepts, meta-relations linking meta-concepts, meta-attributes characterizing meta-concepts and meta-relations, and meta-constraints upon several kinds of components. The meta-model uses the "meta" prefix referring to the meta-level, where domain-independent abstractions are defined. This level is different to other levels involved: the domain level, where concepts specific to the application domain are defined, and the instance level, where particular instances of domain-specific concepts are introduced.

The requirements meta-model (see Figure 1) is based on instances of meta-concepts, linked to instances of the meta-relations, and featured by instances of meta-attributes. This model emphasizes both conceptual and structural aspects. Natural language is not considered in this meta-model as the source of the descriptions for the scenarios and controlled languages are not intended to represent the formal elements of the meta-model. Also, the usage of some sort of semantic network for describing the meta-model gives the orientation toward structural descriptions, excluding dynamic elements. Finally, from this meta-model we cannot deduce the process we must follow for transforming the scenarios into specifications.

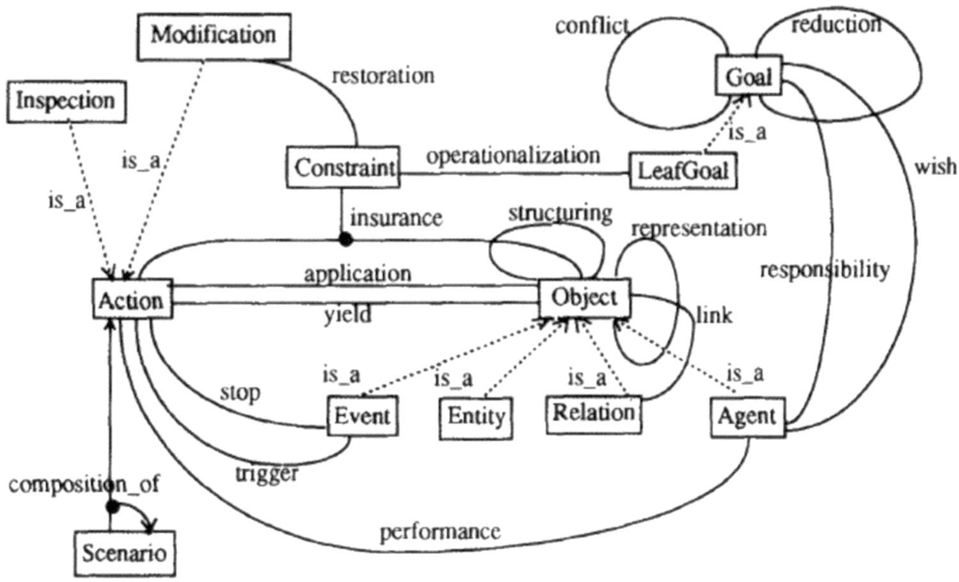

Fig. 1. The KAOS meta-model (Dardenne *et al.*, 1991)

Hu *et al.* (2010) propose a 'requirements meta-model' from the perspectives of *Role, Goal, Process*, and *Service* (RGPS). The meta-model is focused on modeling requirements from early requirements elicitation processes and, then, the process can be used to dynamically capture the stakeholder needs. The Relationships of the RGPS are defined in four layers (see Figure 2). The *Role Layer* contains actors (human or software), who are involved in the requirements engineering process, and information about what roles they play, respectively. The *Goal layer* depicts strategic goals (*i.e.*, Functional or Non-Functional goals) of service-oriented requirements. The *Process layer* is a multiple model, where processes can be composed by other processes. Finally, the *Service layer* represents the services composed when they are selected from the service repository. The RPGS model refers to the roles involved in requirements elicitation processes. Besides, it represents the functional elements implicated in the elicitation process.

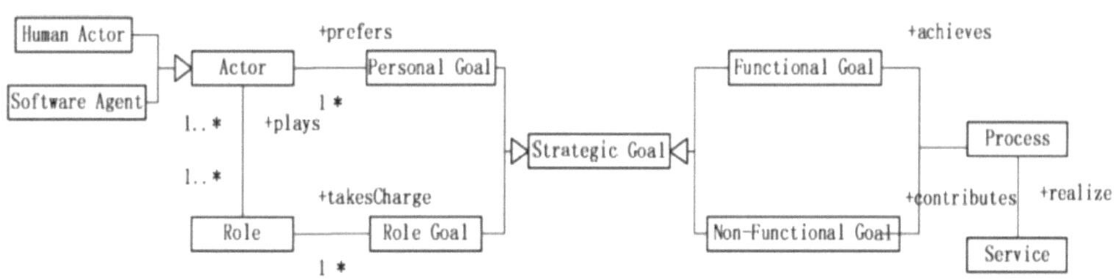

Fig. 2. The RPGS meta-model (Hu *et al.*, 2010)

Hu *et al.* (2010) use a class diagram for representing the meta-model, but avoiding the behavioral component of this kind of diagram (mainly directed by the class operations.) The diagram is structural in nature, without elements leading to transformation processes. Also, the contents of natural language discourses or controlled languages specifications are not established in the meta-model. Consequently, the transformation process from natural language to controlled language cannot be identified.

Wei *et al.* (2008) present an approach nearest to the knowledge representation of requirements expressed in natural language. Also, they show how to define natural language patterns like the abstraction of the requirement statement. In this model, *patterns* (a part of the sentence) could be composed for describing several requirement statements, *i.e.*, a complete sentence of various requirements. The proposal can be seen in Figure 3, where the *behavior* represents a basic functional requirement, which is a kind of simple sentence. *Constraint* and *status* are other kinds of simple sentences. A *constraint* represents non-functional requirements (like quantitative and qualitative constrains), and the *status* represents the context requirements and services belonging to the stakeholders. An *event* is a behavioral trigger, which activates changes in either the entity state or the system state. A *condition* is a test of the current state of an entity or a test of the current system state.

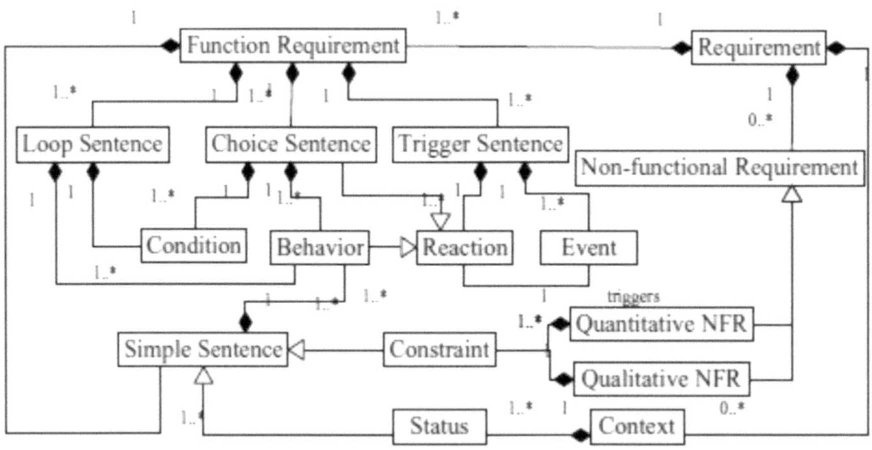

Fig. 3. Requirements statement model (Wei *et al.*, 2008)

As in the case of Hu *et al.* (2010), Wei *et al.* (2008) select a class diagram for representing their model, avoiding the behavioral component of the process. This model has a clear distinction between natural language discourses and controlled language requirements, but the transformation process is not clearly identified. However, some of the classes they use will be suitable for describing the entire requirements elicitation process, from natural to controlled language.

Rubin (2009) proposes a meta-model for representing the knowledge about the requirements engineering domain. This model comprises essential concepts belonging to the software development process. In this meta-model, Rubin proposes ontological constructs, that is, ontological components which can be combined to build up a model in a specific domain. The meta-model incorporates the domain-related constructs, their relationships, their link attributes, and their states (see Figure 4). This meta-model is used to bridge the data view (mainly composed by attributes) and the other elements focused on services.

Rubin (2009) expresses the meta-model by using a sort of entity-relationship diagram, mainly focused on structural elements. For this reason, the dynamic components are absent of the representation. Also, the distinction between natural language discourses and controlled languages specifications is absent.

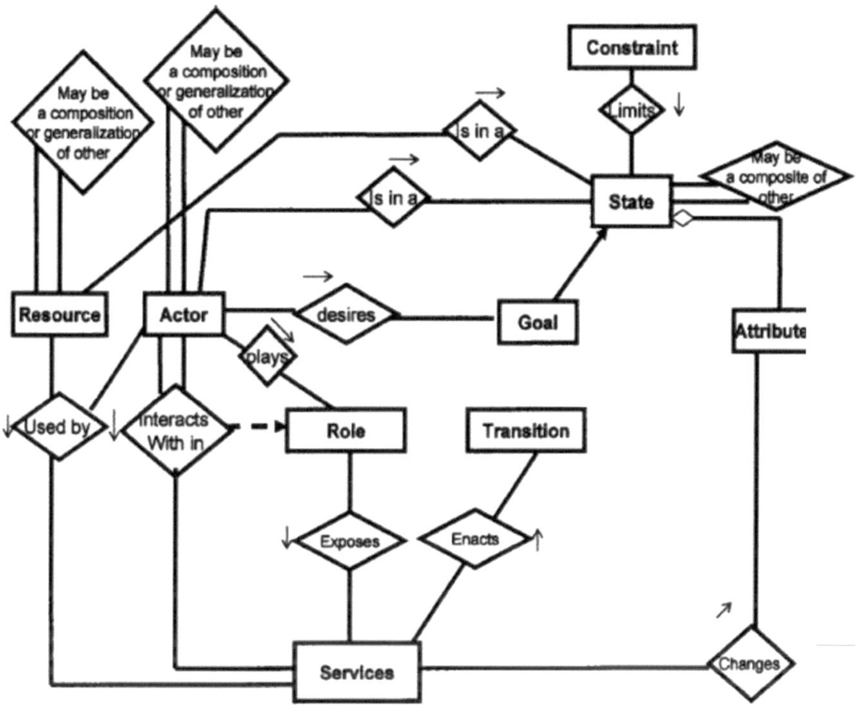

Fig. 4. Meta-model of requirements engineering domain knowledge (Rubin, 2009)

On the other hand, some other approaches have been introduced (*e.g.*, ontologies and meta-ontologies.) Zapata *et al.* (2010) propose a meta-ontology for the requirements elicitation process. This meta-ontology is incremental and independent of the problem domain. Zapata *et al.* (2010) use the meta-ontology to obtain stakeholder concepts from a dialogue expressed in natural language. The concepts identified in the meta-ontology are the following: *object, actor, constrains, actor-function, activity,* and *organization*. The meta-ontology is constructed in Protégé, an ontology editor. Due to the similarities between the hierarchical ontologies and the class diagram, we can say that the concepts of this meta-ontology are represented into a structural class diagram. In Figure 5 we show an image of the proposed meta-ontology. One of the main advantages in the usage of Protégé for representing the meta-ontology is the possibility of creating instances of it. So, we can define questions to be answered by the ontology and the entire process can be clarified by using the instances and the programmed questions.

An ontology to define semantics elements inside requirements descriptions is presented by Kaiya and Saeki (2006). The thesaurus of this proposal has concepts and relationships among the concepts. Also, it has several subclasses of concept classes and relationships (see Figure 6). In Figure 6, an "object" is a sub-class of a concept-class and an "apply" relationship can connect two concepts.

Fig. 5. Meta-ontology for requirements elicitation (Zapata *et al.*, 2010)

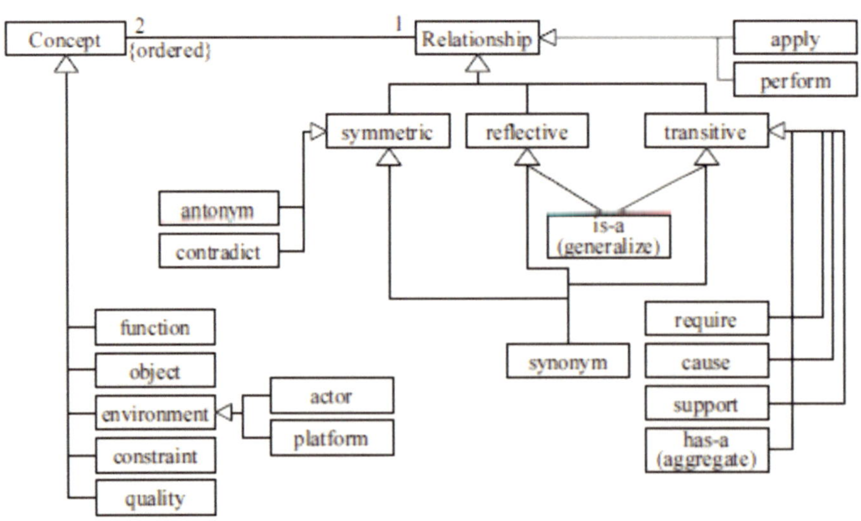

Fig. 6. Meta-model of Ontology for requirements (Kaiya & Saeki, 2006)

Both Zapata *et al.* (2010) and Kaiya and Saeki (2006) describe the meta-ontology in terms of class diagrams without the dynamic elements. Hence, the process for transforming the discourse into specifications is not clearly stated. Also, neither the natural language elements nor the controlled language elements are explicitly identified, leading to subjective interpretation of the meta-ontology concepts. Despite the mentioned drawbacks, the meta-ontology and the ontology can be used for defining some of the important concepts surrounding the requirements elicitation process and the transformation process from natural language discourses into controlled language specifications.

A meta-model for the requirements elicitation process is proposed by Dzung and Ohnishi (2009). This model is based on functional requirements (FR). Each FR is modeled as a node of the ontology, including one verb and several nouns. Inheritance and aggregation relationships can be represented as functional structures belonging to systems of certain domains. Functional requirements can include other relationships, for example: agent of the function (who), location of the function (where), time (when), reason (why), and non-functional requirements (NFR). In Figure 7, one of the diagrams used by Dzung and Ohnishi (2009) for representing the ontology is depicted. As in the case of the meta-ontology of Zapata *et al.* (2010), the main advantage of this approach is the possibility of instantiating the ontology. However, Dzung and Ohnishi (2009) require some other diagrams for representing the features of the ontology.

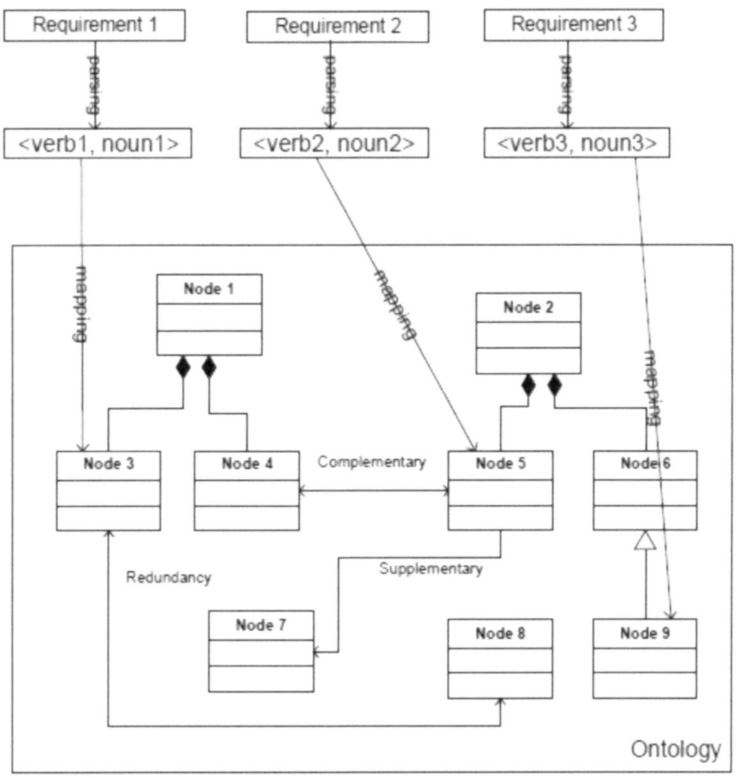

Fig. 7. Ontological meta-model for the requirements elicitation process (Dzung & Ohnishi, 2009).

Finally, another relevant approach is LEL (Language Extended Lexicon; Demitrio, 2005). This proposal focuses on identifying lexical elements from natural language. The lexicon comprises symbols representing: (i) active objects or subjects (perform actions;) (2) passive objects or subjects (actions are performed on them;) (iii) verbs; and (iv) meaningful states of the system. Demitrio (2005) proposes a framework for the automatic generation of LEL, based on information from specific documentation. Based on this lexicon, the analyst could generate the necessary scenarios to represent the knowledge in a specific context (see Figure 8). In this Figure, we can state the scenarios as the center of the model, generating many connections to other elements of the model like context, title, objectives, actors, resources, episodes, and exceptions. The diagram for representing the model is structural in nature, with constraints defined on some of the concepts used.

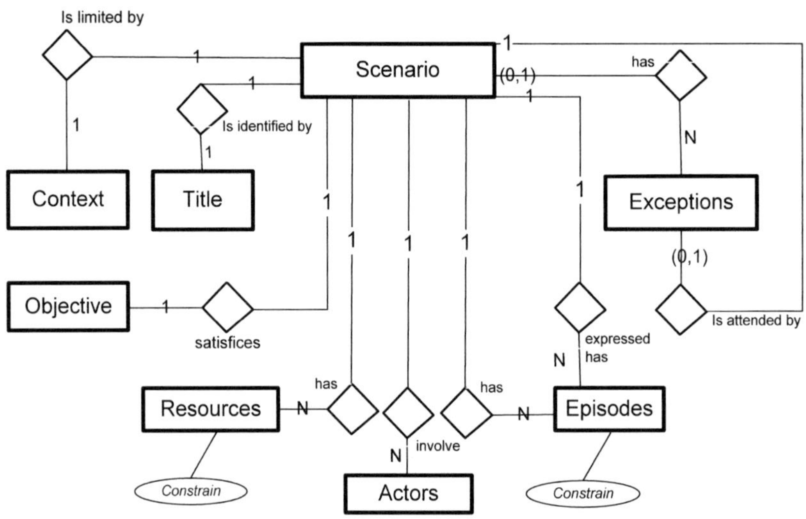

Fig. 8.Model to generate LEL from requirements (Demitrio, 2005)

Both the ontology suggested by Dzung and Ohnishi (2009) and the lexicon presented by Demitrio (2005) are related to the usage of natural language as the starting point for the requirements elicitation process. Dzung and Ohnishi (2009) selected an ontological approach for representing the process, defining the mapping process itself. However, the entire process comprises several diagrams and the whole structure and dynamics cannot be represented into one single diagram. Demitrio (2005) uses an entity-relationship diagram (mostly structural), and the elements of either natural or controlled languages are not explicitly identified. Consequently, the transformation process is also absent from this representation.

4. Knowledge representation proposal

In the state-of-the-art review, we mentioned a number of cases to represent knowledge related to the requirements elicitation process. Just a few of them are focused on the transformation process from natural language into controlled language. Also, they lack some explicit definition of the elements belonging either to natural or controlled language. Finally, the relationship between structural and dynamic elements is also absent from several knowledge representations, because they are structural in essence.

As we will describe in this Section, we propose a knowledge representation for this *transformation* from natural language discourses into controlled language specifications by using a dynamic and structural viewpoint in the requirements elicitation process. This knowledge representation approach is based on the pre-conceptual schemas (PS). A PS is an intermediate stage between natural language and conceptual schemas. The following are the main elements we can identify in the PS syntax:

- PS concepts (see Figure 9) are restricted to only two elements of the stakeholder discourse: nominal phrases noun-type (*e.g.*, grammatical element, domain-model, and technical-document), and single nouns (*e.g.*, analyst, user, requirement, and so forth.)

Fig. 9. Examples of PS Concepts (author elaboration).

- PS relationships (see Figure 10) are restricted to verbs from the stakeholder discourse. There are three kinds of PS relationships: structural relationships (single solid line), which refer to structural verbs or permanent relationships between concepts ("to be", "to have", and "to uniquely have" ,) dynamic relationships (with dotted line) which refer to dynamic verbs or temporal relationships between concepts (verbs such as "to review", "to generate", "to build", and so forth,) and achievement relationships (with double solid line) which refer to goal verbs (for example "to maximize", "to guarantee", and so on).

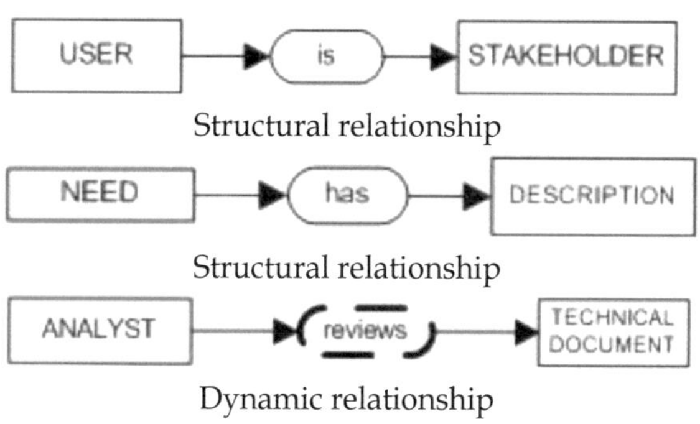

Fig. 10. Examples of PS relationships (author elaboration).

- PS conditionals represent preconditions—expressed in terms of concepts—that trigger some dynamic relationship. PS conditionals are formed by sets of concepts with comparative operators, such as "grade mark is greater than three."
- PS references (see Figure 11) are links between the same elements posted in different places at different distances from the PS.
- PS implications (see Figure 12) represent cause-and-effect relationships between dynamic relationships. Two uses of PS implications are: linking a dynamic relationship to another one and linking a PS conditional to a dynamic relationship.

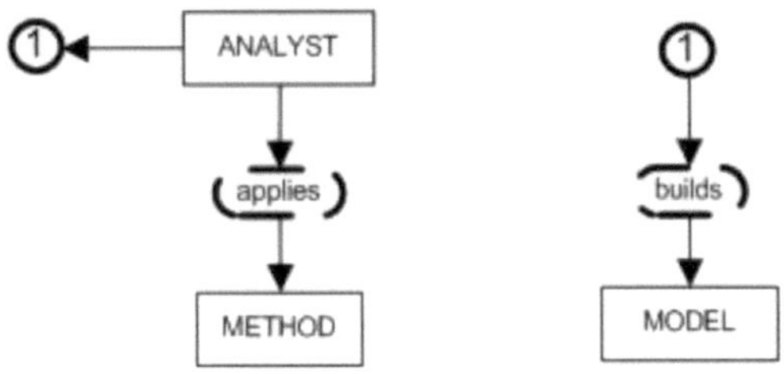

Fig. 11. Examples of PS references (author elaboration).

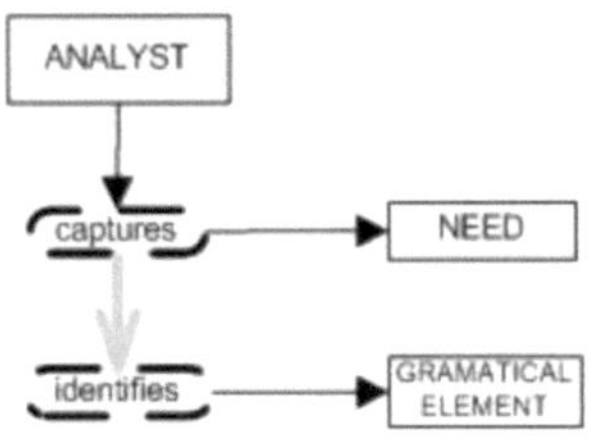

Fig. 12. Example of PS implication (author elaboration).

- Frames (represented by thick-lined rectangles with rounded edges as shown in Figure 13) are useful for gathering portions of the PS.

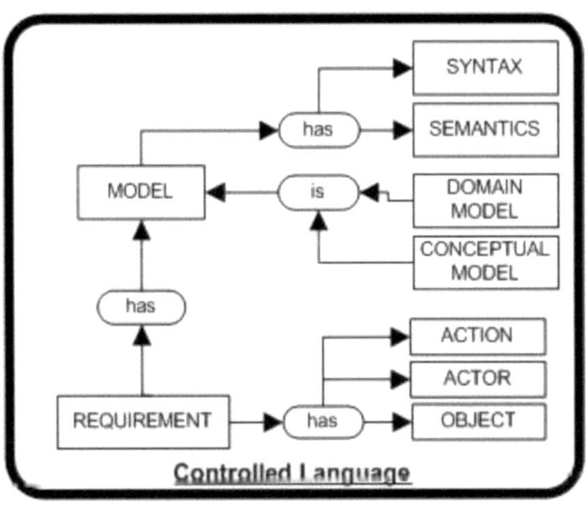

Fig. 13. Example of PS frame (author elaboration).

As mentioned before, we use a PS to represent several elements involved in the requirements elicitation process made by analysts. Furthermore, we represent the transformation process from natural language to controlled language. The proposed PS includes the relationship between structural and dynamic elements of the process. Analysts can use this PS to understand the transformation of stakeholder needs and expectations (from a discourse expressed in natural language) into requirements specifications and models (expressed in a controlled language.) We will explain the entire pre-conceptual schema as follows (see Figure 14).

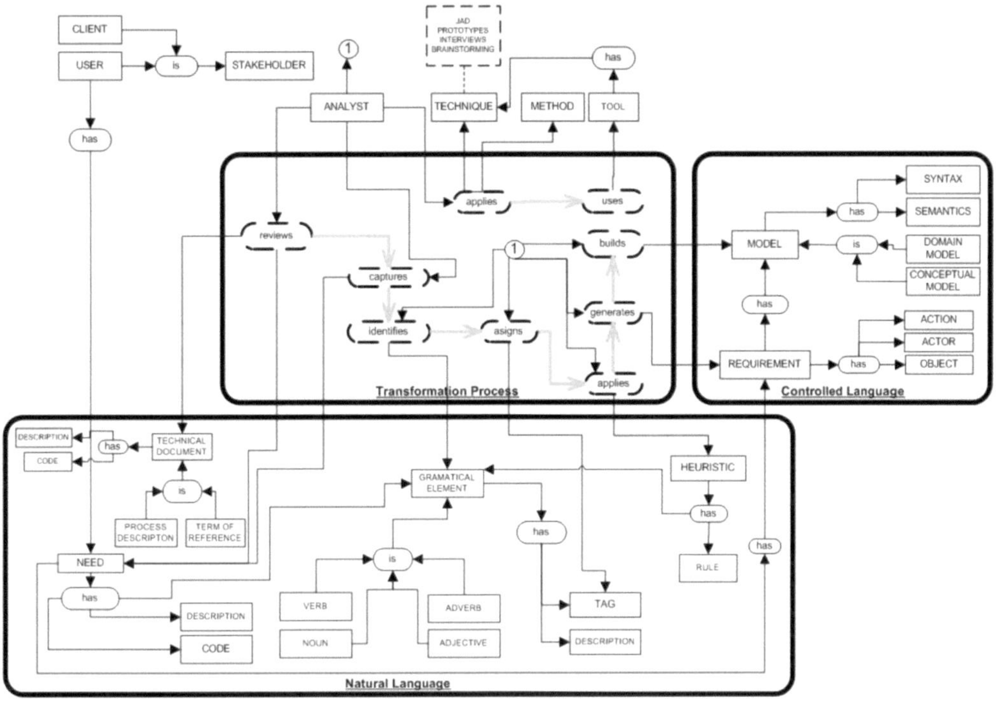

Fig. 14. Pre-conceptual Schema (author elaboration).

Analysts and stakeholders are involved in Requirements Elicitation. A STAKEHOLDER can be the CLIENT or the USER. A USER has a NEED. The ANALYST captures that NEED, based on a review of the TECHNICAL DOCUMENTATION, PROCESS DESCRIPTION, and TERM OF REFERENCE. The NEED has a *code*, a *description*, and a *grammatical element*. After capturing the NEEDS, the ANALYST identifies the GRAMATICAL ELEMENTS from NEED description. A GRAMATICAL ELEMENT can be: *Verb, Noun, Adverb*, or *Adjective*. It also has a TAG and a DESCRIPTION. Is the ANALYST who assigns a TAG to each GRAMATICAL ELEMENT identified, and applies a particular HEURISTIC as the tag. Immediately after, she/he generates a REQUIREMENT. The REQUIREMENT has an *action*, an *actor*, and an *object* associated. Finally, the ANALYST builds a MODEL, which has a particular *syntax* and *semantics*.

This way the NEED identified first by the ANALYST has a set of REQUIREMENTS, which will be drawn in a MODEL. The model can be a CONCEPTUAL MODEL or a DOMAIN MODEL. Through the whole process, the ANALYST applies a METHOD. This METHOD has a TECHNIQUE or set of techniques, supported by the use of one TOOL or more.

We include three frames in the PS: natural language, controlled language, and transformation process. By doing this, we are explicitly defining the elements of the requirements elicitation process regarding either natural or controlled language. With the third frame, we are signaling the activities belonging to the transformation process from natural language discourse into controlled language specifications defined by models and requirements. The natural language frame comprises the concepts belonging to the stakeholder discourse, headed by the description of the needs. Also, the grammatical elements are included, and the tags related to the type of element we are using. The controlled language frame has the concepts related to the translated information originated from the description of the needs, mainly the requirements and the models. In the current state of the art, this information must be generated by the analyst, but in the proposed environment, some tools could help in elaborating the models and the requirements. Particularly, the environment surrounding the PS is currently searching for automated generation of diagrams and source code. Finally, the transformation process frame includes all the dynamic relationships we can identify in the process, like capturing needs, identifying grammatical elements, assigning tags, applying heuristics, generating requirements, and building models. Some PS elements are not grouped by frames, because they are related either to the agents who generates the activities of the process or to some properties we need to take for granted in the process, like the methods and tools.

With the proposed PS, we address the aforementioned drawbacks of the previous work in the following way:

- With frames we describe the elements represented in the natural language discourse and the results of the transformation process in terms of controlled language requirements and models.
- A third frame is used for describing the entire transformation process from natural to controlled language. The different dynamic relationships involved in this framework are the steps we need to follow for completing the transformation process.
- The distinction between structural and dynamic elements is accomplished by the nature of the pre-conceptual schema. The concepts are structural and the dynamic relationships are behavioral. They are linked by the intervention of the agents in the process, mainly the analyst and the stakeholder.

In order to illustrate how the process of transforming NL into controlled language occurs, we show—by means of an example—both the values assigned to each element and the fulfilled conditions to perform an action. This illustration shows the attribute values that bind with each concept and is based on executable pre-conceptual schemas (Zapata *et al.*, 2011). An executable PS adds elements to the basic notation; essentially differentiating concepts that contains attributes (class concepts) and atomic concepts (attribute concepts).

In the natural language frame, a User, which is a stakeholder, has a need. The scenario is characterized by steps, as follows. In the first step an *analyst* reviews a type of *technical document*. In this case the *technical document* is a *Term of Reference*, which has a *code* and a *description*. In our proposed example, the value of description is *Commonly, the manager is in charge of authorizing the payments represented by the payroll* and the code is labeled as *001*. The first step is represented in Figure 15.

This process is currently made by hand. The *need* has a *description*, a *code*, and *grammatical elements*. The need *description* is *Only the manager authorizes the payroll*, and the code is set as *001*, as shown in Figure 16.

In the step 3, the *analyst* identifies the *grammatical elements* from the *need*, which can be a *verb*, *adverb*, *noun*, or *adjective*. Each *grammatical element* has a *tag* and a *description*. The *analyst* assigns a *tag* to each *grammatical element*, after identifies it (implication). For the need coded

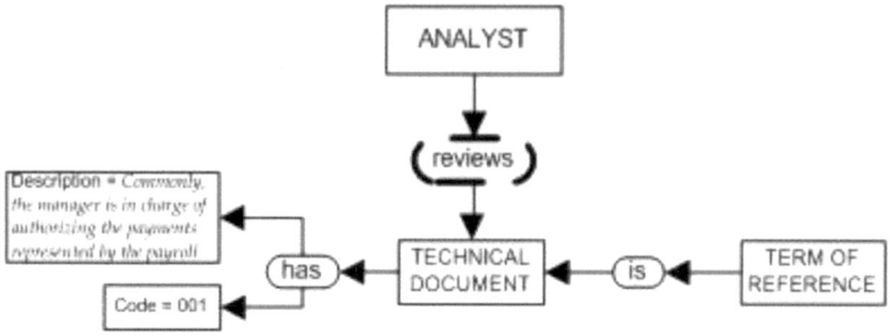

Fig. 15. PS including values of the step 1 (author elaboration).

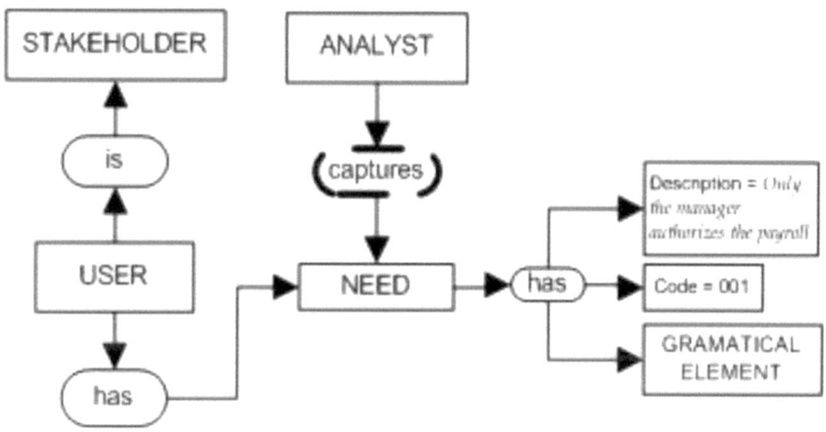

Fig. 16. PS including values of the step 2 (author elaboration).

001, he creates a list of the following values (Table 1). The PS (Figure 17) is supported by a table, such that for each concept-class containing another concept-class, analyst writes the attribute-concepts in a list, which describes the name as a head.

Type Grammatical Element	Tag	Description
Adverb	ADV	*Only*
Noun	N	*The manager*
Verb	VB	*Authorizes*
Noun	N	*The payroll*

Table 1. List attribute concept, Step 3 (author elaboration)

Finally, in the step 4, the analyst applies a heuristic, which in turn has rules and grammatical elements, to generate a requirement. The value of the rule to be applied is *transforming the noun before the verb into actor, the verb into action, and the noun after the verb in object*. Requirement has an action, an object, and an actor, as we show in Figure 18. The exemplification of the class-concept model and its attribute-concepts is beyond the scope of this chapter.

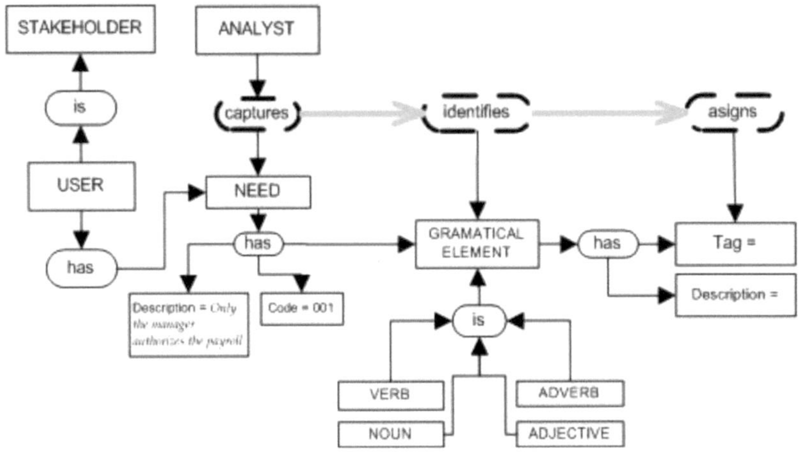

Fig. 17. PS including values of the step 3 (author elaboration).

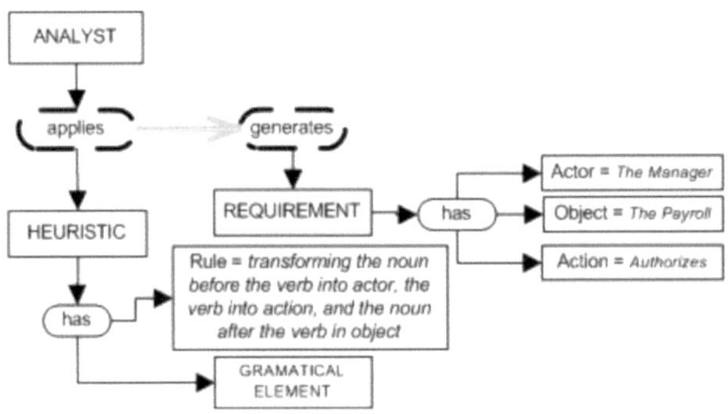

Fig. 18. PS including values of the step 4 (author elaboration).

For the sake of simplicity, we assume the entry of information in multiple attribute-concepts. The executable PS might be much more complex, e.g., using predefined descriptions for each of the values.

5. Conclusions

The requirements engineering research community has proposed several models to understand the requirements elicitation process. These models try to represent knowledge about this conceptual domain, by using ontologies, meta-ontologies, and meta-models. Most of such models fail to describe some issues: the elements belonging either to natural or controlled language, the transformation of natural language into controlled language in the requirements elicitation process made by the analysts, and the relationship between structural and dynamic elements in the process.

In this Chapter, we proposed a model for knowledge representation of the transformation process from a natural language discourse into controlled language specifications (within the context of the requirements elicitation process) by using pre-conceptual schemas. The model helps analysts to systematically understand the requirements elicitation process by taking into account both the dynamic and structural aspects of requirements. In the model, we defined the behavior and functionality of the aforementioned transformation process.

In the proposed knowledge representation model, the following two kinds of structures are shown: functional structure and logical structure of the transformation process. The requirements elicitation process can be performed, based on the structural features in the model.

6. Acknowledgment

This work is founded by the Vicerrectoría de Investigación from both the Universidad de Medellín and the Universidad Nacional de Colombia, under the project: "Método de transformación de lenguaje natural a lenguaje controlado para la obtención de requisitos, a partir de documentación técnica."

7. References

Andrade, J., Ares, J., García, R., Pazos, J., Rodríguez, S., & Silva, A. (2003). A methodological framework for generic conceptualization: problem-sensitivity in software engineering. *Information and Software Technology*, Vol. 46, No. 10, (August 2004), pp. (635–649), 0950-5849

Berry, D. M. (2003) Natural language and requirements engineering - Nu?, In: *CSD & SE Program University of Waterloo*, 20-05-2011, Available from: http://www.ifi.unizh.ch/groups/req/IWRE/papers&presentations/Berry.pdf

Assmann, U., Zschaler, S., & Wagner, G. (2006). *Ontologies, Metamodels, and the Model-Driven Paradigm* (first edition), Springer, 978-3-540-34517-6, New York

Chomsky, N. (1965). Aspects of the Theory of Syntax. MIT Press, Cambridge, MA

Dardenne, A., Fickas, S., & van Lamsweerde, A. (1991). Goal-directed Concept Acquisition in Requirements Elicitation. *Proceedings of the 6th international workshop on Software specification and design*, 0-8186-2320-9, Italia, October 1991

Demitrio, D. (2005) *Framework para Elicitación Automática de Conocimientos*, Tesis Magíster en Ingeniería de software, Facultad de Informática Universidad Nacional de La Plata, Retrieved from http://postgrado.info.unlp.edu.ar/Carrera/Magister/Ingenieria%20de%20Software/Tesis/Daniel%20Demitrio.pdf

Dzung, D. & Ohnishi, A. (2009). Ontology-based Reasoning in Requirements Elicitation. *Seventh IEEE International Conference on Software Engineering and Formal Methods*, 978-0-7695-3870-9, Hanoi, November 2009

Falbo, R.A., Arantes, D.O., & Natali, A.C.C. (2004) Integrating knowledge management and groupware in a software development environment. *Proceedings of the International Conference on Practical Aspects of Knowledge Management*, 978-3-540-24088-4, Vienna, Austria, December 2004

Hu, B., He, K., Liang, P., & Li, R. (2010) REMO: A RGPS-based Requirements Modeling Process for Service Oriented Architecture. *Proceedings of Sixth International Conference on Networked Computing and Advanced Information Management (NCM)*, 978-1-4244-7671-8, Seoul, September 2010

Jiang T. & Li, M. (1998). Formal Grammars and Languages. In Handbook on Algorithms and Theory of Computation. Editor: Mikhail J. Atallah, November 1998

Kaiya, H. & Saeki, M. (2006). Using Domain Ontology as Domain Knowledge for Requirements Elicitation. *Proceedings of the 14th IEEE International Requirements Engineering Conference (RE'06)*, 0-7695-2555-5, Minessota USA, September 2006.

Leite, J.C. (1987). *A survey on requirements analysis*. Department of Information and Computer Science, Advanced Software Engineering Project Technical Report RTP071, California, Irvine

Li, K., Dewar, R.G., & Pooley, R.J. (2003) *Requirements capture in natural language problem statements*, Heriot-Watt University. Retrieved from http://www.macs.hw.ac.uk:8080/techreps/docs/files/HW-MACS-TR-0023.pdf

Mitamura, T. & Nyberg, E. (1995). Controlled English for Knowledge Based Machine Translation: Experience with the KANT System, *Proceedings of the International Conference on Theoretical and Methodological Issues in Machine Translation (TMI)*, Belgium, July 1995

Robertson, S., & Robertson, J. (2006). *Mastering the Requirements Process* (second edition), Addison Wesley, New Jersey

Ruohonen, K. (2009). Formal Languages. In lecture notes for the TUT course "Formaalit kielet". Available on http://math.tut.fi/~ruohonen/FL.pdf

Rubin, E. (2009) *Domain Knowledge Representation in Information Systems*, Thesis of Doctor of Philosophy, University of British Columbia, Retrieved from https://circle.ubc.ca/handle/2429/15229

Seidewitz, Ed. (2003) What models mean. *IEEE Software*, Vol. 20, No. 5, (September 2003), pp. 26-32, 0740-7459

Wei, L., Ke-Qing, H., Kui, Z., & Jian, W. (2008) Combining Domain-Driven Approach with Requirement Assets for Networked Software Requirements Elicitation. *Proceedings of IEEE International Conference on Semantic Computing*, 978-0-7695-3279-0, California, August 2008

Zapata, C.M., Gelbukh, A., & Arango, F. (2006). Pre-conceptual Schema: A Conceptual-Graph-Like Knowledge Representation for Requirements Elicitation, *Lecture Notes in Computer Science*, Vol. 4293, pp. 17-27, 0302-9743

Zapata, C.M., Giraldo, G.L., & Londoño, S. (2011). Executable pre-conceptual schemas, *Revista Avances en Sistemas e Informática*, Vol.7 No.3, pp. 15-23, Medellín, December 2010

Zapata, C.M., Giraldo, G.L., & Mesa, J.E. (2010). A Proposal of Meta-Ontology for Requirements Elicitation, *Ingeniare. Revista chilena de ingeniería*, Vol. 18, No. 1, August 2010, pp. 26-37, 0718-3305

Section 3

Usage of Representations

6

Intelligent Information Access Based on Logical Semantic Binding Method

Rabiah A. Kadir[1], T.M.T. Sembok[2] and Halimah B. Zaman[2]
[1]*Universiti Putra Malaysia /Faculty of Computer Science and IT*
[2]*Univeristi Kebangsaan Malaysia /Faculty of Science and IT*
Malaysia

1. Introduction

The idea of the computer system capable of simulating understanding with respect to reading a document and answering questions pertaining to it has attracted researchers since the early 1970s. Currently, the information access has received increased attention within the natural language processing (NLP) community as a means to develop and evaluate robust question answering methods. Most recent work has stressed the value of information access as a challenge in terms of their targeting successive skill levels of human performance and the existence of independently developed scoring algorithm and human performance measures. It is an exciting research implementation in natural language understanding, because it requires broad-coverage techniques and semantic knowledge which can be used to determine the strength of understanding the natural language in computer science.

In 2003, MITRE Corporation defined a new research paradigm for natural language processing (NLP) by implementing question answering system on reading comprehension. Reading comprehension offers a new challenge and a human-centric evaluation paradigm for human language technology. It is an exciting testbed for research in natural language understanding towards the information access research problem.

The current state-of-the-art development in computer-based language understanding makes reading comprehension system as a good project (Hirschman et al., 1999). It can be a valuable state-of-the-art tool to access natural language understanding. It has been proven by series of work on question answering for reading comprehension task, and it reported an accuracy of 36.3% (Hirschman et al., 1999) on answering the questions in the test of stories. Subsequently, the work of Charniak et al. (2000), Riloff & Thelen (2000), Ng et al. (2000) and Bashir et al. (2004) achieved 41%, 39.8%, 23.6% and 31.6%-42.8% accuracy, respectively. However, all of the above systems used a simple bag-of word matching, bag-of verb stem, hand-crafted heuristic rules, machine learning and advanced BOW and BOV approach. In contrast, this topic will discuss a logic representation and logical deduction approach for an inference. We aim to expand upon proposed logical formalisms towards semantic for question answering rather than just on surface analysis. Set of words, lexical and semantic clues, feature vector and a list of word token were utilized for knowledge representation in this approach.

This topic describes a method for natural language understanding that concerned with the problem of generating an automated answer for open-ended question answering processes that involve open-ended questions (ie. WHO, WHAT, WHEN, WHERE and WHY). The problem of generating an automated answer involves the context of sophisticated knowledge representation, reasoning, and inferential processing. Here, an existing resolution theorem prover with the modification of some components will be explained based on experiments carried out such as: knowledge representation, and automated answer generation. The answers to the questions typically refer to a string in the text of a passage and it only comes from the short story associated with the question, even though some answers require knowledge beyond the text in the passage. To provide a solution to the above problem, the research utilizes world knowledge to support the answer extraction procedure and broadening the scope of the answer, based on the theory of cognitive psychology (Lehnert, 1981, Ram & Moorman, 2005). The implementation used the backward-chaining deduction reasoning technique of an inference for knowledge based which are represented in simplified logical form. The knowledge based representation known as Pragmatic Skolemized Clauses, based on first order predicate logic (FOPL) using Extended Definite Clause Grammar (X-DCG) parsing technique to represent the semantic formalism.

This form of knowledge representation implementation will adopt a translation strategy which involves noun phrase grammar, verb phrase grammar and lexicon. However, the translation of stored document will only be done partially based on the limited grammar lexicon. The queries will be restricted to verb and noun phrase form to particular document. The restriction adopted in the query is appropriate, since the objective is to acquire inductive reasoning between the queries and document input. Logical-linguistic representation is applied and the detailed translation should be given special attention. This chapter deals with question answering system where the translation should be as close as possible to the real meaning of the natural language phrases in order to give an accurate answer to a question. The aim of the translation is to produce a good logical model representation that can be applied to information access process and retrieve an accurate answer. This means that logical-linguistic representation of semantic theory chosen is practically correct for the intended application.

The representation of questions and answers, and reasoning mechanisms for question answering is of concern in this chapter. To achieve a question answering system that is capable of generating the automatic answers for all types of question covered, implementation of logical semantic binding with its argument into existing theorem prover technique will describe in this chapter. Different types of questions require the use of different strategies to find the answer. A semantic model of question understanding and processing is needed, one that will recognize equivalent questions, regardless of the words, syntactic inter-relations or idiomatic forms. The process of reasoning in generating an automated answer began with the execution of resolution theorem proving. Then, the answer extraction proceeded with logical semantic binding approach to continue tracking the relevant semantic relation rules in knowledge base, which contained the answer key in skolem constant form that can be bounded. A complete relevant answer is defined as a set of skolemize clauses containing at least one skolem constant that is shared and bound to each other. The reasoning technique adopted by the system to classify answers, can be classed into two types: satisfying and hypothetical answers. Both classes were formally distinguished based on its answers; either explicitly or implicitly as stated in the text. The goal of using logical semantic binding approach over logical forms has allow for more complex cases, such as in *Why* question where the information extracted is an implicit context from a text passage. The types of questions conducted using this approach are considered as causal antecedent, causal consequent, instrumental or procedural, concept completion, judgemental and feature specification.

The enhancement of logical-linguistic also depends on the discourse understanding from the external knowledge as an additional input in order to understand the text query and produce as its output some description or hypernyms of the information conveyed by the text. World knowledge is a knowledge about the world, that is, particularly referred to the experience or compilations of experience with other information that are not referring to a particular passage that is being asked and it would be true in real world. Real world knowledge refers to the type of knowledge from the end-user, the architectural or implementation knowledge from the software developer and other levels of knowledge as well. World knowledge is used to support the information extraction procedure and to broaden the scope of information access based on the theory of cognitive psychology (Ram & Moorman, 2005). However, several research which started in 2001, tried to exploit world knowledge to support the information extraction (Golden & Goldman, 2001; Ferro et al., 2003).

Information access task is retrieves a set of most relevant answer literal for a query is attempted. Therefore, binding are performed between the query given and the stored documents that are represented in Pragmatic Skolemize Clauses logical form. This chapter presents a comprehensive discussion of how logical semantic binding approach is practical to access the information semantically.

2. Syntax-semantic formalism

In addition to handling the semantic of a language which involves in ascertaining the meaning of a sentence, this section describes the nature of reading comprehension that includes the understanding of a story. Generally, the understanding of a document can be deciphered based on case-by-case sentences. This can be done by sentence understanding through the study of context-independent meaning within individual sentence which must include event, object, properties of object, and the thematic role relationship between the event and the object in the sentences. Based on this theory of sentence understanding, an experiment was executed based on logical linguistics and DCG was chosen as the basis of semantic translation.

2.1 Document understanding

Document understanding focused on inferential processing, common sense reasoning, and world knowledge which are required for in-depth understanding of documents. These efforts are concerned with specific aspects of knowledge representation, an inference technique, and question types (Hirschman et al. 1999; Lehnert et al. 1983; Grohe & Segoyfin 2000).

The challenge to computer systems on reading a document and demonstrating understanding through question answering was first addressed by Charniak (1972) in Dalmas et al. (2004). This work showed the diversity of both logical and common sense reasoning which needed to be linked together with what was said explicitly in the story or article and then to answer the questions about it. More recent works have attempted to systematically determine the feasibility of reading comprehension as a research challenge in terms of targeting successive skill levels of human performance for open domain question answering (Hirschman et al. 1999; Riloff & Thelen 2000; Charniak et al. 2000; Ng et al., 2000; Wang et al. 2000; Bashir et al. 2004; Clark et al. 2005). The work initiated by Hirschman (1999), also expressed the same data set. Earlier works from years 1999 until 2000 introduced the 'bag-of-word' to represent the sentence structure. Ferro et al. (2003) innovated knowledge diagram and conceptual graph to their sentence structure respectively. This thesis, however, shall focus on the logical relationship approach in handling syntactic and semantic variants to sentence structure. This approach will be discussed thoroughly in the following sections and chapters.

The input of document understanding is divided into individual sentences. Intersentential interactions, such as reference is an important aspect of language understanding and the task of sentence understanding. The types of knowledge that are used in analyzing an individual sentence (such as syntactic knowledge) are quite different from the kind of knowledge that comes into play in intersentential analysis (such as knowledge of discourse structure).

2.1.1 Sentence understanding

A sentence can be characterised as a linear sequence of words in a language. The output desired from a sentence understander must include the event, object, properties of object, and the thematic role relationship between the event and the object in the sentence (Ram & Moorman 2005). In addition, it is also desirable to include the syntactic parse structure of the sentence. A fundamental problem in mapping the input to the output in terms of showing sentence understanding is the high degree of ambiguity in natural language. Several types of knowledge such as syntactic and semantic knowledge can be used to resolve ambiguities and identify unique mappings from the input to the desired output. Some of the different forms of knowledge relevant for natural language understanding (Allen 1995; Doyle 1997; Mahesh 1995; Mueller 2003; Dowty et al. 1981; Capel et al. 2002; Miles 1997) are as follows:

i. Morphological knowledge - this concerns how words are constructed from more basic meaning units called morphemes. A morpheme is the primitive unit of meaning in a language. For example, the meaning of word *friendly* is derivable from the meaning of the noun *friend* and the suffix *-ly*, which transforms a noun into an adjective.
ii. Syntactic knowledge - this concerns how words can be put together to form correct sentences and determines what structural role each word plays in the sentence and what phrases are subparts of other phrases.
iii. Semantic knowledge - this concerns what words mean and how these meanings combine in sentences to form sentence meanings. This involves the study of context-independent meaning.
iv. Pragmatic knowledge - this concerns how sentences are used in different situations and how its use affects the interpretation of a sentence.
v. Discourse knowledge - this concerns how the immediately preceding sentences affect the interpretation of the next sentence. This information is especially important for interpreting pronouns and temporal aspects of the information conveyed.

vi. World knowledge - this includes the general knowledge pertaining to the structure of the world that the language user must have in order to, for example, maintain a conversation. It includes what each language user must know about the other user's beliefs and goals.

Recognizing Textual Entities

There is various textual entities in a document that must be recognized. Following are an examples of textual entities:

Words: *was, pushed*

Phrases: *freight elevator, buffer springs*

Times: *yesterday,* last week

Places: *downtown Brooklyn,* East End

Names: *John J. Hug, Mary-Ann*

Numbers: *$1,200, 12 inches*

These entities may be detected using various techniques. Regular expressions and pattern matching are often used (Mueller 1999; Zamora 2004; Li & Mitchell 2003). For example, in the system ThoughtTreasure developed by Mueller (1998), provides text agents for recognizing lexical entries, names, places, times, telephone numbers, media objects, products, prices, and email headers.

Anaphora

A document understanding system must resolve various anaphoric entities on the objects to which they refer (Mitkov 1994). Examples of anaphoric entities are pronouns (*she, they*), possessive determiners (*my, his*), and arbitrary constructions involving the following:

Adjectives (*the pink milk*)

Genitives (*Jim's milk*)

Indefinite and definite articles (*an elevator salesman, the shaft, the buffer springs*)

Names (*John J. Hug*)

Relative clauses (*the $1,200 they had forced him to give them, the milk that fell on the floor*)

Anaphora resolution is a difficult problem to tackle. However, in this research, the anaphora resolution will be attained by adding world knowledge as an input to the original passage.

Commonsense Knowledge Bases

A commonsense knowledge base is a useful resource for a document understanding system. Most importantly, the commonsense knowledge base can evolve along with the document understanding system. Whenever a piece of commonsense knowledge comes in handy in the document understanding system, it can be added to the database. The database can then be expanded, thus becomes useful for the document understanding application.

The above databases have various advantages and disadvantages such as WordNet (Fellbaum 1998), which was designed as a lexical rather than a conceptual database. This means that it lacks links between words in different syntactic categories. For example, there is no link between the noun *creation* and the verb *create*.

2.2 First-order predicate logic syntax-semantic formalism

A crucial component of understanding involves computing a representation of the meaning of sentences and texts. The notion of representation has to be defined earlier, because most words have multiple meanings known as senses (Fillmore & Baker 2000; Sturgill & Segre 1994; Vanderveen & Ramamoorthy 1997). For example, the word *cook* can be sensed as a verb and a sense as a noun; and still can be sensed as a noun, verb, adjective, and adverb. This ambiguity would inhibit the system from making appropriate inferences needed to model understanding.

To represent meaning, a more precised language is required. The tools to do this can be derived from mathematics and logic. This involves the use of formally specified representation languages. Formal languages are comprised of very simple building blocks. The most fundamental is the notion of an atomic symbol, which is distinguishable from any other atomic symbol that is simply based on how it is written.

2.2.1 Syntax

It is common, when using formal language in computer science or mathematical logic, to abstain from details of concrete syntax in term of strings of symbols and instead work solely with parse trees. The syntactic expressions of FOPLs consist of terms, atomic formulas, and well-formed formulas (wffs) (Shapiro 2000; Dyer 1996). Terms consist of individual constants, variables and functional terms. Functional terms, atomic formula, and wffs are nonatomic symbol structures. The atomic symbols of FOPLs are individual constants, variable, function symbols, and predicate symbols. Individual Constants comprised the following:

i. Any letter of the alphabet (preferable early)
ii. Any (such) letter with a numeric subscript
iii. Any character string not containing blanks or other punctuation marks. For example, *Christopher, Columbia.*

Variables comprised the following:

i. Any letter of the alphabet (preferably late)
ii. Any (such) letter with a numeric subscript. For example, *x, xy, g/.*

Function Symbols comprised the following:

i. Any letter of the alphabet (preferably early middle)
ii. Any (such) letter with a numeric subscript
iii. Any character string not containing blanks. For example, *read_sentence, gensym.*

Predicate Symbols comprised the following:

i. Any letter of the alphabet (preferably late middle)
ii. Any (such) letter with a numeric subscript
iii. Any character string not containing blanks. For example, *noun, prep.*

Each function symbol and predicate symbol must have a particular arity. The arity need not be shown explicitly if it is understood. In any specific predicate logic language individual constant, variables, function symbols, and predicate symbols must be disjointed.

Syntax of Terms: Every individual constant and every variable are considered a term.

If f^n is a function symbol of arity n, and $t1, \ldots, tn$ are terms, then $f^n(t1, \ldots, tn)$ is a (functional) term.

example:

free_vars(C,FreeVars),
free_vars([C0 | Cs], Fvs, FVs)

Syntax of Atomic Formulas:

If P^n is a predicate symbol of arity n, and $t1, \ldots, tn$ are terms, then $P^n(t1, \ldots, tn)$ is an atomic formula.

example:

proper_noun(male, christopher).
noun(bear, bears).

Syntax of Well-Formed Formulas (Wffs): Every atomic formula is a wffs. If P is a wff, then so is $\neg P$. if P and Q are wffs, then so are $(P \wedge Q)$, $(P \vee Q)$, $(P \Rightarrow Q)$, and $(P \Leftrightarrow Q)$. If P is a wffs and x is a variable, then $\forall x(P)$ and $\exists x(P)$ are wffs. $\forall$ is called the universal quantifier. $\exists$ is called the existential quantifier. P is called the scope of quantification.

Parentheses are not accounted with when there is no ambiguity, in which case $\forall$ and $\exists$ will have the highest priority, then $\wedge$ and $\vee$ will have higher priority than $\Rightarrow$, which, in turn will have higher priority than $\Leftrightarrow$. For example, $\forall x P(x) \wedge \exists y Q(y) \Leftrightarrow \neg P(a) \Rightarrow Q(b)$ will be written instead of $((\forall x(P(x)) \wedge \exists y(Q(y))) \Leftrightarrow (\neg P(a) \Rightarrow Q(b)))$.

Every concurrence of x in P, not on the scope of some occurrence of $\forall x$ or $\exists x$, is said to be free in P and bound in $\forall xP$ and $\exists xP$. Every occurrence of every variable other than x that is free in P is also free in $\forall xP$ and $\exists xP$. A wff with at least one free variable is called open, no free variables are called closed, and an expression with no variables is called ground.

Syntactic Category: Below, is a syntactic category of English fragment covered by DCG that is given by the set SynCat (Partee 2006; Partee 2001):

SynCat = {S, NP, VP, DET, CNP, ProperN, ADJ, REL, CN, TV, IV, PP}

The elements of SynCat are symbols representing the English categories as follows:

S: sentences

NP: noun phrases

VP: verb phrases

DET: determiners

CNP: common noun phrases

ProperN: proper nouns

ADJ: adjectives

REL: relative clauses

CN: common nouns

TV: transitive verbs

IV: intransitive verbs

PrepP: prepositional phrase

2.2.2 Semantic

Although the intensional semantics of a FOPL depend on the domain being formalized, and the extensional semantics depend also on a particular situation, specification on the types of entities is usually given as the intensional and the extensional semantic of FOPL expressions.

The usual semantic of FOPL assumes a Domain, *D*, of individuals, function on individuals, sets of individuals, and relations on individuals. Let *I* be the set of all individuals in the Domain *D*.

Semantic of Atomic Symbols

Individual Constants:

If *a* is an individual constants, [*a*] is some particular individual in I.

Function Symbols:

If f^n is a function symbol of arity *n*, $[f^n]$ is some particular function in D,

$$[f^n]: \mathrm{I} \times \ldots \times \mathrm{I} \rightarrow \mathrm{I} \ (n \text{ times})$$

Predicate Symbols:

If P^1 is a unary predicate symbol, $[P^1]$ is more particular subset of I. If P^n is a predicate symbols of arity *n*, $[P^n]$ is some particular subset of the relation I × … × I (*n* times).

Semantic of Ground Terms

Individual Constants:

If *a* is an individual constant, [*a*] is some particular individual in I.

Functional Terms:

If f^n is a function symbol of arity *n*, and $t_1, \ldots, t_n$ are ground terms, then $[f^n(t_1, \ldots, t_n)] = [f^n]([t_1], \ldots, [t_n])$.

Semantic of Ground Atomic Formulas

i. If P^1 is unary predicate symbol, and *t* is a ground term, then $[P^1(t)]$ is True if $[t] \in [P^1]$, and False otherwise.

ii. If P^n is an n-ary predicate symbol, and $t1, \ldots, tn$ are ground terms, then $[P^n(t_1, \ldots, t_n)]$ is True if $\langle[t_1], \ldots, [t_n]\rangle \in [P^n]$, and False otherwise.

Semantic of Wffs

i. If P is a ground wff, then $[\neg P]$ is True if $[P]$ is False, otherwise, it is False.
ii. If P and Q are ground wffs, then $[P \wedge Q]$ is True if $[P]$ is True and $[Q]$ is True, otherwise, it is False.
iii. If P and Q are ground wffs, then $[P \vee Q]$ is False if $[P]$ is False and $[Q]$ is False, otherwise, it is True.
iv. If P and Q are ground wffs, then $[P \Rightarrow Q]$ is False if $[P]$ is True and $[Q]$ is False, otherwise, it is True.
v. If P and Q are ground wffs, then $[P \Leftrightarrow Q]$ is True if $[P]$ and $[Q]$ are both True or both False, otherwise, it is False.
vi. $[\forall xP]$ is True if $[P\{t/x\}]$ is True for every ground term, t. Otherwise, it is False.
vii. $\exists xP]$ is True if there is some ground term, t such that $[P\{t/x\}]$ is True. Otherwise, it is False.

Semantic Types of FOPL

Every English expression of a particular syntactic category is translated into semantic expression of a corresponding type. The semantic types are defined as in Table 1.

Syntactic Category	Semantic Type	Expressions
S	t	sentences
ProperN	e	names (*Chris*)
CN(P)	$e \to t$	common noun phrases (*cat*)
NP	e	"e-type" or "referential" NPs (*Chris, the president*)
	$e \to t$	NPs as predicates (*an animal, a president*)
ADJ(P)	$e \to t$	predicative adjectives (*pretty, big*)
REL	$e \to t$	relative clauses (*who(m) read the book*)
VP, IV	$e \to t$	verb phrases, intransitive verbs (*read the book, is big*)
TV	$<e, e> \to t$	transitive verbs (*read, lives*)
is	none	temporary treatment: pretend it is not there
DET	$e \to t$ to e	universal quantifier (*the*)
	$e \to t$ to $e \to t$	existential quantifier (*a*)

Table 1. Semantic Types of Syntactic Category in FOPL

where:

e is a type, representing object of sort entity

t is a type, representing truth values

Based on Table 1, some of the compositional semantics are as follows:

S: Denotes a truth value, relative to an assignment of the values to free variables

NP: Is of two kinds. First, referential NP formed with definite article *the* is of type e and denotes an individual, as in *The boy writes*. Second, Predicate NP formed with indefinite article *a* is of type e → t and denotes a set, as in *Christopher is a boy*. There are lexical NPs of the referential kind, including proper nouns (*George, Robin*) and indexed pronoun (he_i) which will be interpreted as individual variable x_i.

CN, CNP, ADJ, VP, IV, REL: All of type e → t, one-place predicates, denoting sets of individuals. For this type, the parser will freely go back and forth between sets and their characteristic function, treating them as equivalent.

TV: Is a type of <e, e> → t, a function from ordered pairs to truth values, i.e. the characteristic function of a set of ordered pairs. A 2-place relation is represented as a set of ordered pairs, and any set can be represented by its characteristic function.

DET (a): Form predicate nominals as an identity function on sets. It applies to any set as argument and gives the same set as value. For example, the set of individuals in the model who are student, <a student> = | | a | | (| | student | |) = | | student | |

DET (the): Form e-type NPs as the *iota* operator, which applies to a set and yields an entity if its presuppositions are satisfied, otherwise it is undefined. It is defined as follows:

| | ια | | = *d* if there is one and only one entity *d* in the set denoted by | | α | |

| | ια | | is undefined otherwise

For example: the set of animals who Chris love contains only Pooh, then *the animal who Chris loves* will denotes Pooh. If Chris loves no animal or loves more than one animal, then *the animal who Chris loves* is undefined, i.e. has no semantic value.

Semantic Representation of English Expression in FOPL

Table 2 shows the semantic representation or syntax-semantic formalism that represents a number of simple basic English expressions and phrases, along with a way of representing the formula in Prolog.

Syntactic Category	**Semantic Representation**	**As written in Prolog**
Christopher (PN)	**logical constant** *Christopher*	christopher
animal (CN)	**1-place predicate** *(λx)animal(x)*	X^animal(x)
young (ADJ)	**1-place predicate** *(λx)young(x)*	X^young(x)
young animal (CN with ADJ)	1-place predicate joined by 'and' *(λx)young(x)∧ animal(x)*	X^young(X),animal(X)
writes (TV)	**2-place predicate** *(λy)(λx)writes(x,y)*	Y^X^writes(X,Y)
read (IV)	**1-place predicate** *(λx)read(x)*	X^read(X)
is an animal (Copular VP)	**1-place predicate** *(λx)animal(x)*	X^animal(x)
with (PrepP)	**1-place predicate** *(λy)(λx)with(x,y)*	Y^X^with(X,Y)

Table 2. Representation of Simple Words and Phrases

The basic expression *animal* and *young*, is a category of CN and ADJ, are translated into predicate (λx)animal(x) and (λx)young(x) respectively. However, the word *young* is considered as a property, not as a thing. This has to do with the distinction between sense and reference. A common noun such as *owl* can refer to many different individuals, so its translation is the property that these individuals share. The reference of *animal* in any particular utterance is the value of *x* that makes animal(x) true.

These are different with phrases, such as verbs which require different numbers of arguments. For example, the intransitive verb *read* is translated into one-place predicate (λx)read(x). Meanwhile, a transitive verb such as *writes* translates to a two-place predicate such as (λy)(λx)writes(x,y). The copula (*is*) has no semantic representation. The representation for *is an animal* is the same as for *animal,* (λx)animal(x).

Basic expressions can be combined to form complex expressions through unification process, which can be accomplished by arguments on DCG rules. The following shows the illustration of combining several predicates in the N^1 by joining them with ∧ (and) symbol (Covington 1994). From

young = (λx)young(x)
smart = (λx)smart(x)
animal = (λx)animal(x)

then, the complex expression will be presented as:

young smart animal = (λx)(young(x)∧ smart(x)∧ animal(x))

DCG rules for the lexicon entries for the particular words:

```
adj(X^young(X)) --> [young].
adj(X^smart(X)) --> [smart].
adj(X^green(X)) --> [green].
noun(X^animal)) --> [animal].
noun(X^cat)) --> [cat].
```

The syntactic and translation rules of DCG are equivalent to the rules defined in PS. For the PS rules, the semantic of the whole N^1 is as follows:

```
n1(Sem) --> n(Sem).
```

and below is the rule that combines an adjective with an N^1:

```
n1(X^(P,Q)) --> adj(X^P), n1(X^Q).
```

Through these implementation rules, basic English expressions are combined to form complex expressions, and at the same time translated into FOPL expressions using Prolog unification process. The implementation rule for the determiner in natural language corresponds to the quantifiers in formal logic. The determiner (DET) can be combined with a common noun (CN) to form a noun phrase. The determiner or quantifier ∃ normally goes with the connective ∧, and ∀ with →. The sentence *An animal called Pooh* contains quantifier and its semantic representation is presented as *(∃x)(animal(x)^called(x,Pooh))*. In this case, Prolog notation is written as exist(X,animal(X),called(X,Pooh)).

3. Knowledge representation

Knowledge representation is the symbolic representation aspects of some closed universe of discourse. They are four properties in a good system for knowledge representations in our domain, which are representation adequacy, inferential adequacy, inferential efficiency, acquisition efficiency (Mohan, 2004). The objective of knowledge representations is to make knowledge explicit. Knowledge can be shared less ambiguously in its explicit form and this became especially important when machines started to be applied to facilitate knowledge management. Knowledge representation is a multidisciplinary subject that applies theories and techniques from three other fields (Sowa, 2000); logic, ontology, and computation.

Logic and Ontology provide the formalization mechanisms required to make expressive models easily sharable and computer aware. Thus, the full potential of knowledge accumulations can be exploited. However, computers play only the role of powerful processors of more or less rich information sources. It is important to remark that the possibilities of the application of actual knowledge representation techniques are enormous. Knowledge is always more than the sum of its parts and knowledge representation provides the tools needed to manage accumulations of knowledge.

To solve the complex problems encountered in artificial intelligent, it needs both a large amount of knowledge and some mechanisms for manipulating that knowledge to create solution to new problems. Putting human knowledge in a form with which computers can reason it is needed to translate from such 'natural' language form, to some artificial language called symbolic logic. Logic representation has been accepted as a good candidate for representing the meaning of natural language sentences (Bratko, 2001) and also allows more subtle semantic issues to be dealt with. A complete logical representation of open-ended queries and the whole text of passages need an English grammar and lexicon (Specht, 1995; Li, 2003). The output requested for reading comprehension task from each input English phrase must include the event, object, properties of object, and the thematic role relationship between the event and the object in the sentence (Ram & Moorman, 2005).

The translation strategy involves noun phrase grammar, verb phrase grammar and lexicon which are built entirely for the experiment purposes. However, the translation of stored passages will only be done partially based on the limited grammar lexicon. The queries will be restricted to verb and noun phrase form. The restriction adopted in the query is appropriate, since the objective of the reading comprehension task in this research, is to acquire deductive reasoning between the queries and passage input. Therefore, this can be done using verb and noun phrase. Some evidence has been gathered to support this view (Ferro et al., 2003; Bashir et al., 2004).

This work deals with question answering system where the translation should be as close as possible to the real meaning of the natural language phrases in order to give an accurate answer to a question. The query given and the stored passages are represented in PragSC logical form. In general, the translation of the basic expressions or English words into semantic templates are based on their syntactic categories as shown in Table 3, where, X stand for object CN, Y stand for object CN or ADJ, 'predicate' stands for the English word, λ stand for exists or all, and 'app-op' stand for & or $\rightarrow$.

Categories	Template Forms
CN	[X | predicate(X)]
TV	[[X | A], Y | A & predicate(X, Y)]
IV	[[X | A] | A & predicate(X)]
ADJ	[X | predicate(X)]
DET	[[X | A],[X | C] | λ (X, A app-op C)]
Prep	[[X | A], Y | A & predicate(X, Y)]
AUX	Temporary treatment as in FOPL: pretend it is not there

Table 3. Syntax-semantic formalism of english fragment

The syntax and semantic formalism to define the notion of representation due to shows the meaning of a sentence. A new logical form, known as PragSC has been proposed for designing an effective logical model representation that can be applied to question answering process and retrieve an accurate answer. The main advantage of logical representation in this problem is its ability to gives names to the constituents such as noun phrase and verb phrase. This means that it recognizes a sentence as more than just a string of words. Unlike template and keyword approach, it can describe recursive structure, means the longer sentence have shorter sentences within them. Figure 1 illustrates the example of English phrase (an animal called pooh) translation:

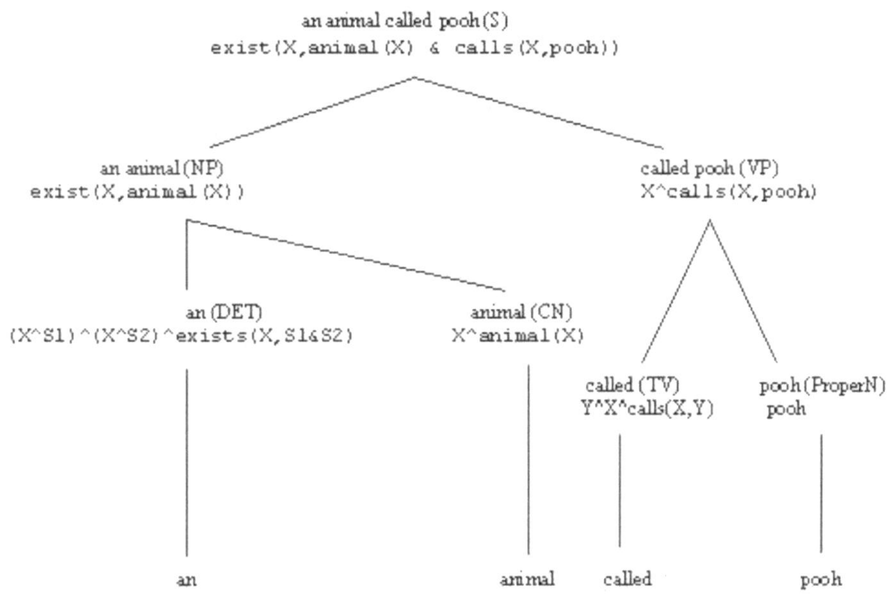

Fig. 1. Semantic tree

Each Natural language text is directly translated into PragSC form which can be used as a complete content indicator of a passage or query. The passages and queries are processed to form their respective indexes through the translation and normalization process which are composed of simplification processes. The similarity values between the passage and query indexes are computed using the skolemize clauses binding of resolution theorem prover technique. This representation is used to define implication rules for any particular question answering and for defining synonym and hypernym words.

A query is translated into its logical representation as documents are translated. This representation is then simplified and partially reduced. The resulting representation of the query is then ready to be proven with the passage representation and their literal answers are retrieved. The proving is performed through uncertain implication process where predicates are matched and propagated, which finally gives a literal answer value between the query and the passage. In the following section, a more detailed description of the query process and its literal answer value will be discussed.

4. Logical semantic binding inference engine

Work on open-ended question answering requires sophisticated linguistic analysis, including discourse understanding and deals with questions about nearly everything, and not only relying on general ontologies and world knowledge. To achieve a question answering system that is capable of generating the automatic answers for all types of question covered, implementation of skolemize clauses binding with its argument into existing theorem prover technique is introduced. Automated theorem proving served as an early model for question answering in the field of AI (Wang et al., 2000). Whereas, skolemize clauses binding approach over logical forms has allow for more complex cases, such as in Why question where the information extracted is an implicit context from a text passage. Skolemize clauses binding approach relates how one clause can be bound to others. Using this approach, the proven theorem need only to determine which skolem constant can be applied to, and valid clauses will be produced automatically.

Skolemize clauses binding is designed to work with simplified logical formula that is transformed into Pragmatic Skolem Clauses form. The basic idea is that if the key of skolemize clause match with any skolemize clauses in knowledge base, then both clauses are unified to accumulate the relevant clauses by connecting its normalize skolem constant or atom on the subject side or the object side of another. The normalize skolem constant or atom is a key for answer depending on the phrase structure of the query. Given a key of skolemize clause in negation form and a set of clauses related in knowledge base in an appropriate way, it will generate a set of relevant clauses that is a consequence of this approach. Lets consider the example of English query Why did Chris write two books of his own? to illustrate the idea of skolemize clauses binding.

Example: Why did Chris write two books of his own?

Key skolemize clause:

~write(chris,g15).Unification:

~ write(chris,g15) :- write(chris,g15)

Key of answer (Object):

g15Set of relevant clauses:
two(g15)
book(g15)
his(g9)
own(g9)
of(g15,g9)
write(chris,g15)
two(g15)
book(g15)
famous(g18)
be(likes(tells(g15,it)),g18)

The example considered that write(chris,g15) is the key skolemize clauses. g15 is the key of answer that is used to accumulate the relevant clauses through linking up process either to its subject side or object side.

Implementation of skolem clauses binding is actually more complicated when the clauses contain variables. So two skolemize clauses cannot be unified. In this experiment, the operation involves "normalization" of the variables just enough so that two skolemize clauses are unified. Normalization is an imposition process of giving standards atom to each common noun that exists in each input text passage which was represented as variable during the translation process. The skolem clauses normalization involves X-DCG parsing technique that has been extended with functionality of bi-clausifier. The detail of X-DCG parsing technique has been explained in chapter 5. Skolem constants were generated through the first parsing process. Then, the process of normalization was implemented in second parsing, which is a transformation process identifying two types of skolem constant to differentiate between quantified (f_n) and ground term (g_n) variable names.

Whereas, binding is a term within this experiment, which refers to the process of accumulating relevant clauses by skolem constant or atom connected to any clauses existing in knowledge base. Each skolemize clause is conceived as connected if each pair of clause in it is interrelated by the key answer which consists of a skolem constant or atom. The idea that it should be specific is based on coherent theory which deals with this particular set of phenomena, originated in the 1970s, based on the work in transformational grammar (Peters & Ritchie, 1973; Boy, 1992).

This work was conducted to solve the problem by connecting the key of an answer that has been produced through resolution theorem prover. Skolemize clauses binding technique gives the interrelation of skolemize clauses that could be considered as a relevant answer by connecting its key of answer. To establish this logical inference technique, Figure 2 illustrates the inference engine framework.

An answer is literally generated by negating a query and implementing skolemize clauses binding. This will enable a resolution theorem prover to go beyond a simple "yes" answer by providing a connected skolem constant used to complete a proof. Concurrently, a semantic relation rule is also specified in pragmatic skolemize clauses as a knowledge base representation. In the example provided, this can be seen as binding process proceeds. If the semantic relation rule being searched contains rules that are unified to a question through its skolem constant, the answers will be produced. Consider the following sample as a semantic relation rule used as an illustration that was originally based on a children passage entitled "School Children to Say Pledge" from Remedia Publications.

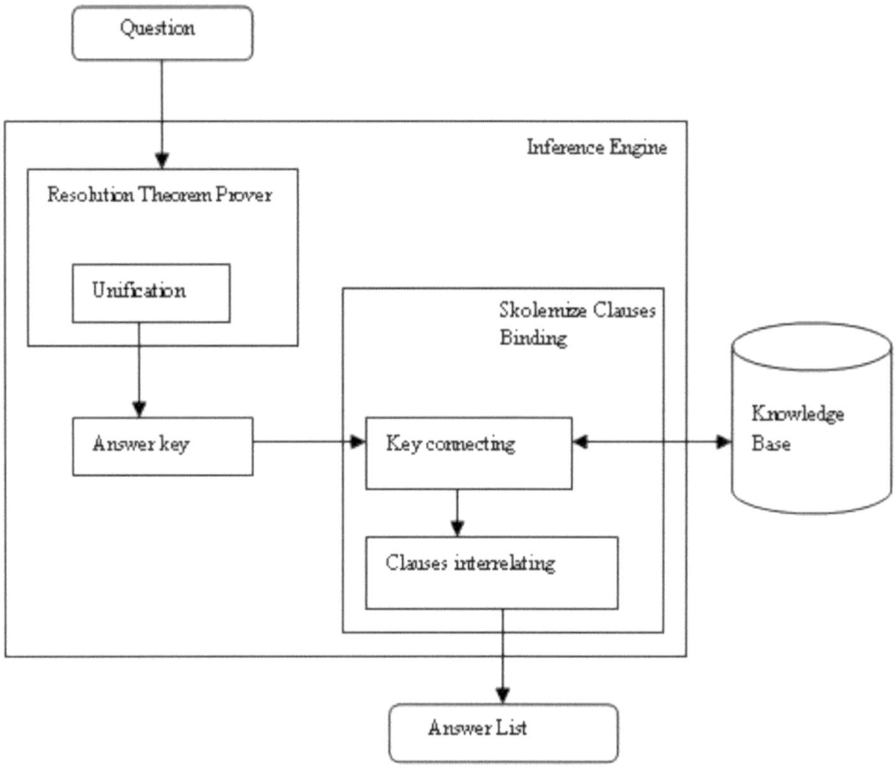

Fig. 2. The architecture of an inference engine framework

Semantic relation rules in PragSC form:

cl([pledge(f25)],[])
cl([young(g37)],[])
cl([people(g37)],[])
cl([proud(g38)],[])
cl([feels(g37,g38)],[])
cl([makes(f25,g37)],[])
cl([writes(r(frances & bellamy),f25)],[])

Given above is the simple semantic relation rules, and the question Why did Frances Bellamy write the pledge?, then, the following logical form of question are produced.

~ pledge(f25) # ~ writes(r(frances & bellamy),f25) # answer(f25)

Based on the above representation, f25 and r(frances & bellamy) is unified with the semantic relation rules in knowledge base;

~ pledge(f25) :- pledge(f25)

~ writes(r(frances & bellamy),f25) :- writes(r(frances & bellamy),f25)

then, bind both entities to any relevant semantic relation rule to find the answer.

a. cl([pledge(f25)],[])
b. cl([young(g37)],[])
c. cl([people(g37)],[])
d. cl([proud(g38)],[])
e. cl([feels(g37,g38)],[])
f. cl([makes(f25,g37)],[])
g. cl([writes(r(frances & bellamy),f25)],[])

The skolemized clauses (a) to (g) are a collection of answer sets that are unified to the question given because each clause is bound with at least one skolem constant. The semantic relation rule base indicates that r(frances & bellamy) is bound to clause (g), meanwhile f25 (pledge) is bound to clause (a) and (g). The system continue tracking any relevant semantic relation rules in knowledge base, which contain skolem constant f25 that can be bounded. In this case clause (f) is picked out. Clause (f) gives more binding process by another skolem constant, g37, represent young people predicate. The process of skolem constant binding was retained until there are no skolem clauses which can be bounded. It is a process of accumulating of relevant clauses by *skolem constant (x)* or *atom* connected to any clauses existing in knowledge base.

$$x \rightarrow P(x,x_1) \wedge P(x_1,x_2) \wedge \ldots \wedge P(x_{n-1},x_n) \wedge P(x_n) \quad (1)$$

The example is motivated by showing what happened when the facts, r(frances & bellamy) and pledge are bound to other clauses or semantic relation rules. Then, the resulting answer is:

makes(f25,g37)
young(g37)
people(g37)
feels(g37,g38)
proud(g38)

All the skolemized clauses were considered as a set of answer that is relevant to the question, and they may be the best information available. Another examples are shown in Table 2. Each example begins with part of a collection of semantic rules in knowledge base, represented in skolemized clauses. In this research, a question Q is represented as a proposition, and a traditional proof initiated by adding the negation of the clause form of Q to a consistent knowledge base K. If an inconsistency is unified, then skolemized clauses binding process proceed to find the relevant answer.

4.1 Relevant answer

A relevant answer to a particular question can be generally defined as an answer that implies all clauses to that question. Relevance for answers has been defined as unifying the skolem constant by the question. In a rule base consisting solely of skolem constants, the unifying of a single skolem constant to a question would be considered a relevant answer. When rules are added, the experiment becomes more complicated. When taxonomic relationship is represented in a rule base, a relevant answer can be defined as an interconnection of all clauses that unify and bind the same skolem constants. Table 4 depicts two examples illustrate the skolemized clauses binding process to extract relevant answer.

	Example 1	**Example 2**
Semantic relation rules (*K*)	cl([now(g1)],[]) cl([new(f1)],[]) cl([faster(f1)],[]) cl([way(f1)],[]), cl([sents(g1,f1)],[]) cl([now(g1)],[]) cl([end(r(pony & express),g1)],[])	cl([two(g46)],[]) cl([book(g46)],[]) cl([own(his)],[]) cl([writes(chris,g46)],[]) cl([famous(g52)],[]) cl([be(like (tells(g46,it)),g52)],[])
Proposition (*Q*)	~ end(r(pony & express),g1) # answer(g1)	~ two(g46)) # ~ book(g46) # ~ writes(chris,g46)) # answer(g46)
Unifying process	~ end(r(pony & express),g1) :- end(r(pony & express),g1)	~ two(g46) :- two(g46) ~ book(g46) :- book(g46) ~ writes(chris,g46) :- writes(chris,g46)
SCB Key connecting	*g1* connecting: now(g1) mail(g1) sents(g1,f1)	*g46* connecting: two(g46) book(g46) be(like (tells(g46,it)),g52)
SCB Clauses interrelating	now(g1) mail(g1) new(f1) faster(f1) way(f1)] sents(g1,f1)	two(g46) book(g46) famous(g52) be(like(tells(g46,it)),g52)

Table 4. Example of question answering process

The first example in Table 4, g1 is considered as a skolem constant to be unified to a skolemized clause in knowledge base, ~ end(r(pony & express),g1) :- end(r(pony & express),g1). Then g1 binds to any skolemized clauses consisting of the same skolem constant, and tracks all possible skolemized clauses in knowledge base by binding skolem constant exists, f1, until all skolem constants bindings are complete. The relevant answer consists of several clauses that are bound by g1. The output is as follows:

sents(g1,f1).
now(g1).
mail(g1).
new(f1).
faster(f1).
way(f1).

Same as the first example, this second example recognised g46 as a skolem constant to be unified to a skolemized clauses in knowledge base which involve more than one clauses to be unified, ~ two(g46) :- two(g46); ~ book(g46) :- book(g46); ~ writes(chris,g46) :- writes(chris,g46). Then, g46 binds to any skolemized clauses consisting of the same skolem constant, and tracks all possible skolemized clauses in knowledge base by binding skolem constant exists, g52, until all skolem constants bindings are complete. The relevant clauses are as follows:

two(g46)
book(g46)
famous(g52)
be(like(tells(g46,it)),g52).

Throughout this experiment, providing information in a form of pragmatic skolemized clauses is just a method to collect the keywords for relevant answers. The issues related to the problem of providing an answer in correct English phrases can be considered another important area of research in question answering. In this research this problem has been considered, but thus far it has taken the form of observations rather than formal theories. This represents an area for further research interest.

5. Intelligent information access

This topic aims is to extract some relevant answers which are classified into satisfying and hypothetical answers. When the idea of an answer is expanded to include all relevant information, question answering may be viewed as a process of searching for and returning of information to a questioner that takes different places in time. As one of the most challenging and important processes of question answering systems is to retrieve the best relevant text excerpts with regard to the question, Ofoghi et al. (2006) proposed a novel approach to exploit not only the syntax of the natural language of the questions and texts, but also the semantics relayed beneath them via a semantic question rewriting and passage retrieval task. Therefore, in our experiment, we used logics description to provide a natural representation and reasoning mechanism to answer a question which is a combination of resolution theorem prover and a new approach called skolemize clauses binding.

On the other hand, external knowledge sources are added in order to give more understanding of text and produce some descriptions of the information conveyed by the text passages. External knowledge sources consist of two components with different roles of usage and motivation. First, world knowledge is used to solve the outstanding problem related to the ambiguity introduced by anaphora and polysemy. Meanwhile, in the second component, hypernyms matching procedure constitute the system in looking for the meaning of superordinates words in the question given. The purpose of this component is to produce a variety of answers based on different ways on how it is asked. This thesis has clearly demonstrated their importance and applicability to question answering, including their relationship to the input passage in natural language. In particular, this thesis is focused on providing detailed formal definition of world knowledge.

Situating a query as a concept in a taxonomic hierarchy makes explicit the relationship among type of questions, and this is an important part of intelligent intelligent extraction. A logical technique solves a constraint satisfaction problem by the combination of two different methods. Logical reasoning applied an inference engine to extract an automatic answer. Logical technique exploits the good properties of different methods by applying them to problems they can efficiently solve. For example, search is efficient when the problem has many solutions, while an inference is efficient in proving unsatisfiability of overconstrained problems.

This logical technique is based on running search over a set of variables and inference over the other ones. In particular, backtracking or some other form of search is executed with a number of variables; whenever a consistent partial assignment over these variable is found, an inference is executed on the remaining variables to check whether this partial assignment can be extended to form a solution based on logical approach. This affects the choice of the variables evaluated by the search. Indeed, once a variable is evaluated, it can be effectively extracted from the knowledge base, restricting all constraints it is involved with in its value. Alternatively, an evaluated variable can be replaced by a skolem constant, one for each constraint, all having a single-value domain. This mixed technique is efficient if the search variables are chosen in a manner where duplicating or deleting them turns the problem into one that can be efficiently solved by inference.

6. Discussion and conclusion

To appreciate fully the significance of the findings of this research, it helps to firstly understand the level of scientific rigor used to guide the formation of conclusions from the research. The experiments are considered complete when the expecting results or findings replicate across previous research and settings. Findings with a high degree of replicability are finally considered as incontrovertible findings and these form the basis for additional research. Each research study within this research domain network usually follows the most rigorous scientific procedures.

The study does not embrace any a priori theory, but represent the linguistic knowledge base into logical formalisms to build up the meaning representation and enforce syntactic and semantic agreements that include all information that are relevant to a question. In a true scientific paradigm, the study is tested in different behaviour or condition which involve two kinds of external knowledge sources. This contrasts with the usual nature of previous researches in the same domain, where none was ever tested against all four conditions as in this study. The detail of the research works and experiences are as follows:

- **Logical Interpreter Process.** The interpreter process, whether it be for translation or interpreting, can be described as decoding the meaning of the source text and re-encoding this meaning in the target representation. In this experiment the target representation is in simplified logical model. To decode the meaning of a text, the translator must first identify its component "interpreter units," that is to say, the segments of the text to be treated as a cognitive unit. A interpreter unit may be a word, a phrase or even one or more sentences. Behind this seemingly simple procedure lies a complex cognitive operation. To decode the complete meaning of the source text, the interpreter must consciously and methodically interpret and analyze all its features. This process requires thorough knowledge of the interpreter, grammar, semantics, syntax, dictionary, lexicons and the like, of the source language. The interpreter needs the same in-depth knowledge to re-encode the meaning in the target language. In fact, in general, interpreters' knowledge of the target language is more important, and needs to be deeper than their knowledge of the source language.

The interpreter is a domain-independent embodiment of logical inference approach to generate a clauses form representation. The translation process is guided by a set of phrase structure rules of the sentence and build a tree structure of sentence. The rules mean: An S can consist of an NP followed by a VP. An NP can consist of a D followed by an N. A VP can consist of a V followed by an NP, and etc. This set of rules is called a Definite-Clause Grammar (DCG) as shown below:

S :- NP, VP
NP :- D, N
VP :- V, NP

The parsing process is like left-right top-down parsers, DCG-rule parsers go into a loop when they encounter a rule of the form. Each position in the tree has labels, which may indicate procedure to be run when the traversal enters or leaves that position. The leaves of the tree will be words, which are picked out after morphological processing, or pieces of the original text passage. In the latter case, the interpreter looks up the phrase structure in the lexicon dictionary to find realization for the words that satisfied the lexical items. Below is shown an example of lexical items.

D(a, singular).
N(animal, animals).
V(amaze, amazes, amazed, amazed, amazing, amazes).

The result is a new logical form representation of phrase structure tree, possibly with part(s) of the original text passage. In this way, the entire text passage is gradually translated into logical form as shown below.

alive(_36926 ^ isa(r(christopher & robin),_36926))
& well(_36926 ^ isa(r(christopher & robin),_36926))

exists(_46238,((pretty(_46238) & home(_46238))
& calls(_46238,r(cotchfield & farm))) & lives(chris,_46238))

After got a way of putting logical formula into a nice tidy form, an obvious thing to investigate was need a way of writing something in clausal form known as Pragmatic Skolemize Clauses (PragSC). PragSC form is a collection of clauses with at most one unnegated literal. The logical formula must turns out into PragSC form, to work with logical inference approach as proposed. The interpreter does some additional work in translation process, therefore, some modification to its was required. Before PragSC can be generated, it is required to generate a new unique constant symbol known as Skolem Constant using multi-parsing approach. The first parsing used to generate skolem constant, introducing two types of skolem constant to differentiate between quantified (f_n) and ground term (g_n) variable names. Meanwhile, the second parsing was implemented an algorithm to convert a simplified logical formula into PragSC form.

cl([alive(g34)],[]).
cl([isa(r(christopher & robin),g34)],[]).
cl([well(g35)],[]).
cl([isa(r(christopher & robin),g35)],[]).

cl([pretty(f29)],[]).
cl([home(f29)],[]).
cl([calls(f29,r(cotchfield & farm))],[]).
cl([lives(chris,f29)],[]).

- **Identifying Inference Engine Methodology.** In this experiment, the inference procedure has to identify the type to generate a relevant answer. The inference procedure is a key component of the knowledge engineering process. After all preliminary information gathering and modeling are completed queries are passed to the inference procedure to get answers. In this step, the inference procedure operates on the axioms and problem-specific facts to derive at the targeted information. During this process, inference is used to seek out assumptions which, when combined with a theory, can achieve some desired goal for the system without contradicting known facts. By seeking out more and more assumptions, worlds are generated with non-contradicting knowledge.

In inference process, implementation of skolemize clauses binding with its argument into existing theorem prover technique is introduced. The answer literal enables a resolution refutation theorem prover to keep track of variable binding as a proof proceeds. Resolution refutation can be though as the bottom-up construction of a search tree, where the leaves are the clause produced by knowledge base and the negation of the goal. For example, if the question asked has the logical form $\exists y\ P(x, y)$, then a refutation proof is initiated by adding the clause $\{\neg P(x, y)\}$ to the knowledge base. When the answer literal is employed, the clause $\{\neg P(x, y), ANSWER(x)\}$ is added instead. The x in the answer literal (ANSWER(x)) will reflect any substitutions made to the x in ¬P(x, y), but the *ANSWER* predicate will not participate in (thus, will not effect) resolution. Then, the inference process preceded using skolemize clauses binding approach relates how one clause can be bound to others. For example, if the key of skolemize clause (x) match with any skolemize clauses in knowledge base, then both clauses are unified to accumulate the relevant clauses by connecting its normalize skolem constant or atom on the subject side or the object side of another, formulated as $x \rightarrow P(x,x1) \wedge P(x1,x2) \wedge \ldots \wedge P(xn\text{-}1,xn) \wedge P(xn)$.

7. References

Allen, J. 1995. *Natural Language Understanding*. 2nd Ed. Redwood City, CA: Benjamin/Cummings.

Bashir, A., Kantor, A., Ovesdotter C. A., Ripoche, G., Le, Q., & Atwell, S. (2004). Story Comprehension. Retrieved April 11, 2005 from http://12r.cs.uiuc.edu/~danr/Teaching/CS598-04/Projects/First/Term2.pdf

Capel, A., Heaslip, L., & Williamson, D. 2002. *English Grammar*. H. P. 1990. 1st Ed. Westerhill Road, Bishopbriggs, Glasgow G64 2QT: HarperCollins Publishers.

Charniak, E. 1972. Toward a Model of Children's Story Comprehension. PhD Thesis. Institute of Technology, Massachusetts.

Charniak, E., Altun, Y., Braz, R.d.S., Garret, B., Kosmala, M., Moscovich, T., Pang, L., Pyo, C., Sun, Y., Wy, W., Yang, Z., Zeller, S., and Zorn, L. (2000). Reading Comprehension Programs in an Statistical-Language-Processing Class. In Proceeding of the ANLP/NAACL 2000 Workshop on Reading Comprehension Test as Evaluation for Computer-Based Language Understanding Systems, (pp. 1-5).

Clark, C., Hodges, D., Stephan, J., & Moldovan, D. 2005. Moving QA Towards Reading Comprehension Using Context and Default Reasoning. American Association for Artificial Intelligence, CA.

Dalmas, T., Leidner, J.L., Webber, B., Grover, C., & Bos, J. 2004. Generating Annotated Corpora for Reading Comprehension and Question Answering Evaluation. http://remote.science.uva.nl/~mdr/NLPQA/07dalmas-et-al.pdf [2 April 2004].

Dowty, D. R., Wall, R. E., & Peters, S. 1981. *Introduction to Montague Semantics*. Dordrecht, Holland: D. Reidel Publishing Co.

Doyle, P. 1997. Natural Language Understanding: AI Qual Notes. http://www1.cs.columbia.edu/nlp/paper.html [14 November 2003].

Dyer, C. R. 1996. Lecture Notes: First-Order Logic (Chapter 8 - 9). http://www.cs.wisc.edu/~dyer/cs540/notes/fopc.html [10 March 2004].

Fellbaum, C. 1998. *WordNet: An Electronic Lexical Database*. Cambridge: MIT Press.

Ferro, L., Greiff, W., Hirschman, L., & Wellner, B. 2003. Reading, Learning, Teaching. http://www.mitre.org/news/events/ [2 April 2004].

Fillmore, C. J., & Baker, C.F. 2000. Frame Semantic for Text Understanding. *International Journal of Lexicography* 16 (3): 363-366.

Golden, T. M., & Goldman, S.R. 2001. Development and Evaluation of an Automatized Comprehension Assessment Tool. 0113369. University of Texas at Dallas.

Grohe, M., & Segoyfin, L. 2000. On First-Order Topologies Queries. *15th Annual IEEE Symposium on Logic in Computer Science (LICS '00)*, pp. 349 - 361

Hirschman, L., Light, M., Breck, E., & Burger, J.D. (1999). Deep Read: A Reading Comprehension System. Proceeding of the 37th Annual Meeting of the Association for Computational Linguistics, (pp. 325 – 332).

Lehnert, W. G. (1981). A Computational Theory of Human Question Answering. In A. K. Joshi, Weber, B.J., & Sag, I.A. Elements of Discourse Understanding, (pp.145-176). Cambridge: Cambridge University Press.

Lehnert, W., Micheal, D., Johnson, P., Yang, C.J., & Harley, S. 1983. BORIS - an Experiment in In-Depth Understanding of Narrative. *Journal of Artificial Intelligence* 20 (1): 55-68.

Mahesh, K. 1995. Syntax-Semantic Interaction in Sentence Understanding. PhD Thesis. Georgia Institute of Technology, Georgia.

Miles, W. S. 1997. Natural Language Understanding. WSM Information Systems Inc.

Mitkov, R. 1994. An Integrated Model for Anaphora Resolution. *Proceedings of the 15th Conference on Computational Linguistics*, pp. 1170 -1176

Mueller, E. T. 2003. Story Understanding through Multi-representation Model Construction. *Proceeding of HLT-NAACL 2003 Workshop.*, pp. 46 - 53.

Ng, H. T., Teo, L.H., & Kwan, J.L.P. (2000). A Machine Learning Approach to Answering Questions for Reading Comprehension Tests. Proceedings of the 2000 Joint SIGDAT Conference on Empirical Methods in Natural Language Processing and Very Large Corpora (EMNLP/VLC-2000), (pp. 124-132).

Ram, A., & Moorman, K. (2005). Towards a theory of reading and understanding. *In Understanding Language Understanding: Computational Models of Reading, Cambridge:* MIT Press.

Riloff, E., & Thelen, M. (2000). A Rule-based Question Answering System for Reading Comprehension Tests. Proceeding of ANLP/NAACL 2000 Workshop on Reading Comprehension Tests as Evaluation for Computer-Based Language Understanding Systems, (pp. 13 - 19).

Shapiro, S. C. 2000. Propositional, First-Order and Higher-Order Logics: Basic Definitions, Rules of Inference, and Examples. *In Natural Language Processing and Knowledge Representation: Language for Knowledge and Knowledge for Language* April: 379 - 395

Sturgill, D. B., & Segre, A. M. 1994. Using Hundreds of Workstations to solve First-order Logic problems. *12th National Conf. on Artificial Intelligence,* pp. 187-192

Vanderveen, K. B., & Ramamoorthy, C. V. 1997. Anytime Reasoning in First-Order Logic. *Proc. of the 9th Int. Conf. on Tools with Artificial Intelligence (ICTAI '97),* pp. 142 - 148

7

Knowledge Representation in a Proof Checker for Logic Programs

Emmanouil Marakakis, Haridimos Kondylakis and Nikos Papadakis
Department of Sciences, Technological Educational Institute of Crete, Greece

1. Introduction

Lately the need for systems that ensure the correctness of software is increasing rapidly. Software failures can cause significant economic loss, endanger human life or environmental damage. Therefore, the development of systems that verify the correctness of software under all circumstances is crucial.

Formal methods are techniques based on mathematics which aim to make software production an engineering subject as well as to increase the quality of software. *Formal verification,* in the context of software systems, is the act of proving or disproving the correctness of a system with respect to a certain formal specification or property, using formal methods of mathematics. *Formal program verification* is the process of formally proving that a computer program does exactly what is stated in the program specification it was written to realize. Automated techniques for producing proofs of correctness of software systems fall into two general categories: 1) *Automated theorem proving* (Loveland, 1986), in which a system attempts to produce a formal proof given a description of the system, a set of logical axioms, and a set of inference rules. 2) *Model checking,* in which a system verifies certain properties by means of an exhaustive search of all possible states that a system could enter during its execution.

Neither of these techniques works without human assistance. Automated theorem provers usually require guidance as to which properties are "interesting" enough to pursue. Model checkers can quickly get bogged down in checking millions of uninteresting states if not given a sufficiently abstract model.

Interactive verifiers or *proof checkers* are programs which are used to help a user in building a proof and/or find parts of proofs. These systems provide information to the user regarding the proof in hand, and then the user can make decisions on the next proof step that he will follow. Interactive theorem provers are generally considered to support the user, acting as clerical assistants in the task of proof construction. The *interactive systems* have been more suitable for the systematic formal development of mathematics and in mechanizing formal methods (Clarke & Wing, 1996). *Proof editors* are interactive language editing systems which ensure that some degree of "semantic correctness" is maintained as the user develops the proof. The *proof checkers* are placed between the two extremes, which are the automatic theorem provers and the proof editors (Lindsay, 1988).

In this chapter we will present a proof *checker* or an *interactive verifier* for logic programs which are constructed by a schema-based method (Marakakis, 1997), (Marakakis & Gallagher, 1994) and we will focus on the knowledge representation and on its use by the core components of the system. A *meta-program* is any program which uses another program, the object program, as data. Our proof checker is a meta-program which reasons about object programs. The logic programs and the other elements of the theory represented in the Knowledge Base (KB) of our system are the object programs. The KB is the data of the proof checker. The proof checker accesses and changes the KB. The representation of the underlying theory (object program) in the proof checker (meta-program) is a key issue in the development of the proof checker. Our System has been implemented in Sicstus Prolog and its interface has been implemented in Visual Basic (Marakakis, 2005), (Marakakis & Papadakis, 2009)

2. An Overview of the main components of the proof checker

This verifier of logic programs requires a lot of interaction with the user. That is why emphasis is placed on the design of its interface. The design of the interface aims to facilitate the proof task of the user. A screenshot of the main window of our system is shown in Fig. 1.

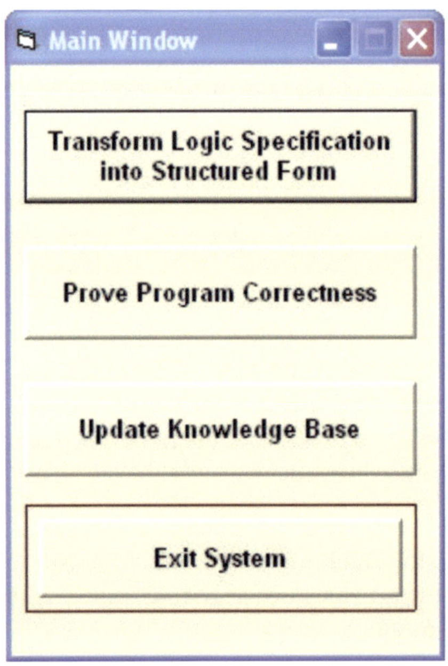

Fig. 1. The main window of the proof-checker.

Initially, all proof decisions are taken by the programmer. The design of the interface aims to facilitate the proof task of the user. This interactive verifier of logic programs consists of three distinct parts the *interface,* the *prover* or *transformer and the knowledge base (KB).* The interface offers an environment where the user can think and decide about the proof steps that have to be applied. The user specifies each proof step and the prover performs it. A high-level design of our system is depicted in Fig. 2. The main components of the proof checker with their functions are shown in this figure. The prover of the system consists of the following two components. 1) The component *"Spec Transformer"* transforms a specification expressed in typed FOL into structured form which is required by our correctness method (Marakakis, 1997), (Marakakis, 2005). 2) The component "*Theorem Proof Checker* supports the proof task of the selected correctness theorem.

The "*KB Update*" subsystem allows the user to update the KB of the system through a user-friendly interface. The knowledge base (KB) and its contents are also shown in Fig. 2. The KB contains the representation of specifications, theorems, axioms, lemmas, and programs complements. It also has the representation of FOL laws in order to facilitate their selection for application. These entities are represented in ground representation (Hill & Gallagher, 1998). The main benefit of this representation is the distinct semantics of the object program variables from the meta-variables. It should be noted that the user would like to see theorems, axioms, lemmas and programs in a comprehensible form which is independent of their representation. However, the ground representation cannot be easily understood by users. Moreover, the editing of elements in ground representation is error-prone. Part of the interface of the system is the "*Ground-Nonground Representation Transformer*" component which transforms an expression in ground representation into a corresponding one in the standard formalism of FOL and vice-versa. The standard form of expressions helps users in the proof task and for the update of the KB.

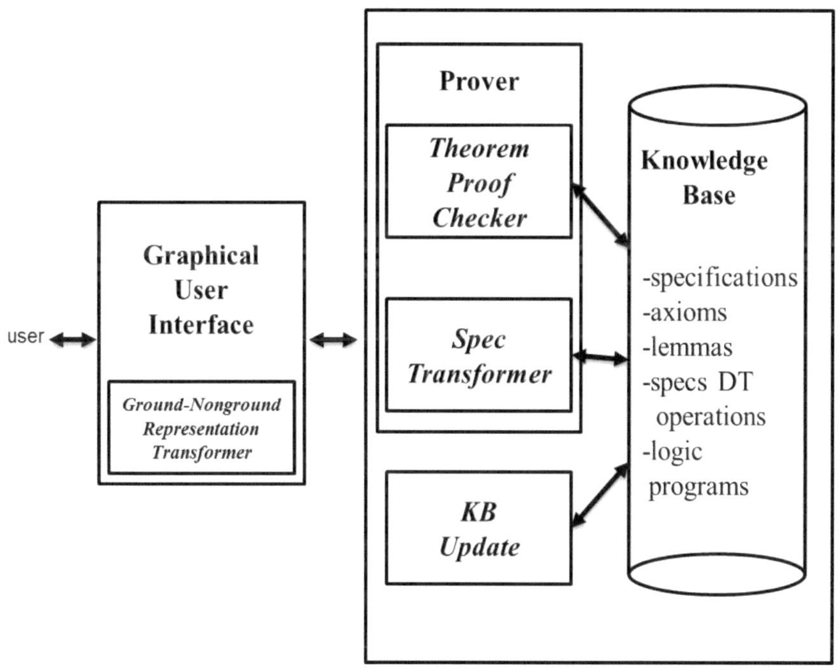

Fig. 2. Main components of the proof-checker.

3. Knowledge representation

Knowledge and *representation* are two distinct concepts. They play a central role in the development of intelligent systems. *Knowledge* is a description of the world, i.e. the problem domain. *Representation* is how knowledge is encoded. *Reasoning* is *how* to extract more information from what is explicitly represented.

Different types of knowledge require different types of representation. Different types of knowledge representation require different types of reasoning. The most popular knowledge representation methods are based on *logic, rules, frames* and *semantic nets*. Our discussion will be focused on knowledge representation based on logic.

Logic is a language for reasoning. It is concerned with the truth of statements about the world. Each statement is either "true" or "false". Logic includes the following: a) *syntax* which specifies the symbols in the language and how they can be combined to form sentences, b) *semantics* which specify how to assign a truth to a sentence based on its meaning in the world and c) *inference rules* which specify methods for computing new sentences from existing sentences. There are different types of logic, i.e. propositional logic, first-order predicate logic, fuzzy logic, modal logic, description logic, temporal logic, etc. We are concerned on knowledge representation and reasoning based on typed first-order predicate logic because our correctness method is based on typed FOL.

Another classification of knowledge representation is *procedural* and *declarative* knowledge representation. *Declarative knowledge* concerns representation of the problem domain (world) as a set of truth sentences. This representation expresses "*what something is*". On the other hand, the procedural *knowledge* concerns tasks which must be performed to reach a particular goal. In procedural representation, the control information which is necessary to use the knowledge is embedded in the knowledge itself. It focuses on "*how something is done*". In the same way, *declarative programming* is concerned with writing down "*what*" should be computed and much less with "*how*" it should be computed (Hill & Lloyd, 1994). Declarative programming separates the control component of an algorithm (the "*how*") from the logic component (the "*what*"). The key idea of declarative programming is that a program is a theory (in some suitable logic) and computation is deduction from the theory (Lloyd, 1994). The advantages of declarative programming are: a) teaching, b) semantics, c) programmer productivity, c) meta-programming and e) parallelism. Declarative programming in Logic Programming means that programs are theories. The programmer has to supply the intended interpretation of the theory. Control is usually supplied automatically by the system, i.e. the logic programming language. We have followed the declarative knowledge representation for the representation of the knowledge base of our system.

3.1 Meta-programming, ground and non-ground representation

A language which is used to reason about another language (or possibly itself) is called *meta-language* and the language reasoned about is called the *object language*. A *meta-program* is a program whose data is another program, i.e. the *object program*. Our proof-checker is a meta-program which manipulates other logic programs. It has been implemented in Prolog and the underlying theory, i.e. the logic programs being verified and the other elements of the KB, is the object program. An important decision is how to represent programs of the object language (i.e. the KB elements in our case) in the programs of the meta-language, i.e. in the meta-programs. *Ground representation* and non-*ground representation* are the two main approaches to the representation of object programs in meta-programs. We have followed the ground representation approach for the representation of the elements of the KB of our system. Initially, ground and non-ground representation will be discussed. Then, we will see the advantages and the drawbacks of the two representations.

In logic programming there is not clear distinction between programs and data because data can be represented as program clauses. The semantics of a meta-program depend on the way the object program is represented in the meta-program. Normally, a distinct representation is given to each symbol of the object language in the meta-language. This is called *naming relation* (Hill & Gallagher, 1998). Rules of construction can be used to define the representation of the constructed terms and formulas. Each expression in the language of the object program should have at least one representation as an expression in the language of the meta-program. The *naming relation* for constants, functions, propositions, predicates and connectives is straightforward. That is, constants and propositions of the object language can be represented as constants in the meta-language. Functions and predicates of the object language can be represented as functions in the language of meta-program. A connective of the object language can be represented either as a connective or as a predicate or as a function in the meta-language. The main problem is the representation of the variables of the object language in the language of the meta-program. There are two approaches. One approach is to represent the variables of the object program as ground terms in the meta-program. This representation is called *ground representation*. The other approach is to represent the variables of the object program as variables (or non-ground terms) in the meta-program. This representation is called *non-ground representation*.

Using non-ground representation of the object program is much easier to make an efficient implementation of the meta-program than using ground representation. In non-ground representation, there is no need to provide definitions for *renaming*, *unification* and *application* of substitutions of object language formulas. These operations which are time consuming do not require special treatment for the object language terms. The inefficiency in ground representation is mainly due to the representation of the variables of the object program as constants in the meta-program. Because of this representation complicated definitions for *renaming*, *unification* and *application* of substitutions to terms are required. On the other hand, there are semantic problems with non-ground representation. The meta-program will not have clear declarative semantics. There is not distinction of variables of the object program from the ones of the meta-program which range over different domains. This problem can be solved by using a typed logic language instead of the standard first-order predicate logic. The ground representation is more clear and expressive than the non-ground one and it can be used for many meta-programming tasks. Ground representation is suitable for meta-programs which have to reason about the computational behavior of the object program. The ground representation is required in order to perform any complex meta-programming task in a sound way. Its inherent complexity can be reduced by specialization. That is, such meta-programs can be specialized with respect to the representation of the object program (Gallagher 1993).

Another issue is how the theory of the object program is represented in the meta-program. There are again two approaches. One approach is the object program to be represented in the meta-program as program statements (i.e. clauses). In this case, the components of the object program are fixed and the meta-program is specialized for just those programs that can be constructed from these components. The other approach is the object program to be represented as a term in a goal that is executed in the meta-program. In this case the object program can be either fixed or it can be constructed dynamically. In this case the meta-program can reason about arbitrary object programs. This is called *dynamic meta-*

programming. The object program in our proof checker is represented as clauses. The underlying theory is fixed for each proof task.

3.2 Ground representation of object programs in the proof-checker

The KB shown in Fig. 2 contains the representation of specifications, theorems, axioms, lemmas and programs complements. It also has the representation of FOL laws in order to facilitate their selection for application. These KB elements are represented in ground representation (Hill & Gallagher, 1998).. The representation of the main symbols of the object language which are used in this chapter is shown below.

Object language symbol	**Representation**
constant	constant
object program variable	term *v(i)*, *i* is natural
function	term *g(i)*, *i* is natural
proposition, formulas of FOL	term *f(i)*, *i* is natural
predicate	term *p(i)*, *i* is natural
connectives (∨,∧,~,→,↔)	\/, /\, ~, -> , <->
exist (∃)	*ex*
for all (∀)	*all*
length of sequence *x1*(#x1)	*len(v(1):Type):nat*
operation plus (+)	*plus*
operation minus (-)	*minus*
type variable	term *tv(i)*, *i* is natural
type sequence	*seq*
empty sequence (<>)	*nil_seq*
sequence constructor (*Head* :: *Tail*)	*seq_cons*(*Head*, *Tail*) where *Head* and *Tail* are defined in ground representation accordingly.
operator / (*Object*/*Type*)	(*Object* : *Type*)
$x1_i$ / *Type* (e.g. $x_1/a1$)	*v(1, i:nat):Type (e.g. v(1, 1:nat):tv(1))*
equality (=)	*eq*
inequality (≠)	*~eq*
less-equal (≤)	*le*
greater-equal (≥)	*ge*
type natural (N)	*nat*
type integer (Z)	*int*
nonzero naturals (N_1)	*posInt*

Predicates are represented by their names assuming that each predicate has a unique name. In case of name conflicts, we use the ground term *p(i)* where *i* is natural. Sum of n elements, i.e. $\sum_{i=1}^{n} x_i$ is represented as the following ground term: *sum(1:nat, v(2):nat, v(3, v(4):nat):Type):Type* where "*Type*" is the type of x_i.

3.3 Representation of variables

3.3.1 Type variables

The type variables are specified by the lower case Greek letter *α* followed by a positive integer which is the unique identifier of the variables e.g. *α1, α2, α3, α4* etc. Each type variable is represented in ground form by a term of the form *tv(N)* or in simplified form *tvN* where *N* stands for the unique identifier of the variable. For example, the ground representation of type variables *α1, α2, α3* could be *tv(1)* or *tv1, tv(2)* or *tv2, tv(3)* or *tv3* respectively.

3.3.2 Object program variables

Object program variables and variables in specifications are expressed using the lower case English letter *x* followed by a positive integer which is the unique identifier of the variables e.g. *x1, x2, x3, x4* etc. Each object variable is represented in ground form by a term of the form *v(N)* where *N* stands for the unique identifier of the variable. For example, the ground representation of the object variables *x1, x2, x3* is *v(1) ,v(2) and v(3)* respectively. Note that, the quantifier of each variable comes before the variable in the formula. Subscripted variables of the form $x1_i$ represent elements from constructed objects. They are represented by a term of the form *v(Id, i:nat):ElementType* where the first argument "*Id*" represents its unique identifier and the second one represents its subscript. "*Id*" is a natural number. This type of variables occurs mainly in specifications. A term like *v(Id, i:nat):ElementType* can be assumed as representing either a regular compound term or an element of a structured object like a sequence. The distinction is performed by checking the types of the elements *x* and *x(i)*. For example, for *i=1* by checking *x1:seq(α1)* and *x1(1:nat):α1*, it can be inferred that *x1(1:nat):α1* is an element of *x1:seq(α1)*.

3.4 Representation of axioms and lemmas

A set of axioms is applied to each DT including the "*domain closure*" and the "*uniqueness*" axioms which will be also presented later on Section 3.7. Each axiom is specified by a FOL formula. Axioms are represented by the predicates "*axiom_def_ID/1*" and "*axiom_def/4*" as follows. The predicate

"*axiom_def_ID(Axiom_Ids)*"

represents the identifiers of all axioms in the KB. Its argument "*Axiom_Ids*" is a list with the identifiers of the axioms. For example, the representation "axiom_def_ID([1,2,3,4])" says that the KB has four axioms with identifiers 1,2,3 and 4.

The specification of each axiom is represented by a predicate of the following form

"*axiom_def(Axiom_Id, DT_name, Axiom_name, Axiom_specification)*".

The argument "*Axiom_Id*" is the unique identifier of the axiom, i.e. a positive integer. "*DT_name*" is the name of the DT which the axiom is applied to. "*Axiom_name*" is the name of axiom. "*Axiom_specification*" is a list which has the representation of the specification of the axiom.

Example: *Domain closure axiom for sequences.* Informally, this axiom says that a sequence can be either empty or it will consist from head and tail.

Specification:

$$[\forall x1/seq(a2),[x1= < > \vee (\exists x3/a2,\ \exists x4/seq(a2),[x1=x3::x4])]]$$

Representation:

```
axiom_def (1, sequences, 'domain closure',
  [all v(1):seq(tv(1)), (eq(v(1):seq(tv(1)),nil_seq) \/
    [ex v(2):tv(1), ex v(3):seq(tv(1)), eq(v(1):seq(tv(1)),seq_cons(v(2):tv(1),
          v(3):seq(tv(1))):seq(tv(1))) ])]).
```

Similarly, lemmas are represented by the predicates "*lemma_sp_ID/1*" and "*lemma_sp/4*".

3.5 Representation of first-order logic laws

The FOL laws are equivalence preserving transformation rules. Each FOL law is specified by a FOL formula. They are represented by predicates *fol_law_ID/1* and *fol_law/3* as follows. The predicate

"*fol_law_ID(FOL_laws_Ids)*"

represents the identifiers of all FOL laws in the KB. Its argument "*FOL_laws_Ids*" is a list with the identifiers of all FOL laws. The specification of each FOL law is represented by a predicate of the form

"*fol_law(FOL_law_Id, FOL_law_description, FOL_law_specification).*".

The argument "*FOL_law_Id*" is the unique identifier of the FOL law, i.e. a positive integer. "*FOL_law_description*" is the name of a FOL law. "*FOL_law_specification*" is a list which has the ground representation of the specification of FOL law.

Example: (∧ distribution)

Specification:

$$P \wedge (Q \vee R) \leftrightarrow (P \wedge Q) \vee (P \wedge R)$$

Representation:

```
fol_law(2,' ∧ distribution',
      [f1 /\ (f2 \/ f3) <-> (f1 /\ f2) \/ (f1 /\ f3)]).
```

3.6 Representation of theorems

3.6.1 Initial theorem

The theorems that have to be proved must also be represented in the KB. Each theorem is specified by a FOL formula. They are represented by the predicates "*theorem_ID/1*" and "*theorem/4*" as follows. The predicate

"*theorem_ID(Theorems_Ids)*"

represents the identifiers of all theorems that are available in the KB. Its argument "*Theorems_Ids*" is a list with the identifiers of all theorems. The specification of each theorem is represented by a predicate of the form

"*theorem(Theorem_Id, Program_Id, Spec_struct_Id, Theorem_specification).*"

The argument "*Theorem_Id*" is the unique identifier of the theorem, i.e. a positive integer. The arguments "*Program_Id*" and "*Spec_struct_Id*" are the unique identifiers of the program and the structured specifications respectively. "*Theorem_specification*" is a list which has the representation of the specification of theorem.

Example: The predicate *sum(x1, x2)* where $Type(sum) = seq(Z) \times Z$ is true iff *x2* is the sum of the sequence of integers *x1*. The correctness theorem for predicate *sum/2* and the theory which is used to prove it is as follows.

$$Comp(Pr) \cup Spec \cup A \models \forall x1/seq(Z), x2/Z\ (sum(x1,x2) \leftrightarrow sum^S(x1, x2))$$

Pr is the logic program for predicate *sum*/2, excluding the DT definitions. *Comp(Pr)* is the complement of the program *Pr*. *Spec* is the specification of predicate *sum*/2, i.e. $sum^S(x1,x2)$. *A* is the theory for sequences, i.e. the underlying DTs for predicate *sum*/2, including the specifications of the DT operations.

Theorem Specification:

$$\forall x1/seq(Z),\ \forall x2/Z\ (sum(x1,x2) \leftrightarrow sum^S(x1,x2))$$

Representation:

```
theorem(1, progr1, spec_struct1,
   [all v(1):seq(int),all v(2):int, (sum(v(1):seq(int), v(2):int):int <->
      sum_s(v(1):seq(int), v(2):int))]).
```

3.6.2 Theorems in structured form

The specification of a theorem may need to be transformed into structured form in order to proceed to the proof. The structure form of theorems facilitates the proof task. Each theorem in structured form is specified by a FOL formula. They are represented by the predicates "*theorem_struct_ID/1*" and "*theorem_struct/4*" as follows. The predicate

"*theorem_struct_ID(Theorems_Ids)*"

represents the identifiers of all theorems available in the KB with the specification part in structured form. Its argument "*Theorems_Ids*" is a list with the identifiers of all theorems in structured form. The specification of each theorem is represented by a predicate of the form

"*theorem_struct(Theorem_struct_Id,Program_Id,Spec_struct_Id, Theorem_specification).*".

The argument "*Theorem_struct_Id*" is the unique identifier, i.e. a positive integer, of the theorem whose specification part is in structured form. The arguments "*Program_Id*" and "*Spec_struct_Id*" are the unique identifiers of the program and the structured specifications respectively. "*Theorem_specification*" is a list which has the representation of the specification of theorem.

Example

In order to construct the theorem in structured form the predicate specification must be transformed into structured form. The initial logic specification for predicate *sum*/2 is the following.

$$\forall x1/seq(Z),\ x2/Z\ (sum^{S}(x1,x2) \leftrightarrow x2 = \sum_{i=1}^{\#x1} x1_i\ )$$

The logic specification of $sum^{S}(x1,x2)$ in structured form and its representation are following.

Theorem Specification:

$$\forall x1/seq(Z),\ \forall x2/Z\ (sum^{S}(x1,x2) \leftrightarrow [x1{=}{<>} \wedge x2{=}0 \vee [\exists x4/Z,\ \exists x5/Z,$$
$$\exists x6/seq(Z),[x1{=}x5{::}x6 \wedge x2{=}x5{+}x4 \wedge sum^{S}(x6,x4)]]])$$

Representation:

theorem_struct(1, progr1, spec_struct1,
[all v(1):seq(int), all v(2):int, (sum(v(1):seq(int), v(2):int) <->
((eq(v(1):seq(int),nil_seq:seq(tv(1))) /\ eq(v(2):int,0:int)) \/ [ex v(3):int,
ex v(4):int, ex v(5):seq(int), (eq(v(1):seq(int), seq_cons(v(4):int,
v(5):seq(int)):seq(int)) /\ eq(v(2):int,plus(v(4):int, v(3):int)) /
sum_s(v(5):seq(int), v(3):int))]))]).

3.7 An example theory and theorem

Throughout this Chapter we use the correctness theorem and theory for predicate *sum/2*. That is,

$$Comp(Pr) \cup Spec \cup A \ |= \forall x1/seq(Z),\ x2/Z\ (sum(x1,x2) \leftrightarrow sum^{S}(x1,\ x2))$$

The ground representation of theory is also illustrated.

Theory

The logic program completion *Comp(Pr)* of *Pr* is as follows.

$\forall$x1/seq(Z), $\forall$x2/Z,[sum(x1,x2) $\leftrightarrow$ (p1(x1) $\wedge$ p2(x1,x2) $\vee$ [$\exists$x3/Z, $\exists$ x4/seq(Z),
$\exists$ x5/Z,[$\neg$p1(x1) $\wedge$ p3(x1,x3,x4) $\wedge$ p4(x1,x3,x5,x2) $\wedge$ sum(x4,x5)]])]
$\forall$x1/seq(Z),[p1(x1) $\leftrightarrow$ empty_seq(x1)]
$\forall$ x1/seq(Z), $\forall$x2/Z,[p2(x1,x2) $\leftrightarrow$ neutral_add_subtr_int(x2)]
$\forall$ x1/seq(Z), $\forall$x2/Z, $\forall$x3/seq(Z),[p3(x1,x2,x3) $\leftrightarrow$ p5(x1,x2,x3) $\wedge$ p6(x1,x2,x3)]
$\forall$ x1/seq(Z), $\forall$x2/Z, $\forall$x3/seq(Z),[p5(x1,x2,x3) $\leftrightarrow$ head(x1,x2)]
$\forall$ x1/seq(Z), $\forall$x2/Z, $\forall$x3/seq(Z),[p6(x1,x2,x3) $\leftrightarrow$ tail(x1,x3)]
$\forall$ x1/seq(Z), $\forall$x2/Z, $\forall$x3/Z, $\forall$x4/Z,[p4(x1,x2,x3,x4) $\leftrightarrow$ plus_int(x3,x2,x4)]

Representation:

- *progr_clause(progr1, 1,[all v(1):seq(int), all v(2):int, [sum(v(1):seq(int),v(2):int) <-> ((p1(v(1):seq(int)) /\ p2(v(1):seq(int), v(2):int)) \/ [ex v(3):int, ex v(4):seq(int), ex v(5):int,*

[~p1(v(1):seq(int)) /\ p3(v(1):seq(int), v(3):int,v(4):seq(int)) /\ p4(v(1):seq(int),v(3):int, v(5):int, v(2):int) /\ sum(v(4):seq(int),v(5):int)]])]]).

- *progr_clause(progr1, 2, [all v(6):seq(int),[p1(v(6):seq(int)) <-> empty_seq(v(6):seq(int))]]).*
- *progr_clause(progr1, 3, [all v(7):seq(int), all v(8):int,[p2(v(7):seq(int), v(8):int) <-> neutral_add_subtr_int(v(8):int)]]).*
- *progr_clause(progr1, 4, [all v(9):seq(int), all v(10):int, all v(11):seq(int), [p3(v(9):seq(int), v(10):int, v(11):seq(int))<-> p5(v(9):seq(int), v(10):int, v(11):seq(int)) /\ p6(v(9):seq(int), v(10):int, v(11):seq(int))]]).*
- *progr_clause(progr1, 5, [all v(12):seq(int), all v(13):int, all v(14):seq(int),[p5(v(12):seq(int), v(13):int, v(14):seq(int)) <-> head(v(12):seq(int), v(13):int)]]).*
- *progr_clause(progr1, 6, [all v(15):seq(int), all v(17):int, all v(16):seq(int),[p6(v(15):seq(int), v(17):int, v(16):seq(int))<-> tail(v(15):seq(int), v(16):seq(int))]]).*
- *progr_clause(progr1, 7, [all v(18):seq(int), all v(19):int, all v(20):int, all v(21):int,[p4(v(18):seq(int), v(19):int, v(20):int, v(21):int) <-> plus_int(v(20):int, v(19):int, v(21):int)]]).*

The logic specification (*Spec*) is shown in Section 3.6 and its representation in ground form.

The theory *A* of the DT operations including the specification of the DT operations is as follows.

Axioms

Domain closure axiom for sequences

$$\forall x1/seq(a2),[x1=<\,> \ \forall(\exists x3/a2,\ \exists x4/seq(a2),[x1=x3::x4])]$$

Its ground representation is shown in section 3.4.

Uniqueness axioms for sequences

i $\forall x1/a2,\ \forall x3/seq(a2),[\sim[x1::x3/a2=<\,>]]$

ii $\forall x1/a2,\ \forall x3/a2,\ \forall x4/seq(a2),\ \forall x5/seq(a2),[x1::x4=x3::x5 \wedge x1=x3 \wedge x4=x5]$

Representation:

- *axiom_def(2, sequences, "uniqueness i", [all v(1):tv(1), all v(2):seq(tv(1)), [~[eq(seq_cons (v(1):tv(1), v(2):seq(tv(1))):tv(1),nil_seq:seq(tv(1)))]]]).*
- *axiom_def(3, sequences, "uniqueness ii", [all v(1):tv(1), all v(2):tv(1), all v(3):seq(tv(1)), all v(4):seq(tv(1)),[eq(seq_cons(v(1):tv(1), v(3):seq(tv(1))):seq(tv(1)), seq_cons(v(2):tv(1), v(4):seq(tv(1))):seq(tv(1))) -> (eq(v(1):tv(1), v(2):tv(1)) /\ eq(v(3):seq(tv(1)), v(4):seq(tv(1))))]]).*

Definition of summation operation over 0 entities

$$\forall x1/seq(Z),[x1=<\,> \rightarrow \Sigma((i=1 \text{ to } \#x1)\ x1_i)=0]$$

Representation:

- *axiom_def(4, sequences, "summation over 0 entities", [all v(1):seq(int), [eq(v(1):seq(int),nil_seq) -> eq(sum(1:int,len(v(1):seq(int)):int, v(1,v(3):nat):int), 0:int)]]).*

Lemmas

∀x1/seq(a2),[x1 ≠ < > ↔ [∃x3/a2, ∃x4/seq(a2),[x1=x3::x4/a2]]]
∀x1/a2, ∀x3/seq(a2), ∀x4/seq(a2),[x3=x1::x4→(∀x5/N,[2≤x5≤#x3→x3(x5)=x4(x5-1)])]
∀x1/seq(a2), ∀x3/seq(a2), ∀x4/a2,[x1=x4::x3→#x1=#x3+1]
∀x1/a2, ∀x3/seq(a2), ∀x4/seq(a2),[x3=x1::x4/a2→x1=$x3_1$/a2]

Representation:

- lemma_sp(1, sequences, "Non-empty sequences have at least one element",[all v(1):seq(tv(1)), [~eq(v(1):seq(tv(1)),nil_seq:seq(tv(1))) <-> [ex v(2):tv(1), ex v(3):seq(tv(1)), [eq(v(1):seq(tv(1)), seq_cons(v(2):tv(1), v(3):seq(tv(1))):tv(1))]]]]).
- lemma_sp(2,sequences,"if sequence s has tail t then the element si is identical to the element ti-1",[all v(1):tv(1), all v(2):seq(tv(1)), all v(3):seq(tv(1)),[eq(v(2):seq(tv(1)), seq_cons(v(1):tv(1), v(3):seq(tv(1))):seq(tv(1))) -> (all v(4):nat, [le(2:nat, v(4):nat) /\ le(v(4):nat, len(v(2):seq (tv(1))):nat) -> eq(v(2, v(4):nat):tv(1), v(3, minus(v(4): nat,1:nat)))])]]).
- lemma_sp(3, sequences, "If sequence s has tail t then the length of s is equal to the length of t plus 1", [all v(1):seq(tv(1)), all v(2):seq(tv(1)), all v(3):tv(1), [eq(v(1):seq(tv(1)), seq_cons(v(3):tv(1), v(2):seq(tv(1))):seq(tv(1))) -> eq(len(v(1):seq(tv(1))): nat,plus(len(v(2): seq(tv(1))):nat,1:nat))]]).
- lemma_sp(4, sequences, "If sequence s is non-empty then its head h is identical to its first element", [all v(1):tv(1), all v(2):seq(tv(1)), all v(3):seq(tv(1)),[eq(v(2):seq(tv(1)), seq_cons(v(1):tv(1), v(3):seq(tv(1))):tv(1)) -> eq(v(1):tv(1), v(2, 1:int):tv(1))]]).

Logic specifications of DT operations

∀x1/seq(a2),[empty_seq(x1) ↔ x1= < >]
∀x1/Z,[neutral_add_subtr_int(x1) ↔ x1=0]
∀x1/seq(a2), ∀x3/a2,[head(x1,x3) ↔ [x1≠ < > ∧ [∃x4/seq(a2),[x1=x3::x4/a2]]]]
∀x1/seq(a2), ∀x3/seq(a2),[tail(x1,x3) ↔ [∃x4/a2,[x1≠< > ∧ x1=x4::x3/a2]]]
∀x1/Z, ∀x2/Z, ∀x3/Z,[plus_int(x1,x2,x3) ↔ x3=x2+x1]

Representation:

- dtOp_sp(empty_seq, 1, "seq: empty", [all v(1):seq(tv(1)), [empty_seq(v(1):seq(tv(1))) <-> eq(v(1):seq(tv(1)),nil_seq:seq(tv(1)))]]).
- dtOp_sp(head, 2, "seq: head", [all v(1):seq(tv(1)), all v(2):tv(1),[head(v(1):seq(tv(1)), v(2):tv(1)) <-> [~eq(v(1):seq(tv(1)),nil_seq:seq(tv(1))) /\ [ex v(3):seq(tv(1)), [eq(v(1):seq (tv(1)),seq_cons(v(2):tv(1), v(3):seq(tv(1))):tv(1))]]]]]).
- dtOp_sp(tail, 3, "seq: tail", [all v(1):seq(tv(1)), all v(2):seq(tv(1)), [tail(v(1):seq(tv(1)), v(2):seq(tv(1))) <-> [ex v(3):tv(1),[~eq(v(1):seq(tv(1)), nil_seq:seq (tv(1))) /\ eq(v(1), seq_cons(v(3):tv(1),v(2):seq(tv(1))):tv(1))]]]]).
- dtOp_sp(neutral_add_subtr_int, 8, "int: neutral_add_subtr_int", [all v(1):int, [neutral_add_subtr_int(v(1):int) <-> eq(v(1):int,0:int)]]).
- dtOp_sp(plus_int, 9,"int: plus_int", [all v(1):int, all v(2):int, all v(3):int, [plus_int(v(1):int,v(2):int,v(3):int) <-> eq(v(3):int,plus(v(2):int,v(1):int))]]).

4. Schematic view of the Interaction of the main components

In this section, a schematic view of the proof checker and the interaction of its main components will be shown. In addition, the functions of its components will be discussed. An example of a proof step will illustrate the use of the KB representation in the proof task.

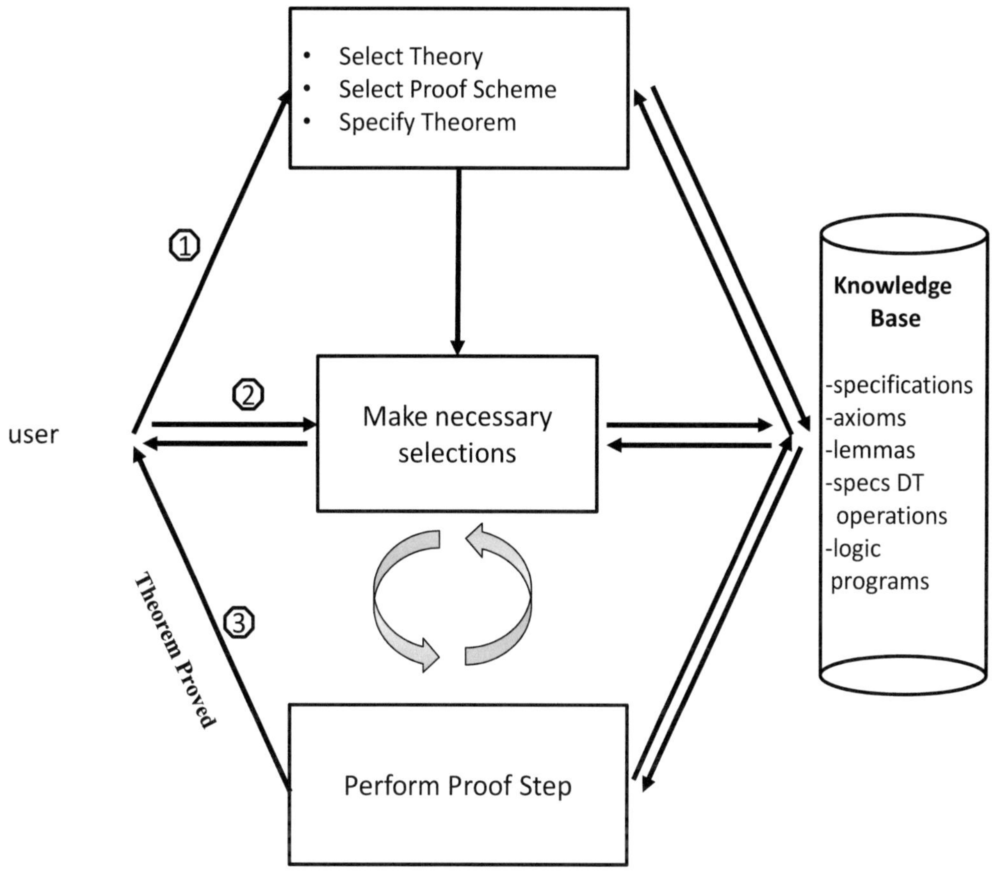

Fig. 3. Schematic View of the Theorem Proof Checker.

4.1 Schematic view of the theorem proof checker

The process of proving a theorem is shown in Fig. 3 and consists of three steps.

- Step 1: In order to prove the correctness of a theorem the user initially has to specify the theorem that is going to be proved and to select the theory and the proof scheme that will be used for the proof. The theory is retrieved from the *KB* and it is presented to the user for selection. It consists of a *program complement*, a *logic specification*, *axioms* and *lemmas*. The corresponding window of the interface which allows the user to make these selections is shown in Fig. 6.
- Step 2: After the selection the user proceeds to the actual proof of the specific theorem. In order to do that he has to select specific parts from the theorem, the theory and the transformation rules that will be applied. The transformation rules that can be applied are first order logic (FOL) laws, folding and unfolding.
- Step 3: In this step the selected transformation is applied and the equivalent form of the theorem is presented to the user. The user can validate the result. He is allowed to approve or cancel the specific proof step.

The last two steps are performed iteratively until the theorem is proved.

4.2 Schematic view of specification transformer

Fig. 4 depicts the procedure for transforming a specification in the required structured form, which is similar to the previous case. In this case however, the underlying theory consists of *Spec* U *Axioms* U *Lemmas*. Initially, the user selects a specification, then the rest elements of the theory are automatically selected by the system. Next, in step 2, the user has to select specific theory elements and transformation rules. In step 3, the selected transformation rule is performed. Step 2 and step 3 are performed iteratively until the specification is transformed in the required structured form.

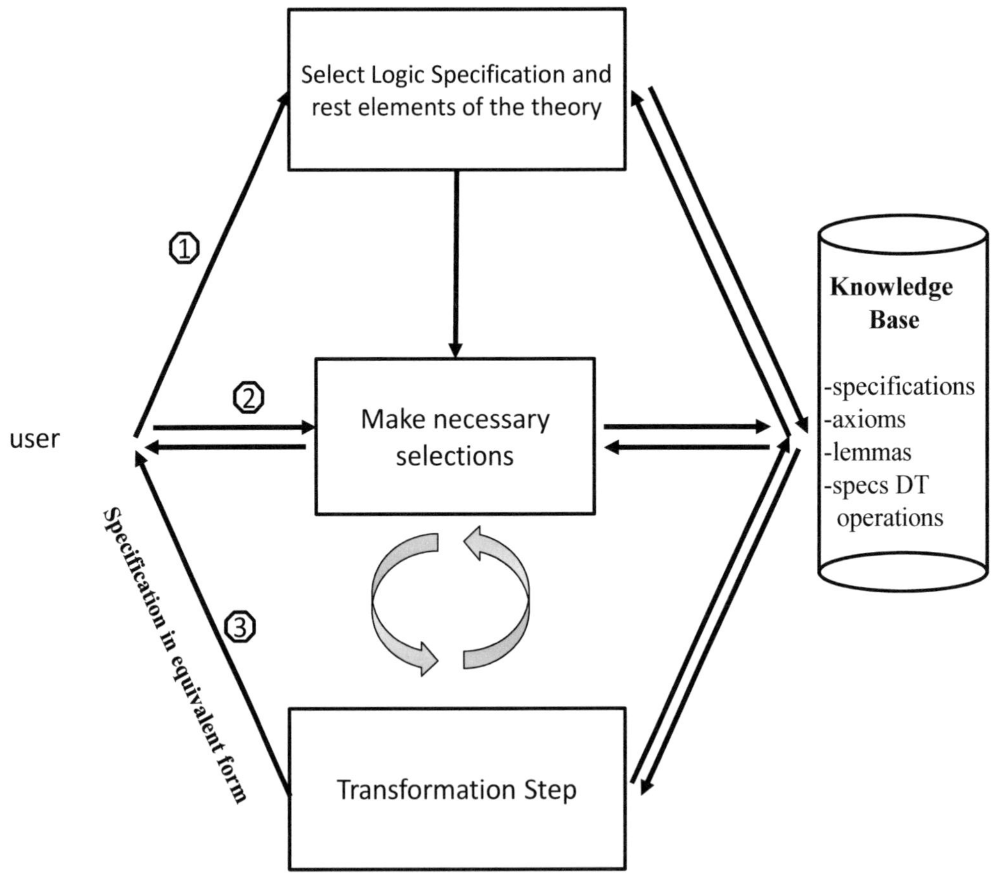

Fig. 4. Schematic View of Specification Transformer.

4.3 Illustration of a proof step

The *"Transformation Step"* procedure is actually a sub-procedure of the *"Perform Proof Step"* procedure and that is why we will not present it. The schematic view of the main algorithm for the procedure which performs a proof step, i.e. *"performProofStep", is* shown in Fig. 5. It is assumed that the user has selected some theory elements, and a transformation rule that should be applied to the current proof step.

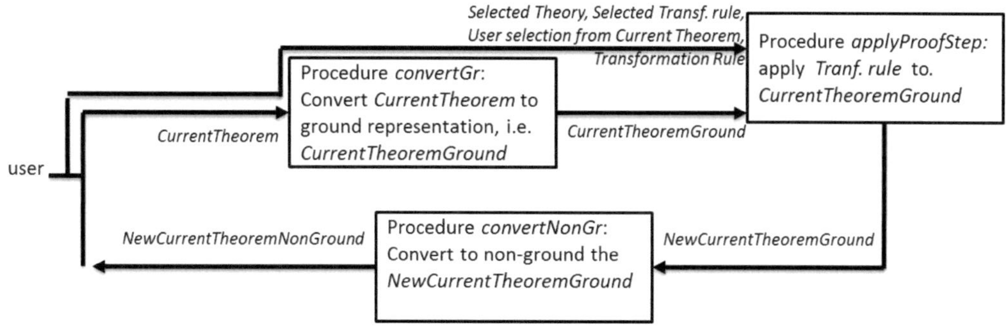

Fig. 5. Schematic view of the "performProofStep" procedure.

The function block diagram of the algorithm "*performProofStep*" shown in Fig. 5 will be discussed through an example. Consider that our theorem has been transformed and its current form is the following:

$$\forall x1/seq(Z),\ \forall x2/Z\ (sum^S(x1,x2) \leftrightarrow$$
$$(x1=<> \wedge x2=0 \vee [\exists x3/Z,[\ \exists x4/seq(Z),false \wedge x2=x4+x3 \wedge sum^S(x4,x3)]]))$$

The user has selected the following FOL law to be applied to the above theorem:

$$P \wedge false \leftrightarrow false$$

Initially, the current theorem is converted to the corresponding ground representation by the procedure "*ConvertGr*" and we get:

[all v(1):seq(int),[all v(2):int,sum_s(v(1):seq(int),v(2):int)<->
(eq(v(1):seq(int),nil_seq:seq(int))/\eq(v(2):int,0:int) \/
[ex v(3):int,[ex v(4):int,[ex v(5):seq(int),
false/\eq(v(2):int,plus(v(4):int,v(3):int):int)/\sum_s(v(5):seq(int),v(3):int)]]])]]

Then, the procedure "*applyProofStep*" applies the transformation rule to the current theorem and derives the new theorem. In order to do that, this procedure constructs and asserts a set of clauses which implement the selected transformation rule. Then, it applies this set of clauses and derives the new theorem in ground representation. That is,

[all v(1):seq(int),[all v(2):int,sum_s(v(1):seq(int),v(2):int)<->
(eq(v(1):seq(int),nil_seq:seq(int))/\eq(v(2):int,0:int) \/
[ex v(3):int,[ex v(4):int,[ex v(5):seq(int),
false /\ sum_s(v(5):seq(int),v(3):int)]]])]]

The new theorem is then converted to the corresponding non-ground form in order to be presented to the user. That is,

$$[\ \forall x1/seq(Z),[\ \forall x2/Z,sum^S(x1,x2) \quad \leftrightarrow \quad (x1=<> \quad \wedge x2=0 \quad \vee \quad [\exists x3/Z,[\ \exists x4/seq(Z),$$
$$false \wedge sum^S(x4,x3)]])]]$$

5. System interface

To enable users to guide this proof checker it is necessary to provide a well-designed user interface. The design of the interface of an interactive verifier depends on the intended user. In our verifier we distinguish two kinds of users, the "*basic users*" and the "*advanced* or *experienced users*". We call "*basic user*" a user who is interested in proving a theorem. We call an "*advanced user*" a user who in addition to proving a theorem he/she may want to enhance the KB of the system in order to be able to deal with additional theorems. Such a user is expected to be able to update the KB of axioms, lemmas, predicate specifications, specifications of DT operations and programs. We will use the word "*user*" to mean both the "*basic user*" and the "*advanced user*". Both kinds of users are expected to know very well the correctness method which is supported by our system (Marakakis, 2005).

Initially, the system displays the main, top-level window as shown in Fig. 1. This window has a button for each of its main functions. The name of each button defines its function as well, that is, "*Transform Logic Specification into Structured Form*", "*Prove Program Correctness*" and "*Update Knowledge Base*". The selection of each button opens a new window which has a detailed description of the required functions for the corresponding operation. Now we will illustrate the "*Prove Program Correctness*" function to better understand the whole interaction with the user.

5.1 Interface illustration of the "Prove Program Correctness" task

If the user selects the button "*Prove Program Correctness*" from the main window, the window shown in Fig. 6 will be displayed. The aim of this window is to allow the user to select the appropriate theory and proof scheme that he will use in his proof. In addition, the user can either select a theorem or define a new one.

After the appropriate selections, the user can proceed to the actual proof of the theorem by selecting the button "*Prove Correctness Theorem*". The window that appears next is shown in Fig. 7. The aim of this window is to assist the user in the proof task. The theorem to be proved and its logic specification are displayed in the corresponding position on the top-left side of the window. This window has many functions. The user is able to choose theory elements from the KB that will be used for the current proof step. After selection by the user of the appropriate components for the current proof step the proper inference rule is selected and it is applied automatically. The result of the proof step is shown to the user. Moreover, the user is able to cancel the last proof step, or to create a report with all the details of the proof steps that have been applied so far.

5.1.1 Illustration of a proof step

Let's assume that the user has selected a theorem to be proved, its corresponding theory and a proof scheme. Therefore, he has proceeded to the verification task. For example, he likes to prove the following theorem:

$$Comp(Pr) \cup Spec \cup A \mid= \forall x1/seq(Z), x2/Z\ (sum(x1,x2) \leftrightarrow sum^{S}(x1,x2))$$

The user has selected the "*Incremental*" proof scheme which requires proof by induction on an inductive DT. Let assume that the correctness theorem has been transformed to the following form:

$$\forall x1/seq(Z),\ \forall x2/Z,\ sum(x1,x2) \leftrightarrow [\exists x3/Z,\ \exists x4/Z,\ \exists x5/seq(Z),\ x1 \neq <> \wedge x1=x4::x5 \wedge x1 \neq <> \wedge x1=x4::x5 \wedge x2=x4+x3 \wedge sum(x5,x3)]$$

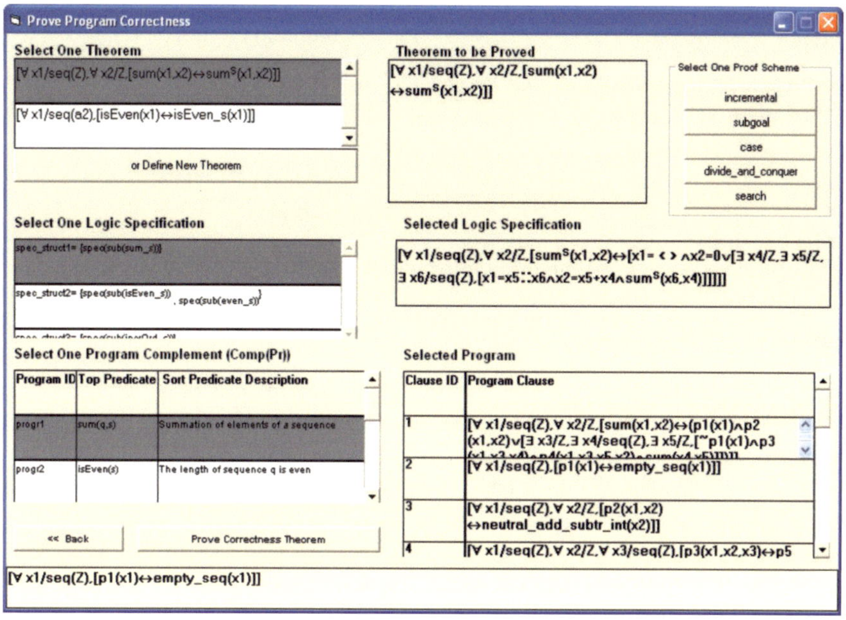

Fig. 6. The window for selecting Theory, Theorem and Proof Scheme

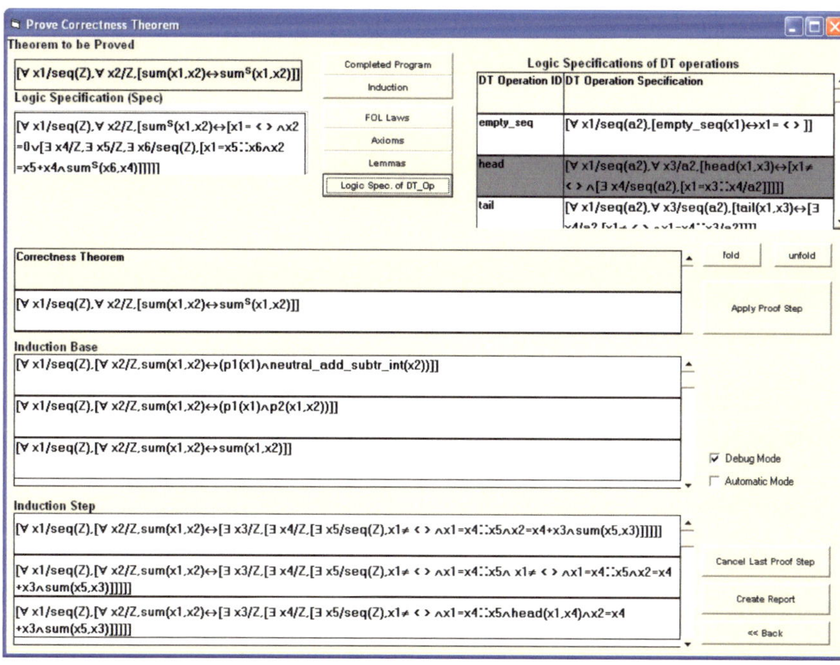

Fig. 7. The window for proving a correctness theorem

In order to proceed to the next proof step the following steps should be performed:

- First, the user selects *"Logic Spec. of DT_Op"* and then he selects the *"Head"* DT operation:

$\forall x1/seq(a2),\ \forall x3/a2,[head(x1,x3)\ \leftrightarrow [x1 \neq <> \wedge [\exists x4/seq(a2),[x1=x3::x4/a2]]]]$

- Then he selects the button *"Apply Proof Step"* and the result is shown in the next line of the *"Induction Step"* area:

$\forall x1/seq(Z),\ \forall x2/Z,\ sum(x1,x2)\ \leftrightarrow [\exists x3/Z,\ \exists x4/Z,\ \exists x5/seq(Z),$
$x1 \neq <> \wedge x1=x4::x5 \wedge head(x1,\ x4) \wedge x2=x4+x3 \wedge sum(x5,x3)]$

The user continues applying proof steps until to complete the proof of the theorem.

6. Results

The results of this research work involve the development of a proof checker that can be used efficiently by its users for the proof of correctness theorems for logic programs constructed by our schema-based method (Marakakis, 1997). The system has been tested and allows the verification of non-trivial logic programs. Our proof checker is highly modular, and allows the user to focus on proof decisions rather than on the details of how to apply each proof step, since this is done automatically by the system. The update of the KB is supported by the proof-checker as well. The overall interface of our system is user-friendly and facilitates the proof task.

The main features of our system which make it to be an effective and useful tool for the interactive verification of logic programs constructed by the method (Marakakis, 1997) are the following.

- The proof of the correctness theorem is guided by the logic-program construction method (Marakakis, 1997). That is, the user has to select a proof scheme based on the applied program schema for the construction of the top-level predicate of the logic program whose correctness will be shown.
- Proof steps can be cancelled at any stage of the proof. Therefore, a proof can move to any previous state.
- The system supports the proof of a new theorem as part of the proof of the initial theorem.
- The update of the theories stored in the KB of the system is supported as well.
- The overall verification task including the update of the KB is performed through a user-friendly interface.
- At any stage during the verification task the user can get a detailed report of all proof steps performed up to that point. So, he can get an overall view of the proof performed so far.

7. Conclusions

This chapter has presented our proof checker. It has been focused on the knowledge representation layer and on its use by the main reasoning algorithms. Special importance on the implementation of the proof checker has been given on flexibility so the system being developed could be enhanced with additional proof tasks. Finally, the main implementation criteria for the knowledge representation are the support for an efficient and modular implementation of the verifier.

In our proof checker, a proof is guided by the selected proof scheme. The selection of a proof scheme is related with the construction of the top-level predicate of the program that will be verified. The user-friendly interface of our system facilitates the proof task in all stages and the update of the KB. Its modular implementation makes our proof checker extensible and amenable to improvements.

The natural progression of our proof checker is the addition of automation. That is, we intend to move proof decisions from the user to the system. The verifier should have the capacity to suggest proof steps to the user. Once they are accepted by the user they will be performed automatically. Future improvements aim to minimize the interaction with the user and to maximize the automation of the verification task.

8. References

Clarke, E. & Wing, J. (1996). Formal Methods: State of the Art and Future Directions, *ACM Computing Surveys*, Vol. 28, No. 4, pp. 626-643, December, 1996.

Gallagher, J. (1993). Tutorial on Specialization of Logic Programs, *Proceedings of PERM'93, the ACM Sigplan Symposium on Partial Evaluation and Semantics-Based Program Manipulation*, pp. 88-98, ACM Press, 1993.

Hill, P. M. & Gallagher, J. (1998). Meta-programming in Logic Programming, *Handbook of Logic in Artificial Intelligence and Logic Programming*, vol. 5, edited by D. Gabbay, C. Hogger, J. Robinson, pp. 421-497, Clarendon Press, Oxford, 1998.

Hill, P. M. & Lloyd, J. W. (1994). The Gödel Programming Language, The MIT Press, 1994.

Lindsay, P. (1988). A Survey of Mechanical Support for Formal Reasoning, *Software Engineering Journal*, vol. 3, no. 1, pp.3-27, 1988.

Lloyd, J.W. (1994). Practical Advantages of Declarative Programming. In Proceedings of the Joint Conference on Declarative Programming, GULP-PRODE'94, 1994.

Loveland, D. W. (1986). Automated Theorem Proving: Mapping Logic in AI, *Proceedings of the ACM SIGART International Symposium on Methodologies for Intelligent Systems*, pp. 214-229, Knoxville, Tennessee, United States, October 22-24, 1986.

Marakakis, E. (1997). Logic Program Development Based on Typed, Moded Schemata and Data Types, *PhD thesis*, University of Bristol, February, 1997.

Marakakis, E. (2005). Guided Correctness Proofs of Logic Programs, *Proc. the 23th IASTED International Multi-Conference on Applied Informatics*, edited by M.H. Hamza, pp. 668-673, Innsbruck, Austria, 2005.

Marakakis, E. & Gallagher. J.P. (1994). Schema-Based Top-Down Design of Logic Programs Using Abstract Data Types, *LNCS 883, Proc. of 4th Int. Workshops on Logic Program Synthesis and Transformation - Meta-Programming in Logic*, pp.138-153, Pisa, Italy, 1994.

Marakakis, E. & Papadakis, N. (2009). An Interactive Verifier for Logic Programs, *Proc. Of 13th IASTED International Conference on Artificial Intelligence and Soft Computing* , pp. 130-137, 2009.

8

Knowledge in Imperfect Data

Andrzej Kochanski, Marcin Perzyk and Marta Klebczyk
Warsaw University of Technology
Poland

1. Introduction

Data bases collecting a huge amount of information pertaining to real-world processes, for example industrial ones, contain a significant number of data which are imprecise, mutually incoherent, and frequently even contradictory. It is often the case that data bases of this kind often lack important information. All available means and resources may and should be used to eliminate or at least minimize such problems at the stage of data collection. It should be emphasized, however, that the character of industrial data bases, as well as the ways in which such bases are created and the data are collected, preclude the elimination of all errors. It is, therefore, a necessity to find and develop methods for eliminating errors from already-existing data bases or for reducing their influence on the accuracy of analyses or hypotheses proposed with the application of these data bases. There are at least three main reasons for data preparation: (a) the possibility of using the data for modeling, (b) modeling acceleration, and (c) an increase in the accuracy of the model. An additional motivation for data preparation is that it offers a possibility of arriving at a deeper understanding of the process under modeling, including the understanding of the significance of its most important parameters.

The literature pertaining to data preparation (Pyle, 1999, 2003; Han & Kamber, 2001; Witten & Frank, 2005; Weiss & Indurkhya, 1998; Masters, 1999; Kusiak, 2001; Refaat, 2007) discusses various data preparation tasks (characterized by means of numerous methods, algorithms, and procedures). Apparently, however, no ordered and coherent classification of tasks and operations involved in data preparation has been proposed so far. This has a number of reasons, including the following: (a) numerous article publications propose solutions to problems employing selected individual data preparation operations, which may lead to the conclusion that such classifications are not really necessary, (b) monographs deal in the minimal measure with the industrial data, which have their own specific character, different from that of the business data, (c) the fact that the same operations are performed for different purposes in different tasks complicates the job of preparing such a classification.

The information pertaining to how time-consuming data preparation is appears in the works by many authors. The widely-held view expressed in the literature is that the time devoted to data preparation constitutes considerably more than a half of the overall data exploration time (Pyle, 2003; McCue, 2007). A systematically conducted data preparation can reduce this time. This constitutes an additional argument for developing the data preparation methodology which was proposed in (Kochanski, 2010).

2. A taxonomy of data preparation

Discussing the issue of data preparation the present work uses the terms *process, stage, task,* and *operation*. Their mutual relations are diagrammatically represented in Fig. 1 below. The data preparation process encompasses all the data preparation tasks. Two stages may be distinguished within it: the introductory stage and the main stage. The stages of the process involve carrying out tasks, each of which, in turn, involves a range of operations. The data preparation process always starts with the introductory stage. Within each stage (be it the introductory or the main one) different tasks may be performed. In the introductory stage, the performance of the first task (the choice of the first task is dictated by the specific nature of the case under analysis) should always be followed by data cleaning. It is only after data cleaning in the introductory stage that performing the tasks of the main stage may be initiated. In the main stage, the choice of the first task, as well as ordering of the tasks that follow are not predetermined and are dependent on the nature of the case under consideration. As far as the data collected in real-life industrial (production) processes are concerned, four tasks may be differentiated:

- data cleaning is used in eliminating any inconsistency or incoherence in the collected data
- data integration makes possible integrating data bases coming from various sources into a single two-dimensional table, thanks to which algorithmized tools of data mining can be employed
- data transformation includes a number of operations aimed at making possible the building of a model, accelerating its building, and improving its accuracy, and employing, among others, widely known normalization or attribute construction methods
- data reduction limits the dimensionality of a data base, that is, the number of variables; performing this task significantly reduces the time necessary for data mining.

Each of the tasks involves one or more operations. An operation is understood here as a single action performed on the data. The same operation may be a part of a few tasks.

In Fig. 1, within each of the four tasks the two stages of the process are differentiated: the introductory stage of data preparation (in the diagram, this represented as the outer circles marked with broken lines) and the main stage of data preparation (represented as inner circles marked with solid lines). These two separate stages, which have been differentiated, have quite different characters and use quite different tools. The first stage - that of the introductory data preparation - is performed just once. Its performance in particular tasks is limited to a single operation. This operation is always followed by the task of data cleaning. The stage of the introductory data cleaning is a non-algorithmized stage. It is not computer-aided and it is based on the knowledge and the experience of the human agent preparing the data.

The second - that is, the main - stage is much more developed. It can be repeated many times at each moment of the modeling and of the analysis of the developed model. The repetition of the data preparation tasks or the change in the tools employed in particular tasks is aimed at increasing the accuracy of the analyses. The order in which the tasks are carried out may change depending upon the nature of the issue under analysis and the form of the collected data. According to the present authors, it seems that it is data cleaning which should always be performed as the first task. However, the remaining tasks may be performed in any order. In some cases different tasks are performed in parallel: for instance the operations performed in the task of data integration may be performed simultaneously with the operations involved in data transformation, without deciding on any relative priority. Depending on the performed operations, data reduction may either precede data integration (attribute selection) or go at the very end of the data preparation process (dimensionality selection).

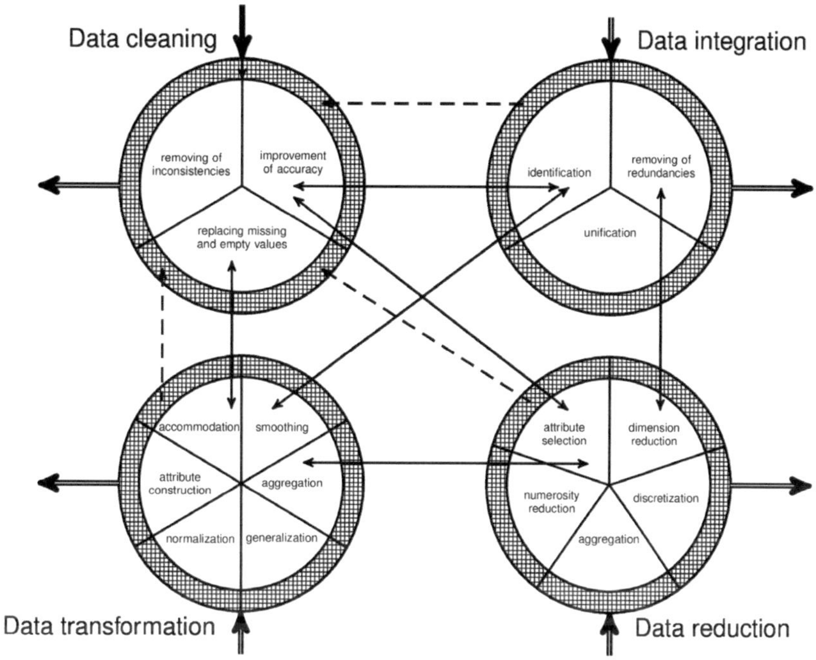

Fig. 1. Tasks carried out in the process of data preparation with the distinction into the introductory and the main stage (Kochanski, 2010)

3. Task of data preparation

A task is a separate self-contained part of data preparation which may be and which in practice is performed at each stage of the data preparation process. We can distinguish four tasks (as represented in Fig. 1): data cleaning, data transformation, data integration, and data reduction. Depending upon the stage of the data preparation process, a different number of operations may be performed in a task - at the introductory stage the number of operations is limited. These operations, as well as the operations performed in the main stage will be discussed below, in the sections devoted to particular tasks.

The data preparation process, at the stage of introductory preparation, may start with any task, but after finishing the introductory stage of this task, it is necessary to go through the introductory stage of data cleaning. It is only then when one can perform operations belonging to other tasks, including the operations of the task with which the process of data preparation has started. This procedure follows from the fact that in the further preparation, be it in the introductory or in the main stage, the analyst should have at his disposal possibly the most complete data base and only then make further decisions.

It is only after the introductory stage is completed in all tasks that the main stage can be initiated. This is motivated by the need to avoid any computer-aided operations on raw data.

3.1 Data cleaning

Data cleaning is a continuous process, which reappears at every stage of data exploration. However, it is especially important at the introductory data preparation stage, among others, because of how much time these operations take. At this phase, it involves a one-time data correction, which resides in the elimination of all kind of errors resulting from human negligence at the stage of data collection. The introductory data cleaning is a laborious process of consulting the source materials, often in the form of paper records, laboratory logs and forms, measuring equipment outprints, etc., and filling in the missing data by hand. The overall documentation collected at this stage may also be used in the two other operations of this task: in accuracy improvement and in inconsistency removal.

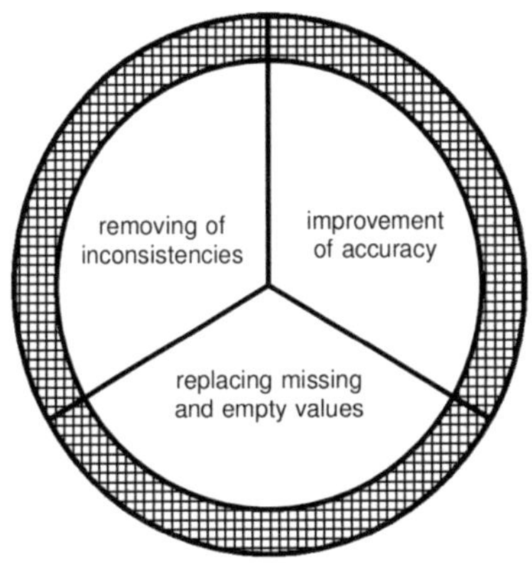

Fig. 2. Operations performed in the data cleaning task (with the introductory stage represented as the squared area and the main stage represented as the white area)

As shown in Fig. 2, the data cleaning task may involve three operations, the replacement of the missing or empty values, the accuracy improvement, and the inconsistency removal, which in the main stage employ algorithmized methods:

- replacement of missing or empty values employs the methods of calculating the missing or empty value with the use of the remaining values of the attribute under replacement or with the use of all attributes of the data set;
- accuracy improvement is based on the algorithmized methods of the replacement of the current value with the newly-calculated one or the removal of this current value;
- inconsistency removal most frequently employs special procedures (e.g. control codes) programmed in data collection sheets prior to the data collecting stage.

In what follows, these three operations will be discussed in detail because of their use in the preparation of the data for modeling.

a. The replacement of missing or empty values

The case of the absent data may cover two kinds of data: an empty value – when a particular piece of data could not have been recorded, since - for instance - such a value of the measured quantity was not taken into consideration at all, and a missing value - when a particular piece of data has not been recorded, since - for instance - it was lost. The methods of missing or empty value replacement may be divided into two groups, which use for the purpose of calculating the new value the subset of the data containing:

either

- only the values of the attribute under replacement (simple replacement)

or

- either the specially selected or all the values of the collected set (complex replacement).

The methods of simple replacement include all the methods based on statistical values (statistics), such as, for instance the mean value, the median, or the standard deviation. The new values which are calculated via these methods and which are to replace the empty or the missing values retain the currently defined distribution measures of the set.

The complex replacement aims at replacing the absent piece of data with such a value as should have been filled in originally, had it been properly recorded (had it not been lost). Since these methods are aimed at recreating the proper value, a consequence of their application is that the distribution measures of the replacing data set may be and typically are changed.

In complex replacement the absent value is calculated from the data collected in the subset which contains selected attributes (Fig. 3a) or selected records (Fig. 3b) and which has been created specifically for this purpose. The choice of a data replacement method depends on the properties of the collected data - on finding or not finding correlations between or among attributes. If there is any correlation between, on the one hand, selected attributes and, on the other, the attribute containing the absent value, it is possible to establish a multilinear regression which ties the attributes under analysis (the attribute containing the absent value and the attributes which are correlated with it). In turn, on this basis the absent value may be calculated. An advantage of this method is the possibility of obtaining new limits, that is, a new minimal and maximal value of the attribute under replacement, which is lower or higher than the values registered so far. It is also for this reason that this method is used for the replacement of empty data.

When there is no correlation between the attribute of the value under replacement and the remaining attributes of the set, the absent value is calculated via a comparison with the selected records from the set containing complete data. This works when the absent value is a missing value.

The choice of a data replacement method should take into consideration the proposed data modeling method. Simple replacement may be used when the modeling method is insensitive to the noise in the data. For models which cannot cope with the noise in the data complex data replacement methods should be used.

It is a frequent error commonly made in automatized absent data replacement that no record is made with respect to which pieces of the data are originally collected values and which have been replaced. This piece of information is particularly important when the model quality is being analyzed.

X	X_1	X_2	X_3	X_4	X_5	X_6	X_7	X_8
1	0,44264	0,33500	0,25427	0,35923	0,16962	0,00716	0,48662	0,32565
2	0,22330	0,28883	0,83385	0,47689	0,70585	0,37254	0,93544	0,56954
3	0,27493	0,33005	0,58590	0,34546	0,01733	0,31112	0,85849	0,45207
4	0,98221	0,48329	0,60996	0,63946	0,36832	0,47123	0,20616	0,87007
5	0,13867	0,04751	0,82575	0,95047	0,74808	0,51304	0,12866	0,92690
6	0,19544	0,64661	0,54804	0,54047	0,19131	0,03098	0,49135	0,71928
7	0,30852	0,16328	0,55166	0,54092	0,54074	0,04924	0,58695	0,66732
8	0,00041	0,25978	0,31942	0,45177	0,03746	0,01925	0,14991	0,46064
9	0,19001	0,25658	0,05029	0,15835	0,33636		0,80948	0,15902
10	0,96184	0,46663	0,95992	0,54820	0,04761	0,80451	0,27177	0,48748
11	0,66559	0,95384	0,84559	0,76149	0,79613	0,99048	0,73015	0,97383
12	0,44050	0,31420	0,95545	0,69524	0,19512	0,47188	0,56926	0,95379
13	0,34064	0,64198	0,61337	0,27064	0,18290	0,48872	0,95916	0,69138
14	0,54202	0,40815	0,69619	0,49253	0,33158	0,64028	0,37219	0,78562
15	0,19946	0,10397	0,62387	0,90537	0,85044	0,66453	0,30543	0,80890
16	0,41862	0,48597	0,93570	0,73022	0,73567	0,42406	0,68604	0,82964
17	0,06957	0,49556	0,57802	0,45966	0,56085	0,35513	0,91340	0,75443
18	0,45747	0,98770	0,43052	0,36385	0,56939	0,14738	0,62208	0,65532
19	0,09304	0,95937	0,44208	0,61713	0,06287	0,65605	0,26071	0,67018
20	0,07758	0,17060	0,62618	0,93290	0,19343	0,88051	0,74191	0,94996

(a)

X	X_1	X_2	X_3	X_4	X_5	X_6	X_7	X_8
1	0,44264	0,33500	0,25427	0,35923	0,16962	0,00716	0,48662	0,32565
2	0,22330	0,28883	0,83385	0,47689	0,70585	0,37254	0,93544	0,16954
3	0,27493	0,33005	0,58590	0,34546	0,01733	0,41112	0,85849	0,45207
4	0,98221	0,48329	0,60996	0,63946	0,36832	0,47123	0,20616	0,87007
5	0,13867	0,04751	0,82575	0,95047	0,74808	0,10304	0,12866	0,82690
6	0,19544	0,64661	0,54804	0,54047	0,19131	0,03098	0,49135	0,71928
7	0,30852	0,16328	0,81166	0,54092	0,54074	0,84924	0,58695	0,66732
8	0,00041	0,25978	0,51942	0,45177	0,03746	0,10925	0,14991	0,46064
9	0,19001	0,25658	0,05029	0,15835	0,33636	0,59725	0,80948	0,15902
10	0,96184	0,46663	0,95992	0,54820		0,50451	0,27177	0,28748
11	0,66559	0,95384	0,84559	0,76149	0,79613	0,99048	0,73015	0,97383
12	0,44050	0,31420	0,95545	0,69524	0,19512	0,47188	0,56926	0,95379
13	0,34064	0,64198	0,14337	0,27064	0,18290	0,48872	0,95916	0,09138
14	0,94202	0,40815	0,69619	0,49253	0,33158	0,64028	0,37219	0,48562
15	0,19946	0,10397	0,32387	0,90537	0,85044	0,36453	0,30543	0,80890
16	0,91862	0,48597	0,93570	0,53022	0,73567	0,52406	0,18604	0,29636
17	0,06957	0,49556	0,07802	0,45966	0,56085	0,35513	0,31340	0,35443
18	0,45747	0,98770	0,43052	0,36385	0,56939	0,14738	0,62208	0,65532
19	0,09304	0,95937	0,14208	0,61713	0,06287	0,65605	0,26071	0,67018
20	0,07758	0,17060	0,62618	0,93290	0,19343	0,88051	0,74191	0,54996

(b)

Fig. 3. (a) Selected attributes (X_3, X_8) will serve in calculating the absent value in attribute X_6 (b) Selected records (4, 14, 16) will serve in calculating the absent value in attribute 10

b. Accuracy improvement

The operation of accuracy improvement, in the main stage of data preparation, is based on algorithmized methods of calculating a value and either replacing the current value (the value recorded in the database) with the newly-calculated one or completely removing the current value from the base. The mode of operation depends upon classifying the value under analysis as either noisy or an outlier. This is why, firstly, this operation focuses on identifying the outliers within the set of the collected data. In the literature, one can find reference to numerous techniques of identifying pieces of the data which are classified as outliers (Alves & Nascimento, 2002; Ben-Gal, 2005; Cateni et al., 2008; Fan et al., 2006; Mohamed et al., 2007). This is an important issue, since it is only in the case of outliers that their removal from the set may be justified. Such an action is justified when the model is developed, for instance, for the purpose of optimizing an industrial process. If a model is being developed with the purpose of identifying potential hazards and break-downs in a process, the outliers should either be retained within the data set or should constitute a new, separate set, which will serve for establishing a separate pattern. On the other hand, noisy data can, at best, be corrected but never removed - unless we have excessive data at our disposal.

In the literature, there are two parallel classifications of the outlier identification methods. The first employs the division into one-dimension methods and multidimension methods. The second divides the relevant methods into the statistical (or traditional) ones and the ones which employ advanced methods of data exploration.

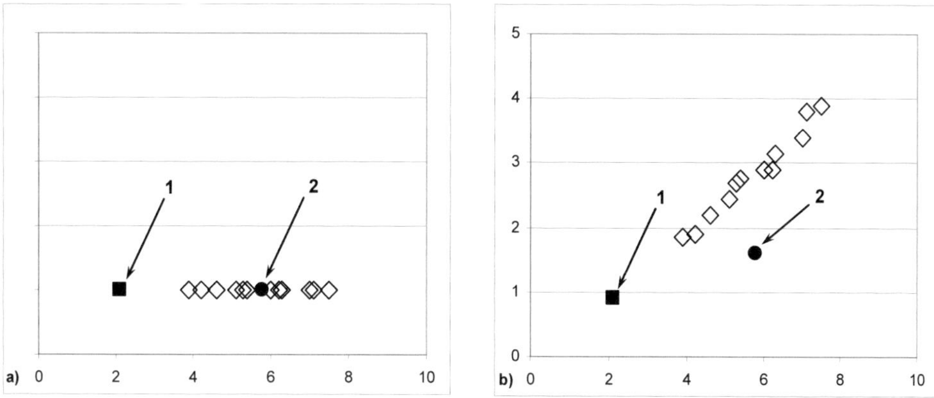

Fig. 4. Outliers a) one-dimension, b) multidimension; 1, 2 outliers - a description in the text

The analysis of one-dimension data employs definitions which recognize as outliers the data which are distant, relative to the assumed metric, from the main data concentration. Frequently, the expanse of the concentration is defined via its mean value and the standard error. In that case, the outlier is a value (the point marked as 1 in Fig. 4a) which is located outside the interval (X_m - k* 2SE, X_m + k* 2SE), where: SE - standard error, k - coefficient, X_m - mean value. The differences between the authors pertain to the value of the k coefficient and the labels for the kinds of data connected with it, for instance the outliers going beyond the boundaries calculated for k = 3,6 (Jimenez-Marquez et al., 2002) or the outliers for k = 1,5 and the extreme data for k = 3 (StatSoft, 2011). Equally popular is the method using a box plot (Laurikkala et al., 2000), which is based on a similar assumption concerning the calculation of the thresholds above and below which a piece of data is treated as an outlier.

For some kind of data, for instance those coming from multiple technological processes and used for the development of industrial applications, the above methods do not work. The data of this kind exhibit a multidimensional correlation. For correlated data a one-dimension analysis does not lead to correct results, which is clearly visible from the example in Fig. 4 (prepared from synthetic data). In accordance with the discussed method, Point 1 (marked as a black square) in Fig. 4a would be classified as an outlier. However, it is clearly visible from multidimensional (two-dimensional) data represented in Fig. 4b that it is point 2 (represented as a black circle) which is an outlier. In one-dimension analysis it was treated as an average value located quite close to the mean value.

Commonly used tools for finding one-dimension outliers are statistical methods. In contrast to the case of one-dimension outliers, the methods used for finding multidimensional outliers are both statistical methods and advanced methods of data exploration. Statistical methods most frequently employ the Mahalanobis metric. In the basic Mahalanobis method for each vector x_i the Mahalanobis distance is calculated according to the following formula (1) (Rousseeuw & Zomeren, 1990):

$$\mathrm{MD}_i = \left(\left(\mathbf{x}_i - T(\mathbf{X})\right)\mathbf{C}(\mathbf{X})^{-1}\left(\mathbf{x}_i - T(\mathbf{X})\right)^{t}\right)^{1/2} \qquad \text{for } i = 1, 2, 3, \ldots n \tag{1}$$

where: $T(\mathbf{X})$ is the arithmetic mean of the data set, $\mathbf{C}(\mathbf{X})$ is the covariance matrix.

This method takes into account not only the central point of the data set, but also the shape of the data set in multidimensional space. A case with a large Mahalanobis distance can be identified as a potential outlier. On the basis of a comparison with the chi-square distribution, an outlier can be removed as was suggested in (Filzmoser, 2005). In the literature, further improvements of the Mahalanobis distance method can be found, for example the one called the Robust Mahalanobis Distance (Bartkowiak, 2005). The outlier detection based on the Mahalanobis distance in industrial data, was performed in e.g. (Jimenez-Marquez et al., 2002). As far as data exploration is concerned, in principle all methods are used. The most popular ones are based on artificial neural networks (Alves & Nascimento, 2002), grouping (Moh'd Belal Al- Zgubi, 2009), or visualization (Hasimah et al., 2007), but there are also numerous works which suggest new possibilities of the use of other methods of data mining, for example of the rough set theory (Shaari et al., 2007). An assumption of methodologies employing data exploration methods is that the data departing from the model built with their help should be treated as outliers.

c. Inconsistency removal

At the introductory stage inconsistencies are primarily removed by hand, via reference to the source materials and records. At this stage it will also encompass the verification of the attributes of the collected data. It is important to remove all redundancies at this stage. Redundant attributes may appear both in basic databases and in databases created via combining a few smaller data sets. Most often, this is a consequence of using different labels in different data sets to refer to the same attributes. Redundant attributes in merged databases suggest that we have at our disposal a much bigger number of attributes than is in fact the case. An example of a situation of this kind is labeling the variables (columns) referring to metal elements in a container as, respectively, *element mass, the number of elements in a container,* and *the mass of elements in the container.* If the relevant piece of information is not repeated exactly, for example, if instead of the attribute *the mass of elements in the container* what is collected is *the mass of metal in the container,* then the only problem is increasing the model development time. It is not always the case that this is a significant problem, since the majority of models have a bigger problem with the number of records, than with the number of attributes. However, in the modeling of processes aimed at determining the influence of signal groups, an increase in the number of inputs is accompanied with an avalanche increase in the number of input variable group combinations (Kozlowski, 2009). It should also be remembered that some modeling techniques, especially those based on regression, cannot cope with two collinear attributes (Galmacci, 1996). This pertains also to a small group of matrix-based methods (Pyle, 1999).

At the main stage of data preparation inconsistency removal may be aided with specially designed procedures (e.g. control codes) or tools dedicated to finding such inconsistencies (e.g. when the correlations/interdependencies among parameters are known).

3.2 Data integration

Because of the tools used in knowledge extraction it is necessary that the data be represented in the form of a flat, two-dimensional table. It is becoming possible to analyze the data recorded in a different form, but the column-row structure - as in a calculation sheet - is the best one (Pyle, 2003). The task of data integration may be both simple and complicated, since it depends on the form in which the data is collected. In the case of synthetic data, as well as in appropriately prepared industrial data collecting systems this is unproblematic. However, the majority of industrial databases develop in an uncoordinated way. Different departments of the same plant develop their own databases for their own purposes. These databases are further developed without taking into consideration other agencies. This results in a situation in which the same attributes are repeated in numerous databases, the same attributes are labeled differently in different databases, the same attributes have different proportions of absent data in different bases, the developed databases have different primary keys (case identifiers), etc. The situation gets even worse when the databases under integration have been developed not within a single plant but in more distant places, for example in competing plants.

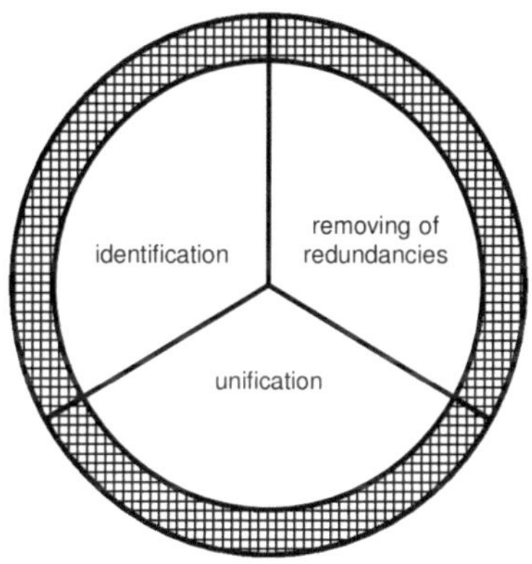

Fig. 5. The operations performed in the data integration task (with the introductory stage represented as the squared area and the main stage represented as the white area)

As represented in Fig 5, data integration consists of three operations. The introductory stage of data integration focuses on two of them: identification and redundancy removal. Both these operations are closely connected with one another. The first operation - identification - is necessary, since the task of data integration starts with identifying the quantity around which the database sets may be integrated. Also, at the data integration introductory stage the removal of obvious redundancies should be performed. Their appearance may result, for instance, from the specific way in which the industrial production data is recorded. The results of tests conducted in centrally-operated laboratories are used by different factory departments, which store these results independently of one another, in their own databases. The result of data integration performed without introductory analysis may be that the same quantities may be listed in the end-product database a number of times and, moreover, they may be listed there under different labels. A person who knows the data under analysis will identify such redundant records without any problem.

At the main stage, unlike in other data preparation tasks, the integration operations are only performed with the aid of algorithmized tools and are still based on the knowledge about the process under analysis. At this stage, the operations represented in Fig. 5 are performed with the following aims:

- identification - serves the purpose of identifying the attributes which could not have been identified at the introductory stage, for instance, in those cases in which the label does not explain anything,
- redundancy removal - just like the attribute selection in the data reduction task, which is characterized below, uses algorithmized methods of comparing the attributes which have been identified only in the main stage with the aim of removing the redundant data,
- unification - this is performed so that the data collected in different sets have the same form, for instance the same units.

The operation of identification uses methods which make it possible to identify the correlation between the attribute under analysis and other identified process attributes. In this way it is possible to establish, for instance, what a particular attribute pertains to, where the sensor making the recorded measurement could have been installed, etc.

The second performance of the redundancy removal operation pertains only to attributes which have been identified only in the second, main stage of data integration. As far as this second performance is concerned, redundancy removal may be identified with the attribute selection operation from the data reduction task and it uses the same methods as the attribute selection operation.

Unification is very close to the data transformation task. In most cases it amounts to transforming all the data in such a way that they are recorded in a unified form, via converting part of the data using different scales into the same units, for instance, converting inches into millimeters, meters into millimeters, etc. A separate issue is the unification of the data collected in different sets and originating from measurements employing different methods. In such cases one should employ the algorithms for converting one attribute form into another. These may include both analytical formulas (exact conversion) and approximate empirical formulas. When this is not possible, unification may be achieved via one of the data transformation operations, that is, via normalization (Liang & Kasabov, 2003).

The main principle that the person performing the data integration task should stick to is that the integrated database should retain all the information collected in the data sets which have been integrated. Seemingly, the suggestion, expressed in (Witten & Frank, 2005), that data integration should be accompanied by aggregation, is misguided. Aggregation may accompany integration, but only when this is absolutely necessary.

3.3 Data transformation

Data transformation introductory stage usually amounts to a single operation dictated by data integration, such as aggregation, generalization, normalization or attribute (feature) construction. Performing aggregation may be dictated by the fact that the data collected in multiple places during the production process may represent results from different periods:

a different hour, shift, day, week or month. Finding a common higher-order interval of time is necessary for further analyses. The same reasons make necessary the performance of generalization or normalization. Generalization may be dictated, for instance, by the integration of databases in which the same attribute is once recorded in a nominal scale (e.g. ultimate tensile strength - ductile iron grade 500/07) and once in a ratio scale (ultimate tensile strength - UTS = 572 MPa). We can talk about normalization in the introductory stage only when we understand this term in its widest sense, that is, as a conversion of quantities from one range into those of another range. In that case, such a transformation as measurement unit conversion may be understood as normalization at the introductory stage.

Data transformation encompasses all the issues connected with transforming the data into a form which makes data exploration possible. At the introductory stage it involves six operations represented in Fig. 6:

- smoothing - this resides in transforming the data in such a way that local data deviations having the character of noise are eliminated. Smoothing encompasses, among others, the techniques such as, for example, binning, clustering, or regression;
- aggregation - this resides in summing up the data, most frequently in the function of time, for example from a longer time period encompassing not just a single shift but a whole month;
- generalization - this resides in converting the collected data containing the measurements of the registered process quantity into higher-order quantities, for instance via their discretization;
- normalization - this resides in the rescaling (adjustment) of the data to a specified, narrow range, for instance, from 0.0 to 1.0;
- attribute (feature) construction - this resides in mathematical transformations of attributes (features) with the aim of obtaining a new attribute (feature), which will replace in modeling its constituent attributes;
- accommodation - this resides in transforming the data into a format used by a specific algorithm or a tool, for example into the ARFF format (Witten & Frank, 2005).

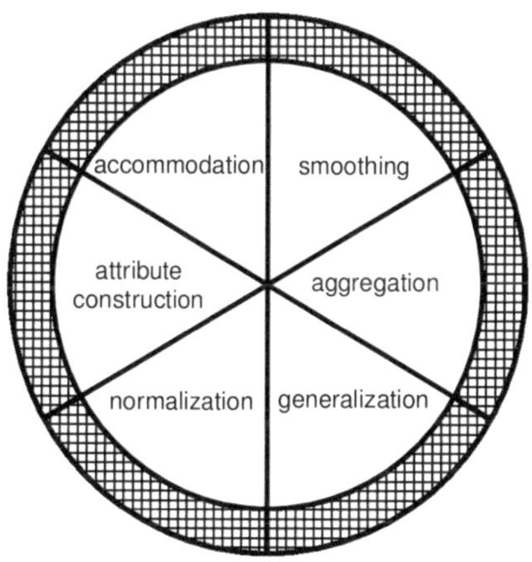

Fig. 6. Operations performed in the data transformation task (with the introductory stage represented as the squared area and the main stage represented as the white area).

Smoothing is an operation which follows from the assumption that the collected data are noisy with random errors or with divergence of measured attributes. In the case of industrial (also laboratory) data such a situation is a commonplace, unlike in the case of business data (the dollar exchange rate cannot possibly be noisy). Smoothing techniques are aimed at removing the noise, without at the same time interfering with the essence of the measured attributes. Smoothing methods may be of two kinds: (a) those which focus on comparing the quantity under analysis with its immediate neighborhood and (b) those which analyze the totality of the collected data.

Group (a) includes methods which analyze a specified lag or window. In the former case, the data are analyzed in their original order, while in the latter they are changed in order. These methods are based on a comparison with the neighboring values and use, for instance, the mean, the weighted moving mean, or the median. Group (b) includes methods employing regression or data clustering. The method of loess - local regression could be classified as belonging to either group.

In the first group of methods (a) a frequent solution is to combine a few of techniques into a single procedure. This is supposed to bring about a situation in which further smoothing does not introduce changes into the collected data. A strategy of this kind is resmoothing, in which two approaches may be adopted: either 1) smoothing is continued up to the moment when after a subsequent smoothing the curve does not change or 2) a specified number of smoothing cycles is performed, but this involves changing the window size. Two such procedures, 4253H and 3R2H were discussed in (Pyle, 1999). A method which should also be included in the first group (a) is the PVM (peak - valley - mean) method.

Binning, which belongs to group (a) is a method of smoothing (also data cleaning) residing in the creation of bins and the ascription of data to these bins. The data collected in the respective bins are compared to one another within each bin and unified via one of a few methods, for example, via the replacement with the mean value, the replacement with the median, or the replacement with the boundary value. A significant parameter of smoothing via binning is the selection of the size of bins to be transformed. Since comparing is performed only within the closest data collected in a single bin, binning is a kind of local smoothing of the data.

As was already mentioned above, the second important group of smoothing methods (b) are the techniques employing all the available data. Among others, this includes the methods of regression and of data clustering.

Fig.7 represents the smoothing of the laboratory data attribute (ultimate compressive strength) of greensand in the function of moisture content. The data may be smoothed via adjusting the function to the measured data. Regression means the adjustment of the best curve to the distribution of two attributes, so that one of these attributes could serve for the prediction of the other attribute. In multilinear regression the function is adjusted to the data collected in the space which is more than two-dimensional.

An example of smoothing with the use of data clustering techniques was discussed in (Kochanski, 2006). In the data which is grouped the outliers may easily be detected and either smoothed or removed from the set. This procedure makes possible defining the range of variability of the data under analysis.

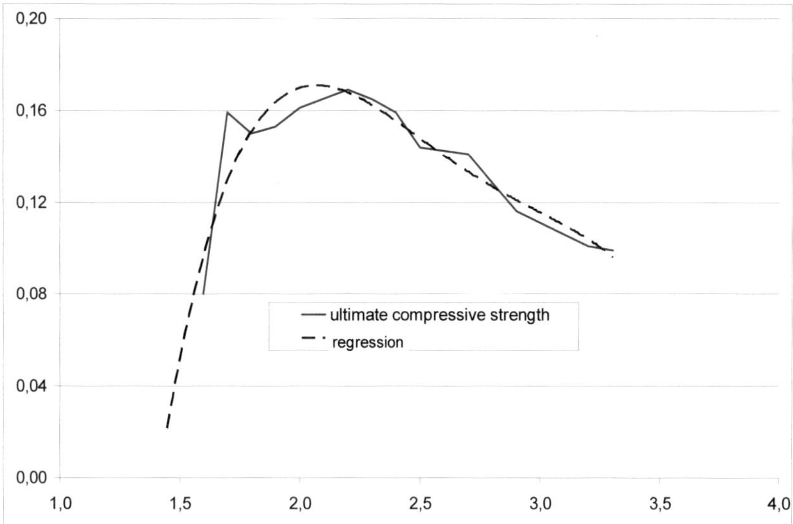

Fig. 7. The regression method applied to the industrial data: the ultimate compressive strength of greensand in the function of moisture content (the authors' own research)

In the case of industrial data the issue of smoothing should be treated with an appropriate care. The removal or smoothing of an outlier may determine the model's capability for predicting hazards, break-downs or product defects. The industrial data often contain quantities which result from the process parameter synergy. The quantity which may undergo smoothing is, for instance, the daily or monthly furnace charge for the prediction of the trend in its consumption, but not the form moisture content for the prediction of the appearance of porosity.

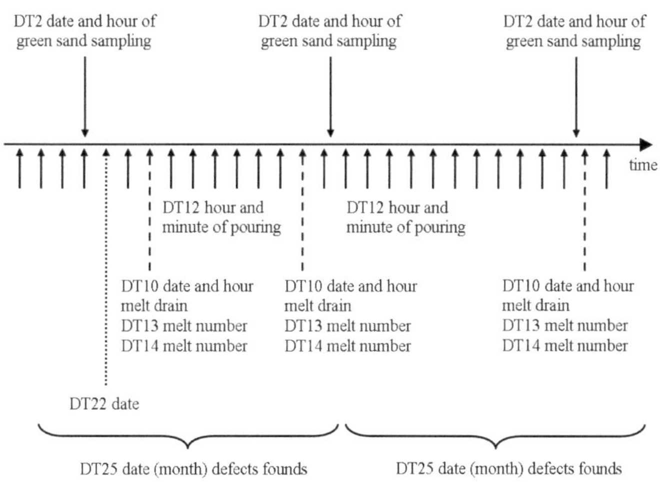

Fig. 8. Measurements performed with different frequency and encompassing different time periods: from a measurement encompassing 1 minute to a measurement encompassing the data from an entire month; (the data are collected in different places: DTxx – a symbol for the process technical documentation) (Research report, 2005)

In manufacture processes, when different operations are performed in different places and records are collected in separate forms, a frequent situation is the impossibility of integrating the separate cases into a single database. The absence of a single key makes data integration impossible. (Research report, 2005) discusses data integration with the use of aggregation. Data aggregation (represented as parentheses) and data location on the time axis, which makes possible further integration, are diagrammed in Fig. 8.

Generalization in data preparation is an operation which is aimed at reducing the number of the values that an individual attribute may take. In particular, it converts a continuous quantity into an attribute which takes the value of one of the specified ranges. The replacement of a continuous quantity with a smaller number of labeled ranges makes easier grasping the nature of the correlation found in the course of data exploration. Generalization applies to two terms: discretization and notional hierarchy.

Discretization is a method which makes possible splitting the whole range of attribute variation into a specified number of subregions. Discretization methods in the two main classifications are characterized in terms of the direction in which they are performed or in terms of whether or not in feature division they employ information contained in the features other than the one under discretization. In the first case, we talk about bottom-up or top-down methods. In the second case, we distinguish between supervised and unsupervised methods.

The notional hierarchy for a single feature makes possible reducing the number of the data via grouping and the replacement of a numerical quantity, for instance the percentage of carbon in the chemical composition of an alloy, with a higher-order notion, that is, *a low-carbonic* and *a high-carbonic alloy*. This leads to a partial loss of information but, in turn, thanks to the application of this method it may be easier to provide an interpretation and in the end this interpratation may become more comprehensible.

There are many commonly used methods of data normalization (Pyle, 1999; Larose, 2008). The effect of performing the operation of normalization may be a change in the variable range and/or a change in the variable distribution. Some data mining tools, for example artificial neural networks, require normalized quantities. Ready-made commercial codes have special modules which normalize the entered data. When we perform data analysis, we should take into consideration the method which has been employed in normalization. This method may have a significant influence on the developed model and the accuracy of its predictions (Cannataro, 2008; Ginoris et al., 2007; Al Shalabi et al., 2006).

The following are the main reasons for performing normalization:

- a transformation of the ranges of all attributes into a single range makes possible the elimination of the influence of the feature magnitude (their order 10, 100, 1000) on the developed model. In this way we can avoid revaluing features with high values,
- a transformation of the data into a dimensionless form and the consequent achievement of commensurability of a few features makes possible calculating the case distance, for instance with the use of the Euclid metric,
- a nonlinear transformation makes possible relieving the frequency congestion and uniformly distributing the relevant cases in the range of features,
- a nonlinear transformation makes it possible to take into consideration the outliers,

- data transformation makes possible a comparison of the results from different tests (Liang & Kasabov, 2003).

The following may be listed as the most popular normalization methods:

- min-max normalization - it resides, in the most general form, in the linear transformation of the variable range in such a way that the current minimum takes the value 0 (zero), while the current maximum takes the value 1 (one). This kind of normalization comes in many variants, which differ from one another, among others, with respect to the new ranges, for instance (-1,1); (-0,5, 0,5);
- standarization - it resides in such a transformation in which the new feature has the expectation mean value which equals zero and the variance which equals one. The most frequently used standardization is the Z-score standardization, which is calculated according to the following formula (2):

$$Z = \frac{x - \mu}{\sigma} \tag{2}$$

where: x - feature under standarization, μ – mean value, σ – standard population deviation;

- decimal normalization, in which the decimal separator is moved to the place in which the following equation (3) is satisfied:

$$X^1 = \frac{X}{10^j} \tag{3}$$

where: j is the smallest integer value, for which *Max* (| X^1 |) < 1.

A weakness of the normalization methods discussed above is that they cannot cope with extreme data or with the outliers retained in the set under analysis. A solution to this problem is a linear - nonlinear normalization, for example the soft-max normalization or a nonlinear normalization, for example the logarithmic one (Bonebakker, 2007).

As was mentioned above, the nonlinear normalization makes it possible to include into the modeling data set extreme data or even outliers, as well as to change the distribution of the variable under transformation. The logarithmic transformation equations given in (4a,b) and the tangent transformation equation in (5) were employed in (Olichwier, 2011):

$$X_i^{'} = w \cdot \lg(c + X_i) \tag{4a}$$

$$X_i^{'} = w \cdot \lg(1 + cX_i) \tag{4b}$$

where: w, c - coefficients

$$X_i^{'} = \frac{1}{2}[\tanh(k \cdot (\frac{X_i - \mu}{\sigma}) + 1] \tag{5}$$

where: k - coefficient, μ – mean value, σ – standard population deviation.

The use of the logarithmic transformation made it possible to locally spread the distributions of the selected parameters. The original skew parameter distribution after the transformation approached the normal distribution. One effect of the transformation in question was a visible increase in the prediction quality of the resulting model.

The data in the databases which are under preparation for mining may be collected in many places and recorded in separate sets. As a result of integrating different data sources it is possible to perform their transformation, for instance in the domain of a single manufacture process. The data represented by two or more features may be replaced with a different attribute. A classical example of this is the replacement of the two dates defining the beginning and the end of an operation, which were originally recorded in two different places, with a single value defining the duration of the operation, for instance the day and the hour of molding, as well as the day and the hour of the mould assembly are replaced with the mould drying time. A deep knowledge of the data makes possible using mathematical transformations which are more complex than a mere difference. As a consequence, new, semantically justified feature combinations are created. An example of this was discussed in (Kochanski, 2000).

The knowledge of the properties of the algorithm employed in data mining is a different kind of reason behind the creation of new attributes. In the case of algorithms capable only of the division which is parallel to the data space axis (for instance in the case of the majority of decision trees) it is possible to replace the attributes pertaining to features characterized with linear dependence with a new attribute which is the ratio of the former attributes (Witten & Frank, 2005).

It is possible to perform any other transformations of attributes which do not have any mathematical justification but which follow from the general world knowledge: the names of the days of the week may be replaced with the dates, the names of the elements may be replaced with their atomic numbers, etc.

The last encountered way of creating attributes is the replacement of two attributes with a new attribute which is their product. A new attribute created in this way may have no counterpart in reality.

The common use of accommodation suggests that it should be considered as one of the issues of data transformation. What is used in data mining are databases which have been created without any consideration for their future specific application, that is, the application with the use of selected tools or algorithms. In effect, it is often the case that the collected data format does not fit the requirements of the tool used for mining, especially in a commercial code. The popular ARFF (attribute - relation file format) makes use only of the data recorded in a nominal or interval scale. The knowledge gathered in the data recorded in a ratio scale will be lost as a result of being recorded in the ARFF format.

The calculation spreadsheet Excel, which is popular and which is most frequently used for gathering the industrial data, may also be the cause of data distortion. Depending upon the format of the cell in which the registered quantity is recorded, the conversion of files into the txt format (which is required by a part of data mining programs) may result in the loss of modeling quality. This is a consequence of the fact that a defined cell contains the whole number which was recorded in it but what is saved in file conversion is only that part of this number which is displayed (Fig.9).

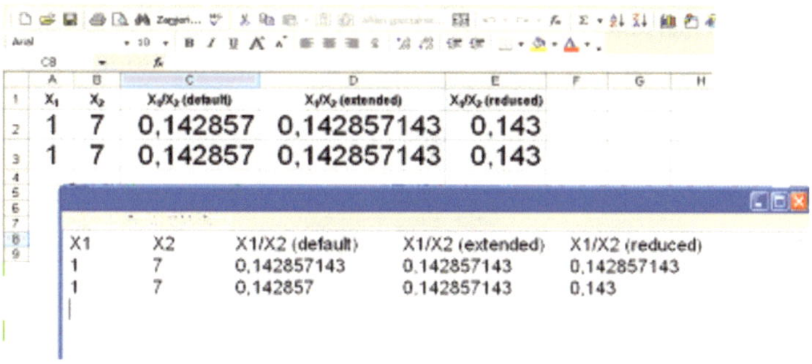

Fig. 9. Data conversion - the conversion of a file from the xls to the txt format brings about a partial loss of information (the authors' own work)

3.4 Data reduction

At the introductory stage of data preparation this task is limited to a single operation - attribute selection - and it is directly connected with the expert opinion and experience pertaining to the data under analysis. It is only as a result of a specialist analysis (for example, of brainstorming) that one can remove from the set of collected data those attributes which without question do not have any influence on the features under modeling.

The aim of the main stage data reduction techniques is a significant decrease in the data representation, which at the same time preserves the features of the basic data set. Reduced data mining makes then possible obtaining models and analyses which are identical (or nearly identical) to the analyses performed for the basic data.

Data reduction includes five operations, which are represented in Fig. 10:

- attribute selection - this resides in reducing the data set by eliminating from it the attributes which are redundant or have little significance for the phenomenon under modeling;
- dimension reduction - this resides in transforming the data with the aim of arriving at a reduced representation of the basic data;
- numerosity reduction - this is aimed at reducing the data set via eliminating the recurring or very similar cases;
- discretization - this resides in transforming a continuous variable into a limited and specified number of ranges;
- aggregation - this resides in summing up the data, most frequently in the function of time, for instance from a longer time period encompassing not just the period of a single shift but e.g. the period of a whole month.

The collected industrial database set may contain tens or even hundreds of attributes. Many of these attributes may be insignificant for the current analysis. It is frequently the case that integrated industrial databases contain redundant records, which is a consequence of the specific way in which the data is collected and stored in a single factory in multiple places. Keeping insignificant records in a database which is to be used for modeling may lead not only to - often a significant - teaching time increase but also to developing a poor quality model. Of course, at the introductory stage, a specialist in a given area may identify the group of attributes which are relevant for further modeling, but this may be very time-consuming, especially given that the nature of the phenomenon under analysis is not fully known. Removing the significant attributes or keeping the insignificant ones may make it very difficult, or even impossible, to develop an accurate model for the collected data.

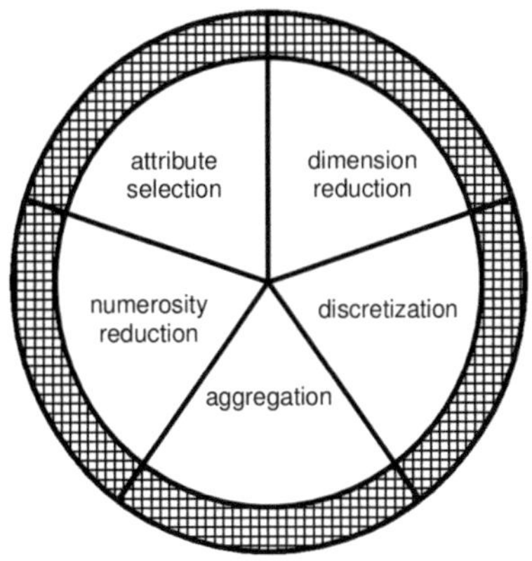

Fig. 10. The operations performed in the data reduction task (with the introductory stage represented as the squared area and the main stage represented as the white area)

At the main stage, attribute selection is performed without any essential analysis of the data under modeling, but only with the help of selection algorithms. This is supposed to lead to defining the intrinsic (or effective) dimensionality of the collected data set (Fukunaga, 1990) The algorithms in question are classified as either *filters* or *wrappers*, depending on whether they are employed as the operation preceding the modeling proper (filters) or as the operation which is performed alternately with the modeling (wrappers).

Attribute selection is performed for four reasons: (a) to reduce the dimensionality of the attribute space, (b) to accelerate the learning algorithms, (c) to increase the classification quality, and (d) to facilitate the analysis of the obtained modeling results (Liu et al., 2003). According to the same authors, it may - in particular circumstances - increase the grouping accuracy.

Dimensionality reduction is the process of creating new attributes via a transformation of the current ones. The result of dimensionality reduction is that the current inventory of attributes $X\{x_1,x_2,\ldots,x_n\}$ is replaced with a new one $Y\{y_1,y_2,\ldots,y_m\}$ in accordance with the following equation (6):

$$Y = F(x_1, x_2, \ldots, x_n) \tag{6}$$

where F() is a mapping function and $m < n$. In the specific case $Y_1 = a_1x_1 + a_2x_2$, where a_1 and a_2 are coefficients (Liu & Motoda, 1998). The same approach, which takes into consideration in its definition the internal dimensionality, may be found in (Van der Maaten et al., 2009). The collected data are located on or in the neighborhood of a multidimensional curve. This curve is characterized with m attributes of the internal dimensionality, but is placed in the n-dimensional space. The reduction frees the data from the excessive dimensionality, which is important since it is sometimes the case that $m<<n$.

The operation of dimensionality reduction may be performed either by itself or after attribute selection. The latter takes place when the attribute selection operation has still left a considerable number of attributes used for modeling. The difference between dimensionality reduction and attribute selection resides in the fact that dimensionality reduction may lead to a partial loss of the information contained in the data. However, this often leads to the increase in the quality of the obtained model. A disadvantage of dimensionality reduction is the fact that it makes more difficult the interpretation of the obtained results. This results from the impossibility of naming the new (created) attributes. In some publications attribute selection and dimensionality reduction are combined into a single task of data dimensionality reduction[1] (Chizi & Maimon, 2005; Fu & Wang, 2003; Villalba & Cunningham, 2007). However, because of the differences in the methods, means, and aims, the two operations should be considered as distinct.

Discretization, in its broadest sense, transforms the data of one kind into the data of another kind. In the literature, this is discussed as the replacement of the quantitative data with the qualitative data or of the continuous data with the discrete data. The latter approach is the approach pertaining to the most frequent cases of discretization. It should be remembered, however, that such an approach narrows down the understanding of the notion of discretization. This is the case since both the continuous and the discrete data are numerical data. The pouring temperature, the charge weight, the percent element content, etc. are continuous data, while the number of melts or the number of the produced casts are discrete data. However, all the above-mentioned examples of quantities are numbers. Discretization makes possible the replacement of a numerical quantity, for instance, the ultimate tensile strength in MPa with the strength characterized verbally as high, medium, or low. In common practice ten methods of discretization method classification are used. These have been put forward and characterized in (Liu et al., 2002; Yang et al., 2005). A number of published works focus on a comparison of discretization methods which takes into account the influence of the selected method on different aspects of further modeling, for instance, decision trees. These comparisons most frequently analyze three parameters upon which data preparation – discretization exerts influence:

- the time needed for developing the model,
- the accuracy of the developed model,
- the comprehensibility of the model.

Comparative analyses are conducted on synthetic data, which are generated in accordance with a specified pattern (Ismail & Ciesielski, 2003; Boullé, 2006), on the widely known data sets, such as Glass, Hepatitis, Iris, Pima, Wine, etc. (Shi & Fu 2005, Boullé, 2006; Ekbal, 2006; Wu QX et al., 2006; Jin et al., 2009; Mitov et al., 2009), and on production data (Perzyk, 2005).

As has been widely demonstrated, the number of cases recorded in the database is decisive with respect to the modeling time. However, no matter what the size of the data set is, this time is negligibly short in comparison with the time devoted to data preparation. Because of that, as well as because of a small size, in comparison, for instance, with the business data sets, numerosity reduction is not usually performed in industrial data sets.

---

[1]Data Dimensionality Reduction DDR, Dimension Reduction Techniques DRT

The operation of aggregation was first discussed in connection with the discussion of the data transformation task. The difference between these two operations does not reside in the method employed, since the methods are the same, but in the aims with which aggregation is performed. Aggregation performed as a data reduction operation may be treated, in its essence, as the creation of a new attribute, which is the sum of other attributes, a consequence of this being a reduction in the number of events, that is, numerosity reduction.

4. The application of the selected operations of the industrial data preparation methodology

For the last twenty years, many articles have been published which discuss the results of research on ductile cast iron ADI. These works discuss the results of research conducted with the aim of investigating the influence of the parameters of the casting process, as well as of the heat treatment of the ductile iron casts on their various properties. These properties include, on the one hand, the widely investigated ultimate tensile strength, elongation, and hardness, and, on the other, also properties which are less widely discussed, such as graphite size, impact, or austenite fraction. The results discussed in the articles contain large numbers of data from laboratory tests and from industrial studies. The data set collected for the present work contains 1468 cases coming both from the journal-published data and from the authors' own research. They are characterized via 27 inputs, such as: the chemical composition (characterized with reference to 14 elements), the structure as cast (characterized in terms of 7 parameters), the features as cast (characterized in terms of 2 parameters), the heat treatment parameters (characterized in terms of 4 parameters), as well as via 11 outputs: the cast structure after heat treatment, characterized in terms of the retained austenite fraction and the cast features (characterized in terms of 10 parameters). 13 inputs were selected from the set, 9 of them characterizing the melt chemical composition and 4 characterizing the heat treatment parameters. Also, 2 outputs were selected - the mechanical properties after treatment - the ultimate tensile strength and the elongation. The set obtained in this way, which contained 922 cases, was prepared as far as data cleaning is concerned, in accordance with the methodology discussed above.

Prior to preparation, the set contained only 34,8 % of completely full records, containing all the inputs and outputs. The set contained a whole range of cases in which outliers were suspected.

For the whole population of the data set under preparation outliers and high leverage points were defined. This made possible defining influentials, that is, the points exhibiting a high value for Cook's distance. In Fig 11, which represents the elongation distribution in the function of the ultimate tensile strength, selected cases were marked (a single color represents a single data source). The location of these cases in the diagram would not make it possible to unequivocally identify them as outliers. However, when this is combined with an analysis of the cases with a similar chemical composition and heat treatment parameters, the relevant cases may be identified as such.

Fig. 12 below represents the generated correlation matrix of the collected data. The high level of the absent data in the database is visible, among others, in the form of the empty values of the correlation coefficient - for instance, the database contains no case of a simultaneous appearance of both *Al contents* and *participation of graphite nodules*.

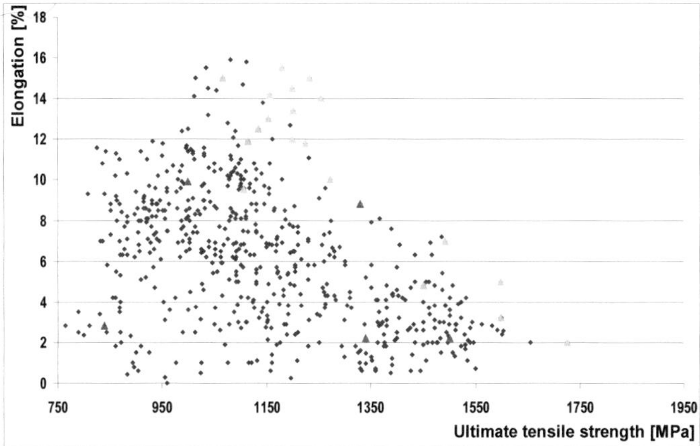

Fig. 11. The elongation distribution in the function of the ultimate tensile strength. The colored pints represent cases identified as outliers (the authors' own work)]

With the use of the methodology discussed above, the database was filled in, which resulted in a significant decrease in the percentage of the absent data for the particular inputs and outputs. The degree of the absent data was between 0,5 and 28,1% for inputs and 26,9% for the UTS and 30,6% for the elongation. The result of filling in the missing data was that the degree of the absent data for inputs was reduced to the value from 0,5 to 12,8%, and for strength and elongation to, respectively, 1,3% and 0,8%. Fig. 13 represents the proportion of the number of records in the particular output ranges "before" and "after" this replacement operation. Importantly, we can observe a significant increase in the variability range for both dependent variables, that is, for elongation from the level of 0÷15% to the level of 0÷27,5%, and for strength from the level of 585÷1725MPa to the level of 406÷1725MPa, despite the fact that the percentage of the records in the respective ranges remained at a similar level for the data both "before" and "after" the filling operation. Similar changes occurred for the majority of independent variables - inputs. In this way, via an increase in the learning data set, the reliability of the model was also increased. Also, the range of the practical applications of the taught ANN model was increased, via an increase in the variability range of the parameters under analysis.

The data which was prepared in the way discussed above were then used as the learning set for an artificial neural network (ANN). Basing on the earlier research [4], two data sets were created which characterized the influence of the melt chemical composition and the heat treatment parameters (Tab. 1) of ductile cast iron ADI alloys on the listed mechanical properties. The study employed a network of the MLP type, with one hidden layer and with the number of neurons hidden in that layer equaling the number of inputs. For each of the two cases, 10 learning sessions were run and the learning selected for further analysis was the one with the smallest mean square error.

A qualitative analysis of the taught model demonstrated that the prediction quality obtained for the almost twice as numerous learning data set obtained after the absent data replacement was comparable, which is witnessed by a comparable quantitative proportion of errors obtained on the learning data set for both cases (Fig. 14).

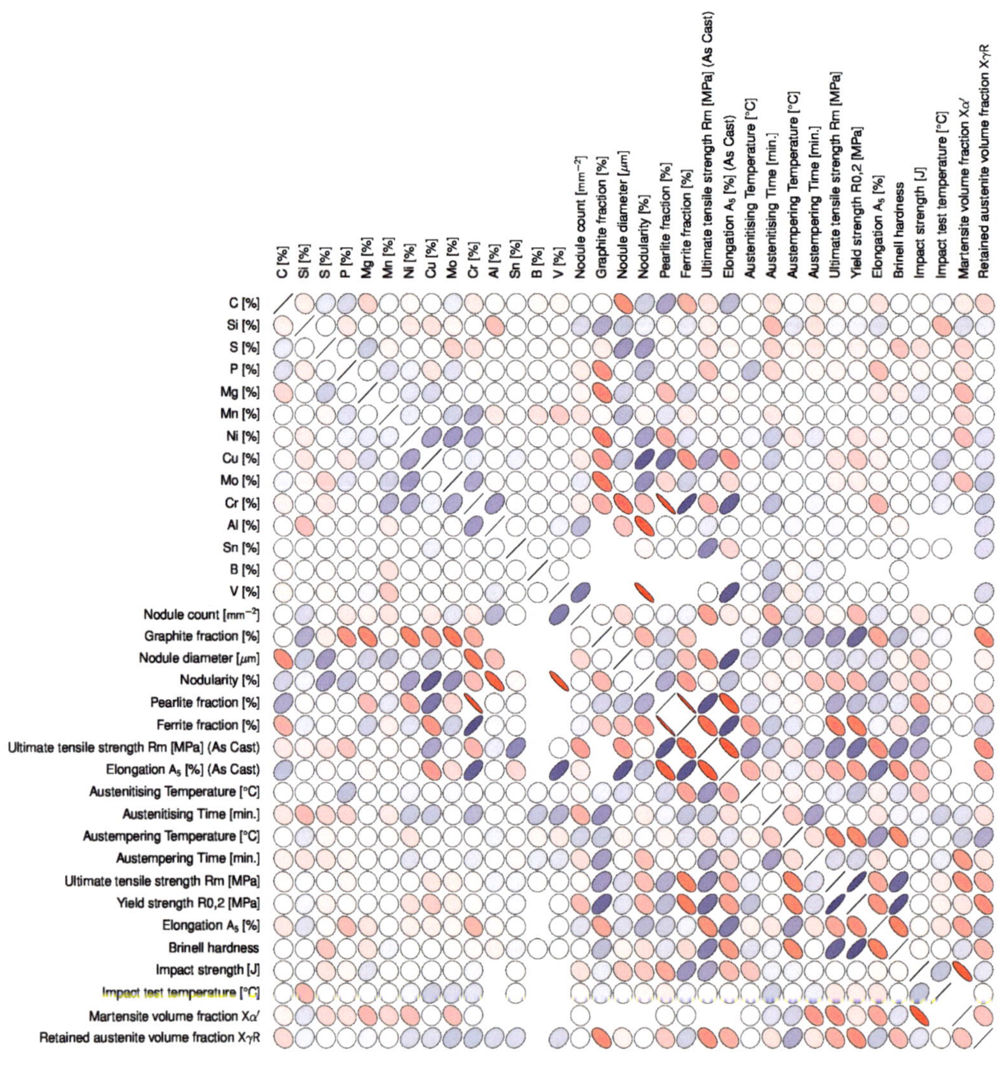

Fig. 12. The input and output correlation matrix. The blue color represents the positive correlation while the red color represents the negative one; the deformation size correlation, of the circle (ellipsoidality) and the color saturation indicate the correlation strength (Murdoch & Chow, 1996)

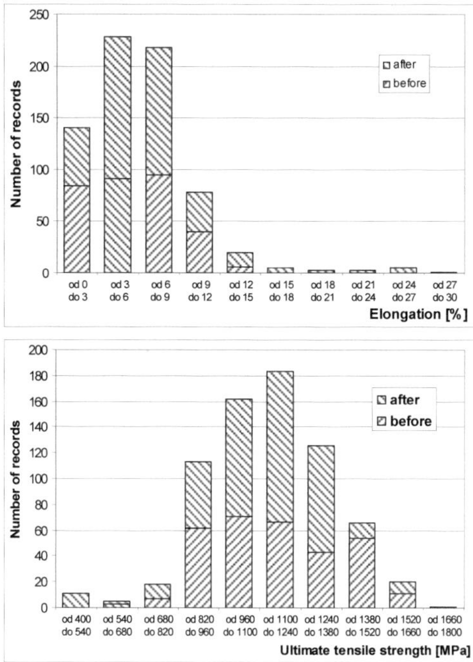

(a)

(b)

Fig. 13. The proportions of the numbers of records in the specified ranges of the output variables a) elongation [%], b) ultimate tensile strength [MPa] before and after replacing the missing and empty values

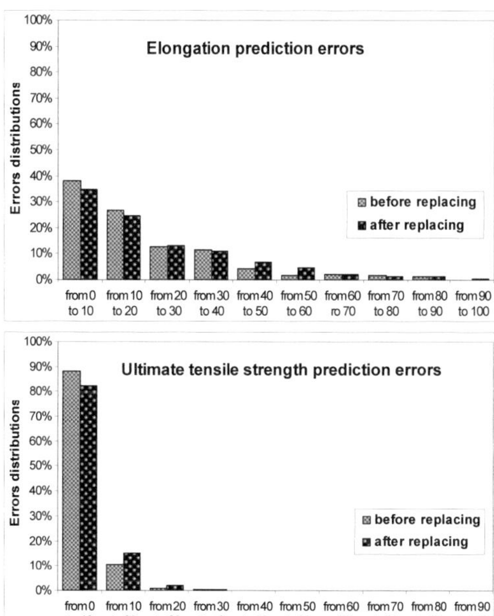

(a)

(b)

Fig. 14. Output prediction error distribution a) elongation [%], b) ultimate tensile strength [MPa]

A further confirmation of this comes from a comparative analysis of the real results and the ANN answers which was based on correlation graphs and a modified version of the correlation graph, taking into account the variable distribution density (Fig. 15 and 16). In all cases under analysis we can observe that the ANN model shows a tendency to overestimate the minima and to underestimate the maxima. This weakness of ANNs was discussed in (Kozlowski, 2009).

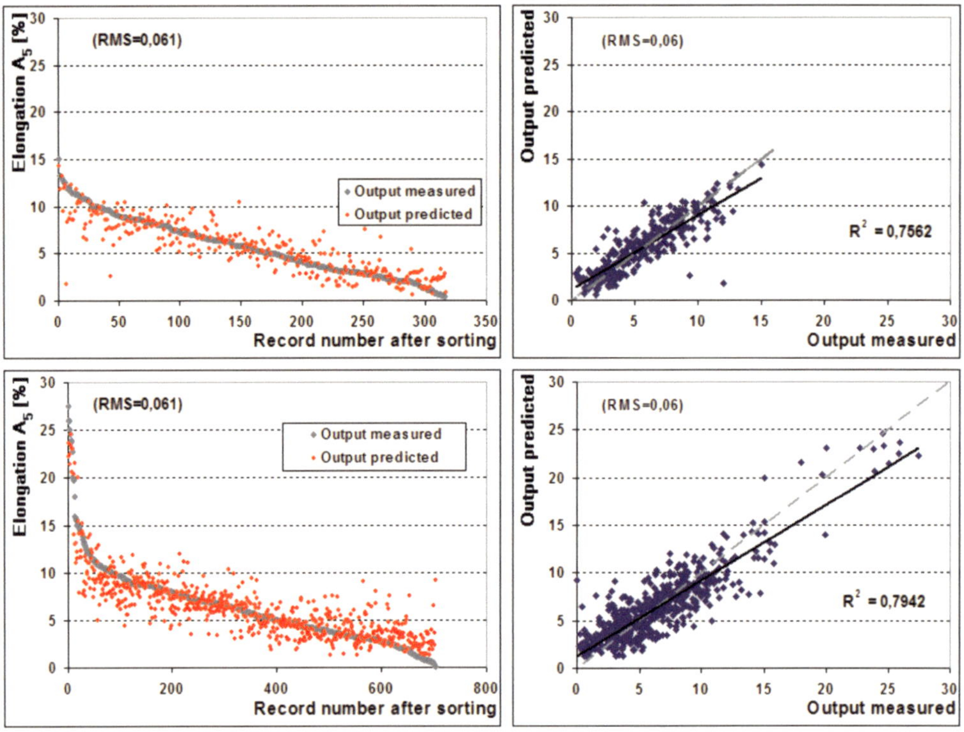

Fig. 15. The distribution of the real results and the predictions of the elongation variable for a) the data set without replacement; b) the data set after replacement

The analyzed cases suggest that an ANN model taught on a data set after absent data replacement exhibits similar and at the same high values of the model prediction quality, that is, of the mean square error, as well as of the coefficient of determination R^2. In the case of predicting A_5, the more accurate model was the ANN model based on the data set after replacement (for R_m the opposite was the case). However, the most important observable advantage following from data replacement and from the modeling with the use of the data set after replacement is the fact that the ANN model increased its prediction range with respect to the extreme output values (in spite of a few deviations and errors in their predictions). This is extremely important from the perspective of the practical model application, since it is the extreme values which are frequently the most desired (for instance, obtaining the maximum value R_m with, simultaneously, the highest possible A_5), and, unfortunately, the sources - for objective reasons - usually do not spell out the complete data, for which these values were obtained. In spite of the small number of records characterizing the extreme outputs, an ANN model was successfully developed which can make predictions in the whole possible range of dependent variables. This may suggest that the absent data was replaced with appropriate values, reflecting the obtaining general tendencies and correlations. It should also be noted that the biggest prediction errors occur for the low values of the parameters under analysis (e.g.: for A_5 within the range 0÷1%), which may be directly connected with the inaccuracy and the noise in the measurement (e.g.: with a premature break of a tensile specimen resulting from discontinuity or non-metallic inclusions).

The application of the proposed methodology makes possible a successful inclusion into data sets of the pieces of information coming from different sources, including also uncertain data.

An increase in the number of cases in the data set used for modeling results in the model accuracy increase, at the same time significantly widening the practical application range of the taught ANN model, via a significant increase, sometimes even doubling, of the variability range of the parameters under analysis.

Multiple works suggested that ANN models should not be used for predicting results which are beyond the learning data range. The methodology proposed above makes possible the absent data replacement and therefore, the increase of the database size. This, in turn, makes possible developing models with a significantly wider applicability range.

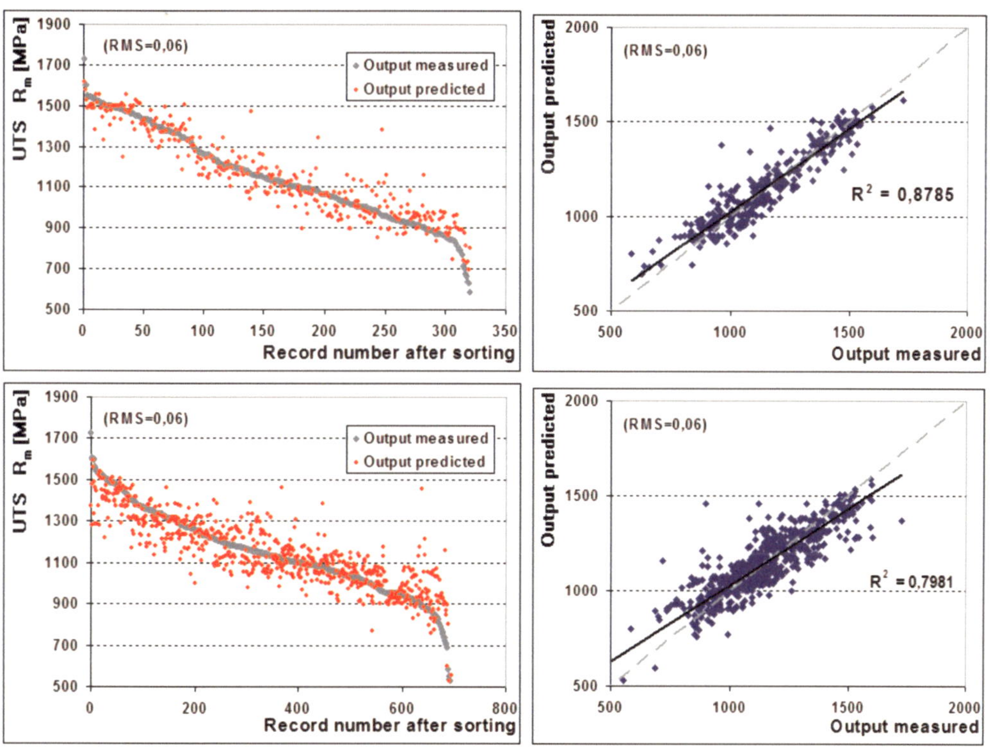

Fig. 16. The distribution of the real results and the predictions of the UTS (ultimate tensile strength) variable for a) the data set without replacement; b) the data set after replacement

5. Conclusion

The proposed methodology makes possible the full use of imperfect data coming from various sources. Appropriate preparation of the data for modeling via, for instance, absent data replacement makes it possible to widen, directly and indirectly, the parameter variability range and to increase the set size. Models developed on such sets are high-quality models and their prediction accuracy can be more satisfactory.

The consequent wider applicability range of the model and its stronger reliability, in combination with its higher accuracy, open a way to a deeper and wider analysis of the phenomenon or process under analysis.

6. References

Agre G. & Peev S. (2002). On Supervised and Unsupervised Discretization, *Cybernetics and information technologies*, Vol. 2, No. 2, pp. 43-57, Bulgarian Academy of Science, Sofia

Al Shalabi L. & Shaaban Z. (2006). Normalization as a Preprocessing Engine for Data Mining and the Approach of Preference Matrix, *Proceedings of the International Conference of Dependability of Computer Systems (DEPCOS-RELCOMEX'06)*, ISBN: 0-7695-2565-2

Al Shalabi L.; Shaaban Z. & Kasasbeh B. (2006). Data Mining: A Preprocessing Engine, *Journal of Computer Science* 2 (9); pp. 735-739, ISSN 1549-3636

Alves R.M.B. & Nascimento C.A.O. (2002). Gross errors detection of industrial data by neural network and cluster techniques, *Brazilian Journal of Chemical Engineering*, Vol. 19, No. 04, pp. 483 - 489, October - December 2002

Bartkowiak A. (2005). Robust Mahalanobis distances obtained using the 'Multout' and 'Fast-mcd' methods, *Biocybernetics and Biomedical Engineering*, Vol. 25, No. 1, pp. 7-21,

Ben-Gal I. (2005). Outlier detection, *In Data Mining and Knowledge Discovery Handbook: A Complete Guide for Practitioners and Researchers*, edited by Maimon O. and Rockach L., Kluwer Academic Publishers, ISBN 0-387-24435-2

Bensch M.; Schröder M.; Bogdan M. & Rosenstiel W. (2005). Feature Selection for High-Dimensional Industrial Data, *ESANN2005 proceeding – European Symposium on Artificial Neural Networks*, Bruges, Belgium, ISBN2-930307-05-6, 27-29 April, 2005

Bonebakker J. L. (2007). Finding representative workloads for computer system design, *Sun Microsystems*, ISBN/EAN: 978-90-5638-187-5

Boullé M. (2006). MODL: A Bayes optimal discretization method for continuous attributes, *Journal Machine Learning*, Vol. 65, No. 1, pp. 131 – 165, ISSN 0885-6125 (Print) 1573-0565 (Online)

Cannataro M. (2008). Computational proteomics: management and analysis of proteomics data, *Briefings in Bioinformatics*, Vol. 9, No. 2, pp. 97-101

Cateni S.; Colla V. & Vannucci M. (2008). Outlier Detection Methods for Industrial Applications in Advances and Robotics, *Automation and Control*, edited by Aramburo J. and Trevino A.R., Publisher InTech, ISBN 978-953-7619-16-9

Chizi B. & Maimon O. (2005). Dimension reduction and feature selection, *In Data Mining and Knowledge Discovery Handbook*, Ch. 5, pp. 93–111, edited by: Maimon O., Rokach L., *Springer Science+Business Media*, ISBN 978-0-387-24435-8 (Print) 978-0-387-25465-4 (Online)

Chuanng-Chien Ch.; Tong-Hong L. & Ben-Yi L. (2005). Using correlation coefficient in ECG waveform for arrhythmia detection, *Biomedical Engineering - Applications, Basis & Communications*, 2005(June), 17, 147-152

Ekbal A. (2006). Improvement of Prediction Accuracy Using Discretization and Voting Classifier, *18th International Conference on Pattern Recognition*, Vol. 2, pp: 695 - 698

Fan H.; Zaïane O.R.; Foss A. & Wu J. (2006). A Nonparametric Outlier Detection for Effectively Discovering Top-N Outliers from Engineering Data, *Advances in Knowledge Discovery and Data Mining, Lecture Notes in Artificial Intelligence*, 2006, Vol. 3918

Filzmoser P. (2005). Identification of multivariate outliers: A performance study, *Austrian Journal of Statistics*, Vol. 34, No. 2, pp. 127-138,

Fu X. & Wang L.(2003). Data Dimensionality Reduction With Application to Simplifying RBF Network Structure and Improving Classification Performance, *IEEE Transactions on systems, man and cybernetics – part B: Cybernetics*, Vol. 33, No. 3, June 2003, pp. 399 - 409

Fukunaga K. (1990). Introduction to Statistical Pattern Recognition, 2nd ed., *Academic Press*, San Diego, ISBN 0-12-269851-7

Galmacci G. (1996). Collinearity detection in linear regression models, *Computational Economics*, Vol. 9, pp. 215-227

Ginoris Y.P.; Amaral A.L.; Nicolau A.; Coelho M.A.Z. & Ferreira E.C. (2007). Raw data pre-processing in the protozoa and metazoa identification by image analysis and multivariate statistical techniques, *Journal of chemometrics*, Vol. 21, pp. 156–164

Han J. & Kamber M. (2001). Data Mining. Concepts and Techniques, Morgan Kaufmann Publisher, ISBN 1-55860-489-8

Hasimah Hj M.; Abdul Razak H. & Azuraliza Abu B.(2007). Pixel-based Parallel-Coordinates technique for outlier detection in Cardiac Patient Dataset, *Proceedings of the International Conference on Electrical Engineering and Informatics*, Institut Teknologi Bandung, Indonesia June 17-19, 2007

Ismail M.K. & Ciesielski V. (2003). An empirical investigation of the impact of discretization on common data distributions, *Proc. of the Third International Conference on Hybryd Intelligent Systems (HIS'03)*, edited by Abraham A., Koppen M., Franke K., pp.692-701, IOS Press

Jimenez-Marquez S.A.; Lacroix C. & Thibault J.(2002). Statistical Data Validation Methods for Large Cheese Plant Database, *Journal of Dairy Science*, Vol. 85, No. 9, 2081–2097, American Dairy Science Association, 2002

Jin R.; Breitbart Y. & Muoh Ch.(2009).Data discretization unification, *Journal Knowledge and Information Systems*, Vol. 19, No.1, (April, 2009), pp. 1 - 29, ISSN 0219-1377 (Print) 0219-3116 (Online)

Kochanski A. (2000)., Combined methods of ductile cast iron modeling, *III Polski Kongres Odlewnictwa, Zbior Materialow*, str. 160-165, Warszawa (in Polish)

Kochanski A. (2006). Aiding the detection of cast defect causes. Polish Metallurgy 2002 - 2006, *Komitet Metalurgii Polskiej Akademii Nauk*, red. K. Swiatkowski, ISBN 83-910-159-4-4, Krakow (in Polish)

Kochanski A. (2010). Data preparation, *Computer Methods in Materials Science*, Vol. 10, No. 1, pp. 25-29

Kozlowski J. (2009). Aiding the foundry process control with the use of advanced artificial neural network analysis methods, *PhD thesis, (in Polish)*, Warsaw University of Technology, Faculty of Production Engineering

Kusiak A. (2001). Feature Transformation Methods in Data Mining, *IEEE Transactions on Electronics Packaging Manufacturing*, Vol. 24, No. 3, July 2001

Larose D. T. (2005). Discovering Knowledge in Data. An Introduction to DATA MINING, John Wiley & Sons, Inc.

Laurikkala, J.; Juhola M.& Kentala E. (2000). Informal Identification of Outliers in Medical Data, *Proceeding in the Fifth International Workshop on Intelligent Data Analysis on Medicine and Pharmacology IDAMAP-2000*, Berlin

Liang Goh & Kasabov, N.(2003). Integrated gene expression analysis of multiple microarray data sets based on a normalization technique and on adaptive connectionist model, *Proceedings of the International Joint Conference on Neural Networks*, Vol. 3, pp. 1724 - 1728, 20-24 July, 2003

Liu H., Hussain F.; Tan C.L. & Dash M. (2002). Discretization: An Enabling Technique, Data Mining and Knowledge Discovery, Vol. 6, No. 4, pp. 393–423, Kluwer Academic Publishers, ISSN: 1384-5810 (Print) 1573-756X (Online)

Liu H. & Motoda H.(1998). Feature extraction, construction and selection: a data mining perspective, Kluwer Academic Publishers, ISBN 0-7923-8196-3,print. 2001

Liu H.; Motoda H. & Yu L. (2003). Feature Extraction, Selection, and Construction, In: *The Handbook of Data Mining* ed. Nong Ye, Lawrence Erlbaum Associates, ISBN 0-8058 – 4081-8

Loy Ch. Ch.; Lai MW. K. & Lim Ch. P. (2006). Dimensionality reduction of protein mass spectrometry data using Random Projection, *Lecture Notes in Computer Science*, Vol. 4233, ISBN 978-3-540-46481-5

Van der Maaten L.; Postma E. & Van den Herik J. (2009) *Dimensionality Reduction: A Comparative Review*, preprint

Masters T. (1993). Practical Neural Network Recipes in C++, Academic Press Inc.

McCue C.(2007). Data Mining and Predictive Analysis: Intelligence Gathering and Crime Analysis, Butterworth-Heinemann, ISBN 0750677961, 9780750677967

Mitov I.; Ivanova K.; Markov K.; Velychko V.; Stanchev P. & Vanhoof K. (2009). Comparison of discretization methods for preprocessing data for Pyramidal Growing Network classification method, *New Trends in Intelligent Technologies Supplement to International Journal - Information Technologies and Knowledge* Volume 3

Moh'd Belal Al- Zgubi (2009). An Effective Clustering-Based Approach for Outlier Detection, *European Journal of Scientific Research*, ISSN 1450-216X Vol.28 No.2, pp.310-316

Mohamed H. Hj. ; Hamdan A.R. & Bakar A.A. (2007). Pixel-based Parallel-Coordinates technique for outlier detection in Cardiac Patient Dataset, *Proceedings of the*

International Conference on Electrical Engineering and Informatics, Institut Teknologi Bandung, Indonesia June 17-19, 2007

Murdoch, D.J. & Chow, E.D. (1996). A graphical display of large correlation matrices. The American Statistician 50, 178-180

Olichwier J. (2011). The influence of data preparation on the accuracy of the modeling with the use of the laboratory and literature ADI ductile cast iron data, *MSc thesis, (in Polish)*, supervised by A. Kochanski, Warsaw University of Technology, Faculty of Production Engineering

Perzyk M. ; Biernacki R.& Kochanski A.(2005). Modelling of manufacturing processes by learning systems: the naive Bayesian classifier versus artificial neural networks, *Journal of Materials Processing Technology*, Elsevier, Vol. 164-165, pp. 1430-1435

Pyle D. (1999). Data Preparation for Data Mining, Morgan Kaufmann Publisher, ISBN 1-55860-529-0

Pyle D. (2003). Data Collection, Preparation, Quality, and Visualization, In: *The Handbook of Data Mining* edited by Nong Ye, Lawrence Erlbaum Associates, ISBN 0-80584-081-8

Research raport KBN Nr 003353/C.T08-6/2003 (in Polish)

Refaat M. (2007). Data Preparation for Data Mining Using SAS, Morgan Kaufmann Publisher, ISBN 13-978-0-12-373577-5

Rousseeuw P.J. & Zomeren B.C. van (1990). Unmasking multivariate outliers and leverage points, *Journal of the American Statistical Association*, Vol. 85, No. 411, pp. 633-651, American Statistical Association

Saeys Y.; Inza I. & Larrañaga P. (2007). A review of feature selection techniques in bioinformatics, *Bioinformatics*, Vol. 23, No. 19, pp. 2507–2517

Shaari F.; Abu Bakar A. & Razak Hamdan A. (2007). On New Approach in Mining Outlier, *Proceedings of the International Conference on Electrical Engineering and Informatics Institut Teknologi Bandung*, Indonesia, June 17-19, 2007

Shi H.& Fu J-Z.(2005). A global discretization method based on rough sets, *Proceedings of the Fourth International Conference on Machine Learning and Cybernetics*, Guangzhou, 18-21 August, 2005

StatSoft (2011) web page http://www.statsoft.pl/textbook/stathome.html

Villalba S. D. & Cunningham P. (2007). An Evaluation of Dimension Reduction Techniques for One-Class Classification, *Technical Report UCD-CSI-2007-9*, University College Dublin, , August 13th, 2007

Weiss S. M. & Indurkhya N. (1998). Predictive Data Mining: a practical guide, Morgan Kaufmann Publisher, ISBN 1-55860-403-0

Witten I.H. & Frank E.(2005). Data Mining. Practical Machine Learning Tools and Techniques, 2nd ed., Elsevier Inc., ISBN-13: 978-0-12-088407-0

Wu QX.; Bell D.; McGinnity M.; Prasad G.; Qi G. & Huang X. (2006). Improvement of Decision Accuracy Using Discretization of Continuous Attributes, *Lecture Notes in Computer Science*, Vol. 4223, Publisher Springer Berlin / Heidelberg, ISSN 0302-9743 (Print) 1611-3349 (Online)

Yang Y.; Webb G.I. & Wu X. (2005). Discretization Methods, In: *Data Mining and Knowledge Discovery Handbook*, Ch. 6, pp. 113–130, edited by: Maimon O., and Rokach L., Springer Science+Business Media, ISBN 978-0-387-24435-8 (Print)

9

A Knowledge Representation Formalism for Semantic Business Process Management

Ermelinda Oro and Massimo Ruffolo
High Performance Computing and Networking Institute of the National Research Council,
Altilia srl
Italy

1. Introduction

Business process models are increasingly used to create clarity about the logical sequence of activities in public and private organizations belonging to different industries and areas. To improve *Business Process Management* (BPM), semantic technologies (like ontologies, reasoners, and semantic Web services) should be integrated in BPM tools in order to enable semantic BPM. Semantic Business Process Management (SBPM) approaches and tools aim at allowing more efficient and effective business process management across complex organizations. By semantic BPM decision makers can get transparent, fast, and comprehensive view of relevant business processes for better analyzing and driving processes. In defining semantic BPM tools aimed at improving the quality of process models and subsequent process analyses, a key aspect to take into account is to represent in combined way static knowledge regarding a specific application domain (i.e. domain ontologies) and dynamic knowledge related to process schemas and instances that are typically performed in a given domain. For example, in the health care domain, where the evidence-based medicine has contributed to define and apply clinical processes for caring a wide variety of diseases, a process-oriented vision of clinical practices may allow for enhancing patient safety by enabling better risks management capabilities.

In this Chapter is firstly summarized the large body of work currently available in the field of knowledge representation formalisms and approaches for representing and managing business processes. Then a novel ontology-based approach to business process representation and management, named Static/Dynamic Knowledge Representation Framework (SD-KRF), is presented. The SD-KRF allows for expressing in a combined way domain ontologies, business processes and related business rules. It supports semantic business process management and contributes to enhancing existing BPM solutions in order to achieve more flexible, dynamic and manageable business processes. More in detail, the presented framework allows methods for:

1. Creating ontologies of business processes that can be queried and explored in a semantic fashion.
2. Expressing business rules (by means of *reasoning tasks*) that can be used for monitoring processes.
3. Extracting information from business documents. Semantic information extraction allows the acquisition of information and metadata useful for the correct execution of business

processes from unstructured sources and the storage of extracted information into structured machine-readable form. Such a facility makes available large amount of data on which data mining techniques, can be performed to discover patterns related to adverse events, errors and cost dynamics, hidden in the structure of the business processes, that are cause of risks and of poor performances.

4. Querying directly enterprise database in order to check activity status.
5. Executing business processes and acquiring process instances by means of either *workflow enactment* (predefined process schemas are automatically executed) or *workflow composition* (activity to execute are chosen step-by-step by humans).
6. Monitoring business processes during the execution by running reasoning tasks.
7. Analyzing acquired business process instances, by means of querying and inference capabilities, in order to recognize errors and risks for the process and the whole organization.

SD-KRF is an homogeneous framework where the domain knowledge, the process structures, and the behavioral semantics of processes are combined in order to allow querying, advanced analysis and management of business processes in a more flexible and dynamic way.

2. Semantic business process management at a glance

BPM links processes and information systems. One of the most important aspect of BPM is the modeling of processes. Historically, process modeling has mainly been performed with general purpose languages, such as Activity Diagrams (AD), Business process Modeling Notation (BPMN) or Event-driven Process Chains (EPC). Such instruments are not suitable for an automated semantic process analysis because semantic modeling of structural elements and domain knowledge are missing. In recent years different languages and approaches for semantic business process management have emerged. In this Section will be briefly described languages for representing processes and their semantics.

By considering the abilities of representing business processes, as described in van der Aalst (2009), existing languages for processes modeling can be classified in:

- **Formal languages**. Processes are described by using formal models, for examples Markov chains and Petri nets. Such languages have unambiguous semantics.
- **Conceptual languages**. Processes are represented by user-friendly semi-formal languages. Example of well known conceptual languages are UML activity diagrams, BPMN (Business Process Modeling Notation), and EPCs (Event- Driven Process Chains). Activity diagrams (or control flow diagrams) is a type of UML (unified modeling language OMG (2011)) diagrams. They provide a graphical notation to define the sequential, conditional, and parallel composition of lower-level behaviors, therefore they are suitable for modeling business processes. The Event-driven Process Chain (EPC) van der Aalst (1999) is a type of flowchart used for business process modeling and compared to UML activity diagrams, the EPC covers more aspects such as a detailed description of business organization units together with their respective functions as well as information and material resources used in each function. These essential relationships are not explicitly shown in activity diagrams. The Business Process Model and Notation (BPMN) White (2006) is a graphical notation for drawing business processes, proposed as a standard notation. The language is similar to other informal notations such as UML activity diagrams and extended

event-driven process chains. Models expressed in terms of BPMN are called Business Process Diagrams (BPDs). A BPD is a flowchart having different elements: Flow Objects, Connecting Objects, Swim-lanes, Artifacts, Events, Activities, and Gateways. Events are comparable to places in a Petri net, in fact they are used to trigger and/or connect activities. Whereas in UML Activity Diagrams and in BPMN resource types are captured as swim-lanes, with each task belonging to one or more swim-lane, in Event-driven Process Chains (EPC) resource types are explicitly attached to each task. These type of languages describe only the desired behavior of processes, and do not have a formal semantics, therefore they are not suitable for enabling processes execution.

- **Execution languages**. Because formal languages are too general and conceptual languages are aiming at the representation of processes and not directly at execution, languages that consider the processes enactment have been defined. The most common language in this category is BPEL (Business Process Execution Language) Wohed et al. (2006). BPMN diagrams are refined into BPEL specifications, but such translation is a difficult task because BPMN lacks of formal semantics. Therefore, several attempts have been made to provide semantics for a subset of BPMN Weske (2007). Other proprietary enactment languages have been defined. For example, XPDL XPDL (2011) is a very common language based on BPMN.

2.1 Semantic business process management

BPM is a difficult task because the semantic of a business processes is frequently hidden in complex models obtained by different description and enactment languages. The explicit representation of domain knowledge related to business processes combined to explicit description of the semantic processes could help to obtain advices, alerts, and reminders. Furthermore, reasoning capabilities allow for representing and managing business rules and better enacting and monitoring of processes Peleg (2009). Classical languages adopted for representing process models provide a low degree of automation in the BPM lifecycle. In particular, there are many difficulties in the translations of business modeling (performed by business expert analist) to workflow models (which are executable IT representations of business processes). Like Semantic Web Services achieve more automation in discovery and mediation with respect to conventional Web services, BPM systems can obtain more automation by using knowledge representation and reasoning, and therefore semantic technologies Hepp et al. (2005).

Initially, knowledge representation and reasoning is been used for artificial intelligence tasks Newell (1980) to support humans in decision making. Then, rule-based systems were introduced. An important example is Mycin Shortliffe (1976) that represented clinical knowledge and contained if-then-else rules in order to derive diagnoses and treatments for a given disease. After, it was integrated database for representing knowledge in decision support systems. An important example is the Arden System for Medical Logic Modules (MLMs) Hripcsak et al. (1994) system. MLMs, in Arden Syntax, define decision logic via a knowledge category that has data, event, logic, and action slots useful in representing processes. Finally, ontologies Gruber (1995) were used for formally representing the knowledge as a set of concepts within a domain, and the relationships between those concepts. An ontology may be used to describe the domain, and to reason about the entities and relations within that domain in order to provide decision support. It is noteworthy that to add, delete or modify knowledge in rule-based systems was a difficult task, whereas ontologies are more simply modifiable. Ontologies and Semantic Web service technologies can be used throughout the BPM lifecycle Hepp et al. (2005); Wetzstein et al. (2007).

The use of semantics in BPM creates Semantic Business Process Management (SBPM) System. The goal of Semantic Business Process Management is to achieve more automation in BPM by using semantic technologies. In Wetzstein et al. (2007) the SBPM lifecycle is described. There are 4 principal phases: *Process Modeling*, *Process Implementation*, *Process Execution*, and *Process Analysis*. The usage of semantic technologies increases the automation degree and the BPMS functionalities.

During the *process modeling phase*, the annotation of business process models allows for associating semantics to task and decisions in the process. The annotation is usually performed by using ontologies that describe domains or processes components. Generally, ontologies are created by ontology engineers, domain experts and business analysts. Different types of ontologies are relevant to business process management Hepp & Roman (2007). For instance, an organizational ontology is used to specify which organizational tasks have to be performed, in combination with a Semantic Web Service (SWS) ontology that specify the IT services that implement tasks, and domain ontologies that describe data used in the processes. The processes annotation enables additional semantics functionalities. In fact, ontological annotation of tasks enables the reuse of process fragments in different business processes in the *implementation phase*. During the *execution phase*, semantic instances are created, semantic checks of obtained instances can be automatically evaluated by calling reasoning tasks. During the semantic BP *analysis phase*, two different features are distinguished: (i) process monitoring which aims at providing relevant information about running process instances in the process execution phase, (ii) process mining that analyzes already executed process instances, in order to detect points of improvement for the process model. Such features take advantages by the semantic annotation. For instance, business analysts can formulate semantic queries and use reasoning to deduce implicit knowledge. Analysis allows for improving business processes for decreasing costs or risks in processes executions Medeiros & Aalst (2009).

There exist a lot of work addressing the enhancement of Business Process Management Systems ter Hofstede et al. (2010) by using Semantic Web techniques and, in particular, computational ontologies Hepp et al. (2005).

Robust and effective results have been obtained from European research projects CORDIS (2011), such as SUPER SUPER (2011), PLUG-IT PLUG-IT (2011) and COIN COIN (2011). They implemented new semantics-based software tools that enhance BPs of companies, and lower costs and risks. SUPER SUPER (2011), that means Semantics Utilised for Process Management within and between Enterprises, is an European Project financed from the Europen Union 6th Framework Program, within Information Society Technologies (IST) priority. The project successfully concluded at 31st of March 2009. The objective of SUPER was to make BPM accessible for business experts adding semantics to BP. Semantic Web and, in particular, Semantic Web Services (SWS) technology allows for integrating applications at the semantic level. Based on ontologies, Semantic Web (SW) technologies provide scalable methods and tools for the machine readable representation of knowledge. Semantic Web Services (SWS) use SW technologies to support the automated discovery, substitution, composition, and execution of software components (Web Services). BPM is a natural application for SW and SWS technology. The project SUPER combines SWS and BPM, provided a semantic-based and context-aware framework, and created horizontal ontologies which describe business processes and vertical telecommunications ontologies to support domain-specific annotation. SUPER ontologies allow telecoms business managers to search existing processes, to model new business processes, to modify process models, to search for semantic web services that compose business processes and to execute implemented business process models.

The project plugIT PLUG-IT (2011), that means Plug Your Business into IT, has been co-funded by the European Union Intelligent Content and Semantics. It is based on the observation of the necessity to align Business and Information Technology (IT). The result of the project was the IT-Socket Knowledge portal. The project is based on the idea that IT can be consumed by plugging in business, like electric power is consumed when plugging in electronic devices in a power socket. ITSocket externalizes the expert knowledge by using graphical semi-formal models, such a knowledge is formalized in order to enable a computer-supported alignment using semantic technologies. Figure 1 shows business and IT experts that formalize the knowledge and so they enable automated support of business and IT alignment. In particular the alignment can be delegated to semantic technologies.

COIN, that means Enterprise COllaboration and INteroperability, COIN (2011) is an integrated project in the European Commission Seventh Framework Programme, that stars in 2008 and ends in 2011. The scope of the project is create a pervasive and self-adapting knowledge that enable enterprise collaboration and interoperability services in order to manage and effectively operate different forms of business collaborations.

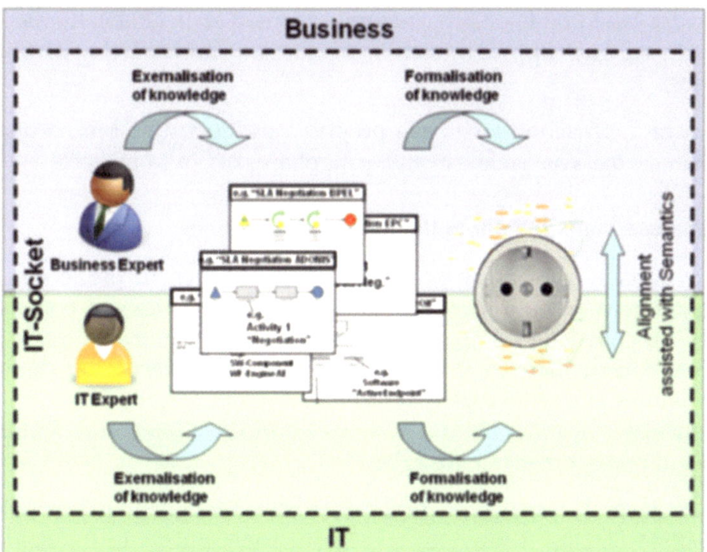

Fig. 1. IT-Socket for business and IT alignment

In literature a lot of ontology-based approaches to business process management have been proposed. Initially, a set of approaches was proposed to apply techniques borrowed from the Semantic Web to the BP management context SUPER (2011). In Missikoff et al. (2011) an ontology-based approach for querying business process repositories for the retrieval of process fragments to be reused in the composition of new BPs is presented. The proposed solution is composed by an ontological framework (OPAL) aimed at capturing the semantics of a business scenario, and a business process modelling framework (BPAL) to represent the workflow logic of BPs. In Markovic (2008) a querying framework based on ontologies is presented. In Francescomarino & Tonella (2008) a visual query language for business Process is described. Processes are represented trough a BPMN meta-model ontology annotated by using domain ontologies, SPARQL queries are visually formulated.

Other approaches based on meta-model ontologies have been presented in Haller et al. (2008; 2006) In Hornung et al. (2007) the authors present an initial idea for an automatic approach for completion of BP models. Their system recommends appropriate completions to initial process fragments based on business rules and structural constraints. The main elements are modeled by using an OWL representation of Petri nets that allows for efficiently computing the semantic similarity between process model variants. Additionally the approach makes use of the Semantic Web Rule Language (SWRL), which is based upon a combination of OWL DL with Unary/Binary Datalog RuleML Boley et al. (2001), to model additional constraints imposed by business rules. Ontoprocess system Stojanovic & Happel (2006) for semantic business process management semantically described, business processes are combined with SWRL rules by using a set of shared ontologies that capture knowledge about a business domain. These formal specifications enable to automatically verify if a process description satisfies the consistency constraints defined by business rules. In order to query BPs, some graph-matching-based approaches have been proposed Awad et al. (2008); Haller et al. (2006) . In Awad et al. (2008) BPs are compiled to finite state models, so model checking techniques allow for verifying structural features of process schemas. However, the semantics of the business domain is not considered. Other approaches that allow for modeling and reasoning over workflows are based on logic programming Montali et al. (2008); Roman & Kifer (2007) have been introduced. Such approaches allow for checking and enacting BPs, but they are not used for querying.

As shown, a lot of approaches have been proposed in litterature, but no one is capable to semantically manage in a comprehensive way all phases of SBPM lifecycle.

2.2 Business process management in the health care domain

The health care domain is of great interest for BPM. In fact, in the recent past, a strong research effort has been taken to provide standard representations of both declarative and procedural medical knowledge. In particular, in the area of medical knowledge and clinical processes representation, there exist one of the most rich collection of domain ontologies available worldwide and a wide variety of formalisms for clinical process representation. In the following, available approaches and systems for medical ontologies and clinical process representation and management are described.

A very famous and widely adopted medical thesaurus is Mesh, the Medical Subject Headings classification MESH (2011). It provides a controlled vocabulary in the fields of medicine, nursing, dentistry, veterinary medicine, etc. MeSH is used to index, catalogue and retrieve the world's medical literature contained in PubMed. Another classification, that has become the international standard diagnostic classification for all medical activities and health management purposes, is ICD10-CM ICD (2011); WHO (2011) the International Classification of Diseases Clinical Modification, arrived to its 10th Revision. The most comprehensive medical terminology developed to date is SNOMED-CT SNOMED (2011), the Systematized Nomenclature of Medicine Clinical Terms, based on a semantic network containing a controlled vocabulary. Electronic transmission and storing of medical knowledge is facilitated by LOINC, the Logical Observation Identifiers Names and Codes LOINC (2011), that consists in a set of codes and names describing terms related to clinical laboratory results, test results and other clinical observations. Machine-readable nomenclature for medical procedures and services performed by physicians are descried in CPT, the Current Procedural Terminology CPT (2011), a registered trademark of the American Medical Association. A comprehensive meta-thesaurus of biomedical terminology is the NCI-EVS NCI-EVS (2011) cancer ontology. Some medical ontologies are, also, due to European medical organizations. For example, CCAM the Classification Commune des Actes Medicaux CCAM (2011), is a French coding system of clinical procedures that consists in a multi-hierarchical classification of medical terms related to physician and dental surgeon procedures. A classification of the terminology related to surgical operations and procedures that may be carried out on a patient is OPCS4, the Office of Population Censuses and Surveys Classification of Surgical Operations and Procedures 4th Revision OPCS-4 (2011), developed in UK by NHS. The most famous and used ontology in the field of healthcare information systems is UMLS, the Unified Medical Language System UMLS (2011), that consists in a meta-thesaurus and a semantic network with lexical applications. UMLS includes a large number of national and international vocabularies and classifications (like SNOMED, ICD-10-CM, and MeSH) and provides a mapping structure between them. This amount of ontologies constitutes machine-processable medical knowledge that can be used for creating semantically-aware health care information systems.

The evidence-based medicine movement, that aims at providing standardized clinical guidelines for treating diseases Sackett et al. (1996), has stimulated the definition of a wide set of approaches and languages for representing clinical processes. A well known formalisms is GLIF, the Guideline Interchange Format GLIF (2011). It is a specification consisting of an object-oriented model that allows for representing sharable computer-interpretable and executable guidelines. In GLIF3 specification is possible to refer to patient data items defined by a standard medical vocabularies (such as UMLS), but no inference mechanisms are provided. Pro*forma* Sutton & Fox (2003) is essentially a first-order logic formalism extended to support decision making and plan execution. Arden Syntax HL7 (2011); Peleg et al. (2001); Pryor & Hripcsak (1993) allows for encoding procedural medical knowledge in a knowledge base that contains so called Medical Logic Modules (MLMs). An MLM is a hybrid between a production rule (i.e. an "if-then" rule) and a procedural formalism. It is less declarative than GLIF and Pro*forma*, its intrinsic procedural nature hinders knowledge sharing. EON Musen et al. (1996) is a formalism in which a guideline model is represented as a set of scenarios, action steps, decisions, branches, synchronization nodes connected by a "followed-by" relation. EON allows for associating conditional goals (e.g. if patient is diabetic, the target blood pressures are 135/80) with guidelines and subguidelines. Encoding of EON guidelines is done by Protégé-2000 Protégé (2011) knowledge-engineering environment.

3. Static/dynamic knowledge representation framework

The key idea which the Static and Dynamic Knowledge Representation Framework (SD-KRF) is based on is that elements of the workflow meta-model (i.e. processes, nodes, tasks, events, transitions, actions, decisions) are expressed as ontology classes Oro & Ruffolo (2009); Oro et al. (2009b). This way workflow elements and domain knowledge can be easily combined in order to organize processes and their elements as an ontology. More in detail, the SD-KRF allows for representing extensional and intensional aspects of both declarative and procedural knowledge by means of:

- *Ontology and Process Schemas*. The former expresses concepts related to specific domains. Ontology contents can be obtained by importing other existing ontologies and thesaurus or by means of direct manual definition. The latter are expressed according with the workflow meta-model illustrated in Section 3.1.

- *Ontology and Process Instances* both expressed in term of ontology instances. In particular, ontology class instances can be obtained by importing them from already existing ontologies or by creating them during process execution. Process instances are created exclusively during process execution. Instances are stored in a knowledge base.
- *Reasoning Tasks* that express, for instance, decisions, risks and business rules.
- *Concept Descriptors* that express information extraction rules capable to recognize and extract ontology instances contained in unstructured documents written in natural language. By concept descriptors ontology instances can be automatically recognized in documents and used for both enriching the knowledge base and annotating unstructured documents related to given domains and processes.

The SD-KRF constitutes an innovative approach for semantic business process management in the field of healthcare information systems. Main features of the presented semantic approach (founded on logic programming) is that it, conversely to already existing systems and approaches, enables to represent process ontologies that can be equipped with expressive business rules. In particular, the proposed framework allows for jointly managing declarative and procedural aspects of domain knowledge and express reasoning tasks that exploit represented knowledge in order to prevent errors and risks that can take place during processes execution. The framework enables, also: (i) manual process execution in which each activity to execute in a given moment is chosen by a human actor on the base of the current configuration of patient and disease parameters, and (ii) automatic execution by means of the enactment of an already designed process schema (e.g. guidelines execution). During process execution, process and ontology instances are acquired and stored in a knowledge base. The system is able to automatically acquire information from electronic unstructured medical documents, exploiting a semantic information extraction approach. Extracted information are stored into a knowledge base as concept instances. The processes execution can be monitored by running (over clinical process schemas and instances) reasoning tasks that implements business rules.

3.1 Modelling process

A significant amount of research has been already done in the specification of mechanisms for process modeling (see, Georgakopoulos et al. (1995) for an overview of different proposals). The most widely adopted formalism is the control flow graph, in which a workflow is represented by a labeled directed graph whose nodes correspond to the activities to be performed, and whose arcs describe the precedences among them. In the SD-KRF we adopt the graph-oriented workflow meta-model shown in Figure 2.a and 2.b, inspired by the JPDL JPDL (2011) process modeling approach. The adopted meta-model: (i) covers the most important and typical constructs required in workflow specification; (ii) allows for executing processes in the SD-KRF by using the JBPM workflow engine; (iii) allows for using workflow mining techniques grounded on graph-oriented meta-models.

Since our scope is to allow the semantic representation of processes, we need firstly to formally define the process meta-model as the following 6-tuple:

$$\mathcal{P} = \langle N, A_r, E_v, A_n, T_k, E \rangle$$

where:

- N is a finite set of *nodes* partitioned in the following subsets: task nodes N_T (that represent activities in which a humans or machines perform tasks), subprocess nodes N_{SP} (that model activities referring processes external to the current one), group nodes N_G (that represent a set of nodes that can be executed without a specific order), custom nodes N_C (that model activities in which custom methods can be executed and handled automatically), wait nodes N_W (that represent activities that temporary stop the execution while they execute methods), join nodes N_J, and fork nodes N_F (that are respectively used to combine or split execution paths) and decision nodes N_D (that allow for controlling the execution flow on the base of conditions, variables or choices performed automatically or by human actors).
- A_r is a set of *actors*. Actors can be human or automatic. They represent the agents that execute a given task or activity.
- A_n is a set of *actions*. An action is a special activity that can be performed as answer to the occurrence of an event.
- T_k is a set of *tasks* that represent tasks to execute in task nodes.
- $E = \{\langle x, y\rangle : x \in N_{From} \wedge y \in N_{To}\}$ is a set of *transitions* in which the following restrictions hold, when $N_{From} \equiv N_{FN} \cup N_D$ then $N_{To} \equiv N_{FN} \cup N_{FCN} \cup N_{end}$ and when $N_{From} \equiv N_{FCN}$ then $N_{To} \equiv N_{FN} \cup N_D$. Moreover, for each process there is a transition of the form $e_{start} = \langle N_{start}, y\rangle$ where $y \in N_{FN}$ and one of the form $e_{end} = \langle x, N_{end}\rangle$ where $x \in \{N_{FN} \cup N_D\}$. The subset $E_d \subset E$ where $E_d = \{\langle x, y\rangle : x \in N_D \wedge y \in N_{FN}\}$ is the set of *decisions*. A decision relates a decision node to a flow node and could hold a *decision rule* that is used at run-time to automatically control the execution flow of a process.
- E_v is a set of *events*. An event causes the execution of an action that constitutes the answer to the event. An event can be, for example, the throwing of an exception during the execution of a task.

3.2 Modeling static and dynamic knowledge

Formally the Static/Dynamic Knowledge Representation Framework (SD-KRF) is the 5-tuple having the following form:

$$\mathcal{O} = \langle D, A, C, R, I\rangle.$$

Where ontology/process schemas are expressed by using elements of D, A, C and R in $\mathcal{O}$ that are *finite* and *disjoint* sets of entity names respectively called *data-types*, *attribute-names*, *classes* and *relations*. The set of classes C is organized in taxonomies and partitioned in two subsets:

- The set of process classes $C_P = N \cup A_r \cup A_n \cup T_k \cup E_v$ that represents elements of the workflow meta-model. It is constituted by the union of classes representing nodes, actors, actions, tasks and events.
- The set of ontology classes C_O that represent concepts related to a specific knowledge domains.

The set R is a set of ontological relations partitioned in two subsets: the set of transition $R_P = E$, and the set of relations R_M used for representing relations between ontology concepts. In the following meaning and usage of $\mathcal{O}$ is explained by describing the implementation of a running example.

4. An example: representing ontologies and a process schemas in the medical domain

The medical domain offers many ontologies and thesaura describing diseases, drugs, medical examinations, medical treatments, laboratory terms, anatomy, patients administration, and clinical risks. Examples of medical ontologies are UMLS UMLS (2011), LOINC LOINC (2011), ICD10-CM ICD (2011), SNOMED SNOMED (2011). Many of such ontologies can be freely obtained from international organization that maintain them and can be automatically imported in the SD-KRF or manually entered by means of direct manual definition.

This section describes a clinical process for caring the breast neoplasm (Figure 2.c). Such an example in the medical domain, that will be used in the rest of the chapter as running example, allows for describing the ability of the SD-KRF to enable the representation of ontologies representing in combined way process schemas, ontological concepts and relations, and instances of both processes and ontologies.

The example considers practices carried out in the oncological ward of an Italian hospital, hence it is not general but specific for the domain of the considered ward. The clinical process is organized in the following 10 activities:

1. Task node *Acceptance* models patient enrollment. A patient arrives to the ward with an already existing clinical diagnosis of a breast neoplasm. This activity can be performed manually by an oncologist that collects patient personal data, and directly acquiring information from electronic medical records in natural language. The information extraction task is performed by exploiting the semantic information extraction approach described in Section 5. Extracted information are stored as ontology instances Oro et al. (2009a).
2. Group node *Anamnesis* represents a set of anamnesis activities: *general anamnesis* in which physiological general data (e.g. allergies, intolerances) are being collected; *remote pathological anamnesis*, concerning past pathologies; *recent pathological anamnesis*, in which each data or result derived from examinations concerning the current pathologies are acquired. These activities can be manually executed without a specific order or by exploiting semantic extraction rules (descriptors) that enable the recognition of information into unstructured source like pre-existing EMR.
3. Task node *Initial clinical evaluation* allows for acquiring the result of an examination of the patient by an oncologist.
4. Decision node *More clinical test requested* represents the decision to perform or not additional examination on the patient.
5. Group node *Other exams* models possible additional clinical tests. If requested these tests are conducted to find out general or particular conditions of patient and disease not fully deducible from the test results already available.
6. Task node *Therapeutic strategy definition* models the selection of a guideline with related drug prescription. At execution time the physician picks a guideline (selected among the guidelines already available in the knowledge base) that depends upon actual pathology state as well as other collected patient data.
7. Task node *Informed agreement sign* models the agreement of the patient concerning understanding and acceptance of consequences (either side effects or benefits) which may derive from the chosen chemotherapy, and privacy agreements.

8. Sub-process *Therapy administration*, models a subprocess that constitutes the guideline to execute for caring the patient.
9. Decision node *Therapy ended* models a decision activity about effects of the therapy and the possibility to stop or continue cares.
10. Task node *Discharging* models the discharging of the patient from the ward end allows for acquiring final clinical parameter values.

In the activities (6) and (8) risk and error conditions can be identified. At each guideline, chosen in (6), corresponds a prescription of drugs (chemotherapy). Hence the computation of doses, which may depend on patient's biomedical parameters such as body's weight or skin's surface, is required. Cross-checking doses is fundamental here, because if a wrong dose is given to the patient the outcome could be lethal. Furthermore, therapy administration ((8)-th activity) must contain checks that aims at verify type and quantity of chemotherapeutic drugs to submit to the cared patient.

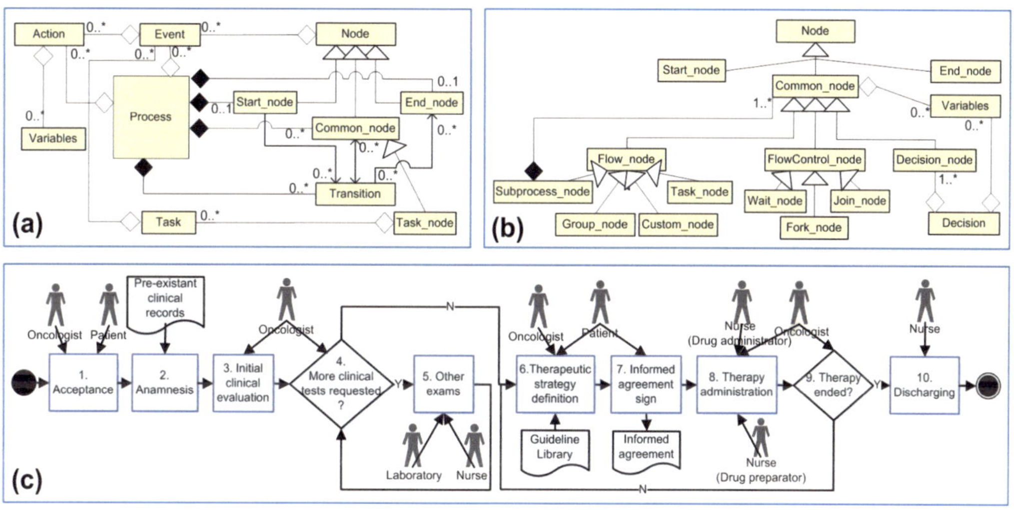

Fig. 2. (a) The process meta-model. (b) The nodes hierarchy. (c) A clinical process for caring the breast neoplasm

4.1 Ontology and process schemas

This section presents the syntax of the SD-KRF language by example. A class in $C \in \mathcal{O}$ can be thought as an aggregation of individuals (objects) that have the same set of properties (attributes $A \in \mathcal{O}$). From a syntactical point of view, a class is a name and an ordered list of attributes identifying the properties of its instances. Each attribute is identified by a name and has a type specified as a data-type or class.

In the following the implementation of the workflow meta-model in the SD-KRF language is firstly presented. In particular, *nodes* in C_P are implemented by using the class hierarchy (built up by using `isa` key-word) shown below.

```
class process(name:string).
class node(name:string, container: process, start_time:integer,
        end_time:integer).
```

```
class start_node() isa{node}.
class end_node() isa{node}.
class common_node () isa{node}.
    class flowControl_node() isa{common_node}.
        class fork() isa{flowControl_node}.
        class join() isa{flowControl_node}.
        class wait_node() isa{flowControl_node}.
    class flow_node() isa{common_node}.
        class task_node(tasks:[task], handler:human_actor)
                        isa{flow_node}.
        class custom_node(handler: automatic_actor, method:string)
                        isa{flow_node}.
        class group_node(nodes:[node]) isa{flow_node}.
        class sub_process_node(sub_proc: process) isa{flow_node}.
    class decision_node(handler:actor) isa{common_node}.
        class automatic_decision_node(handler:automatic_actor)
                        isa{decision_node}.
        class manual_decision_node(task:task, handler:human_actor)
                        isa{decision_node}.
```

Task nodes and manual decision nodes contain *tasks* that are performed by humans. Tasks `class task(name: string).` collects values of activity variables given in input by human actor. *Actors* of a process (that can be human or automatic) represent the agents that execute a given task. They are represented by means of the following classes in C_P:

```
class actor(name:string).
    class human_actor() isa {actor}.
    class automatic_actor(uri:string) isa {actor}.
```

During the process enactment, by running risk and business rules, *events* may occur. Furthermore, an event can be generated by an exception during the execution of a task. Events, and related actions to performs in response, are represented in C_P by the following classes.

```
class event(relativeTo:object, timestamp:integer).
    class node_event(relativeTo:node) isa{event}.
    class task_event(relativeTo:task) isa{event}.
    class process_event(relativeTo:process) isa{event}.
class action(method:string).
```

Relationships among objects are represented by means of relations, which like classes, are defined by a name and a list of attributes. *Transitions* and *decisions*, in R_P, that relate couple of nodes, are represented by means of the following ontology relations.

```
relation transition(name:string, from:node, to:node).
relation decision(name:string, from:decision_node, to:node).
```

When the user defines a specific process schema s/he can specialize original meta-model elements for adding new semantic attribute required by the specific process. In the following are shown some classes representing nodes of the running example depicted in Figure 2.

```
class acceptance_node(tasks:[acceptance_form],handler:physician)
      isa{task_node}.
class anamnesis_node(nodes:[general_anamnesis_node,
      remotePathological_anamnesis_node, recentPathological_anamnesis_node])
      isa {group_node}.
class recentPathological_anamnesis_node(tasks:[pathology_form],
      handler:physician) isa {task_node}.
class therapeutic_strategy_definition_node(tasks:[therapeutic_strategy_form],
      handler:nurse) isa {task_node}.
class therapy_administration_node(sub_process:therapy_administration_process)
      isa{sub_process_node}.
class more_tests_node(task:more_tests_form) isa{manual_decision_node}.
```

`acceptance` and `therapeutic_trategy_definition` process activities are represented as subclasses of `task_node` class, in fact they represent activities in which tasks consist in the execution of forms filled by humans. Whereas `anamnesis_node`, which `Recent Pathological anamnesis` activity belongs to, is represented as a subclass of `group_node` class. `therapy_administration_node` and `more_tests_node` are specializations of `sub_pr oc_node` and `decision_node` respectively. Human actors that operate in this clinical process could be physicians, nurses and patients. They are represented by a person hierarchy that exploits multiple inheritance capabilities in order to express that persons are also human actors of the clinical process.

```
class person(fiscalCode:string,name:string,surname:string,sex:sex_type,
             bornDate:date,address:address).
    class patient(hospitalCard:string, weight:float, heigthCm:float)
             isa {person,human_actor}.
    class healthCareEmploy(occupation:string, role:string)
             isa {person,human_actor}.
        class nurse() isa {healthCareEmploy}.
        class physician() isa {healthCareEmploy}.
```

Class schemas representing tasks related to task-nodes can be expressed by using the following class schemas. Attribute types can be classes represented in C_M expressing different medical concepts (e.g. diseases, drugs, body parts). During task execution values of resulting class instances are obtained from fields filled in forms.

```
class task(name: string).
    class acceptance_form(patient:patient, acc_date:date) isa{task}.
    class pathology_form(disease:disease) isa{task}.
    class chemotherapeutic_strategy_form(strategy:therapeuticStrategy)
          isa{task}.
    class more_tests_form(choice:boolean)isa{task}.
```

In a clinical process, an event can be activated by an exception during the execution of a node or by a reasoning task aimed at control business rules. A reasoning task checks parameters values of running node and already acquired node instances and throws an event related to an error. An example of different kinds of possible errors is shown in the following taxonomy, where the attribute `msg` of the class `view_msg` (action) is the message to display when the error occurs.

```
class task_event(relativeTo:task) isa{event}.
    class medicalError(msg:string) isa{task_event}.
        class drugPrescriptionError() isa {medicalError}.
class view_msg(msg:string) isa {action}.
```

Class schemas in C_M expressing knowledge concerning anatomy, breast neoplasm disease and related therapies and drugs have been obtained (imported) from the Medical Subject Headings (Mesh) Tree Structures , the International Classification of Diseases (ICD10-CM) . and the Anatomical Therapeutic Chemical (ATC/DDD) .

```
class anatomy(name:string).
    class bodyRegion() isa {anatomy}.
class disease(descr:string).
  class neoplasm() isa {disease}.
    class malignant_neoplasm() isa {neoplasm}.
       class primarySited_neoplasm(site:bodyRegion,zone:string)
             isa {malignantNeoplasm}.
          class breast_primarySited_neoplasm() isa {primarySited_neoplasm}.
class drug(name:string, ddd:float, unit:unitOfMeasure,admRoute:[string],
           notes:string).
    class antineoplasticAndImmunomodulatingAgent() isa {drug}.
        class endocrineTherapy() isa {antineoplasticAndImmunomodulatingAgent}.
            class hormoneAntagonistsAndRelatedAgents()isa {endocrineTherapy}.
                class enzymeInhibitors()
                      isa {hormoneAntagonistsAndRelatedAgents}.
            class hormoneAndRelatedAgents()isa {endocrineTherapy}.
                class estrogens() isa {hormoneAndRelatedAgents}.
class code(c:string).
    class icd10Code(chapter:integer, block:string,category:string,
          subCat:string) isa {code}.
    class mesh08Code(category:string, subCat:string) isa {code}.
class therapy(name:string, dru:drug, dose:float).
class therapeuticStrategy(patient:patient, therapy:therapy,startDate:date,
                          nDay:integer).
```

The previous classes are a fragment of a medical ontology inherent (breast) neoplasm cares and are used to model the clinical process shown in Section 4. Class `primarySited_neoplasm` shows the ability to specify user-defined classes as attribute types (i.e. `site:bodyRegion`). Class `drug` has a list-type attribute `admRoute:[string]` representing possible route of administration for a drug (for example inhalation, nasal, oral, parenteral). Relation schemas expressing medical knowledge can be declared by using the following syntax:

```
relation suffers (patient:patient, disease:disease).
relation relatedDrug (dis:disease, dru:drug).
relation sideEffect (dru:drug, effect:string).
relation classifiedAs (dis:disease, c:code).
```

Relation `suffer` asserts diseases suffered by a patient. Relations `relatedDrug` and `sideEffect` associates respectively drugs to a diseases and side effects to drugs. Moreover, relation `classifiedAs` enables users to query the ontologies by using codes defined in the original medical ontologies.

4.2 Ontology and process instances

Clinical process instances are expressed by ontology instances and created exclusively during process execution. Classes instances (objects) are defined by their *oid* (that starts with #) and a list of attributes. Instances obtained by executing the running example, are shown in the following.

```
#1:neoplasm_process(name:"Breast Neoplasm").
#2:therapy_administration_process(name:"Therapy Administration").
#1_1:acceptance_node(name:"Acceptance", container:#1, start_time:6580,
    end_time:16580, tasks:[#1_1_1], handler:#27).
#1_2:anamnesis_node(name:"Anamnesis", container:#1, start_time:16570,
    end_time:26580, nodes:[#1_2_1, #1_2_2, #1_2_3])
#1_2_3:recentPathological_anamnesis_node(name:"Recent Pathological Anamnesis",
       container:#1, start_time:19580, end_time:26570,tasks:[#1_2_3_1],
       handler:#27).
...
```

As described in section 4, instance of `anamnesis_node #1_2` is composed by a set of anamnesis activities represented by means of their *id*. The object `#1_2_3` belongs to `#1_2`. Objects `#1_1`, `#1_2_3` are tasks executed in custom and manual decision node and are stored as their attributes. When execution arrives in a task node or in a manual decision node, task instances are created and the user input is stored as values of the task attributes. Some tasks related to task nodes are shown in the following.

```
#1_1_1:acceptance_form(name:"Acceptance", patient:#21, acc_date:#data_089).
#1_2_3_1:pathology_form(name:"Recent Pathology", disease:#neoB_01).
```

For example, the instance `1_1_1` of the class `acceptance_form` is created by an oncologist that fills in a form. It contains an instance of patient class.

Transition and decision tuples, created during the process execution, are shown in the following. The tuple of `decision` in the following example is obtained as a manual choice of an oncologist, but instances of decisions could be automatically generated by means of reasoning tasks.

```
transition(name:"Acceptance-Anamnesis",from:#1_0, to:#1_1).
decision(name:"More Clinical Tests requested - No",from:#1_4, to:#1_6).
```

Instances of the classes `bodyRegion`, `breast_primarySited_neoplasm`, and of the subclasses of `drug` and `code`, can be obtained by importing them from already existing medical ontologies and can be declared as follows:

```
#A01.236: bodyRegion(name:"breast").
#neoB_01: breast_primarySited_neoplasm(descr:"Malignant neoplasm of breast",
          site:#A01.236, zone:"Nipple and areola").
#L02BG03: enzymeInhibitors(name:"Anastrozole", ddd:1, unit:mg,
          admRoute:["oral"], notes:"").
#L02AA04: estrogens(name:"Fosfestrol", ddd:0.25, unit:g,
          admRoute:["oral","parenteral"], notes:"").
#icd10_C50.0: icd10Code(c:"C50.0", chapter:2, block:"C", category:"50",
          subCat:"0").
#mesh08_C04.588.180: mesh08Code(c:"C04.588.180",category:"C", subCat:"04").
```

The object having ***id*** `#neoB_01`, is an instance of the `breast_primarySited_neoplasm` class. Its attributes `descr` and `zone` (which type is `string`) have string values: `"Malignant neoplasm of breast"` and `"Nipple and areola"`, whereas the attribute `site` has value `#A01.236` that is an ***id*** representing an instance of the class `bodyRegion`. Tuples expressing medical knowledge can be declared by using the following syntax:

```
suffer (pat:#21, dis:#neoB_01).
relatedDrug (dis:#C50.9, dru:#L02BG03).
sideEffect (dru:#L02BG03, effect:"Chest pain").
sideEffect (dru:#L02BG03, effect:"Shortness of breath").
classifiedAs (dis:#neoB 01, c:#icd10 C50.0).
classifiedAs (dis:#neoB 01, c:#mesh08 C04.588.180).
```

The tuple of the relation `suffer` asserts that the patient `#p_002` suffers of the disease `#neoB_01`. The same diseases is classified in the ICD10-CM with identifier code `#icd10_C50.0`, and is stored in Mesh tree structure with identifier code `#mesh08_C04.588.180`. By means of the relation `classifiedAs` an user is enabled to querying concepts in the SD-KRF ontology by using one of the identifiers in the original medical ontologies.

4.3 Reasoning over schemas and instances

Integrity constraints, business rules and complex inference rules can be expressed over schemas and instances respectively by means of *axioms* and *reasoning tasks*. For example, the following axiom prevents the prescription of a drug to a patient that has an allergy to a particular constituent of the drug.

```
::-therapyStrategy(patient:P, therapy:T, drug:D),
   hasActivePrinciple(drug:D,constituent:C),
   allergy(patient:P,actPrin:C).
```

Axioms could be, also, used for: (i) specify constraints about transitions behavior. For example, the axiom `"::-P:process(), not start_node(container:P)."` expresses that a `start_node` must exist for each process. Constraints are also used for expressing that a transition links nodes belonging to the same process, and corresponds to an effective edge of the process model as shown in the following:

```
::-transition(from:N1,to:N2), N1:node(container:P1),
   N2.node(container:P2), P1!=P2.
::-transition(from:N1,to:N2), N1:node(start_time:ST1),
   N2:node(start_time:ST2), ST1>=ST2.
::-P:neoplasm_process(), transition(from:N1,to:N2),
   N1:acceptance_node(container:P),
   not N2:anamnesis_node(container:P).
...
```

A reasoning task can be used for expressing a business rule. The following reasoning task, for instance, throws a medical error event when the prescribed dose exceed the recommended dose based on individual characteristics (i.e. age and weight) of the interested patient. Such a check is useful when a `therapeutic_strategy_form` is created while `therapeutic_strategy_definition_node` is active.

```
ID:drugPrescription_medicalError(relativeTo:TASK,timestamp:TIME,msg:MSG):-
    TASK:chemotherapeutic_strategy_form(strategy:STR),
    STR:therapeuticStrategy(patient:P, therapy:T),
    P:patient(bornDate:DATE,weight:W), @age(date,AGE),
    T:therapy(dru:DRUG,dose:DOSE),
    recommendedDose(drug:DRUG, dose:RD, minAge:MA, MinWeight:MW),
    AGE<MA, W<MW, DOSE>RD,
    MSG:="Prescribed dose " + DOSE + "exceed recommend dose " + RD, @newID(ID),
    @now(TIME).
```

The generated prescription error event must be properly handled in the process, for example an error message is visualized by means of a GUI to the physician.

```
ID:view_msg(method:"exception.jar", msg:MSG):-
   X:drugPrescription_medicalError(relativeTo:TASK, timestamp:TIME, msg:MSG),
   @newID(ID).
```

Queries can be also used for exploring clinical processes ontologies in a semantic fashion. For instance `malNeoplasm_f_patient(patient:P)?` returns every female patients suffering of any malignant neoplasm (e.g `P=#21, P=#34` ids are given for answer), where `malNeoplasm_f_patient(patient:P)`:

```
malNeoplasm_f_patient(patient:P):- P:patient(sex:#F),suffer(patient:P,disease:D),
                                   D:malignant_neoplasm().
```

5. Semantic information extraction

In the Static/Dynamic Knowledge Representation Framework classes and instances can be enriched by *concepts descriptors* that are rules allowing to recognize and extract concepts contained in unstructured documents written in natural language. Concepts extracted by descriptors are stored in the knowledge base as instances of the related classes in the ontology.

Considering the example of clinical process described in Section 4 semantic information extraction tasks can be applied to Electronic Medical Records (EMRs), results of examinations, medical reports, etc. coming from different hospital wards in order to populate the clinical process instance related to a given patient.

In the following, a set of semantic extraction rules (i.e. *descriptors*) that allow for extracting patient name, surname, age and disease is shown. Descriptors exploit concepts and relationships referred to the disease, its diagnosis, cares in term of surgical operations and chemotherapies with the associated side effects. Concepts related to persons (patients), body parts and risk causes are also represented. All the concepts related to the cancer come from the ICD10-CM diseases classification system, whereas the chemotherapy drugs taxonomy, is inspired at the Anatomic Therapeutic Chemical (ATC) classification system. Extracted information are exploited to construct, for each cared patient, an instance of lung cancer clinical process.

```
class anatomy ().
    class bodyRegion (bp:string) isa {anatomy}.
        class organ isa {body_part}.
            lung: organ("Lung").
```

```
            <lung> -> <X:token(), matches(X,"[Ll]ung")>.
        ...
    ...
class disease (name:string).
    tumor: disease("Tumor").
    <tumor> -> <X:token(), matches(X,"[Tt]umor")>.
    cancer: disease("Cancer").
    <cancer> -> <X:token(), matches(X,"[Cc]ancer")>.
    ...
relation synonym (d1:disease,d2:disease)
    synonym(cancer,tumor).
    ...
class body_part_desease () isa {disease}.
    lung_cancer: body_part_disease("Lung cancer").
    <lung_cancer> -> <diagnosis_section> CONTAIN <lung> &
                     <X:desease(),synonym(cancer,X)>
    ...
collection class patient_data (){}
    collection class patient_name (name:string){}
        <patient_name(Y)> -> <T:token(),defBy(T, "name:")>
                             <X:token()> {Y := X;} SEPBY <X:space()>.
    collection class patient_surname (surname:string){}
            <patient_surname(Y)> -> <X:hiStr(),matches(X,"sur(:?name)?:")>
                                    <X:token()> {Y:=X;} SEPBY <X:space()>.
        collection class patient_age (age:integer){}
            <patient_age(Y)> -> <X:token(),matches(X,"age:")>
                                <Z:token()>{Y := $str2int(Z);}
                                SEPBY <X:space()>.
    ...
collection class patient_data (name:string, surname:string,
                               age:integer, diagnosis:body_part_disease){}
     <patient_data(X,Y,Z,lung_cancer)> -> <hospitalization_section>
                                          CONTAIN
                                          <P:patient_name(X1)>{X:=X1} &
                                          <P:patient_surname(Y1)>{Y:=Y1} &
                                          <P:patient_age(Z1)>{Z:=Z1} &
                                          <lung_cancer>.
...
```

The classes diagnosis_section and hospitalization_section, used in the above descriptors, represent text paragraphs containing personal data and diagnosis data recognized by proper descriptors that aren't shown for lack of space. The extraction mechanism can be considered in a WOXM fashion: Write Once eXtract Many, in fact the same descriptors can be used to enable the extraction of metadata related to patient affected by lung_cancer in unstructured EMRs that have different arrangement. Moreover, descriptors are obtained by automatic writing methods (as happens, for example, for the cancer and tumor concepts) or by visual composition (as happens for patient_data)

Metadata extracted by using the descriptors are stored as class instances into a knowledge base. Using descriptors shown above the extraction process generates the following

patient_
data class instance for an EMR: "#1":patient_data("Mario", "Rossi","70",lung_
cancer).

5.1 Implementation issues

A prototype of the SD-KRF has been implemented by combining the JBPM engine JPDL (2011) and the XONTO system Oro et al. (2009a). It is designed to follow a clinical processes life-cycle model based on 3 phases: processes and ontologies *design and implementations, execution and monitoring, analysis*. The first module exploits the XONTO system. It provides functionalities for importing and/or representing (by using direct "on-screen" drawing and manual specification facilities): ontologies and processes. Moreover, semantic extraction rules (descriptors), that enable the recognition and extraction of information from unstructured sources, can be modeled by exploiting the XONTO approach. A set of business/risk/error rules can be described in terms of ontology constraints and/or reasoning tasks. Acquired and/or represented schemas and instances are stored in a knowledge base and can be queried by using querying and meta-querying capabilities. The *Execution & Monitoring* module is mainly constituted by the JBPM engine that interact with the XONTO system. Process execution is performed in two ways: (i) by using a *workflow enactment* strategy. In this case, a process schema is imported in JBPM and automatically executed involving actors that can be humans or machines (e.g. legacy systems supplying results of medical examinations); (ii) by using a dynamic *workflow composition* strategy. In this case, nodes to execute are selected step by step by choosing the most appropriate one in a given moment. Nodes are chosen by using semantic querying capabilities of XONTO system and executed by JBPM. Queries allows for specifying data and each significant information available in the particular moment of the execution. The execution generates process instances that are stored in a knowledge base. Reasoning, querying and meta-querying over schemas and available instances are possible. This way, process execution can be monitored by running business rules that equip process schemas. Events generated by rules alert process actors that can react for preventing risks and errors. The *Analytics* module aims at allowing analysis of the clinical processes instances after their acquisition. The execution of clinical processes makes available process instances that are also ontology instances. This way a large amount of semantically enriched data becomes available for retrieval, querying and analysis. Analysis are performed by creating reports obtained by semantic query of acquired process instances.

The SD-KRF constitutes an innovative approach for semantic business process management in the field of healthcare information systems. Main features of the presented semantic approach (founded on logic programming) is that it, conversely to already existing systems and approaches, enables to represent process ontologies that can be equipped with expressive business rules. In particular, the proposed framework allows for jointly managing declarative and procedural aspects of domain knowledge and express reasoning tasks that exploit represented knowledge in order to prevent errors and risks that can take place during processes execution. The framework enables, also: (i) manual process execution in which each activity to execute in a given moment is chosen by a human actor on the base of the current configuration of patient and disease parameters, and (ii) automatic execution by means of the enactment of an already designed process schema (e.g. guidelines execution). During process execution, process and ontology instances are acquired and stored in a knowledge base. The system is able to automatically acquire information from electronic unstructured medical documents, exploiting a semantic information extraction approach. Extracted information are stored into a knowledge base as concept instances and are also used to fill XML documents enabling interoperability. The processes execution can be monitored by running (over clinical process schemas and instances) reasoning tasks that implements business rules. The framework could be used in many application fields by modeling proper domain ontologies and processes.

6. References

Awad, A., Decker, G. & Weske, M. (2008). Efficient compliance checking using bpmn-q and temporal logic, *BPM*, pp. 326–341.

Boley, H., Tabet, S. & Wagner, G. (2001). Design rationale for ruleml: A markup language for semantic web rules, *SWWS*, pp. 381–401.

CCAM (2011). Classification commune des actes médicaux.
URL: *http://www.ccam.sante.fr/*

COIN (2011). Enterprise collaboration and interoperability.
URL: *http://www.coin-ip.eu/*

CORDIS (2011). Community research and development information service.
URL: *http://cordis.europa.eu/*

CPT (2011). Current procedural terminology (cpt): a registered trademark of the american medical association (ama).
URL: *http://www.ama-assn.org/ama/pub/category/3113.html*

Francescomarino, C. D. & Tonella, P. (2008). Crosscutting concern documentation by visual query of business processes, *Business Process Management Workshops*, pp. 18–31.

Georgakopoulos, D., Hornick, M. & Sheth, A. (1995). An overview of workflow management: from process modeling to workflow automation infrastructure, *Distrib. Parallel Databases* 3(2): 119–153.

GLIF (2011). The guideline interchange format.
URL: *http://www.openclinical.org/gmm_glif.html*

Gruber, T. R. (1995). Toward principles for the design of ontologies used for knowledge sharing?, *Int. J. Hum.-Comput. Stud.* 43(5-6): 907–928.

Haller, A., Gaaloul, W. & Marmolowski, M. (2008). Towards an xpdl compliant process ontology, *SERVICES I*, pp. 83–86.

Haller, A., Oren, E. & Kotinurmi, P. (2006). m3po: An ontology to relate choreographies to workflow models, *IEEE SCC*, pp. 19–27.

Hepp, M., Leymann, F., Domingue, J., Wahler, A. & Fensel, D. (2005). Semantic business process management: A vision towards using semantic web services for business process management, *ICEBE*, pp. 535–540.

Hepp, M. & Roman, D. (2007). An ontology framework for semantic business process management, *Wirtschaftsinformatik (1)*, pp. 423–440.

HL7 (2011). Health Level Seven.
URL: *http://www.hl7.org/*

Hornung, T., Koschmider, A. & Oberweis, A. (2007). Rule-based autocompletion of business process models, *CAiSE Forum*.

Hripcsak, G., Ludemann, P., Pryor, T. A., Wigertz, O. B. & Clayton, P. D. (1994). Rationale for the arden syntax, *Comput. Biomed. Res.* 27: 291–324.
URL: *http://dl.acm.org/citation.cfm?id=188778.188784*

ICD (2011). International Classification of Diseases, Tenth Revision, Clinical Modification (ICD-10-CM).
URL: *http://www.cdc.gov/nchs/about/otheract/icd9/icd10cm.htm*

JPDL (2011). jbpm process definition language.
URL: *http://www.jboss.org/jbossjbpm/jpdl/*

LOINC (2011). Logical observation identifiers names and codes.
URL: *http://loinc.org/*

Markovic, I. (2008). Advanced querying and reasoning on business process models, *BIS*, pp. 189–200.

Medeiros, A. K. A. D. & Aalst, W. M. (2009). Process mining towards semantics, *Advances in Web Semantics I*, number 46, pp. 35–80.

MESH (2011). Medical subject headings.
URL: *http://www.nlm.nih.gov/mesh/*

Missikoff, M., Proietti, M. & Smith, F. (2011). Querying semantically enriched business processes, *DEXA (2)*, pp. 294–302.

Montali, M., Torroni, P., Alberti, M., Chesani, F., Gavanelli, M., Lamma, E. & Mello, P. (2008). Verification from declarative specifications using logic programming, *ICLP*, pp. 440–454.

Musen, M. A., Tu, S. W., Das, A. K. & Shahar, Y. (1996). Eon: A component-based approach to automation of protocol-directed therapy., *Journal of the American Medical Informatics Association* 3(6): 367–388.

NCI-EVS (2011). NCI Enterprise Vocabulary Services (EVS).
URL: *http://ncicb.nci.nih.gov/NCICB/infrastructure/cacore_overview/vocabulary*

Newell, A. (1980). The knowledge level (presidential address), *AI Magazine* 2(2): 1–20.

OMG (2011). Unified modeling language.
URL: *http://www.uml.org/*

OPCS-4 (2011). The office of population censuses and surveys classification of surgical operations and procedures, 4th revision.
URL: *http://www.openclinical.org/medTermOPCS4.html*

Oro, E. & Ruffolo, M. (2009). Towards a semantic system for managing clinical processes, *ICEIS (2)*, pp. 180–187.

Oro, E., Ruffolo, M. & Saccà, D. (2009a). Ontology-based information extraction from pdf documents with xonto, *International Journal on Artificial Intelligence Tools (IJAIT)* 18(5): 673–695.

Oro, E., Ruffolo, M. & Saccà, D. (2009b). A semantic clinical knowledge representation framework for effective health care risk management, *BIS*, pp. 25–36.

Peleg, M. (2009). Executable knowledge, *Encyclopedia of Database Systems*, pp. 1073–1079.

Peleg, M., Ogunyemi, O., Tu, S., Boxwala, A. A., Zeng, Q., Greenes, R. A. & Shortliffe, E. H. (2001). Using features of arden syntax with object-oriented medical data models for guideline modeling, *in American Medical Informatics Association (AMIA) Annual Symposium, 2001*, pp. 523–527.

PLUG-IT (2011). It-socket knowledge portal - plug-it initiatives.
URL: *http://plug-it.org/*

Protégé (2011). Ontology Editor and Knowledge Acquisition System.
URL: *http://protege.stanford.edu*

Pryor, T. A. & Hripcsak, G. (1993). The arden syntax for medical logic modules., *Journal of Clinical Monitoring and Computing* 10(4): 215–224.

Roman, D. & Kifer, M. (2007). Reasoning about the behavior of semantic web services with concurrent transaction logic, *VLDB*, pp. 627–638.

Sackett, D. L., Rosenberg, W. M. C., Gray, M. J. A., Haynes, B. R. & Richardson, S. W. (1996). Evidence based medicine: what it is and what it isn't, *BMJ* 312(7023): 71–72.
URL: *http://bmj.bmjjournals.com/cgi/content/full/312/7023/71*

Shortliffe, E. H. (1976). *Computer-Based Medical Consultations: MYCIN*, Elsevier/North-Holland.

SNOMED (2011). Systematized nomenclature of medicine-clinical terms (snomed ct). URL: *http://www.ihtsdo.org/snomed-ct/*

Stojanovic, L. & Happel, H.-J. (2006). Ontoprocess – a prototype for semantic business process verification using swrl rules, *ESWC*.

SUPER (2011). Semantic utilised for process management within and between enterprises. URL: *http://www.ip-super.org/*

Sutton, D. R. & Fox, J. (2003). The syntax and semantics of the proforma guideline modeling language., *JAMIA* 10(5): 433–443.

ter Hofstede, A. H. M., van der Aalst, W. M. P., Adams, M. & Russell, N. (eds) (2010). *Modern Business Process Automation - YAWL and its Support Environment*, Springer.

UMLS (2011). Unified medical Language System. URL: *http://www.nlm.nih.gov/research/umls/*

van der Aalst, W. M. P. (1999). Formalization and verification of event-driven process chains, *Information & Software Technology* 41(10): 639–650.

van der Aalst, W. M. P. (2009). Business process management, *Encyclopedia of Database Systems*, pp. 289–293.

Weske, M. (2007). *Business Process Management: Concepts, Languages, Architectures*, Springer.

Wetzstein, B., Ma, Z., Filipowska, A., Kaczmarek, M., Bhiri, S., Losada, S., Lopez-Cob, J.-M. & Cicurel, L. (2007). Semantic business process management: A lifecycle based requirements analysis, *SBPM*.

White, S. (2006). Business process modeling notation specification.

WHO (2011). World health organization. URL: *http://www.who.int/classifications/en/*

Wohed, P., van der Aalst, W. M. P., Dumas, M., ter Hofstede, A. H. M. & Russell, N. (2006). On the suitability of bpmn for business process modelling, *Business Process Management*, pp. 161–176.

XPDL (2011). Xpdl2.1 complete specification. URL: *http://www.wfmc.org/xpdl.html*

10

Automatic Concept Extraction in Semantic Summarization Process

Antonella Carbonaro
Computer Science Department, University of Bologna, Mura Anteo Zamboni, Italy

1. Introduction

The Semantic Web offers a generic infrastructure for interchange, integration and creative reuse of structured data, which can help to cross some of the boundaries that Web 2.0 is facing. Currently, Web 2.0 offers poor query possibilities apart from searching by keywords or tags. There has been a great deal of interest in the development of semantic-based systems to facilitate knowledge representation and extraction and content integration [1], [2]. Semantic-based approach to retrieving relevant material can be useful to address issues like trying to determine the type or the quality of the information suggested from a personalized environment. In this context, standard keyword search has a very limited effectiveness. For example, it cannot filter for the type of information, the level of information or the quality of information.

Potentially, one of the biggest application areas of content-based exploration might be personalized searching framework (e.g., [3],[4]). Whereas search engines provide nowadays largely anonymous information, new framework might highlight or recommend web pages related to key concepts. We can consider semantic information representation as an important step towards a wide efficient manipulation and retrieval of information [5], [6], [7]. In the digital library community a flat list of attribute/value pairs is often assumed to be available. In the Semantic Web community, annotations are often assumed to be an instance of an ontology. Through the ontologies the system will express key entities and relationships describing resources in a formal machine-processable representation. An ontology-based knowledge representation could be used for content analysis and object recognition, for reasoning processes and for enabling user-friendly and intelligent multimedia content search and retrieval.

Text summarization has been an interesting and active research area since the 60's. The definition and assumption are that a small portion or several keywords of the original long document can represent the whole informatively and/or indicatively. Reading or processing this shorter version of the document would save time and other resources [8]. This property is especially true and urgently needed at present due to the vast availability of information. Concept-based approach to represent dynamic and unstructured information can be useful to address issues like trying to determine the key concepts and to summarize the information exchanged within a personalized environment.

In this context, a concept is represented with a Wikipedia article. With millions of articles and thousands of contributors, this online repository of knowledge is the largest and fastest growing encyclopedia in existence.

The problem described above can then be divided into three steps:

- Mapping of a series of terms with the most appropriate Wikipedia article (disambiguation).
- Assigning a score for each item identified on the basis of its importance in the given context.
- Extraction of n items with the highest score.

Text summarization can be applied to many fields: from information retrieval to text mining processes and text display. Also in personalized searching framework text summarization could be very useful.

The chapter is organized as follows: the next Section introduces personalized searching framework as one of the possible application areas of automatic concept extraction systems. Section three describes the summarization process, providing details on system architecture, used methodology and tools. Section four provides an overview about document summarization approaches that have been recently developed. Section five summarizes a number of real-world applications which might benefit from WSD. Section six introduces Wikipedia and WordNet as used in our project. Section seven describes the logical structure of the project, describing software components and databases. Finally, Section eight provides some considerations on case study and experimental results.

2. Personalized searching framework

In personalized searching frameworks, standard keyword search is of very limited effectiveness. For example, it does not allow users and the system to search, handle or read concepts of interest, and it doesn't consider synonymy and hyponymy that could reveal hidden similarities potentially leading to better retrieval. The advantages of a concept-based document and user representations can be summarized as follows: (i) ambiguous terms inside a resource are disambiguated, allowing their correct interpretation and, consequently, a better precision in the user model construction (e.g., if a user is interested in computer science resources, a document containing the word 'bank' as it is meant in the financial context could not be relevant); (ii) synonymous words belonging to the same meaning can contribute to the resource model definition (for example, both 'mouse' and 'display' brings evidences for computer science documents, improving the coverage of the document retrieval); (iii) synonymous words belonging to the same meaning can contribute to the user model matching, which is required in recommendation process (for example, if two users have the same interests, but these are expressed using different terms, they will be considered overlapping); (iv) finally, classification, recommendation and sharing phases take advantage of the word senses in order to classify, retrieve and suggest documents with high semantic relevance with respect to the user and resource models.

For example, the system could support Computer Science last-year students during their activities in courseware like Bio Computing, Internet Programming or Machine Learning. In fact, for these kinds of courses it is necessary an active involvement of the student in the acquisition of the didactical material that should integrate the lecture notes specified and released by the teacher. Basically, the level of integration depends both on the student's prior knowledge in that particular subject and on the comprehension level he wants to acquire. Furthermore, for the mentioned courses, it is continuously necessary to update the acquired knowledge by integrating recent information available from any remote digital library.

3. Inside summarization

Summarization is a widely researched problem. As a result, researchers have reported a rich collection of approaches for automatic document summarization to enhance those provided manually by readers or authors as a result of intellectual interpretation. One approach is to provide summary creation based on a natural language generation (as investigated for instance in the DUC and TREC conferences); a different one is based on a sentence selection from the text to be summarized, but the most simple process is to select a reasonable short list of words among the most frequent and/or the most characteristic words from those found in the text to be summarized. So, rather than a coherent text the summary is a simple set of items.

From a technical point of view, the different approaches available in the literature can be considered as follows. The first is a class of approaches that deals with the problem of document classification from a theoretical point of view, making no assumption on the application of these approaches. These include statistical [9], analytical [10], information retrieval [11] and information fusion [12] approaches. The second class deals with techniques that are focused on specific applications, such as baseball program summaries [13], clinical data visualization [14] and web browsing on handheld devices [15]. [16] reports a comprehensive review.

The approach presented in this chapter produce a set of items, but involves improvements over the simple set of words process in two means. Actually, we go beyond the level of keywords providing conceptual descriptions from concepts identified and extracted from the text. We propose a practical approach for extracting the most relevant keywords from the forum threads to form a summary without assumption on the application domain and to subsequently find out concepts from the keyword extraction based on statistics and synsets extraction. Then semantic similarity analysis is conducted between keywords to produce a set of semantic relevant concepts summarizing actual forum significance.

In order to substitute keywords with univocal concepts we have to build a process called Word Sense Disambiguation (WSD). Given a sentence, a WSD process identifies the syntactical categories of words and interacts with an ontology both to retrieve the exact concept definition and to adopt some techniques for semantic similarity evaluation among words. We use MorphAdorner [17] that provides facilities for tokenizing text and WordNet [18], one of the most used ontology in the Word Sense Disambiguation task.

The methodology used in this application is knowledge-based, it uses Wikipedia as a base of information with its extensive network of cross-references, portals, categories and info-boxes providing a huge amount of explicitly defined semantics.

To extract and access useful information from Wikipedia in a scalable and timely manner we use the Wikipedia Miner toolkit [http://wikipedia-miner.sourceforge.net/] including scripts for processing Wikipedia dumps and extracting summaries such as the link graph and category hierarchy.

4. Related works in automatic text summarization

A variety of document summarization approaches have been developed recently. The paper [19] reviews leading notions and developments, and seeks to assess the state of the art for this challenging task. The review shows that some useful summarizing for various purposes can already be done but also, not surprisingly, that there is a huge amount more to do both in terms of semantic analysis and capturing the main ideas, and in terms of improving linguistic quality of the summaries. A further overview on the latest techniques related to text summarization can be found in [20]. Generally speaking, the summarization methods can be either extractive or abstractive. Extractive summarization involves assigning relevant scores to some units (e.g. sentences, paragraphs) of the document and extracting the sentences with highest scores, while abstraction summarization involves paraphrasing sections of the source document using information fusion, sentence compression and reformulation [21]. In general, abstraction can condense a text more strongly than extraction, but the required natural language generation technologies are harder to develop representing a growing field.

Sentence extraction summarization systems take as input a collection of sentences and select some subset for output into a summary. The implied sentence ranking problem uses some kind of similarity to rank sentences for inclusion in the summary [22].

For example, MEAD (http://www.summarization.com/mead/) is based on sentence extraction. For each sentence in a cluster of related documents, MEAD computes three features and uses a linear combination of the three to determine what sentences are most salient. Sentence selection is constrained by a summary length threshold, and redundant new sentences avoided by checking cosine similarity against prior ones.

Extractive summarizers can be based on scoring sentences in the source document. For example, [23] consider each document as a sequence of sentences and the objective of extractive summarization is to label the sentences in the sequence with 1 and 0 (summary or non-summary sentence).

The summarization techniques can also be classified into two groups: supervised and unsupervised techniques. In the first case they rely on pre-existing document-summary pairs, while in the second, they are based on properties and heuristics derived from the text. Supervised extractive summarization techniques treat the summarization task as a two-class classification problem at the sentence level, where the summary sentences are positive samples while the non-summary sentences are negative samples. After representing each sentence by a vector of features, the classification function can be trained in two different manners [24]. Many unsupervised methods have been developed by exploiting different features and relationships of the sentences.

Furthermore, summarization task can also be categorized as either generic or query-based. A query-based summary presents the information that is most relevant to the given queries while a generic summary gives an overall sense of the document content [21].

Text summarization can also be classified on the basis of volume of text documents available distinguishing between single document and multi-document text summarization techniques. The article [25] presents a multi-document, multi-lingual, theme-based summarization system based on modeling text cohesion (story flow). In this paper a Naïve Bayes classifier for document summarization is also proposed. Also in [26] we can find an analysis of multi-document summarization in scientific corpora.

Finally, automatic document summarization is a highly interdisciplinary research area related with computer science, multimedia, statistics, as well as cognitive psychology. In [27] they introduce an intelligent system based on a cognitive psychology model (the event-indexing model) and the roles and importance of sentences and their syntax in document understanding. The system involves syntactic analysis of sentences, clustering and indexing sentences with five indices from the event-indexing model, and extracting the most prominent content by lexical analysis at phrase and clause levels.

5. Applications

Here we summarize a number of real-world applications which might benefit from WSD and on which experiments have been conducted [28].

5.1 Information Retrieval (IR)

Search engines do not usually use explicit semantics to prune out documents which are not relevant to a user query. An accurate disambiguation both of the document base and of the query words, would allow it to eliminate documents containing the same words used with different meanings (thus increasing precision) and to retrieve documents expressing the same meaning with different wordings (thus increasing recall).

Most of the early work on the contribution of WSD to IR resulted in no performance improvement also because only a small percentage of query words are not used in their most frequent (or predominant) sense, indicating that WSD must be very precise on uncommon items, rather than on frequent words. [29] concluded that, in the presence of queries with a large number of words, WSD cannot benefit IR. He also indicated that improvements in IR performance would be observed only if WSD could be performed with at least 90% accuracy. Encouraging evidence of the usefulness of WSD in IR has come from [30]. Assuming a WSD accuracy greater than 90%, they showed that the use of WSD in IR improves the precision by about 4.3%. With lower WSD accuracy (62.1%) a small improvement (1.73% on average) can still be obtained.

5.2 Information Extraction (IE)

In detailed application domains it is interesting to distinguish between specific instances of concepts: for example, in the medical domain we might be interested in identifying all kinds of antidepressant drugs across a text, whereas in bioinformatics we would like to solve the ambiguities in naming genes and proteins. Tasks like named-entity recognition and acronym expansion that automatically spells out the entire phrase represented (a feature found in some content management and Web-based search systems), can all be cast as disambiguation problems, although this is still a relatively new area. Acronym expansion functions for search is considered an accessibility feature that is useful to people who have difficulties in typing.

[31] proposed the application of a link analysis method based on random walks to solve the ambiguity of named entities. [32] used a link analysis algorithm in a semi-supervised approach to weigh entity extraction patterns based on their impact on a set of instances.

Some tasks at Semeval-2007 more or less directly dealt with WSD for information extraction. Specifically, the metonymy task in which a concept is not called by its own name but by the name of something intimately associated with that concept ("Hollywood" is used for American cinema and not only for a district of Los Angeles) required systems to associate the appropriate metonymy with target named entities. Similarly, the Web People Search task required systems to disambiguate people names occurring in Web documents, that is, to determine the occurrence of specific instances of people within texts.

5.3 Machine Translation (MT)

Machine translation (MT), the automatic identification of the correct translation of a word in context, is a very difficult task. Word sense disambiguation has been historically considered as the main task to be solved in order to enable machine translation, based on the intuitive idea that the disambiguation of texts should help translation systems choose better candidates. Recently, [33] showed that word sense disambiguation can help improve machine translation. In these works, predefined sense inventories were abandoned in favor of WSD models which allow it to select the most likely translation phrase. MT tools have become an urgent need also in a multilingual environment. Although there are any available tools, unfortunately, a robust MT approach is still an open research field.

5.4 Content analysis

The analysis of the general content of a text in terms of its ideas, themes, etc., can certainly benefit from the application of sense disambiguation. For instance, the classification of blogs or forum threads has recently been gaining more and more interest within the Internet community: as blogs grow at an exponential pace, we need a simple yet effective way to classify them, determine their main topics, and identify relevant (possibly semantic) connections between blogs and even between single blog posts. [34]. A second related area of research is that of (semantic) social network analysis, which is becoming more and more active with the recent evolutions of the Web.

Although some works have been recently presented on the semantic analysis of content [35], this is an open and stimulating research area.

5.5 Lexicography

WSD and lexicography (i.e., the professional writing of dictionaries) can certainly benefit from each other: sense-annotated linguistic data reduces the considerable overhead imposed on lexicographers in sorting large-scaled corpora according to word usage for different senses. In addition, word sense disambiguation techniques can also allow language learners to access example sentences containing a certain word usage from large corpora, without excessive overhead. On the other side, a lexicographer can provide better sense inventories and sense annotated corpora which can benefit WSD.

5.6 The semantic web

The Semantic Web offers a generic infrastructure for interchange, integration and creative reuse of structured data, which can help to cross some of the boundaries that Web 2.0 is facing. Currently, Web 2.0 offers poor query possibilities apart from searching by keywords or tags. There has been a great deal of interest in the development of semantic-based systems to facilitate knowledge representation and extraction and content integration [36], [37]. Semantic-based approach to retrieving relevant material can be useful to address issues like trying to determine the type or the quality of the information suggested from a personalized environment. In this context, standard keyword search has a very limited effectiveness. For example, it cannot filter for the type of information, the level of information or the quality of information.

Potentially, one of the biggest application areas of content-based exploration might be personalized searching framework (e.g., [38],[39]). Whereas today's search engines provide largely anonymous information, new framework might highlight or recommend web pages or content related to key concepts. We can consider semantic information representation as an important step towards a wide efficient manipulation and discovery of information [40], [41], [42]. In the digital library community a flat list of attribute/value pairs is often assumed to be available. In the Semantic Web community, annotations are often assumed to be an instance of an ontology. Through the ontologies the system will express key entities and relationships describing resources in a formal machine-processable representation. An ontology-based knowledge representation could be used for content analysis and object recognition, for reasoning processes and for enabling user-friendly and intelligent multimedia content exploration and retrieval.

Therefore, the semantic Web vision can potentially benefit from most of the above-mentioned applications, as it inherently needs domain-oriented and unrestricted sense disambiguation to deal with the semantics of documents, and enable interoperability between systems, ontologies, and users.

WSD has been used in semantic Web-related research fields, like ontology learning, to build domain taxonomies. Indeed, any area of science that relies on a linguistic bridge between human and machine will use word sense disambiguation.

5.7 Web of data

Although the Semantic Web is a Web of data, it is intended primarily for humans; it would use machine processing and databases to take away some of the burdens we currently face so that we can concentrate on the more important things that we can use the Web for.

The idea behind Linked Data [43] is using the Web to allow exposing, connecting and sharing linking data through dereferenceable URIs on the Web. The goal is to extend the Web by publishing various open datasets as RDF triples and by setting RDF links between data items from several data sources. Using URIs, everything can be referred to and looked up both by people and by software agents. In this chapter we focus on DBpedia [44], that is one of the main clouds of the Linked Data graph. DBpedia extracts structured content from Wikipedia and makes this information available on the Web; it uses the RDF to represent the extracted information. It is possible to query relationships and properties associated with

Wikipedia resources (through its SPARQL endpoint), and link other data sets on the web to DBpedia data.

The whole knowledge base consists of over one billion triples. DBpedia labels and abstracts of resources are stored in more than 95 different languages. The graph is highly connected to other RDF dataset of the Linked Data cloud. Each resource in DBpedia is referred by its own URI, allowing to precisely get a resource with no ambiguity. The DBpedia knowledge base is served as Linked Data on the Web. Actually, various data providers have started to set RDF links from their data sets to DBpedia, making DBpedia one of the central interlinking-hubs of the emerging Web of Data.

Compared to other ontological hierarchies and taxonomies, DBpedia has the advantage that each term or resource is enhanced with a rich description including a textual abstract. Another advantage is that DBpedia automatically evolves as Wikipedia changes. Hence, problems such as domain coverage, content freshness, machine-understandability can be addressed more easily when considering DBpedia. Moreover, it covers different areas of the human knowledge (geographic information, people, films, music, books, ...); it represents real community agreement and it is truly multilingual.

6. Using Wikipedia and WordNet in our project

For the general public, Wikipedia represents a vast source of knowledge. To a growing community of researchers and developers it also represents a huge, constantly evolving collection of manually defined concepts and semantic relations. It is a promising resource for natural language processing, knowledge management, data mining, and other research areas.

In our project we used WikipediaMiner toolkit [wikipedia-miner.sourceforge.net/], a functional toolkit for mining the vast amount of semantic knowledge encoded in Wikipedia providing access to Wikipedia's structure and content, allowing terms and concepts to be compared semantically, and detecting Wikipedia topics when they are mentioned in documents. We now describe some of the more important classes we used to model Wikipedia's structure and content.

Pages: All of Wikipedia's content is presented on pages of one type or another. The toolkit models every page as a unique id, a title, and some content expressed as MediaWiki markup.

Articles provide the bulk of Wikipedia's informative content. Each article describes a single concept or topic, and their titles are succinct, well-formed phrases that can be used as non-descriptors in ontologies and thesauri. For example, the article about domesticated canines is entitled Dog, and the one about companion animals in general is called Pet. Once a particular article is identified, related concepts can be gathered by mining the articles it links to, or the ones that link to it.

The anchor texts of the links made to an article provide a source of synonyms and other variations in surface form. The article about dogs, for example, has links from anchors like canis familiaris, man's best friend, and doggy.

The subset of keywords related to each article helps to discriminate between concepts. In such a way, two texts characterized using different keywords may result similar considering underling concept and not the exact terms. We use the WordNet to perform the following feature extraction pre-process. Firstly, we label occurrences of each word as a part of speech (POS) in grammar. This POS tagger discriminates the POS in grammar of each word in a sentence. After labeling all the words, we select those ones labeled as noun and verbs as our candidates. We then use the stemmer to reduce variants of the same root word to a common concept and filter the stop words.

WordNet is an online lexical reference system, in which English nouns, verbs, adjectives and adverbs are organized into synonym sets. Each synset represents one sense, that is one underlying lexical concept. Different relations link the synonym sets, such as IS-A for verbs and nouns, IS-PART-OF for nouns, etc. Verbs and nouns senses are organized in hierarchies forming a "forest" of trees. For each keyword in WordNet, we can have a set of senses and, in the case of nouns and verbs, a generalization path from each sense to the root sense of the hierarchy. WordNet could be used as a useful resource with respect to the semantic tagging process and has so far been used in various applications including Information Retrieval, Word Sense Disambiguation, Text and Document Classification and many others.

Noun synsets are related to each other through hypernymy (generalization), hyponymy (speciali-zation), holonymy (whole of) and meronymy (part of) relations. Of these, (hypernymy, hyponymy) and (meronymy, holonymy) are complementary pairs. The verb and adjective synsets are very sparsely connected with each other. No relation is available between noun and verb synsets. However, 4500 adjective synsets are related to noun synsets with pertainyms (pertaining to) and attra (attributed with) relations.

Articles often contain links to equivalent articles in other language versions of Wikipedia. The toolkit allows the titles of these pages to be mined as a source of translations; the article about dogs links to (among many others) chien in the French Wikipedia, haushund in German, and 犬 in Chinese.

Redirects are pages whose sole purpose is to connect an article to alternative titles. Like incoming anchor texts, these correspond to synonyms and other variations in surface form. The article entitled dog, for example, is referred to by redirects dogs, canis lupus familiaris, and domestic dog. Redirects may also represent more specific topics that do not warrant separate articles, such as male dog and dog groups.

Categories: Almost all of Wikipedia's articles are organized within one or more categories, which can be mined for hyponyms, holonyms and other broader (more general) topics. Dog, for example, belongs to the categories domesticated animals, cosmopolitan species, and scavengers. If a topic is broad enough to warrant several articles, the central article may be paired with a category of the same name: the article dog is paired with the category dogs. This equivalent category can be mined for more parent categories (canines) and subcategories (dog breeds, dog sports). Child articles and other descendants (puppy, fear of dogs) can also be mined for hypernyms, meronyms, and other more specific topics.

All of Wikipedia's categories descend from a single root called Fundamental. The toolkit uses the distance between a particular article or category and this root to provide a measure of its generality or specificity. According to this measure Dog has a greater distance than carnivores, which has the same distance as omnivores and a greater distance than animals.

Disambiguations: When multiple articles could be given the same name, a specific type of article—a disambiguation—is used to separate them. For example, there is a page entitled dog (disambiguation), which lists not only the article on domestic dogs, but also several other animals (such as prairie dogs and dogfish), several performers (including Snoop Doggy Dogg), and the Chinese sign of the zodiac. Each of these sense pages have an additional scope note; a short phrase that explains why it is different from other potential senses.

Anchors, the text used within links to Wikipedia articles, are surprisingly useful. As described earlier, they encode synonymy and other variations in surface form, because people alter them to suit the surrounding prose. A scientific article may refer to canis familiaris, and a more informal one to doggy. Anchors also encode polysemy: the term dog is used to link to different articles when discussing pets, star signs or the iconic American fast food. Disambiguation pages do the same, but link anchors have the advantage of being marked up directly, and therefore do not require processing of unstructured text. They also give a sense of how likely each sense is: 76% of Dog links are made to the pet, 7% to the Chinese star sign, and less than 1% to hot dogs.

Wikipedia itself is, of course, one of the more important objects to model. It provides the central point of access to most of the functionality of the toolkit. Among other things, here you can gather statistics about the encyclopedia, or access the pages within it through iteration, browsing, and searching.

We used RitaWn [http://www.rednoise.org/rita/wordnet] to query WordNet.

7. System architecture

This section describes the logical structure of the project, describing software components (Figure1) and database (Figure 2) that allow the system to carry out its task.

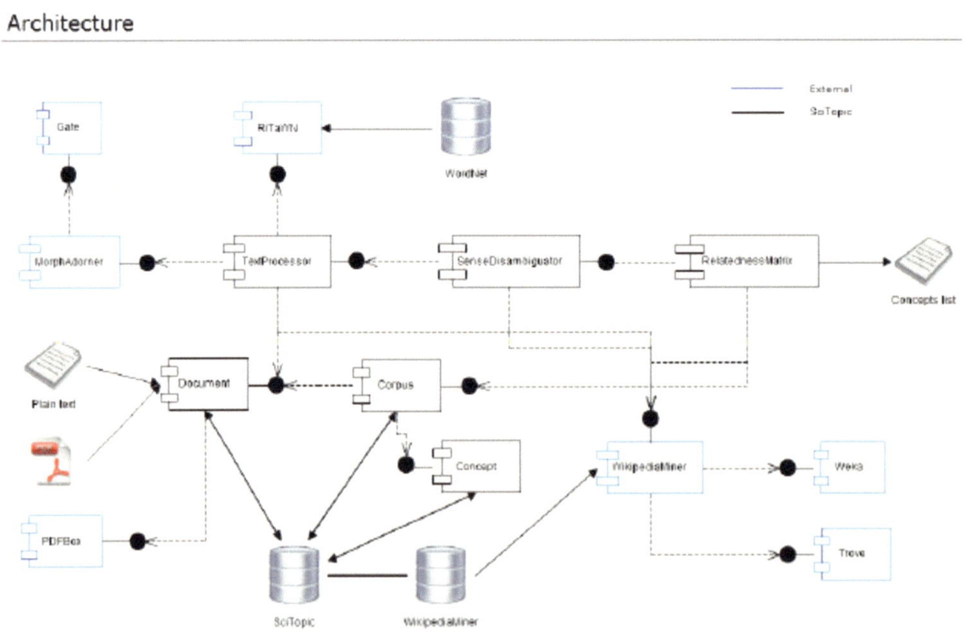

Fig. 1. system architecture

The database maintains documents in plain text and organize them in one or more possibly *Corpus*, a set of documents linked together in a logical manner, for example, by dealing with the topic.

We associate a frequency list of concepts for each corpus (and therefore a set of documents), that is how many times a particular concept is repeated within all the documents of the corpus. A concept corresponds exactly to a Wikipedia article, thus creating a relationship between our project and WikipediaMiner database, more precisely, between the ConceptFrequency and Page tables. These statistics, as we shall see below, are used to better identify those concepts that define a document between similar.

To abstract and manage documents and databases we have created two components, *Corpus* and *Document*, which act as an interface between the other components of the application and the database. They provide editing, creation and deletion functions to facilitate the extraction of content representing the input to all other phases of the main process.

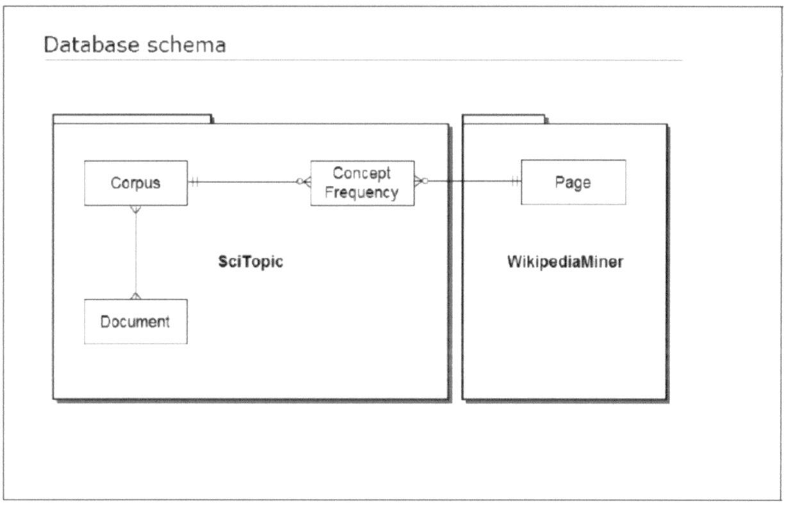

Fig. 2. system database

Starting from a document and a corpus to which it is associated, we proceed to a series of transformations on the text in order to filter all unnecessary components leaving only a set of names in basic form useful for later phases. The component that performs this task is the *TextProcessor* and is configurable, allowing the user to define the desired level of filtering.

The output of the previous phase is used for the disambiguation task, carried out by the component *SenseDisabiguator*; the system maps the most appropriate Wikipedia article to each term or, if this is not possible, it eliminates the term considered unknown. The result is a series of concepts, that is Wikipedia articles.

The component RelatednessMatrix uses this list of concepts to establish the importance of each of them within the context. In particular, the system performs the sum of the degree of relationship between a concept and all the others and evaluates this amount depending on the TFxIDF. So doing, the system associates a weight to each concept, reaching the objective of obtaining the *n* that best define the content of the input document.

7.1 Text processor

Starting from a document and a corpus to which it is associated, *TextProcessor* performs transformations on the text in order to filter all unnecessary components leaving only a set of names in basic form useful for later phases (see Figure 3).

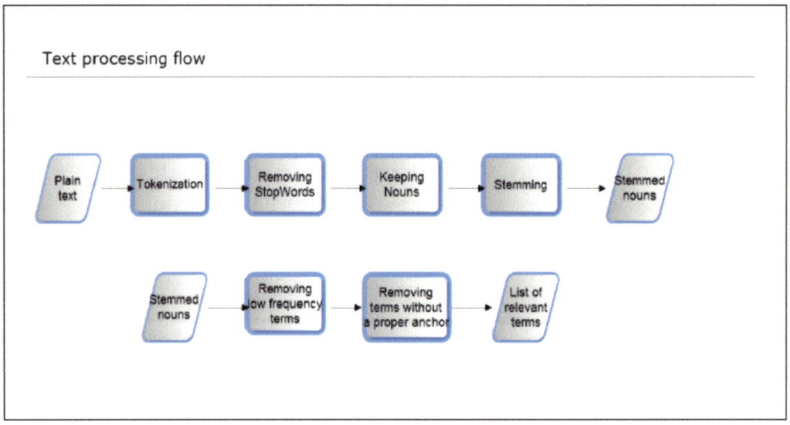

Fig. 3. The text processing flow

The disambiguation process is expensive and it is therefore appropriate to delete any irrelevant term; with this intention the *TextProcessor* module removes both all the remaining words with a frequency less than a given threshold and all those that do not correspond to an appropriate Wikipedia anchor, that is an anchor that has no meaning with probability greater than a defined minimum.

Summarizing, *TextProcessor* has two parameters that affect the selectivity of performed functions: the minimum frequency and the minimum probability of the Wikipedia senses (articles).

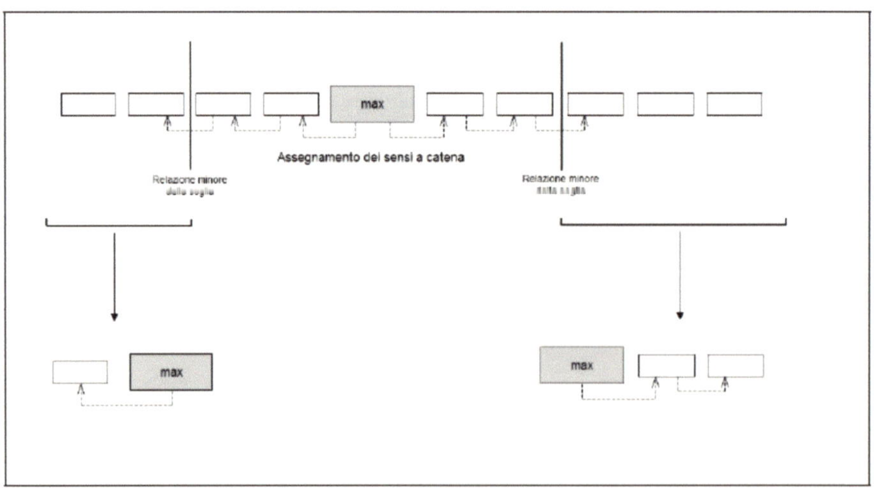

Fig. 4. The SenseDisambiguator recursive procedure

7.2 Sense disambiguator

It is the component that assigns to a specific list of terms (see Figure 4) the most appropriate sense. It is achieved by a recursive procedure (see Figure 5) that takes a list of terms and recursively splits it into slices; for each part it defines a main sense from which disambiguate the others.

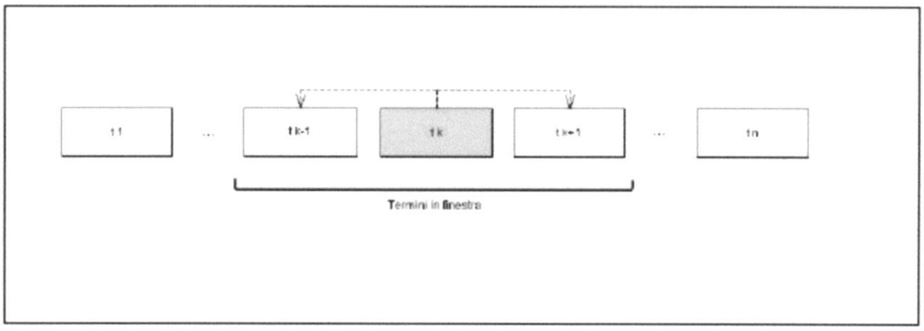

Fig. 5. The sense score is calculated based on the term senses belonging to a window

The pseudo-code of the disambiguation procedure is showed in the following listing.

Listing 6.1: Pseudocodice della procedura di disambiguazione

```

WSD( termini )

//Calcolo dei punteggi dei sensi dei termini
foreach(Termine t1 in termini){
    foreach(Senso s1 in sensi(t1)){
```

7.3 Relatedness matrix

The RelatednessMatrix has the task of both building a relationship matrix using all elements of a given list of senses and of providing various ways of extracting information. It is the component used in the final phase, that is, given a list of senses it extracts the most relevant.

```
        foreach(Termine t2 in finstra(t1)){
            foreach(Senso s2 in sensi(t2)){
                Aggiorna punteggio(s1,t1)
            }
        }
    }
}

AssegnaSensi(termini, 1, n)
```

Listing 6.2: Pseudocodice della procedura di assegnamento dei sensi

```

AssegnaSensi(termini, inizio, fine)

//Termine con senso a punteggio massimo
smax := {s:max{punteggio(s,t)}}
tmax := {t:smax in t}

//Assegno i sensi dei termini a sinistra di tmax
foreach(Termine t1 in termini a sinistra){
    if(Esiste almeno un senso che ha una relazione sufficiente con
        il senso assegnato al termine precedente){
        Assegna al termine t1 il senso s che massimizza relazione(s
            , s_precedente)
    }else{
        // Ricorsione
        AssegnaSensi(termini, inizio, t1)
        break
    }
}

Unisci liste di sensi

//Assegno i sensi dei termini a destra di tmax
foreach(Termine t1 in termini a destra){
    if(Esiste almeno un senso che ha una relazione sufficiente con
        il senso assegnato al termine precedente){
        Assegna al termine t1 il senso s che massimizza punteggio(s
            , s_precedente)
    }else{
        // Ricorsione
        AssegnaSensi(termini, t1, fine)
        break
    }
}

Unisci liste di sensi


return
```

8. Considerations

The work described in this chapter represents some initial steps in exploring automatic concept extraction in semantic summarization process. It could be considered as one possible instance of a more general concept concerning the transition from the Document Web to the Document/Data Web and the consequent managing of these immense volumes of data.

Summarization can be evaluated using intrinsic or extrinsic measures; while the first one methods attempt to measure summary quality using human evaluation, extrinsic methods measure the same through a task-based performance measure such the information retrieval-oriented task. In our experiments we utilized intrinsic approach analyzing [45] as document and [45] [46] [47] [48] [49] [50] [51] [52] [53] [54] [55] as corpus.

This experiment is to evaluate the usefulness of concept extraction in summarization process, by manually reading whole document content and comparing with automatic extracted concepts. The results show that automatic concept-based summarization produces useful support to information extraction. The extracted concepts represent a good summarization of document contents.

For example, we evaluated the influence of chosen window size using 605 terms to be disambiguated. The results are showed in Table 1.

Window	Copertura (C)	Precisione (P)	C%	P%
4	438	268	72.39	61.18
8	461	357	76.19	77.44
12	470	355	77.68	75.53
16	475	369	78.51	77.68
20	480	362	79.33	75.41

Table 1. Change in precision and recall as a function of window size.

Using the best choice of parameter values we obtain the following percentages in precision and recall.

window	minScore	minRelatednessToSplit
8	0.18	0.2

Copertura (C)	Precisione (P)	C%	P%
444	358	73.38	80.63

Table 2. Change in precision and recall using the showed set of parameter values.

Finally, given the document [MW08], Table 3 shows the ten most representative articles automatically extracted from the system.

While the initial results are encouraging, much remains to be explored. For example, many disambiguation strategies with specific advantages are available, so designers now have the possibility of deciding which new features to include in order to support them, but it is particularly difficult to distinguish the benefits of each advance that have often been shown independent of others.

Listing 6.16: I primi dieci articoli che rappresentano il documento [MW08].

```
Language
System
Category theory
Knowledge
Word
Datum (geodesy)
Concept
WordNet
Application software
Accuracy and precision
```

Table 3. Automatically extracted articles representing [MW08]

It would also be interesting to apply the showed method using a different knowledge base, for example YAGO (but always derived from Wikipedia) and use a different measure of relationship between concepts considering not only the links belonging to articles but also the entire link network. That is, considering Wikipedia as a graph of interconnected concepts, we could exploit more than one or two links.

9. References

[1] Henze N., Dolog P., Nejdl W.: Reasoning and Ontologies for Personalized E-Learning in the Semantic Web, Educational Technology & Society, 7 (4), 82-97 (2004)

[2] Bighini C., Carbonaro A.: InLinx: Intelligent Agents for Personalized Classification, Sharing and Recommendation, International Journal of Computational Intelligence. International Computational Intelligence Society. 2 (1), (2004)

[3] Pickens, J., Golovchinsky, G., Shah, C., Qvarfordt, P., and Back, M. Algorithmic Mediation for Collaborative Exploratory Search. To appear in Proceedings of SIGIR

[4] Freyne J., Smyth B.: Collaborative Search: Deployment Experiences, in The 24th SGAI International Conference on Innovative Techniques and Applications of Artificial Intelligence. Cambridge, UK, pp. 121-134 (2004)

[5] Calic J., Campbell N., Dasiopoulou S. and Kompatsiaris Y.: A Survey on Multimodal Video Representation for Semantic Retrieval, in the Third International Conference on Computer as a tool, IEEE (2005)

[6] Carbonaro A., Defining Personalized Learning Views of Relevant Learning Objects in a Collaborative Bookmark Management System, In Z. Ma (Ed.), Web-based Intelligent ELearning Systems: Technologies and Applications (pp. 139-155). Hershey, PA: Information Science Publishing, (2006)

[7] Bloehdorn S., Petridis K., Simou N., Tzouvaras V., AvrithisY., Handschuh S., Kompatsiaris Y., Staab S., Strintzis M. G.: Knowledge Representation for Semantic Multimedia Content Analysis and Reasoning, in Proceedings of the European Workshop on the Integration of Knowledge, Semantics and Digital Media Technology, (2004)

[8] White R. W. and Roth R., Exploratory Search: Beyond the Query-Response Paradigm. Morgan & Claypool, (2009)

[9] McKeown, K., Barzilay, R., Evans, D., Hatzivassiloglou, V., Kan, M., Schiffman, B., and Teufel, S. "Columbia Multi- Document Summarization: Approach and Evaluation". Workshop on Text Summarization, 2001.

[10] Brunn, M., Chali, Y., and Pinchak. C. "Text Summarization Using Lexical Chains". Work. on Text Summarization. 2001.

[11] Aho, A., Chang, S., McKeown, K., Radev, D., Smith, J., and Zaman, K. "Columbia Digital News Project: An Environment for Briefing and Search over Multimedia". Information J. Int. J. on Digital Libraries, 1(4):377-385. 1997.

[12] Barzilay, R., McKeown, K. and Elhadad, M. "Information fusion in the context of multi-document summarization". In Proc. of ACL'99, 1999.

[13] Yong Rui, Y., Gupta, A., and Acero, A. "Automatically extracting highlights for TV Baseball programs". ACM Multimedia, Pages 105-115, 2000.

[14] Shahar, Y. and Cheng, C. "Knowledge-based Visualization of Time Oriented Clinical Data". Proc AMIA Annual Fall Symp., pages 155-9, 1998.

[15] Rahman, A, H. Alam, R. Hartono and K. Ariyoshi. "Automatic Summarization of Web Content to Smaller Display Devices", 6th Int. Conf. on Document Analysis and Recognition, ICDAR01, pages 1064-1068, 2001.

[16] NIST web site on summarization: http://wwwnlpirnist.gov/projects/duc/pubs.html, Columbia University Summarization Resources (http://www.cs.columbia.edu/~hjing/ summarization.html) and Okumura-Lab Resources (http://capella.kuee.kyoto-u.ac.jp/index_e.html).

[17] Burns, Philip R. 2006. MorphAdorner: Morphological Adorner for English Text. http://morphadorner.northwestern.edu/morphadorner/textsegmenter/.

[18] Fellbaum, C., ed (1998), WordNet: An Electronic Lexical Database. MIT Press, Cambridge, Mass

[19] Jones, K. S. (2007). Automatic summarizing: The state of the art. Information Processing and Management, 43, 1449 - 1481

[20] Proceedings of the Workshop on Automatic Text Summarization 2011 Collocated with Canadian Conference on Artificial Intelligence St. John's, Newfoundland and Labrador, Canada May 24, 2011

[21] Wan, X. (2008). Using only cross-document relationships for both generic and topic-focused multi-document summarizations. Information Retrieval, 11, 25-49

[22] Alguliev, R. M., & Alyguliev, R. M. (2007). Summarization of text-based documents with a determination of latent topical sections and information-rich sentences. Automatic Control and Computer Sciences, 41, 132 - 140

[23] Shen, D., Sun, J. -T., Li, H., Yang, Q., & Chen, Z. (2007). Document summarization using conditional random fields. In Proceedings of the 20th international joint conference on artificial intelligence (IJCAI 2007), January 6 - 12 (pp. 2862 - 2867) Hyderabad, India.

[24] Mihalcea, R., & Ceylan, H. (2007). Explorations in automatic book summarization. In Proceedings of the 2007 joint conference on empirical methods in natural language processing and computational natural language learning (EMNLP-CoNLL 2007), 28 - 30 June (pp. 380 - 389) Prague, Czech Republic.

[25] Fung, P., & Ngai, G. (2006). One story, one flow: Hidden Markov story models for multilingual multidocument summarization. ACM Transaction on Speech and Language Processing, 3, 1 - 16.

[26] Ozge Yeloglu, Evangelos Milios, Nur Zincir-Heywood, SAC'11 March 21-25, 2011, TaiChung, Taiwan. Copyright 2011 ACM 978-1-4503-0113-8/11/03

[27] Guo, Y., & Stylios, G. (2005). An intelligent summarization system based on cognitive psychology. Information Sciences, 174, 1 - 36.

[28] Navigli, R. 2009.Word sense disambiguation: A survey. ACM Comput. Surv. 41, 2, Article 10 (2009)

[29] Sanderson, M. 1994. Word sense disambiguation and information retrieval. In Proceedings of the Special Interest Group on Information Retrieval (SIGIR, Dublin, Ireland). 142–151.

[30] Stokoe, C., Oakes, M. J., and Tait, J. I. 2003. Word sense disambiguation in information retrieval revisited. In Proceedings of the 26th Annual International ACM SIGIR Conference on Research and Development in Information Retrieval (Toronto, Onto., Canada). 159–166

[31] Malin, B., Airoldi, E., and Carley, K. M. 2005. A network analysis model for disambiguation of names in lists. Computat. Math. Organizat. Theo. 11, 2, 119–139.

[32] Hassan, H., Hassan, A., and Noeman, S. 2006. Graph based semi-supervised approach for information extraction. In Proceedings of the TextGraphs Workshop in the Human Language Technology Conference of the North American Chapter of the Association of Computational Linguistics (HLT/NAACL, New York, NY). 9–16

[33] Chan, Y. S., Ng, H. T., and Chiang, D. 2007a. Word sense disambiguation improves statistical machine translation. In Proceedings of the 45th Annual Meeting of the Association of Computational Linguistics (Prague, Czech Republic). 33–40.

[34] A. Carbonaro "Forum Summarization to Support Tutor and Teacher in group interaction management" Lytras M.D., De Pablos P.O., Damiani E. (eds.) Semantic Web Personalization and Context Awareness: Management of Personal Identities

and Social Networking, Information Science Reference, chapter 3, pp. 22-31, IGI-Global. 2011, ISBN 978-1-61520-921-7
[35] Semantic Analysis: A Practical Introduction (Oxford Textbooks in Linguistics), Cliff Goddard, 2011
[36] Henze N., Dolog P., Nejdl W.: Reasoning and Ontologies for Personalized E-Learning in the Semantic Web, Educational Technology & Society, 7 (4), 82-97 (2004)
[37] Bighini C., Carbonaro A.: InLinx: Intelligent Agents for Personalized Classification, Sharing and Recommendation, International Journal of Computational Intelligence. International Computational Intelligence Society. 2 (1), (2004)
[38] Pickens, J., Golovchinsky, G., Shah, C., Qvarfordt, P., and Back, M. Algorithmic Mediation for Collaborative Exploratory Search. To appear in Proceedings of SIGIR
[39] Freyne J., Smyth B.: Collaborative Search: Deployment Experiences, in The 24th SGAI International Conference on Innovative Techniques and Applications of Artificial Intelligence. Cambridge, UK, pp. 121-134 (2004)
[40] Calic J., Campbell N., Dasiopoulou S. and Kompatsiaris Y.: A Survey on Multimodal Video Representation for Semantic Retrieval, in the Third International Conference on Computer as a tool, IEEE (2005)
[41] Carbonaro A., Defining Personalized Learning Views of Relevant Learning Objects in a Collaborative Bookmark Management System, In Z. Ma (Ed.), Web-based Intelligent ELearning Systems: Technologies and Applications (pp. 139-155). Hershey, PA: Information Science Publishing, (2006)
[42] Bloehdorn S., Petridis K., Simou N., Tzouvaras V., AvrithisY., Handschuh S., Kompatsiaris Y., Staab S., Strintzis M. G.: Knowledge Representation for Semantic Multimedia Content Analysis and Reasoning, in Proceedings of the European Workshop on the Integration of Knowledge, Semantics and Digital Media Technology, (2004)
[43] Bizer, C. Heath T., and T. Berners-Lee. Linked data - the story so far. International Journal on Semantic Web and Information Systems, 5(3):1, (2009)
[44] Bizer C., Lehmann J., Kobilarov G., Auer S., Becker C., Cyganiak R., and S. Hellmann. Dbpedia - a crystallization point for the web of data. Web Semantics: Science, Services and Agents on the World Wide Web, (2009)
[45] D. Milne and I. H. Witten. An effective, low-cost measure of semantic relatedness obtained from wikipedia links. 2008
[46] F. M. Suchanek, G. Kasneci, and G. Weikum. Yago: A large ontology from wikipedia and wordnet. 2008
[47] J. Yu, J. A. Thom, and A. Tam. Ontology evaluation using wikipedia categories for browsing. 2007
[48] A. Kittur, E. H. Chi, and B. Suh. What's in wikipedia? Mapping topics and conflict using socially annotated category structure. 2009.
[49] T. Zesch, C. M¨uller, and I. Gurevych. Extracting lexical semantic knowledge from wikipedia and wiktionary. 2008.
[50] E. Wolf and I. Gurevych. Aligning sense inventories in Wikipedia and wordnet. 2010.
[51] D. Milne and I. H. Witten. An open-source toolkit for mining wikipedia. 2009
[52] P. Sch¨onhofen. Identifying document topics using the Wikipedia category network. 2009
[53] O. Medelyan, I. H. Witten, and D. Milne. Topic indexing with wikipedia. 2008
[54] H. Amiri, M. Rahgozar, A. A. Ahmad, and F. Oroumchian. Query expansion using wikipedia concept graph. 2008
[55] R. Mihalcea and A. Csomai. Wikify! linking documents to encyclopedic knowledge. 2007

11

Knowledge-Based Approach for Military Mission Planning and Simulation

Ryszard Antkiewicz, Mariusz Chmielewski, Tomasz Drozdowski, Andrzej Najgebauer, Jarosław Rulka, Zbigniew Tarapata, Roman Wantoch-Rekowski and Dariusz Pierzchała
Military University of Technology in Warsaw, Faculty of Cybernetics
Poland

1. Introduction

One of the most complicated and complex decision processes concerns military applications. Military command and control processes are information intensive activities, involving many variables (tasks of friendly forces, expected actions of opposite forces, environmental conditions - terrain, weather, time of the day and season of the year, current state of own (friend) and opposite forces in the sense of personnel, weapon systems and military materiel, etc.) with strong interrelationships and uncertainty. Two of the factors which are especially essential in military decision-making are human battlefield stress and a limited time. Therefore, it is very important to provide, for military decision-makers, computer tools, which support their decisions and try to partially eliminate the negative impact of their stress on the decision being made and shorten the decision-making time (Najgebauer, 1999; Tarapata, 2011). These tools should be a knowledge-based (Tarapata, 2011). An example of a knowledge-based decision support system schema for military applications is presented in Fig.1. There are illustrated two elements, which contain a knowledge base (KB): operational-tactical KB and terrain KB. The first one is used to collect knowledge being used to express the character of the digital battlefield during automation of military decision-making: military rules, decision situation patterns and recognition rules, course of action (CoA) patterns, etc. The second one (terrain KB) collects pre-processed information from the terrain database.

The typical military decision planning process contains the following steps:

- estimation of power of own and opposite forces, terrain, and other factors, which may influence on a task realization,
- identification of a decision situation,
- determination of decision variants (Course of Actions, CoA),
- variants - evaluation (verification),
- recommendation of the best variant (CoA) of the above-stated points, which satisfy the proposed criteria.

Simulation and verification of course of actions (CoA) is considered in many systems and aspects (Antkiewicz et al., 2011a; 2011b; Barry & Koehler, 2005; Mathews, 2004; Najgebauer 2004; Ross et al., 2004; Sokolowski, 2002; Tarapata, 2008; Pierzchała et al., 2011). The most important step of decision planning process is an identification of a decision situation problem: this problem is that we must find the most similar battlefield situation (from earlier defined or ensuing situations, e.g. in battlefield situation knowledge) to current one. Afterwards, the decision situation being identified is a basis for choosing CoA, because with each decision situation a few typical CoA frames are connected. In the chapter we will present a network model of the terrain (with rule-based functions described on the network's nodes and arcs) which is based on pre-processed information from the terrain database, and we will show how to use the operational-tactical KB to identify decision situations.

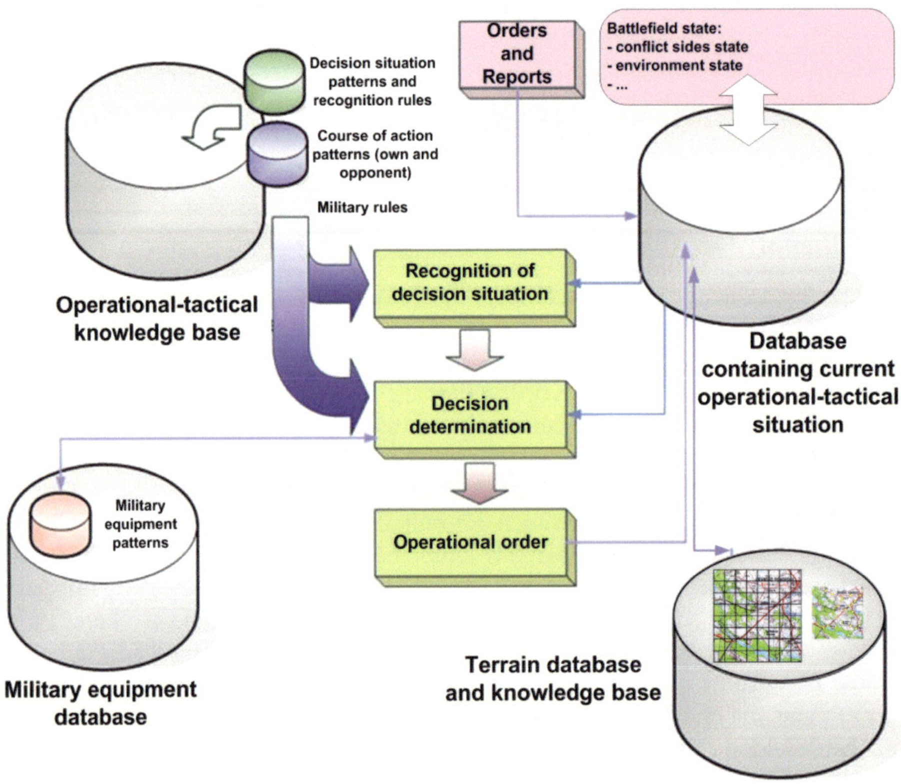

Fig. 1. An example of a knowledge-based decision support system schema for military applications (Tarapata, 2011)

The chapter is organized as follows: in section 2 we present problems connected with modelling the semantics of military domain, section 3 contains battlespace ontology model, in section 4 we present ontology-based reasoning, section 5 contains ontology-based decision situation model and section 6 and 7 present some example of using tool for identification of decision situations.

2. Modelling the semantics of military domain

Recently, knowledge representation in military operations is addressed by application of Network Enabled Capabilities concept. Data, information and knowledge can be distinguished as the following steps in environment understanding. Russell Ackoff defines the content of the human mind separated into: data (basic representation mainly symbols), information (which is data that has been given meaning by definition of relationships), knowledge (appropriate intentional collection of information), understanding (is an interpolative and probabilistic process based on cognitive and analytical characteristics) which synthesize new knowledge. Based on the above definitions the knowledge representation for military domain should be concerned with representing pre-processed inferred information addressing the scenario or course of action. In the following chapter we will discuss the importance of such representations and usefulness of their applications in decision support systems.

In any domain there exists a need to formulate unified semantics shared across multiple heterogeneous components or even systems. The more concealed and specific the domain is, the more detailed terminology we can define. Military domain model is a good example of such case, as the vocabulary is explicit and well-defined moreover the domain experts exchange information using abbreviations and terminology strongly related to this semantic only. Ontology is a model which can be used to achieve this task. It is based on a conceptualisation process and can be understood as a task of identifying and extracting concepts from given domain and formulating their semantics through definitions of binary relationships or axioms. Ontologies can be often regarded as informal or semiformal models of human readable knowledge representations, however in our understanding the need to present such formalisms is to develop model for agent processing.

In the following work, formally we will define ontology as:

"Domain model formulated for the purpose of describing shared knowledge about specific modelling area. Ontology provides both lexical and conceptual point of view separating human view and automata understating of the domain in terms of semantics."

Available in many sources verbal definitions contain blurred vision therefore we can formalise ontology as following tuple:

$$O = \langle C, R_C, H_C, R_{\mathrm{Rel}}, A^O \rangle \tag{1}$$

Consisting of concept set, binary relationships sets defined on that set, characteristics of structural relationships and axiom set containing complex model expressivity. Structural relations between them $R_C = \{r_C : r_C \in C \times C\}$, taxonomical relationships providing information on super-/sub- concepts $H_C = \{h_C : h_C \in (C \setminus \{c_0\}) \times C\}$. To provide capability of describing correspondences between structural relations we provide R_{Rel} which is able to describe inverse relationships, possible relationship taxonomies along with symmetry, transitivity, reflexivity etc. relationship characteristics. The last but not least are the axiom definitions which consist of logical statements describing model restrictions formulated with concept and structural relationship references and involving statements in one of logic based formalisms (First-Order Logic, Description Logic) $A^O = \langle L(G^A), I^L \rangle$. Axioms therefore are defined by the syntax and interpretation function which binds the syntax categories into set of objects forming concepts. The axiom set definition is intentionally generalised as the ontology definitions and can be formulated in any of formal languages meeting the description requirements and offering various expressiveness.

Ontology having those characteristics is a formal model with strong constraints supported by logic languages such as first-order logic (FOL) and description logic (DL). We can also recall other methods (frame representation, topic maps) of such specifications but there are not in the scope of the following work.

We apply ontologies for domain description to:

- Unify understanding of given vocabulary and terminology by formulating concept and relationship semantics inside the domain;
- Use the inference abilities of ontology languages to verify the instance data correctness according to specified in ontology constraints (model consistency, calculate instance membership);
- Merge and map varying data schemas into one unified meaning, integrating multiple representation schemes and standards JC3IEDM, APP-6A, TIDE-BRITE etc.
- Define semantic background for semantic pattern recognition methods applied in decision support procedures;

Specificity of data standards in military systems offer syntactically different representations which correspond to almost the same information scope. The standards themselves have been developed to support various tasks in C2 systems such as: data integration (JC3IEDM), tactical symbology (APP-6A), interoperability services (TIDE-BRITE) and provide specific view on data, its ranges, enumeration types, etc.

Conducted research on the ground of knowledge representation for military applications is mainly concerned with situation awareness assessment and development of common operational picture components. Each of those abstracts require set of techniques which offer inference and cognition in terms of battlespace information discovery. Ontology applications in such areas can help to organise the inference process by application of axiom definitions used by logic reasoners. Depending on the applied ontology language we can obtain domain description with characteristics depending on the utilised language expressivity.

Model expressivity is affected by the language and complexity of constructs contained in the model where the language defines the maximal available expressivity. To sustain traceability and efficiency of reasoning algorithms a set of logic formalisms have been designed called conceptual languages (attributive languages) (Baader et al., 2000). Description Logic is de facto a subset of First-Order Logic designed to restrict some of the constructs which causes undesirability but mostly based on the paper (Baader et al., 2000) we can provide efficient reasoning mechanisms which consider terminology in instance base inference. Synthetic characteristics of such attributive languages, their semantics and inference tasks have been presented in (Baader et al., 2000; Pan, 2004). Study on the complexity of reasoning mechanisms and reasoning capabilities of DL dialects have been described in many publications and summarised on interactive webpage containing synthesised knowledge on that matter - http://www.cs.man.ac.uk/~ezolin/dl.

3. Battlespace ontology model

Ontology design guidelines, which is fairly new discipline, have been gathered on the basis of Tom Gruber's publications (Gruber, 1995; 2009) defining main characteristics of such models and steps of conceptualisation process. Consideration of those guidelines assures model validity and consistency, however it should be remembered that axiom formulation depends on knowledge engineer intent to state stronger ontology commitments which is not always required.

Applied UBOM (Chmielewski, 2009) modelling approach is a result of available in military domain standards for data representation and inference capabilities utilised in prepared decision support procedures. C2 system decision support can specify set of decision and optimisation problems which can be used in situation awareness identification and assessment by inferring possible course of action based on prepared reasoning rules and semantic patterns representing tactical templates and valid blue forces reactions. Many of decision support tasks can be represented in a form of algorithms which we attempt to formalise or provide rules which decision makers should incorporate. Unfortunately, in many cases crisp reasoning methods are not suitable to provide correct answers, therefore the semantic similarity between current scenario and templates in knowledge base provide distance measures which can be adjusted depending on the situation needs.

UBOM design guidelines required to use JC3IEDM similar semantics as this standard is recognised model for C2 systems integration. Having well-defined structures, conceptual model and the most of all meta-model representation JC3 has been chosen as a source which ontology generation process should be implemented on. Having chosen representation language and dialect (OWL DL, $SHOIN^{+}$(D)) we have designed set of transformation rules to reflect the core model entities and their attributes, relationships into corresponding ontology elements. The generation process have been iteratively tuned in order to adjust the final model form, correct domain definitions and a level of model inference capabilities. Early generation attempts showed that JC3 is a very large model and it is not sufficient to reflect the whole model and its elements, instead we have been able to choose the most important elements and their inheritance trees. JC3 is very a specific, sophisticated domain description of battlespace entities, designed to unify meaning in various heterogeneous systems. It uses E-R modelling and OOM design imposing a very rich set of enumeration types and business rules. UBOM ontology is developed using OWL DL language in $SHOIN^{+}$(D) dialect which defines available language expressivity. To provide extensive ontology statements, model extends base attributive language *ALC* with relationship hierarchy *H*, nominals - enumeration concepts *O*, inverse roles *I*, cardinality restrictions *N* and data types support D.

From the beginning of model analysis we have been able to extract true meaning concealed in the model by studying the model's domain types, which turned out to be the most important carriers of semantics. Domains, containing domain values and defined business rules formulate the combinations of allowed, valid values for battlespace entities reflected in the model's structures. Therefore process of designing the ontology axiom set depended in majority on identification of domain values usage and formulation of concept taxonomy tree based on required precision for OBJECT-ITEM and OBJECT-TYPE taxonomies. Due to the large scale of the model and all available descriptions provided by MIP we have chosen a metamodel database MIRD in order to transform chosen entities and relations to the form of semantic model. This operation required extended analysis of the JC3 semantics:

- to choose the most important parts of the model to be transformed;
- to identify transformation rules for JC3 relational model to ontology;
- to filter ontology classes and extract only needed elements.

JC3 model structure consists of entities, composed of attributes. In the most cases, types of attributes are defined by domains. They are composed of domain vales which create similar structure as enumeration types. JC3 defines also business rules which are used to obtain valid domain values combinations for selected attributes. For the purpose of this work we utilize business rules for UNIT-TYPE, EQUIPMENT-TYPE entities to construct available variants of defined units and equipment. The domain knowledge used in this process has been described in MIR Annex G - Symbology Mapping documents and can be used in form of guidelines for extracting meaning from wide range of domain values. Definitions of model transformation rules has been identified for:

- generic guidelines to obtain schematic algorithm for relational model elements transformation into ontology;
- identification of excess relational model elements associated with physical model representation not dealing with its semantic contents;
- definition of uniform naming conventions for generated semantic model elements based on relational model predecessors unifying the element vocabulary;
- development of additional business rules validation scheme to identify combinations of valid domain values and their reflection in form of Description Logic class constructors or SWRL reasoning rules;
- definition of optimal and relevant range of JC3IEDM elements to be transformed providing required ontology expressiveness with compact size and processing efficiency.

Generation of JC3 ontology has been executed several times with different set of transformation rules. The main cause of such approach has been ontology refinement process and optimization of ontology OWL language constructs.

The transformation process assumes that the main goal is to reflect the semantics of the model and not its structure. Due to this fact some of the entities defined on the level of conceptual model have been erased and replaced by the relations between concepts, e.g. associations between OBJECT-TYPE are represented by the OBJECT-TYPE-ASSOCIATION entity which holds additional enumerated meaning of the relation, to enable reasoning abilities in designed ontology we propose to define set of relations between OBJECT-ITEM stating their hierarchy.

The presented process delivers an interactive algorithm of extending base ontology by generation of JC3IEDM parts in a form of integrated ontology modules. Integration of ontology modules generated on the basis of user request is conducted using a mapping strategy. Time generation of the ontology (ontology module) depends on the number of elements which must be reflected in resulting semantic model. The research shows that generation delays differ depending on the required JC3 model entities (domains) that needed to be reflected but also additional restrictions that are formulated on the basis of object properties defined in ontology. We should point out that tests covered also transformation of the model which required introduction of n-ary relationship pattern.

Knowledge in terms of UBOM model reflects the taxonomy of units, military equipment and conducted activities which are used by aggregation to developed a scenario composed of:

- units and their full identification, type description and spatial location;
- unit's equipment and its characteristics affecting the combat potential;
- Comand&Controll chain following the decision process responsibilities;
- unit activities and assigned tasks, objectives;
- unit's activity constraints regarding the collaboration within the task formation.

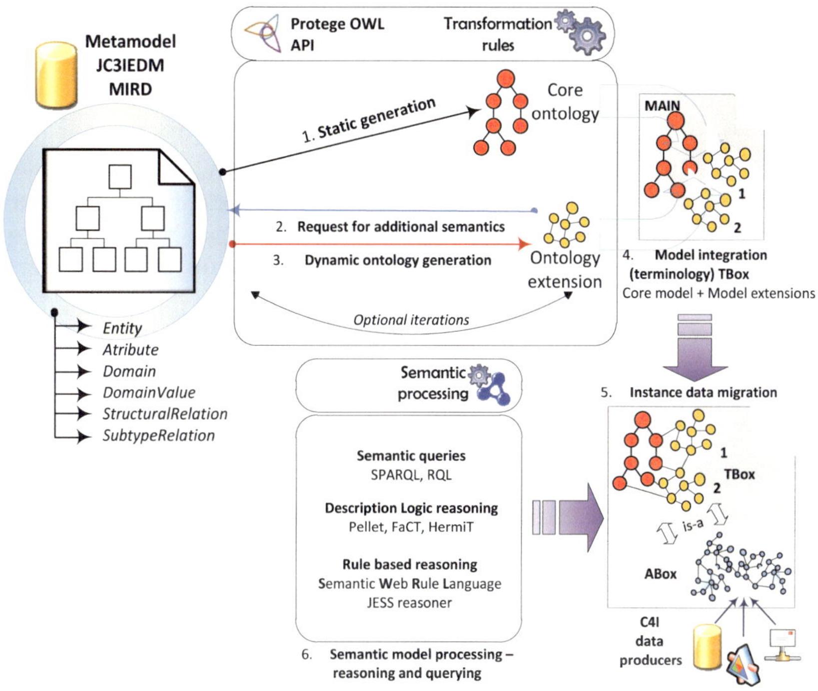

Fig. 2. The ontology adaptive generation process, developing parts of JC3IEDM terminology integrated into the UBOM semantic model

Based on those elements, a part of JC3IEDM description definitions have been reflected and extended in order to match situation assessment requirements. A semantic model therefore needs to reflect meaning of military unit formation, its configuration and potential placement. Those elements, with human and terrain analysis characteristics, may be used to infer some scenario courses or vignettes. Considering such knowledge military experts can evaluate possible hostile forces courses of action therefore preparing variants of counter actions.

Main concepts in UBOM ontology (Chmielewski & Gałka, 2010) following JC3IEDM vocabulary are presented in Fig. 2. Intent of transformation process was to represent the core elements of the data model and its semantics used in data exchange process across multiple functional areas of military domains. Referenced data model version 3.1b consisted of: 290 entities, 1594 attributes, 533 domains (enumeration types), 12409 - domain values, 259 associations, 166 hierarchy relations. Implementation of this model as an ontology in OWL language in the most simplified dialect required more than 20000 ontology constructs (CEA, restrictions, and other axioms). When we additionally consider domain closure axioms - class disjointness, instance uniqueness, etc. - this element count brings us up to 30000 elements. The generated ontology with annotated elements serialised in RDF/OWL requires almost 52456 kB. When we consider that the semantic processing environment must load the model and create additional structures required in reasoning processes the volume of data causes technical issues. Usage of more complex dialect required further ontology refinement towards more restrained logical conditions (existential and cardinality restrictions) and brings the model to even larger size (72213 kB - depending on the quantity of restrictions).

The applied generation process assumed that there is a need for an ontology documentation and reflection of all JC3IEDM entities. However, we can filter the model to consider only necessary elements with minimal annotations requirements, limiting the outcome model size. The core JC3IEDM model after application of those rules consists of base 94 concepts which are mainly associated with OBJECT-ITEM, OBJECT-TYPE hierarchies, CAPABILITIES, ACTION, HOLDING, CONTEXT, REPORTING-DATA. Iterative ontology generation produced ontologies which in majority cases lacked of basic characteristics required by this type of model, mainly in terms of inference capabilities. Therefore a manual knowledge engineering have been additionally applied as a refinement process emphasising those model elements.

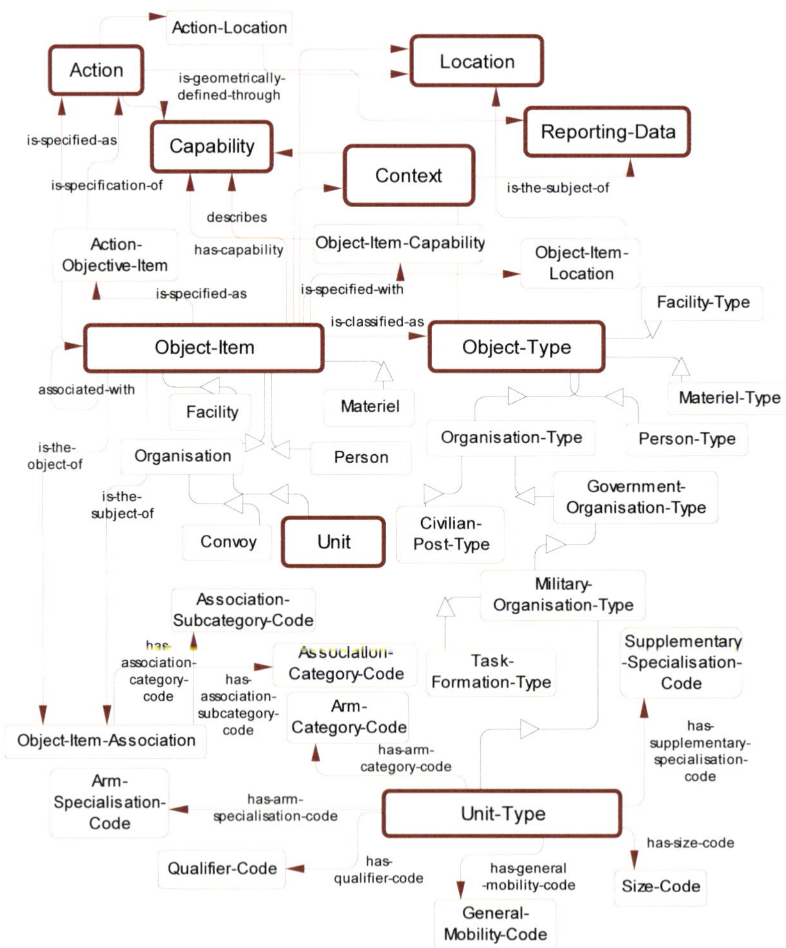

Fig. 3. JC3IEDM based ontology module incorporated into UBOM model

Main entities have been additionally thickened to emphasise important semantics represented in the scenario description. UBOM ontology separates descriptions of military organisations (*Units, TaskForces*) from *Equipment* and *WeaponPlatform* descriptions. This separation is done due to the need for ontology mapping into APP-6A symbology techniques used in Common Operational Picture product composition. We also managed to provide a weaponry branch of a knowledge representation which considers *DamagingFactor, Ammunition, WeaponComponents* in *WeaponPlatform* classification which is not reflected in the JC3IEDM standard. We intentionally choose to present ontology in a form of conceptual graph specifying structural relationships (dark arrows) and concept subsumption (inheritance) empty arrows (also dashed lines). However, such representation cannot provide axiom definitions stated in KB but example definitions will be recalled later in the chapter.

The presented ontology relationships define terminology of *WeaponPlatform* and composition strategies of *Weapons* and other *Equipment* elements forming consistent *DamagingFactor* carrier, affecting specified *Targets*. This way we are able to distinguish *Human* and *Infrastructure* effects, potential *WeaponPlatform* outcomes for both kinetic and non-kinetic engagements. Semantics contained in such definitions allow weapon taxonomy formulation for both conventional and NCB weapons with distinction of multiple *DamagingFactors* and their harming potential in given environment. It is also noticeable that we perceive *WeaponPlatform* as composition of *Equipment, Vehicles, Targeting&AquisitionSystems, Ammunition* and *Weapon* itself resulting in producing a multiple *DamagingFactors* carrier affecting the *Environment* and exploiting given *Target* vulnerabilities.

4. Ontology-based reasoning

Ontology based reasoning techniques are closely connected with the reasoning abilities of language used to express given terminology. We should note that many of available notations and dedicated languages move towards utilising logic based representations and general inference algorithms. Considering such language features as decidability, traceability and efficiency of reasoning, the family of Description Logic languages is most widely used. We should also recognise specific semantics of DL languages, identified reasoning tasks found in DL knowledge bases and how are they coupled in algorithms used by reasoning facilities. Modelling environments and semantic information processing frameworks utilise DL features to perform model consistency checking along with concept and instance classification.

Tasks performed by the reasoning services consist of:

- *Satisfiability of a concept* - determine whether a description of the concept is not contradictory, i.e., whether an individual can exist that would be instance of the concept;
- *Subsumption of concepts* - determine whether concept C subsumes concept D, i.e., whether description of C is more general than the description of D;
- *Consistency of ABox with respect to TBox* - determine whether individuals in ABox do not violate descriptions and axioms described by TBox;
- *Check an individual* - check whether the individual is an instance of a concept;
- *Retrieval of individuals* - find all individuals that are instances of a concept;
- *Realization of an individual* - find all concepts which the individual belongs to, especially the most specialised (leaf classes) ones.

To demonstrate the axiom definitions we can provide simplified DL symbology and semantics which will affect final set of reasoning tasks. Semantics behind such notation come from DL formalisms and have been summarised for convenience of reading.

Using interpretation *I* for C, D being *ALC*- concepts and role name $r \in N_R$ we formulate:

$$\text{Concept conjunction } (C \sqcap D)^I = C^I \cap D^I$$

$$\text{Concept disjunction } (C \sqcup D)^I = C^I \cup D^I$$

$$\text{Universal value restriction } (\forall r.C)^I = \left\{a \in \Delta^I : \forall b \in \Delta^I (a,b) \in r^I \Rightarrow b \in C^I\right\}$$

$$\text{Existential value restriction } (\exists r.C)^I = \left\{a \in \Delta^I : \exists b \in \Delta^I (a,b) \in r^I \wedge b \in C^I\right\}$$

$$\text{Concept subsumption axiom } (C_{subsumption} D)^I = C^I \subseteq D^I$$

$$\text{Concept equivalence axiom } (C_{equivalent} D)^I = \left(C^I \subseteq D^I \wedge D^I \subseteq C^I\right)$$

Following the above formalisms we can recall set of UBOM defined axioms providing ground for ontology-reasoning features.

jc3: Unit-Type *equivalent* ∃ *has-Unit-Type-Supplementary-Specialisation-Code*.**UTSSCode** ⊓ ∃ *has-Unit-Type-General-Mobility-Code*.**UTGMCode** ⊓ ∃ *has-Unit-Type-ARM-Category-Code*.**UTACCode** ⊓ ∃ has-Military-Organization-Type-Service-Code.**MOTSCode**
jc3:MechanisedInfantry-Unit-Type *subsumption* **jc3:Unit-Type** **jc3:MechanisedInfantry-Unit-Type** *equivalent* ∃ *has-Unit-Type-Supplementary-Specialisation-Code*.{Ground-UTSSC} ⊓ ∃ *has-Unit-Type-General-Mobility-Code*.{Land-Tracked-UTGMC} ⊓ ∃ *has-Unit-Type-ARM-Category-Code*.{Armour-UTACC} ⊓ ∃ has-Military-Organization-Type-Service-Code.{Army-MOTSC}

Table 1. Example UBOM based *MilitaryUnit* definitions expressed in JC3 based terminology following unit taxonomy tree Military-Organization-Type-> Unit-Type-> MechanisedInfantry-Unit-Type

Another view represented in UBOM ontology axiom definitions with more human readable meaning can be presented in form of following statements:

MilitaryMan *equivalent* **BattlespaceActor** ⊓ ∃ *Person-member-of-Organisation*. **MilitaryOrganisation**
Commander *equivalent* **MilitaryMan** ⊓ ∃ *Person-manages-Organisation*. **MilitaryOrganisation**
OilRafinery *equivalent* **Infrastructure** ⊓ ∃ *Infrastructure-produces-Supplies*. **FosilFuel**

5. Ontology-based decision situation model

Military unit representation is based on recognised in NATO standards attributes distinguishing battlespace dimension, unit type its rank, affiliation, hostility status etc.

Based on such descriptions we can classify each of the C2 command chain elements and provide detailed information on given formation placed within the battlespace.

Using the *MilitaryUnit*'s relationships between other elements we can establish its function within the command chain, and infer possible responsibilities in combat formation predicting possible intentions. Ontology representation of military units can also be used as a reconnaissance support tool permitting representation of iterative information upgrades on the basis of ReportingData records.

The UBOM ontology does not contain pure OBJECT-TYPE specification - instead proposed taxonomy contains *TargetEffects* form *WeponPlatforms* on specified *Resources*. As the Environment perceived in Network Enabled Capabilities can contain asymmetric threats additional broader approach have been applied through formulation of effect probability *TargetEffect* recorder on some *Resources*. The model itself have been created to place significant interest on the "weapon platform" effects and reflecting those effects depending on the *DamagingFactor* which can be either conventional, psychological or NCB weapons based.

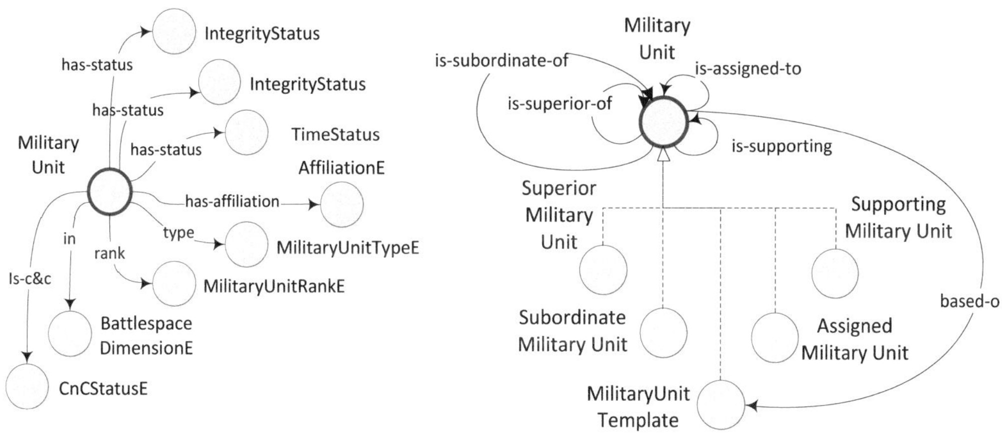

Fig. 4. UBOM *MilitaryUnit* description containing JC3 based attributes (left) and taxonomy reflecting *MilitaryUnit* function in formation and C&C decision chain

UBOM contains also the part of *WeaponPlatform* classification which based on weapon *DamagingFactor* characteristics (*Vulnerability* of *Target*, class of the factor, aim at damaging abilities) permits to model the effects on the *Environment* consisting of *LivingForce*, *Equipment* and *Infrastructure*. Ontology design approach applied in our case was a confrontation of JC3 capacities and terminology used across the other military applications.

Representation of dynamic UBOM constructs affecting the scenario inference have been demonstrated in the Fig. 5. Purpose of such definitions is to describe the nature of activity specification along with classification of conducted tasks their importance in a combat operation implying unit's status in given scenario. Evaluation of prepared instance graphs describing scenarios placed in proper annotated terrain data helps to extend the perception of given scenario and distinct unit roles.

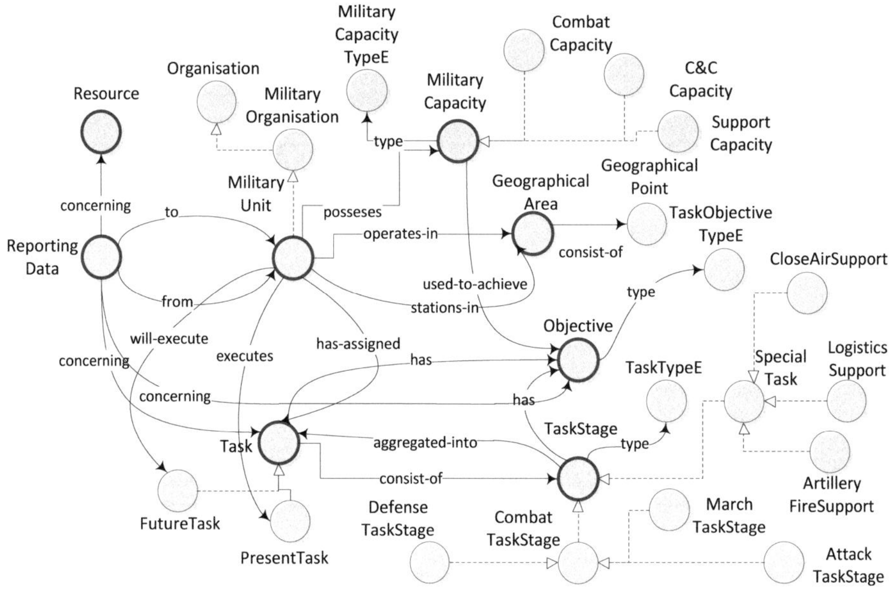

Fig. 5. UBOM decision situation model semantically describing *MilitaryUnits* their *CombatCapacities, Task* formation with executed *Tasks.*

The model addresses also elementary *Organisation* taxonomy which can be identified as *ConflictEntrants* and interaction providers in asymmetric *Environment.* One of the elements of the taxonomy is *MilitaryUnit* serving as main concept for representing an entity of accumulated military force in *Environment* and interacting with it through *Activities* which can be perceived as military *Tasks* for which we define abstract *Objectives.*

Concepts definitions provided in UBOM ontology contains mainly axioms which are used in classification process designed to support current scenario representation. Process of scenario classification assumes that:

- gathered from battlespace information about specific military unit or object is fused and represents consistent, deconflicted information about such entity;
- recorded information produces a graph of connected instances coupled around specific scenario with spatial description of terrain and reconnaissance information gaps declaring uncertain or unreliable information.

Instances of given scenario related entities expressed in UBOM ontology in the process of inference can change type (concept) membership. This is possible due to ontology axiom definitions and specific semantic formulas used by those definitions forming chain of classification rules applied by the DL reasoner. The inferred concept taxonomy graph structure and instance membership assignment is understood as building new knowledge in the given operational KB and is mainly concerned with reasoning about current scenario.

6. Identification of decision situations

Having formulated semantics of the scenario we can apply those elements for the decision situation vector definition, which contains knowledge about the terrain, military potential distribution in a combat formation and assigned tasks formulating a template for recognition process described further in the following chapter. We define a decision situations space as follows:

$$DSS = \{SD: \; SD = (\, SD_r \,)_{r=1,..,8}\} \tag{2}$$

Vector *SD* represents the decision situation, which is described by the following eight elements: SD_1 - command level of opposite forces, SD_2 - type of task of opposite forces (e.g. attack, defence), SD_3 - command level of own forces, SD_4 - type of task of own forces (e.g. attack, defence), SD_5 - net of squares as a model of activities (terrain) area $SD_5 = \left[SD_{ij}^5 \right]_{\substack{i=1,..,SD_7 \\ j=1,..,SD_8}}$, $SD_{ij}^5 = (SD_{ij}^{5,k})_{k=1,..,7}$. The terrain square with the indices (*i,j*) each of the elements denotes: $SD_{ij}^{5,1}$ - the degree of the terrain passability, $SD_{ij}^{5,2}$ - the degree of forest covering, $SD_{ij}^{5,3}$ - the degree of water covering, $SD_{ij}^{5,4}$ - the degree of terrain undulating, $SD_{ij}^{5,5}$ - armoured power (potential) of opposite units deployed in the square, $SD_{ij}^{5,6}$ - infantry power (potential) of opposite units deployed in the square, $SD_{ij}^{5,7}$ - artillery power (potential) of opposite units deployed in the square, $SD_{ij}^{5,7}$ - coordinates of the square (*i,j*), SD_6 - the description of own forces: $SD_6 = \left(SD_i^6 \right)_{i=1,...,4}$, SD_1^6 - total armoured power (potential) of own units, SD_2^6 - total infantry power (potential) of own units, SD_3^6 - total artillery power (potential) of own units, SD_4^6 - total air fire support power (potential); SD_7 - the width of activities (interest) in an area (number of squares), SD_8- the depth of activities (interest) in an area (number of squares).

The set of decision situations patterns are: $PDSS = \{PS : PS \in DSS\}$. For the current decision situation *CS*, we have to find the most similar situation *PS* from the set of patterns. Using the similarity measure function (6) we can evaluate distances between two different decision situations, especially the current and the pattern. We have determined the subset of decision situation patterns $PDSS_{CS}$, which are generally similar to the current situation *CS*, considering such elements like: task type, command level of own and opposite units and own units potential:

$$\begin{aligned} PDSS_{CS} = \{ & PS = (PS_i)_{i=1,..,6} \in PDSS : PS_i = CS_i, \\ & i = 1,..,4, dist_{potwl}(CS, PS) \le \Delta Pot\} \end{aligned} \tag{3}$$

where:

$$dist_{potwl}(CS, PS) = \max\{\left| CS_k^6 - PS_k^6 \right|, k = 1,..4\} \tag{4}$$

ΔPot - the maximum difference of own forces potential.

Afterwards, we formulated and solved the multicriteria optimization problem (5), which allows us to determine the most matched pattern situation (*PS*) to the current one (*CS*) from the point of view of terrain and military power characteristics:

$$Z = \left(PDSS_{CS}, F_{CS}, R_D \right) \tag{5}$$

where:

$$F_{CS} : PDSS_{CS} \rightarrow R^2 \tag{6}$$

$$F_{CS}(PS) = (dist_{ter}(CS,PS), dist_{pot}(CS,PS)) \tag{7}$$

$$dist_{ter}(CS,PS) = \sum_{k=1}^{4} \lambda_k \cdot \left(\sum_{i=1}^{I} \sum_{j=1}^{J} \left(CS_{ij}^{5,k} - PS_{ij}^{5,k} \right)^p \right)^{\frac{1}{p}} \tag{8}$$

$$\sum_{k=1}^{4} \lambda_k = 1, \lambda_k > 0, k = 1,..,4 \tag{9}$$

$$dist_{pot}(CS,PS) = \sum_{k=5}^{7} \mu_k \cdot \left(\sum_{i=1}^{I} \sum_{j=1}^{J} \left(CS_{ij}^{5,k} - PS_{ij}^{5,k} \right)^p \right)^{\frac{1}{p}} \tag{10}$$

$$\sum_{k=5}^{7} \mu_k = 1, \mu_k > 0, k = 5,..,7 \tag{11}$$

$$I = \min\{CS_7, PS_7\}, J = \min\{CS_8, PS_8\} \tag{12}$$

$$R_D = \left\{ \begin{array}{l} (Y,Z) \in PDSS_{CS} \times PDSS_{CS} : \\ dist_{ter}(CS,Y) \le dist_{ter}(CS,Z) \wedge \\ dist_{pot}(CS,Y) \le dist_{pot}(CS,Z) \end{array} \right\} \tag{13}$$

Parameters μ_k and λ_k describe the weights for components calculating the value of functions $dist_{ter}$ and $dist_{pot}$. The domination relation defined by (13) allows us to choose such *PS* from $PDSS_{CS}$, which has the best value of $dist_{ter}$ and $dist_{pot}$, that is the most similar to *CS* (non-dominated *PS* from the R_D point of view). The idea of the identification of a decision situation and CoA selection is presented in Fig. 6.

There are several methods of finding the most matched pattern situation to the current one, which can be used. For example, in the paper (Tarapata, 2007) a concept of multicriteria weighted graphs similarity and its application for pattern matching of decision situations is considered. The approach extends known pattern recognition approaches based on graph similarity with two features: (1) the similarity is calculated as structural and non-structural (quantitative) in weighted graph, (2) choice of the most similar graph to graph representing pattern is based on a multicriteria decision. Application of the presented approach to pattern recognition of decision situations has been described in (Tarapata 2008; Tarapata et al., 2010).

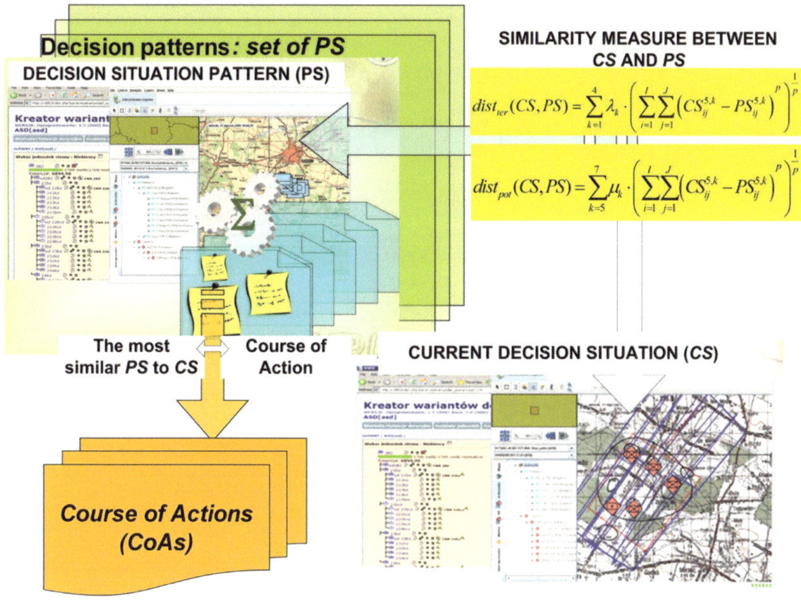

Fig. 6. The idea of identification of the decision situation and CoA selection

7. A practical example of using tool

The tool (called CAVaRS: Course of Action Verification and Recommendation Simulator) allows preparing knowledge base of decision situations patterns with values of characteristic parameters (Antkiewicz et al., 2011b). It also allows to fix the best (nearest) decision situation located in the knowledge base, choose (or create) the best CoA and simulate selected CoAs. The tool CAVaRS has been built at the Cybernetics Faculty of the Military University of Technology in Warsaw (Poland) and authors of this chapter are members of the team, which has created it. The CAVaRS may be used as a part of a Decision Support System (DSS) which supports C4ISR systems or it may work as standalone one. It models two-face land conflict of military units on the company/battalion level. The simulator is implemented in JAVA language as an integrated part of some system for CAXes. The model concerns a couple of processes of firing interaction and movement executed by a single military unit. These two complementary models use a terrain model, described by a network of square areas, which aggregates movement characteristics with 200m×200m granularity.

The example shows elements of knowledge base and the algorithm of the nearest pattern situation searching. The main element of the system is knowledge base which consists of Decision Situations Patterns (DSP). Each DSP is connected to the set of Course of Actions (CoA). The example of two DSPs and their CoAs are presented below.

The first DSP (Fig.7) is connected with two CoAs (Fig.9 and Fig. 10). The second DSP is shown in the Fig. 11. Parameters have been fixed for each DSP. Fig. 8 shows the analyzed area of the opposite forces. Parameters of each DSP are stored in the knowledge base. Finally, Table 2 and Table 3 show values of DSP parameters.

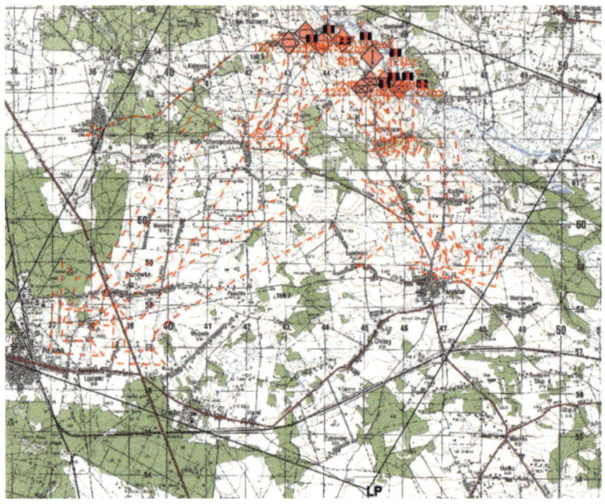

Fig. 7. Graphical representation of DSP 1

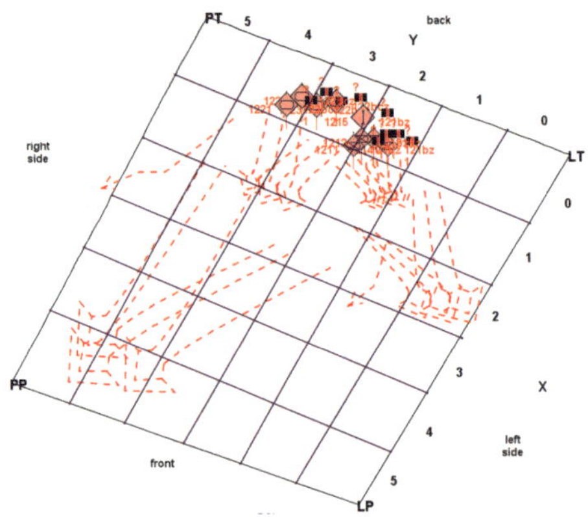

Fig. 8. DSP 1 - area of opposite forces

Coordinates of a terrain area for DSP 1 (NW: north-west corner, NE: north-east corner, SW: south-west corner, SE: south-east corner): NW (LP)=515556N 0213922E, NE (PP)=515740N 0213053E, SW (LT)=520056N 0214431E SE (PT)=520254N 0213541E.

Potential of own forces: mechanized 444; armoured 61.2; artillery 30; antiaircraft 0; other 0.

i	j	$SD_{ij}^{5,1}$	$SD_{ij}^{5,2}$	$SD_{ij}^{5,3}$	$SD_{ij}^{5,4}$	$SD_{ij}^{5,5}$	$SD_{ij}^{5,6}$	$SD_{ij}^{5,7}$
0	0	54%	1%	1%	0.069	0	0	0
0	1	44%	4%	1%	0.116	0	0	0
0	2	42%	15%	2%	0.186	0	17.46	94.13
0	3	45%	9%	4%	0.21	190	16.32	23.75
0	4	41%	8%	2%	0.252	80	5.2	0
0	5	42%	24%	1%	0.176	0	0	0
1	0	46%	23%	2%	0.12	0	0	0
1	1	54%	5%	1%	0.162	0	0	0
1	2	37%	15%	0%	0.231	0	26.98	140.8
1	3	47%	13%	0%	0.158	25	5.71	21.35

i	j	$SD_{ij}^{5,1}$	$SD_{ij}^{5,2}$	$SD_{ij}^{5,3}$	$SD_{ij}^{5,4}$	$SD_{ij}^{5,5}$	$SD_{ij}^{5,6}$	$SD_{ij}^{5,7}$
1	4	45%	10%	0%	0.177	25	1.62	0
1	5	35%	0%	34%	0.168	0	0	0
2	0	2%	0%	58%	0.096	0	0	0
2	1	7%	0%	54%	0.135	0	0	0
2	2	17%	0%	50%	0.183	0	0	0
2	3	11%	0%	38%	0.138	0	0	0
2	4	23%	0%	34%	0.162	0	0	0
2	5	51%	0%	29%	0.179	0	0	0
3	0	2%	0%	46%	0.168	0	0	0
...	...	...	...	...	...	...	...	...
5	5	25%	20%	0%	0.013	0	0	0

Table 2. Detailed values of DSP 1 parameters using notations from (2)

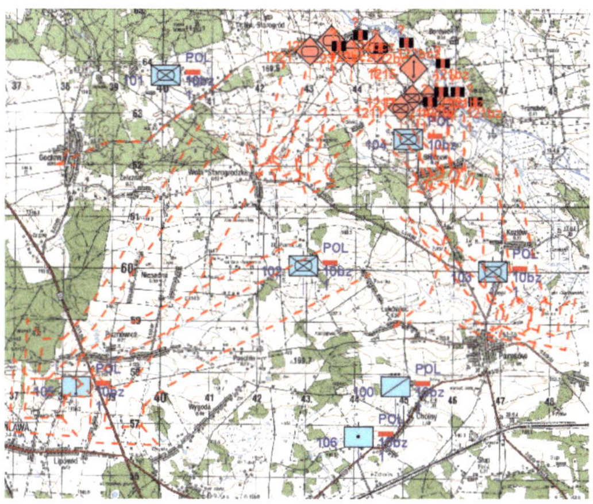

Fig. 9. Graphical representation of DSP 1, CoA 1

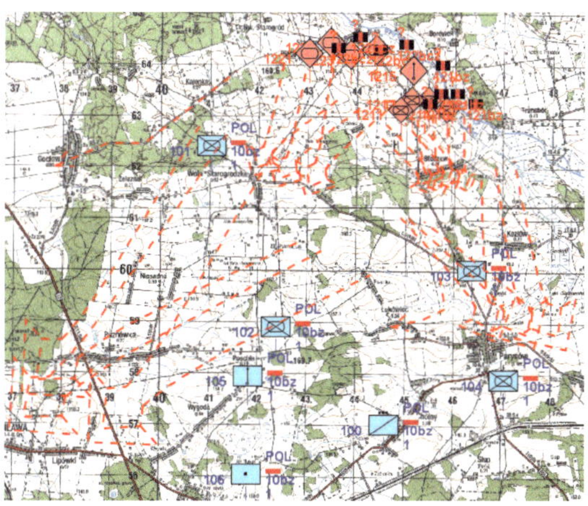

Fig. 10. Graphical representation of DSP 1, CoA 2

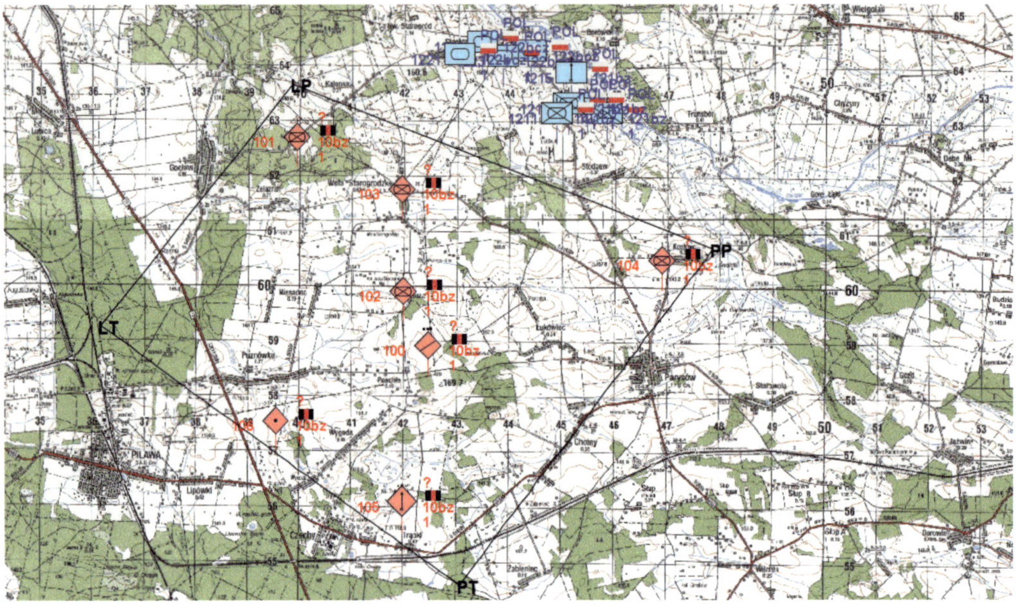

Fig. 11. Graphical representation of DSP 2

Coordinates of a terrain area for DSP 2 (NW: north-west corner, NE: north-east corner, SW: south-west corner, SE: south-east corner): NW (LP)=520120N 0213451E,

NE (PP)=515943N 0214150E, SW (LT)=515858N 0213135E, SE (PT)=515625N 0213736E.

Potential of own forces: mechanized 320; armoured 73.3; artillery 280; antiaircraft 0; other 0.

Each DSP parameter of the current situation (see Fig.12) were calculated. The algorithm for finding the most similar pattern situation compares current situation parameters with each DSP from knowledge base using the method described in section 3. As a result the DSP1 has been fixed according to the *dist* values (equation (8) and (10)) presented in Table 4 because: $dist_{pot}(CS,DSP1) < dist_{pot}(CS,DSP2)$ and $dist_{ter}(CS,DSP1) < dist_{ter}(CS,DSP2)$, hence DSP1 dominates DSP2 from the R_D (formula (13)) point of view.

i	j	$SD_{ij}^{5,1}$	$SD_{ij}^{5,2}$	$SD_{ij}^{5,3}$	$SD_{ij}^{5,4}$	$SD_{ij}^{5,5}$	$SD_{ij}^{5,6}$	$SD_{ij}^{5,7}$
0	0	29%	93%	0%	0.01	0	0	0
0	1	55%	48%	0%	0.06	0	0	0
0	2	91%	1%	0%	0.04	8.62	4.49	0
0	3	84%	10%	0%	0.04	5.38	2.81	0
0	4	84%	11%	0%	0.03	0	5.85	27
0	5	76%	30%	0%	0.01	0	0.65	3
...	...	...	...	...	...	...	...	...
2	2	88%	0%	0%	0.03	13	1.44	0
2	3	84%	10%	0%	0.05	60	6.55	0

i	j	$SD_{ij}^{5,1}$	$SD_{ij}^{5,2}$	$SD_{ij}^{5,3}$	$SD_{ij}^{5,4}$	$SD_{ij}^{5,5}$	$SD_{ij}^{5,6}$	$SD_{ij}^{5,7}$
2	4	59%	44%	0%	0.07	6	0.6	0
2	5	77%	12%	0%	0.06	0	0	0
3	0	66%	33%	0%	0.09	0	0	0
3	1	83%	4%	0%	0.04	0	0	0
3	2	88%	3%	0%	0.02	6.5	0.72	0
3	3	80%	7%	0%	0.08	32.5	3.59	0
3	4	82%	1%	0%	0.1	0	0	0
3	5	81%	0%	0%	0.12	0	0	0
4	0	40%	74%	0%	0.08	66.9	7.39	0
4	1	62%	43%	0%	0.06	32.7	3.61	0
4	2	85%	1%	0%	0.05	93.6	10.4	0
4	3	70%	22%	0%	0.09	0	0	0
4	4	69%	9%	0%	0.15	0	0	0
4	5	87%	4%	0%	0.05	18.9	2.09	0
...	...	...	...	...	...	...	...	...
5	5	85%	6%	0%	0.05	85.1	9.41	0

Table 3. Detailed values of DSP 2 parameters using notations from (2)

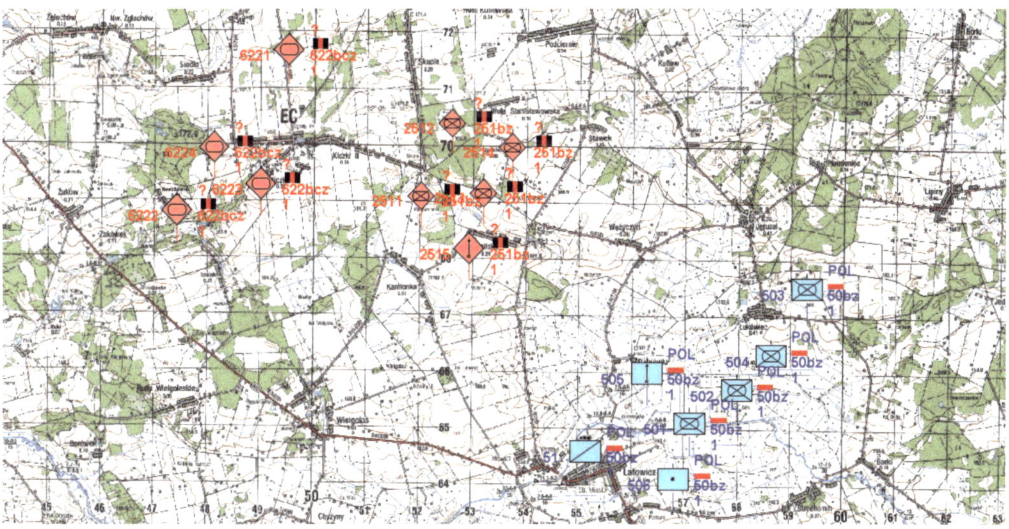

Fig. 12. Current situation (CS)

DSP	$dist_{pot}(CS,DSP)$	$dist_{ter}(CS,DSP)$
DSP1	203.61	1.22
DSP2	222.32	1.47

Table 4. Detailed values of dist parameters from (8) and (10)

8. Conclusions

In this chapter there was presented the problem of using the knowledge base tool for mission planning. The proposed tool (with knowledge base and pattern recognition method) was implemented and verified during the practical experiment. One of the most important problems is to prepare the knowledge base with decision situation patterns and CoAs for each decision situation pattern. The specialized tool for knowledge base management was created - it allows preparing decision situations patterns using GIS functions. The validation process of combat models is very complex, however it is possible to utilize such tools like simulation models calibrator and expert knowledge (Dockery & Woodcock, 1993; Hofmann & Hofmann, 2000; Przemieniecki, 1994). The construction of the simulation model enables testing of different courses of actions including concepts in the area of Network Enabled Capabilities (Moffat, 2003).

9. Acknowledgements

This work was partially done within ATHENA (Asymetric Threat Environment Analysis) supported and funded by 20 cMS within the Joint Investment Program of Force Protection, contacted by the EDA, under the call Mission Planning/Training in an asymmetric environment and secured Tactical Wireless Communications.

10. References

Antkiewicz R., Koszela J., Najgebauer A., Pierzchała D., Rulka J., Tarapata Z., Wantoch-Rekowski R. (2011a): Fast CoA Verification and Recommendation using Tactical Level Land Battle Deterministic Simulator, *Proceedings of the 13th International Conference on Computer Modelling and Simulation (UkSim'2011)*, IEEE Explore, ISBN 978-0-7695-4376-5, Cambridge, United Kingdom, 30 March - 1 April

Antkiewicz R., Najgebauer A., Rulka J., Tarapata Z., Wantoch-Rekowski R. (2011b): Knowledge-Based Pattern Recognition Method and Tool to Support Mission Planning and Simulation, ICCCI'2011, Part I, *Lecture Notes in Computer Science*, vol. 6922 (2011), Springer-Verlag Berlin Heidelberg, pp.478-487

Baader F., Calvanese D., McGuinness D., Nardi D., Patel-Schneider P. (2003): The Description Logic Handbook: Theory, Implementation and Applications. *Cambridge University Press*, ISBN: 9780521781763

Barry P.S., Koehler M.T.K. (2005): Leveraging agent based simulation for rapid course of action development, *Proceedings of the 2005 Winter Simulation Conference*, 4-4 Dec., Orlando (FL)

Chmielewski M., (2009): Ontology applications for achieving situation awareness in military decision support systems. In Nguyen, N.T., Kowalczyk, R. & Chen, S.-M. Computational Collective Intelligence. Semantic Web, Social Networks and Multiagent Systems. Wroclaw: *Springer*, 2009, Volume 5796/2009, 528-539, DOI: 10.1007/978-3-642-04441-0

Chmielewski M. & Gałka A. (2010): Semantic battlespace data mapping using tactical symbology. In Nguyen, N.T., Katarzyniak, R. & Chen, S.-M. Advances in Intelligent Information and Database Systems. Springer, Volume 283/2010, 157-168, DOI: 10.1007/978-3-642-12090-9

Dockery J., Woodcock A.E.R. (1993): The Military Landscape, Mathematical Models of Combat, *Published by Woodhead Publishing* Ltd., Cambridge, England

Gruber, T.R., (1995): Toward Principles for the Design of Ontologies Used for Knowledge Sharing. *International Journal of Human-Computer Studies*, pp.907 - 928

Gruber, T.R., (2009): Ontology. In Liu, L. & Özsu, T.M. Encyclopedia of Database Systems. *Springer-Verlag*

Hofmann, H.W., Hofmann, M. (2000): On the Development of Command & Control Modules for Combat Simulation Models on Battalion down to Single Item Level. In: *Proceedings of the NATO/RTO Information Systems Technology Panel (IST) Symposium "New Information Processing Techniques for Military Systems"*. NATO AC/329 (IST-017) TP/8, Istanbul, Turkey, 9-11 Oct., pp. 85-96

Matthews K. (2004): Development of a Course of Action Simulation Capability, Command and Control Division Information Sciences Laboratory, *DSTO-CR-0376*, Edinburgh (Australia)

Moffat J. (2003): Complexity Theory and Network Centric Warfare, *CCRP Publication Series*, ISBN 1-893723-11-9, Washington

Najgebauer A. (1999): Decision Support Systems for Conflict Situations. Models, Methods and the Interactive Simulation Environments (in Polish). *Ed. Biuletyn WAT*, Warsaw 1999, Poland (294 p.), ISBN 83-908620-6-9

Najgebauer A. (2004): Polish Initiatives in M&S and Training. Simulation Based Operational Training Support System (SBOTSS) Zlocien, *Proceedings of the ITEC'2004*, London, UK

Pan, J.Z., (2004): Description Logics: Reasoning support for the Semantic Web (PHD Thesis). School of Computer Science, *The University of Manchester*

Pierzchała D., Dyk M., Szydłowski A. (2011): Distributed Military Simulation Augmented by Computational Collective Intelligence, in Agent-Oriented Information Systems, ed. Jędrzejowicz P., ICCCI'2011, Part I, Lecture Notes in Computer Science, vol. 6922 (2011), ISBN 978-3-642-23934-2, Springer-Verlag Berlin Heidelberg, pp. 399–408

Przemieniecki J.S. (1994): Mathematical Methods in Defence Analysis, *American Institute of Aeronautics and Astronautics*, Inc., Washington DC

Ross K., Klein G., Thunholm P., Schmitt J., Baxter H. (2004): The Recognition-Primed Decision Model, *Military Review*, July-August, pp.6-10

Sokolowski, J.A. (2002): Can a Composite Agent be Used to Implement a Recognition-Primed Decision Model?, In: *Proceedings of the Eleventh Conference on Computer Generated Forces and Behavioral Representation*, Orlando, FL., May 7-9, pp.473-478

Tarapata Z. (2007): Multicriteria weighted graphs similarity and its application for decision situation pattern matching problem, *Proceedings of the 13th IEEE/IFAC International Conference on Methods and Models in Automation and Robotics*, ISBN 978-83-751803-3-6, 27-30 August 2007, Szczecin, Poland, 1149-1155

Tarapata Z. (2008): Automatization of decision processes in conflict situations: modelling, simulation and optimization, in: Arreguin J.M.R. (edt.): *Automation and Robotics*, pp. 297-328, InTech, ISBN 978-3-902613-41-7, Vienna (Austria)

Tarapata Z., Chmielewski M., Kasprzyk R. (2010): An Algorithmic Approach To Social Knowledge Processing And Reasoning Based On Graph Representation - A Case Study, ACIIDS 2010, *Lecture Notes in Artificial Intelligence*, 5991, Springer-Verlag Berlin Heidelberg, 93-104

Tarapata Z. (2011): Models and algorithms for knowledge-based decision support and simulation in defence and transport applications, *Wojskowa Akademia Techniczna*, ISBN 978-83-62954-15-5, Warszawa